D1627965

Lesbian and Gay Psychology

New Perspectives

Edited by Adrian Coyle and Celia Kitzinger

BPS Blackwell

© 2002 by Blackwell Publishers Ltd
except for editorial arrangement and introduction © 2002 by Adrian Coyle and
Celia Kitzinger
A BPS Blackwell book

Editorial Offices:
108 Cowley Road, Oxford OX4 1JF, UK
    Tel: +44 (0)1865 791100
350 Main Street, Malden, MA 02148-5018, USA
    Tel: +1 781 388 8250

All rights reserved. No part of this publication may be reproduced, stored in a retrieval
system, or transmitted, in any form or by any means, electronic, mechanical,
photocopying, recording or otherwise, except as permitted by the UK Copyright,
Designs and Patents Act 1988, without the prior permission of the publisher.

First published 2002 by The British Psychological Society and Blackwell Publishers Ltd,
a Blackwell Publishing company

Library of Congress Cataloging-in-Publication Data has been applied for

ISBN 1405102217 (hbk)
ISBN 1405102225 (pbk)

A catalogue record for this title is available from the British Library.

Set in Palatino
by Book Production Services, London
Printed and bound in Great Britain by MPG Books Ltd, Bodmin

For further information on
Blackwell Publishers, visit our website:
www.blackwellpublishers.co.uk

STAFFORDSHIRE
UNIVERSITY
LIBRARY

SITE: Thompson

2 8 JUN 2005

CLASS No.
306.766

05219165

Contents

List of contributors

Peter Aggleton is Professor in Education and Director of the Thomas Coram Research Unit at the Institute of Education, University of London. He has worked internationally in the field of health promotion for over 20 years. He has written and edited over 20 books and is the editor of the journal *Culture, Health & Sexuality* and the series editor (and the co-editor of individual volumes) of the *Social Aspects of AIDS* books (published by Taylor & Francis/ Falmer).

Victoria Clarke is a PhD candidate in the Department of Social Sciences at Loughborough University. Her research examines the social construction of lesbian and gay parenting. In 2000, she won the British Psychological Society's Lesbian & Gay Psychology Section inaugural postgraduate prize.

Adrian Coyle is Senior Lecturer and Joint Course Director of the Practitioner Doctorate in Psychotherapeutic & Counselling Psychology in the Department of Psychology at the University of Surrey. Before moving into academia, he worked in HIV/AIDS research, counselling and education. He was one of a group of psychologists (including Celia Kitzinger, Martin Milton, Ian Rivers and Sue Wilkinson) whose campaigning efforts resulted in the establishment of a Lesbian & Gay Psychology Section within the British Psychological Society in 1998 and he is now the co-editor (with Elizabeth Peel) of its publication, *Lesbian & Gay Psychology Review*. His own publications have addressed various issues within lesbian and gay psychology (with a focus upon identity issues, psychological well-being and experiences of therapy), HIV/AIDS, bereavement and qualitative research methods.

Anthony R. D'Augelli is a community psychologist in the Department of Human Development and Family Studies at Pennsylvania State University. He is co-editor (with Charlotte J. Patterson) of *Lesbian,*

Gay, and Bisexual Identities Over the Lifespan: Psychological Perspectives (1995), *Lesbian, Gay, and Bisexual Identities in Families: Psychological Perspectives* (1998) and *Lesbian, Gay, and Bisexual Identities and Youth: Psychological Perspectives* (2001) (all published by Oxford University Press).

Sonja J. Ellis is a Lecturer in Psychology in the School of Social Science and Law at Sheffield Hallam University. Prior to emigrating to the UK, she completed her Bachelor and Master of Social Sciences degrees at the University of Waikato in New Zealand. She completed her PhD at Loughborough University in 2001. Her research within lesbian and gay psychology has focused on lesbian coming out experiences and reasoning about lesbian and gay (human) rights issues.

Brendan Gough is a Lecturer in Qualitative Psychology in the School of Psychology at the University of Leeds. He gained his PhD (on Postmodernism, Social Psychology and Everyday Life) from the School of Psychology at the Queen's University, Belfast in 1993 and took up his first lecturing post at Sheffield Hallam University in 1994, where he taught critical social psychology and qualitative research methods. At Sheffield Hallam, he also initiated the men, masculinities and discourse project - a series of studies by staff and research students which critically explored the social construction of masculinities. In 2000, he took up his present post at the University of Leeds, where he teaches on the newly-developed masters degree in qualitative psychology. His publications to date have focused on the discursive reproduction of sexism, homophobia and male victimhood; with Majella McFadden, he has co-authored a textbook on *Critical Social Psychology: An Introduction* (2001, Macmillan). He continues to research aspects of men and masculinities (such as fatherhood and men's health) and is interested in raising student awareness of qualitative methods and critical approaches to psychology.

Christine Griffin is Senior Lecturer in Social Psychology at the University of Birmingham. Her research interests include young people's experiences of transitions to adulthood, especially for young women; academic and popular representations of youth; feminist perspectives on gender relations; the use of qualitative methods; and the relationship between academics and others working in a professional capacity with young people. She is one of the founding editors of the international journal *Feminism & Psychology* and her publications include *Typical Girls?* (1985, Routledge and Kegan Paul) and *Representations of Youth* (1993, Polity Press). Her research has addressed a number of issues relevant to lesbian and gay psychology, such as the implications of compulsory heterosexuality for young women; lesbians' accounts of their experiences in psychology (with Miriam Zukas); the impact of anti-lesbianism in women's reluctance to identify as feminist; and the role of same-sex desire in young women's friendships.

Celia Kitzinger is Professor of Conversation Analysis, Gender and Sexuality in the Sociology Department at the University of York. She has published nine books and around 100 articles and book chapters on issues related to gender and sexuality. She is the recipient of a Distinguished Publication Award from the Association for Women in Psychology (for her book *The Social Construction of Lesbianism* [1987, Sage]) and a Distinguished Scientific Contribution Award from Division 44 of the American Psychological Association for her contributions to lesbian psychology. She was one of a group of psychologists (including Adrian Coyle, Martin Milton, Ian Rivers and Sue Wilkinson) whose campaigning efforts resulted in the establishment of a Lesbian & Gay Psychology Section within the British Psychological Society in 1998 and is the inaugural Chair of the Section.

Charles Legg is Senior Lecturer in Psychology at City University, London. He graduated in Psychology from Birkbeck College, London, in 1970, obtained his DPhil from Oxford in 1975 and became a Chartered Counselling Psychologist in 1995, after completing the training programme at City University. He teaches on the Advanced Diploma in the Practice of Counselling Psychology at City University and supervises a number of candidates on the DPsych in Counselling Psychology there. His current research involves the analysis of power relations in discourse in and about therapy, based on Foucauldian principles.

Maeve Malley is a systemic psychotherapist and supervisor. She is currently working on a Doctorate in Psychotherapy at Birkbeck College, University of London, examining the use of counselling and therapy by lesbians and gay men.

Laura A. Markowe is Senior Lecturer in the Division of Psychology within the Faculty of Humanities and Social Science at South Bank University in London. She has a PhD from the London School of Economics and Political Science (University of London) and is the author of *Redefining the Self: Coming Out as Lesbian* (1996, Polity Press).

Damian McCann is a systemic psychotherapist, supervisor and trainer and is currently employed as Principal Family and Systemic

Psychotherapist in the Department of Child and Adolescent Psychiatry at Edgware Community Hospital. He is a Clinical Supervisor at the Institute of Family Therapy in London and at the Oxford Family Institute; he was also Co-Founder of the Lesbian and Gay Family Service in London. He is also currently a PhD candidate at Birkbeck College, University of London, researching prospective gay fathers.

Martin Milton is Senior Lecturer and Joint Course Director of the Practitioner Doctorate in Psychotherapeutic & Counselling Psychology in the Department of Psychology at the University of Surrey. He is a Chartered Counselling Psychologist and Registered Psychotherapist and is attached to North East London Mental Health Trust. His specialist interests include lesbian and gay affirmative psychology and psychotherapy, HIV-related psychotherapy and existential psychotherapy. He has been Chair of the British Psychological Society's Division of Counselling Psychology's Standing Committee for Professional Affairs (1994-1998) and has been a member of the Division's Executive Committee (1998-1998). He was one of a group of psychologists (including Adrian Coyle, Celia Kitzinger, Ian Rivers and Sue Wilkinson) whose campaigning efforts resulted in the establishment of a Lesbian & Gay Psychology Section within the British Psychological Society in 1998.

Elizabeth Peel is a PhD candidate in the Department of Social Sciences at Loughborough University and a facilitator of anti-heterosexism training. Her research focuses on the discursive construction of heterosexism and liberalism within lesbian and gay awareness training. She obtained her joint honours degree in Psychology and Sociology and a diploma in Applied Psychology from the University of Nottingham in 1997. She is currently co-editor (with Adrian Coyle) of *Lesbian & Gay Psychology Review* – the publication of the British Psychological Society's Lesbian & Gay Psychology Section.

Ian Rivers is Senior Lecturer in Social Psychology within the School of Sports Science and Psychology at York St John College. He took his first degree in Educational and Community Studies and History at the College of Ripon and York St John (now York St John College) before reading Psychology at the University of Liverpool. He obtained his PhD from the Roehampton Institute, London in 1999 (now the University of Surrey, Roehampton) where he studied the psychosocial correlates and long-term implications of school bullying for lesbians, gay men and bisexual men and women. He was one of a group of psychologists (including Adrian Coyle, Celia

Kitzinger, Martin Milton and Sue Wilkinson) whose campaigning efforts resulted in the establishment of a Lesbian & Gay Psychology Section within the British Psychological Society in 1998. He has published widely in the field of lesbian, gay and bisexual developmental issues and co-ordinates an ESRC-funded seminar series entitled 'Researching lesbian, gay and bisexual issues in statutory, further and higher education'.

Fiona Tasker is a Lecturer in Psychology at Birkbeck College, University of London. She completed her PhD at the University of Cambridge and was a Postdoctoral Research Fellow at City University, London. Her previous publications include papers on children of divorce and children in lesbian and gay families. With Susan Golombok, she is the co-author of *Growing Up in a Lesbian Family: Effects on Child Development* (1997, Guilford). Her current research (funded by the Wellcome Trust) involves a study of gay fathers and their sons and daughters.

Gary Taylor is a Clinical and Health Psychologist, currently employed as Assistant Director of Psychological Services at the University of Sussex, where he is also Director of an MSc programme in Counselling Psychology. Having read Developmental Psychology at the University of Sussex, Gary trained as a Clinical Psychologist with South Thames Regional Health Authority, acquiring his Practitioner Doctorate in 1995. He spent the next three years employed within the NHS in Brighton where he worked primarily with those affected by sexual and physical health problems - including HIV/AIDS - and with men who had been sexually abused or raped. His professional appointments and publications to date reflect his wide-ranging clinical, theoretical and research interests but most notably his interest in social constructionism and issues relating to sexuality, gender and health.

Ian Warwick is a Senior Research Officer at the Thomas Coram Research Unit and Associate Director of the Education Policy Research Unit, both at the Institute of Education, University of London. He has been involved in AIDS-related research since 1986. His research interests include identifying young people's sexual health needs and concerns in developing countries, lifeskills education in central and eastern Europe and developing programmatic approaches to gay men's HIV prevention in London. He is the co-author and editor of numerous reports, articles and books, including *AIDS: Working with Young People, Health Promotion with Young People: An Introductory Guide to Evaluation* and *Young People and Mental Health*.

Sue Wilkinson is Professor of Feminist and Health Studies in the Department of Social Sciences at Loughborough University. She was one of a group of psychologists (including Adrian Coyle, Celia Kitzinger, Martin Milton and Ian Rivers) whose campaigning efforts resulted in the establishment of a Lesbian & Gay Psychology Section within the British Psychological Society in 1998. She is the founding and current editor of the international journal *Feminism & Psychology* and is the author/editor of six books, including *Feminist Social Psychologies: International Perspectives* (1996, Open University Press) and, with Celia Kitzinger, *Representing the Other* (1996, Sage) and *Heterosexuality* (1993, Sage).

Foreword
The Cutting Edges of Lesbian and Gay Psychology

Anthony R. D'Augelli

In some respects, the psychological study of lesbian and gay lives has a short history (but see Chapter 1 in this volume). The landmark work of Evelyn Hooker published in the 1950s (for example, Hooker, 1957) was the first to use a traditional psychological research design – an experimental comparison by expert psychodiagnosticians of the projective test responses of matched heterosexual and gay men – in testing a hypothesis with profound importance for lesbian and gay lives. This research provided the empirical foundation for the removal of homosexuality from the American Psychiatric Association's list of mental disorders years later in 1973. Following Hooker, the application of social science methodologies to the study of homosexuality would wait many years and was taken up systematically by several studies conducted by the Kinsey Institute (Weinberg and Williams, 1974; Bell and Weinberg, 1978), including the first to attempt to model developmental pathways to same-sex sexual orientations (Bell *et al.*, 1981). Thereafter, studies were initiated by individual researchers, who often jeopardized their careers by conducting the research. Using convenience samples (which were exceedingly difficult to obtain given the intense social stigmatization of lesbian and gay people), researchers attempted to understand the complex psychological issues facing lesbians and gay men. Among the most important studies of this era was the first paper on the psychosocial experiences of children raised by lesbian mothers (Golombok *et al.*, 1983). This was a landmark study in several ways. It demonstrated the need to go beyond an understanding of gay individuals to attend to core social units (in this case, lesbian mother-child dyads). It also documented the very existence of lesbian mothers and their children in society at a time when these families were neither part of the cultural landscape nor part of the agendas of researchers studying 'normal' children or families. Similar accomplishments can be attributed to *The Male Couple* (McWhirter and Mattison, 1984), which reported a study that documented the existence of long-standing same-sex couples. At the end of the 1980s, another revolutionary research project appeared –

Kitzinger's (1987) analysis of the nature of lesbian identities, a work that challenged both the ideology and the methodology of psychological researchers. Other studies carried out prior to the 1990s could be mentioned. Suffice to say that by the beginning of the 1990s, enough psychological research had appeared to merit an edited volume (Gonsiorek and Weinrich, 1991) summarizing work that could inform social policy about sexual orientation. Furthermore, it would be beyond the scope of these comments to attempt to review the voluminous empirical research that has appeared in the last decade. An interested reader can consult several volumes (for example, Greene and Herek, 1994; D'Augelli and Patterson, 1995, 2001; Patterson and D'Augelli, 1998).

As more research has accumulated, increasing demands have been placed upon research findings to help charter rational approaches through the often volatile waters of societal discussions of homosexuality. The protection of women and men from discrimination and violence based on their sexual orientation, the determination of the age at which sexual behaviour is legal, the inclusion of education about sexual orientation in schools, the nature of same-sex committed relationships and their social value and the impact of growing up within families headed by lesbian or gay parents are among the issues that current research has influenced. Such research has served to prevent bias and bigotry from perpetuating unfair social practices and has led the way to an affirmative psychological approach that emphasizes the strengths of lesbians and gay men, their significant others and their communities. Psychological research on lesbians and gay men has thus been at the cutting edge of social change.

The cutting edge of lesbian and gay psychology is not only directed to social problems but to psychology itself for, until the assertion of a lesbian and gay psychology, psychology was blind to variability in human sexual orientations. The construct was not considered essential to psychological models of human development and behaviour. Because of the stigmatizing of non-heterosexual orientations, no variations in this domain were considered. Now, however, psychological knowledge can be challenged on heterosexist grounds. Just as queer theorists in the humanities have, since the early 1990s, challenged traditional readings of texts for their motivated erasure of homoerotic desire, lesbian and gay psychologists challenge the heterosexism of traditional psychological research and practice. The analysis of every substantive area covered in this volume – development during adolescence, girls' friendships, identity formation and disclosure, parenting and family issues, health issues, psychotherapeutic and other interventions and social attitudes – will need to include findings such as those reported by the psychologists (and other social scientists) represented here. It is no longer intellectually (not to mention empirically) possible to maintain heterosexual hegemony in psychological research. Research in lesbian and gay psychology has the potential to reinvent identity and social processes (including development over the lifespan and the nature of the family) by declaring the existence of different sexual orientations. The field of psychology cannot go back. The weight of the evidence is clear.

The challenge of a lesbian and gay psychology as represented in these chapters goes beyond the ideological to the methodological. A powerful interplay of qualitative and quantitative methods is apparent here; indeed, there may be a critical distinction between British lesbian and gay psychology and its American counterpart in the pre-eminence of qualitative methods and the frequent use of an explicitly deconstructionist approach in British work. Both the ideographic and the nomothetic are required but, in a lesbian and gay psychology, these approaches are deemed epistemologically equivalent. The multiplicity of approaches may reflect an historical dynamic in which the quest for secure (and valued) sexual identity conflicts with an understanding that security in sexual matters is not to be trusted. An unstable cutting edge will be the rule, not a temporary exception. As new dimensions of sexuality are constructed/discovered by psychological researchers, new questions will arise. The assertion of a lesbian and gay psychology is assured in the interplay of qualitative and quantitative methods; using the approaches together, it becomes less possible to marginalize variability in psychological experience. Lesbian and gay psychology, with its relatively short history, is apparently on its way to a long future indeed.

References

BELL, A.P. and WEINBERG, M.S. (1978) *Homosexualities: A Study of Diversity Among Men and Women*. New York: Touchstone Books.

BELL, A.P., WEINBERG, M.S. and HAMMERSMITH, S.K. (1981) *Sexual Preference: Its Development in Men and Women*. Bloomington, IN: Indiana University Press.

D'AUGELLI, A.R. and PATTERSON, C.J. (Eds) (1995) *Lesbian, Gay, and Bisexual Identities Over the Lifespan: Psychological Perspectives*. New York: Oxford University Press.

D'AUGELLI, A.R. and PATTERSON, C.J. (Eds) (2001) *Lesbian, Gay, and Bisexual Identities and Youth: Psychological Perspectives*. New York: Oxford University Press.

GOLOMBOK, S., SPENCER, A. and RUTTER, M. (1983) Children in lesbian and single-parent households: Psychosocial and psychiatric appraisal. *Journal of Child Psychology and Psychiatry*, 24, 551-572.

GONSIOREK, J.C. and WEINRICH, J.D. (Eds) (1991) *Homosexuality: Research Implications for Public Policy*. Newbury Park, CA: Sage.

GREENE, B. and HEREK, G.M. (Eds) (1994) *Lesbian and Gay Psychology: Theory, Research, and Clinical Applications*. Thousand Oaks, CA: Sage.

HOOKER, E. (1957) The adjustment of the male overt homosexual. *Journal of Projective Techniques*, 21, 18-31.

KITZINGER, C. (1987) *The Social Construction of Lesbianism*. London: Sage.

McWHIRTER, D.P. and MATTISON, A.M. (1994) *The Male Couple: How Relationships Develop*. Englewood Cliffs, NJ: Prentice-Hall.

PATTERSON, C.J. and D'AUGELLI, A.R. (Eds) (1998) *Lesbian, Gay, and Bisexual Identities in Families: Psychological Perspectives*. New York: Oxford University Press.

WEINBERG, M.S. and WILLIAMS, C.J. (1974) *Male Homosexuals: Their Problems and Adjustment*. New York: Oxford University Press.

Chapter 1

Introducing Lesbian and Gay Psychology

Celia Kitzinger and Adrian Coyle

Publication of this book marks the 'coming of age' of British lesbian and gay psychology. It celebrates the founding of the British Psychological Society's (BPS) Lesbian and Gay Psychology Section in 1998 after nine years of campaigning and three rejected proposals (two for a Psychology of Lesbianism Section and one for a Lesbian and Gay Psychology Section). The contributors to this book have generously agreed to donate all royalties to Section funds (as, of course, have the editors). As two of the campaigners who (with Martin Milton and Sue Wilkinson – who have also contributed to this book) ushered the successful proposal through the boards, committees and elections required to make the BPS Lesbian and Gay Psychology Section a reality, we are pleased and proud to have helped to create the conditions under which lesbian and gay psychology can flourish in a British context, as it has already blossomed in North America under the guidance of Division 44 (the Society for the Psychological Study of Lesbian, Gay, and Bisexual Issues) of the American Psychological Association. This book is part of a continuing contribution to the development of a vibrant, diverse and challenging lesbian and gay psychology in a European context.

The field of 'lesbian and gay psychology' initially emerged as a protest against the heterosexism of mainstream psychology. Until the mid-1970s, the vast majority of psychological research (both North American and European) presented homosexuality as a form of pathology, with lesbians and gay men characterized as the sick products of disturbed upbringings (Rosario, 1997). Psychology textbooks routinely presented material on lesbians and gay men under headings implying sickness (for example, 'sexual deviation' or 'sexual dysfunction') (Hall, 1985). The overwhelming majority of psychological research studies on the topic relied on samples drawn from prisons, mental hospitals and psychologists' consulting rooms – and most of these studies were conducted on gay male samples, with the findings generalized to 'include' lesbians (Morin, 1977; Morin and Rothblum, 1991). Techniques designed to convert gay men and lesbians into heterosexuals (aversion therapy, systematic desensitization, castration, psychosurgery and some forms of psychotherapy) were commonplace (see Rosario, 1997). Research on lesbian and gay issues was concentrated in clinical and psychotherapeutic psychology (concerned with the causes and cures of pathological conditions), while mainstream psychology – dealing with staple topics such as education, work and leisure, lifespan development, parenting, health and so on – simply ignored lesbians and gay men altogether, as though lesbians and gay men never attended school, didn't have jobs or leisure activities, didn't grow up or grow old, never had children, never got ill and so on. By leaving lesbians and gay men out of the 'everyday' psychology of ordinary human experience and including them only as florid instances of sexual deviation, this traditional psychology provided a grossly distorted picture of the lives, functioning and well-being of lesbians and gay men.

In the first section of this chapter, we answer the question 'what is lesbian and gay psychology?' and deal with some of the misconceptions which have sometimes been raised about the field and which we had to address in convincing the BPS of the need for a Lesbian and Gay Psychology Section. From the mid-1970s until very recently, the field has been overwhelmingly authored by North American psychologists and our discussion in this first section reflects this. In the second section ('Looking Back to the First Wave: On Not Reinventing the Wheel'), we turn to the European context and outline the early emergence of research and activism in late nineteenth and early twentieth century Germany and Britain, including the founding of the British Society for the Study of Sex Psychology in 1914. In the third section, called 'British Lesbian and Gay Psychology: The Second Wave', we turn to more contemporary British work and document the founding of the BPS Lesbian and Gay Psychology Section. Finally, in the last section, entitled 'Current Contributions: Developing Lesbian and Gay Psychology', we consider the contributions made by those who have written chapters for the current volume and indicate the directions in which we would like to see lesbian and gay psychology moving in the future.

What is lesbian and gay psychology?

Lesbian and gay psychology is psychology which is explicit about its relevance to lesbians and gay men, which does not assume homosexual pathology and which aims to counter prejudice and discrimination against people who are not conventionally heterosexual and to create a better world for lesbians and gay men. As such, lesbian and gay psychology is both a scholarly scientific enterprise and, equally, a clearly policy-oriented, practical, real-world undertaking. The relationship between scholarship and advocacy has a troubled history in psychology – as in other disciplines – but today it is generally recognized that psychological research on many topics has policy implications and that we have a responsibility to make our knowledge and skills as psychologists available to a broader audience of non-psychologists – to 'give psychology away' (MacKay, 2000).

Although anti-lesbian and anti-gay prejudice and discrimination are still apparent within some psychological theory and practice (see Garnets *et al.*, 1991; Annesley and Coyle, 1995, 1998; Kitzinger, 1996; Simoni, 1996; Chernin *et al.*, 1997; Milton and Coyle, 1998), it does not now receive explicit support from psychological bodies or from expert researchers and it is rare to find overt reference to homosexuality as pathology within Anglo-American psychological writing (Morin and Rothblum, 1991; see Herek, 1998, for a discussion of some exceptions). Since the mid-1970s, North American psychology has led the way in creating a lesbian and gay psychology that starts from the assumption that homosexuality falls within the 'normal' range of human behaviour (details of the development of lesbian and gay psychology in the British and European context are discussed in the next two sections of this chapter). 'Homosexuality' was removed as an official diagnostic category from the American Psychiatric Association's *Diagnostic and Statistical Manual of Mental Disorders* in 1973. In 1975, the American Psychological Association (APA) adopted the official policy that homosexuality *per se* does not imply any kind of mental health impairment and urged mental health professionals to take the lead in removing the stigma of mental illness that had long been associated with lesbian and gay sexualities. Nine years later, in 1984, the APA approved the establishment of Division 44, dedicated to the psychological study of lesbian and gay (and, later, bisexual) issues. Research on lesbian and gay issues has now moved well beyond simply demonstrating the 'normality' of lesbians and gay men. The field is no longer devoted solely to arguing the case for homosexuality as a normal variant of sexual behaviour but instead attempts to investigate a wide range of issues of concern to lesbians and gay men. Key texts outlining and defining the field of lesbian and gay psychology as it has developed in North America include those of Garnets and Kimmel (1993), Greene and Herek (1994), D'Augelli and Patterson (1995, 2001), Herek and Greene (1995), Bohan (1996), Savin-Williams and Cohen (1996), Greene (1997), Herek (1998), Patterson and D'Augelli (1998) and Greene and Croom (2000).

Key topics in contemporary lesbian and gay psychology include the establishment of lesbian, gay and bisexual identities; building healthy same-sex relationships; lifespan developmental issues in relation to sexuality; homophobia and anti-lesbian and anti-gay discrimination; lesbian and gay parenting; ethnic and cultural diversity among lesbians, gay men and bisexuals; and issues of 'choice', flexibility and flux in sexual behaviours (see Kitzinger *et al.*, 1998, for an overview). As with research in any other area of psychology, a wide range of different theoretical frameworks – from psychobiological to postmodern –

has been fruitfully employed. Lesbian and gay psychology has offered a particularly fertile ground for discussions and debates about the relative utility of essentialist and social constructionist perspectives in creating political change (see Kitzinger, 1995, for an overview). The diversity of perspectives adopted and the often vigorous debate between their adherents attest to the vitality of lesbian and gay psychology as a field of inquiry.

There are four misconceptions about lesbian and gay psychology which can usefully be addressed here. First, we are *not* claiming that lesbians and gay men have unique psychological features, that they possess psychologies so different from those of heterosexuals as to merit special study in their own right. That, in fact, is the kind of psychology we want to challenge. Rather, we believe that the development of a more inclusive psychology of humankind requires a focus on the particular issues confronting a traditionally under-represented and *mis*represented group and a concentrated effort to *include* lesbians and gay men in psychology as a whole. The inclusion of lesbians and gay men into a psychology which has hitherto taken heterosexuality as the norm (like the inclusion of women into a psychology based on men-as-norm and the inclusion of black people into a psychology based on white-as-norm) calls for major changes to the theoretical frameworks and knowledge bases of the discipline of psychology itself.

Secondly, despite its name, lesbian and gay psychology has also historically included work on bisexual, transgender and – indeed – *hetero*sexual issues and many organizations initially set up with a 'lesbian and gay' title have expanded their names so as explicitly to include first 'bisexual' and then 'transgender' issues: this is a development that has been called for and that we foresee as likely to occur in the British context too (Moon, 2000). As yet, however, there is very little by way of an explicitly 'bisexual' or 'transgender' – or, indeed, explicitly 'heterosexual' – British psychology (but see, for example, Coleman, 1981/1982, Coleman, 1985, Fox, 1995, and Firestein, 1996, on bisexuality; Hegarty and Chase, 2000, and Kitzinger, 2000, on intersex; and Wilkinson and Kitzinger, 1993, on heterosexuality) and it was a requirement of establishing the BPS Lesbian and Gay Psychology Section that we demonstrate the prior existence of relevant bodies of work, which is why the name of the Section is currently limited to 'lesbian and gay' psychology. It is, however, important not to draw the boundaries of lesbian and gay psychology too narrowly. In particular, lesbian and gay issues have always been deeply implicated with notions of gender (as in the stereotypes of 'mannish' lesbian women and 'effeminate' gay men), so there is much to be gained by bringing an explicitly feminist analysis to bear on lesbian and gay issues (and, conversely, by incorporating lesbian and gay issues into psychological work on gender). The lack of cross-fertilization between the psychology of women/gender and lesbian and gay psychology to date (see

Kitzinger, 1996, 2001) remains problematic. Another important area of psychology with which lesbian and gay psychology could usefully develop stronger links is the psychology of race/ethnicity. In struggling against oppression, US homosexual organizations owed a great deal to the example of Martin Luther King and the early black movement which came to prominence in the mid 1950s. Arguments based on the similarity between the oppression of black people and of homosexuals were key to one of the earliest North American books dealing with gay life by a gay author: Donald Webster Cory's *The Homosexual in America* (1951) argued that homosexuals shared a 'caste-like' status with ethnic, religious and racial minorities. However, lesbian and gay psychology – like psychology more generally – has historically been predominantly about the lives and experiences of white men and has failed to engage with sexism, racism or other forms of oppression in deriving its own theories of anti-lesbian and gay discrimination or to deal with the intersection of these different forms of oppression. Although there is now increasing work which redresses these absences (for example, Greene, 1997; Phellas, 1998; Coyle and Rafalin, 2000) – and also work in other disciplines which can be drawn upon (for example, Silvera, 1991; Reyes and Yep, 1997; Rhue and Rhue, 1997; Parker and Caceres, 1999) – more needs to be done as a matter of urgency in order to ensure that lesbian and gay psychology does not privilege a narrow range of voices and perspectives and marginalize and silence others. It is not acceptable for lesbian and gay psychology to have critiqued mainstream psychology for ignoring lesbian and gay lives or for attending to them only within limited and negative frameworks (such as frameworks of psychopathology) and then to proceed to do the same to those lesbian and gay experiences and lives which differ from those which have formed the basis of the majority of existing research and writing in the field. One good scientific reason for avoiding this situation is that the study of previously unexplored or poorly charted experiences and perspectives may produce findings which challenge or at least enrich and elaborate some taken-for-granted theories and concepts within lesbian and gay psychology. For example, Phellas's (1998) research with second generation Greek Cypriot gay men living in London found that these men conceptualized their gay identities in ways which would not have been predicted by existing models of gay identity: identity was constructed in terms of relationships with families, peers and other members of their community but gay identity was not necessarily a primary identity component.

Thirdly, perhaps because of the fact that bisexual, transgender and heterosexual issues all fall within the remit of 'lesbian and gay' psychology, it is sometimes suggested that the field should be labelled the 'psychology of sexuality' (Adams, 1992; Martin, 1995). However, this implies a narrow focus on sexual practices, ignoring the broad range of psychosocial issues (such as employment, parenting, ageing) which constitute the core of contemporary lesbian and gay psychology. Such a restricted focus would make it even harder to make links with theories of gender, race, ethnicity and class, other than as variables impacting on sexual practices. It is, however, also worth noting that (with the exception of research on safer sex and HIV/AIDS) there is in fact remarkably little psychological work on lesbian and gay sexual practices. Sexuality research is typically constrained by a heterosexual paradigm which assumes the insertion of a penis into a vagina as the key sexual act and which considers lesbian and gay sexual practices (if it considers them at all) as variations on this theme. Taking heterosexual couples as 'standard' and measuring lesbians and gay men against them has led (even lesbian and gay psychologists) to the conclusion that lesbians have 'too little' sex (and suffer from something called 'merger' or 'fusion') while gay men have 'too much' sex (and suffer from an inability to form lasting commitments) (Krestan and Bepko, 1980; Burch, 1982; Clunis and Green, 1988; Perlman, 1989; Klinkenberg and Rose, 1994; Gray and Isensee, 1996). These findings depend on measuring everyone's sexuality in terms derived from a heterosexual norm (see Kitzinger and Coyle, 1995). Developing lesbian and gay-centred research on sexuality, then, *is* important – but it is certainly not the only or the most central issue in lesbian and gay psychology.

Finally, it is sometimes thought that only lesbians and gay men can practise lesbian and gay psychology. This has never, in fact, been the case. The phrases 'lesbian psychologist' and 'gay psychologist' mean (in this context) psychologists working on this type of psychology – just as the terms 'social psychologist' or 'sports psychologist' refer to psychologists involved in other types of psychology. A 'lesbian and gay psychologist' can be heterosexual, just as a 'social psychologist' can be anti-social or a 'sports psychologist' can be a couch potato. Of course many (but not all) 'lesbian and gay psychologists' are themselves lesbian, gay, bisexual or transgendered and bring to their research an 'insider' perspective. But there are also many important heterosexual contributors to the field. Equally, just as many heterosexual psychologists have researched topics other than heterosexuality, there are many psychologists who happen to be lesbian, gay, bisexual or transgendered who have not chosen to make lesbian and gay issues the focus of their psychological research or practice. Lesbian and gay psychologists have made remarkable inroads in challenging the heterosexism of mainstream psychology but much remains to be done in order for psychology adequately to reflect the full range and diversity of human experience. In the next two sections, we chart some of the history of lesbian and gay psychology from the 'first wave' of scholarship in the late nineteenth and early twentieth century, to the 'second wave' in the closing decades of the twentieth century.

Looking back to the first wave: on not reinventing the wheel

In Britain and mainland Europe, lesbian and gay scholarship started in the late nineteenth and early twentieth centuries, long before North American work in the area. The BPS Lesbian and Gay Psychology Section inherits a long European tradition of emancipatory scholarship and social activism.[1] The first social movement to advance the civil rights of homosexuals was founded (in Germany) more than a century ago, in 1897. The Scientific Humanitarian Committee, founded by a medical doctor, Magnus Hirschfeld, and a lawyer, Karl Ulrichs, adopted the motto 'justice through science', and set the stage for the development of European scholarship on lesbian and gay issues. The Committee sponsored research on sexual issues, edited a journal called the *Yearbook for Intermediate Sexual Types* and produced information for the public, including a leaflet entitled *What You Should Know About the Third Sex* and a film called *Different from Other People*. It also carried out one of the earliest sex surveys (in 1903), distributing over 6 000 questionnaires about sexual practices to students and factory workers and concluding that 2.2 per cent of the population was homosexual. In 1919, the Committee acquired a building, the Institute of Sexual Science, which became an internationally respected centre for sex research and included an extensive library and a museum. Until its suppression by the Nazis in 1933, it was the leading voice in the world for homosexual rights and its impact extended well beyond Germany. In 1906 and 1907, representatives from the Scientific Humanitarian Committee went to the USA to spread the word; Jacob Schorer, a Dutch lawyer, set up a Netherlands committee in 1911; Eric Thorsell, a Swedish steelworker, took its message to Sweden in the 1930s; and it was directly influential in the founding of the British Society for the Study of Sex Psychology in 1914. In 1921, Hirschfeld set up the World League for Sexual Reform, which gained 130 000 members worldwide.

As its motto 'justice through science' indicates, the Scientific Humanitarian Committee was both a scholarly *and* a political organization. Both of its founders had published scientific texts: Ulrichs' two books on love between men are widely recognized as representing the first scientific treatment of homosexuality and Hirschfeld's book, *Sappho und Sokrates*, drew on Ulrichs' ideas, representing homosexuality as 'a deep inner-constituted natural instinct and as a gender stage between the extremes of masculinity and femininity' (Adam, 1987, p. 231). These ideas of homosexuals as 'intersex' or 'third sex' were reflected in the scholarly English writings of the time, by Havelock Ellis (*Sexual Inversion*, 1897) and Edward Carpenter (*The Intermediate Sex*, 1908), in which homosexual men were presented as having the 'female' qualities of gentleness and emotionality, while homosexual women possessed 'male' qualities and were 'fiery, active, bold and truthful'. The decriminalization of (male) homosexuality was a political goal driving these arguments, the logic being that if homosexuality is 'inborn' or 'innate', then homosexuals should not be held accountable for a condition (whether inferior to heterosexuality, or not) over which they had no control. By changing the public conceptualization of homosexuality from one of wilful depravity to biological predisposition, activists hoped to bring about legal reform. In 1860s Germany, Ulrichs had launched this argument as part of his opposition to the new penal code in Germany designed to criminalize same-sex acts between men, Paragraph 175. In an open letter to the Minister of Justice in 1869 (co-authored with a Hungarian doctor, Benkert – pseudonym Kertbeny – who is often credited with inventing the word 'homosexual'), Ulrichs argued that because homosexuality is innate, it can be subject only to the laws of nature and not to penal law. They also listed famous 'homosexuals' from history who had made important contributions to society, such as Napoleon, Frederick the Great and Michelangelo. By the early 1900s, Ulrichs and Hirschfeld were using the argument that homosexuality was innate to oppose Paragraph 175, which had since become law. In 1907, the Scientific Humanitarian Committee was canvassing political parties for their positions on law reform as the Reichstag elections approached: a public debate on Paragraph 175, sponsored by the Committee, attracted more than 2 000 people.

The British Society for the Study of Sex Psychology was likewise both a scholarly scientific organization and one committed to social change. Building on the work of the German pioneers Hirschfeld and Ulrichs, the British Society for the Study of Sex Psychology was founded in 1914 by Edward Carpenter (an open homosexual and socialist reformer) and Havelock Ellis (a doctor, whose wife, Edith, was openly lesbian and campaigned for lesbian rights during her lecture tour in the USA). Formed in the wake of the Oscar Wilde trials, which offered 'a terrifying moral tale' (Weeks, 1977, p. 21) of the consequences of homosexuality, the British organization, unlike the German one, focused almost exclusively on public education. Commenting on the legislative activism of the German counterpart, Carpenter said: 'We do not think the time has yet arrived in England for a similar demand to be made' (Adam, 1987, p. 54) – and in fact decriminalization of male homosexuality (for men over the age of 21, in private) was not successfully achieved in Britain until more than 50 years later. The Society sponsored public lectures and produced pamphlets including Stella Browne's *Sexual Variety and Variability among Women*, Havelock Ellis' *The Erotic Rights of Women* and Laurence Houseman's *The Relation of Fellow-Feeling to Sex*.

By contrast with these large and thriving European homosexual organizations, the first documented emancipation group in the USA was not formed until 1924, in Chicago, by Henry Gerber, a German-

American immigrant. Its aim (using the same argument popular in European contexts but adapted to the US situation) was 'to promote and to protect the interests of people who by reasons of mental and psychic abnormalities are abused and hindered in the legal pursuit of happiness which is guaranteed them by the Declaration of Independence' (Adam, 1987, p. 98). The group never had more than ten members: it was disbanded by the police and its directors dragged through the courts, as the *Chicago Examiner* trumpeted 'Strange sex cult exposed'.

The claim that homosexuality is biological in origin and not the result of 'choice' – and therefore not a 'sin' or a 'crime' – is a recurrent argument across more than a century of lesbian and gay history. The common early twentieth century argument that homosexuals were an essential 'type of being' with an 'innate condition', an 'intermediate' or 'third' sex – perhaps with admitted 'mental and psychic abnormalities' – was intended at the time as an emancipatory claim and was widespread amongst activists. Havelock Ellis' book, *Sexual Inversion*, has been described as 'a trifle old-fashioned, a diffidently elegant monument to past prejudice and ignorance. But to his contemporaries it often seemed daring, even outrageous' (Weeks, 2000, p. 17). Ellis argued that homosexuality (which he called 'inversion') was an 'anomaly' like colour blindness. He maintained that there were male and female 'elements' (what we would now call 'hormones') in everyone but that the 'male invert is a person with an unusual proportion of female elements, the female invert with an unusual proportion of male elements' (Weeks, 2000, p. 18). He meant to suggest through this hypothesis that the condition was not a result of choice. In one case study of a male homosexual, for example, he noted that it 'clearly showed that the case was congenital and not acquired, so that it could not be called a vice' (Ellis, 1897, p. 222):

> The inverted person may be as healthy as a colour-blind person. Congenital sexual inversion is thus akin to a biological variation. It is a variation doubtless due to imperfect sexual differentiation, but often having no traceable connection with any morbid condition in the individual himself.

The publication in 1928 of Radclyffe Hall's novel, *The Well of Loneliness*, drew on this same argument. Published with an introduction by Havelock Ellis, it made tortured pleas for the 'merciful toleration' of the 'pitiful plight of inverts' (p. i).

These arguments are remarkably similar to those used in late twentieth century Britain in opposing Section 28 of the 1988 Local Government Act (which banned the 'promotion' of homosexuality as a 'pretended family relationship' by local authorities) and in arguing for an equal age of consent for gay men. Just as some contemporary femi-

nist and lesbian activists (and, to a lesser extent, some gay male campaigners) consider 'born that way' strategies to be apologetic and
defensive, so too there were alternative pro-homosexual positions at
the turn of the last century. In Germany, a rival homosexual emancipation group called the 'Community of the Special' and led by Benedict
Friedlander campaigned – like the Scientific Humanitarian Committee
– against Paragraph 175 but rejected the claim that homosexuality was
innate. Friedlander criticized Hirschfeld's position as 'a degrading and
beggarly pleading for sympathy' and was openly scornful of the 'third
sex' theory and of the homosexual man as 'a poor womanly soul lan-
guishing away in a man's body' (Adam, 1987, p. 65). Similarly, there
were lesbians and feminists who rejected Radclyffe Hall's 'third sex'
version of female homosexuality. To a reader from the twenty-first century, these debates from a hundred years ago have a curiously
contemporary tone. They reflect questions often debated amongst
activists today: should we reassure heterosexuals that giving us our
rights will not lead to an increase in homosexuality (because it is innate
and nobody can be corrupted or seduced into a sexual orientation
which goes against their nature) or should we highlight the fact that
many people are prevented from same-sex sexual behaviours and
identities by the fact of massive societal oppression and discrimination? The late 1970s feminist slogan that 'any woman can be a lesbian'
and the late 1990s slogan that 'ten per cent is not enough – recruit,
recruit, recruit!' both emphasize and play on heterosexual fears of a
homosexual take-over, as an alternative strategy to reassurance. Both
strategies, it seems, have a long history in lesbian and gay activism.

Early homosexual activism confronted enormous obstacles, including the banning and burning of books, the imprisonment of their
authors and legal discrimination. With the rise of Nazism, there was a
systematic hounding of homosexual organizations and the murder of
homosexual individuals which eventually led to the virtually complete
suppression of homosexual activism and to the deletion of this early
scholarship from the research literature. The Institute for Sexual Science was destroyed on May 6th 1933 when Nazi storm troopers
ransacked the building and burned more than 10 000 volumes from its
extensive library. Hirschfeld was a Jew and fled to Paris where he died
in 1935. His lover, Kurt Giese, the secretary of the Institute, committed
suicide in 1936. Homosexuality was described by Himmler as 'a symptom of racial degeneracy destructive to our race...degenerates should
be exterminated' (Adam, 1987, p. 43). Nazi persecution wiped away
most of early homosexual culture so that the new gay movement of the
1950s grew up largely ignorant of and cut off from all that had gone
before.

The patchy and fragmented lesbian and gay activism that grew up
during the continuing politically repressive context of the 1940s and
1950s seems to have had no sense of its own history. Lesbians and gay

men in the USA were confronting the McCarthy era. An inquisitorial committee, which met to investigate the 'Employment of Homosexuals and Other Sex Perverts in Government', reported that homosexuals were subject to blackmail and were emotionally unstable and of weak moral fibre. Suspected homosexuals were rejected for government jobs and expelled from the military. In Britain similar tactics and government attacks included among their victims Alan Turing, the mathematician who broke the Nazi code for British intelligence and established the early principles of the computer. Both in Britain and in America, the mass media applauded the purge, churches sanctioned it and medical and psychiatric researchers experimented with lobotomies, castration, clitoridectomy and electroshock therapies to 'cure' homosexuals. Lesbian and gay groups formed during this time include, most famously, the Mattachine Society (named for the medieval court jester who expressed unpopular truths from behind a mask), founded in Los Angeles in 1951, and the lesbian group, Daughters of Bilitis, founded by Del Martin and Phyllis Lyon in 1955. Both groups encouraged their members to offer themselves up to 'duly authorized and responsible' experts in sociology and psychology as research subjects, in the hope that scientific knowledge about homosexuality would lead to the shattering of myths and stereotypes and to the acceptance of lesbians and gay men in society. The Homosexual Reform Society founded in Britain in 1958 had the more radical aims of implementing the recommendations of a government committee which had the previous year produced the unexpectedly liberal recommendation that homosexual behaviour between consenting adults in private should no longer be a criminal offence (which was finally implemented in 1967, with an age of consent for gay men of 21).

The birth of the modern lesbian and gay movement in the USA began with Frank Kameny, a Harvard PhD in Astronomy, who was dismissed from his army post in 1957 for being a known homosexual. Taking the lead of African American militants like Stokely Carmichael, Kameny drew explicit parallels between the black and gay civil rights struggles and coined the phrase 'Gay is Good' to parallel 'Black is Beautiful'. Frank Kameny was one of the key people involved in challenging the psychiatric classification of homosexuality as illness. In 1968, the North American Conference of Homophile Organizations resolved that 'homosexuality is in no way inferior to heterosexuality as a valid way of life' (Adam, 1987, p. 102) and accepted the 'Gay is Good' slogan. A series of protests and demonstrations from 1968 onwards – making the most of psychologist Evelyn Hooker's (1957/1992) research showing no mental health differences between homosexual and heterosexual men – finally led to the vote in the American Psychiatric Association, approving the removal of homosexuality *per se* from the *Diagnostic and Statistical Manual of Mental Disorders* five years later. However, something called 'ego-dystonic homosexuality' – describing instances where a person has failed to accept their sexuality and consequently experiences persistent distress and wishes to be heterosexual – remained until 1987: needless to say, there was no parallel category of 'ego-dystonic heterosexuality' to diagnose those heterosexuals who wished they were lesbian or gay, although the lesbian feminist movement by that time had actually led some heterosexual women to a fervent desire to become lesbian (see Wilkinson and Kitzinger, 1993).

The routine symbolic dating of lesbian and gay liberation to the Stonewall riots in 1969 erases a century of homosexual scholarship and activism. When the police raided the small gay bar, the Stonewall Inn, on Christopher Street in New York's Greenwich Village on a Friday night on June 27th-28th 1969, it was already the 100th anniversary of European gay liberation: it was in 1869 that Ulrichs and Benkert had written their open letter to the German Minister of Justice, opposing the criminalization of gay men.

One mechanism by which oppression operates is the systematic deletion of people's history, so that subsequent generations of lesbian and gay (or black or female) people confront discrimination and prejudice anew, as if for the first time, without any knowledge of the lesbian and gay (or black or female) pioneers of the past and their struggles and strategies. Not knowing our own history of resistance, believing ourselves to be the 'first', we are unable to learn from the failures and successes of the past: we are forced to 'reinvent the wheel'. Reclaiming our own history is both an important liberatory strategy and, of course, an index of good scholarship, in properly acknowledging prior research and other work in our area. So far, however, early European lesbian and gay scholarship has apparently been only of interest to historians (for example, Weeks, 2000). The deletion of our history has been so successful that most contemporary British lesbian and gay psychologists and activists refer to the North American context (Stonewall) to locate the symbolic 'birth' of our movement and think of the early homosexual activists (if they think of them at all) as hopelessly outdated apologists for homosexuality – embarrassing anachronisms unworthy to provide any basis for contemporary psychology. This is not the case for other areas of psychology which routinely refer to and engage with the work of their late nineteenth and early twentieth century 'founding fathers' such as William James, Sigmund Freud, John B. Watson, Ivan Pavlov, Kurt Lewin and James Cattell. As with the work of early homosexual scholars, the writings of James, Freud, Watson, Pavlov, Lewin and Cattell reflect their own particular historical and cultural settings and have various blatant failings and limitations by today's standards. But contemporary psychologists still engage with their work because it is ground-breaking, provocative and challenging and because it is part of the history of our discipline, shaping the theories and methods that we use today. So, too, we can benefit by engaging with the work of early homosexual scholars. Lesbian and gay psychology needs its 'founding fathers' (and founding mothers) too.

British lesbian and gay psychology: the second wave

The British Psychological Society's (BPS) Lesbian and Gay Psychology Section was officially inaugurated at the BPS London Conference on 18th December 1998, marking the culmination of nearly a decade of struggle. Here we describe why we became involved in the struggle to set up this organization, how we finally succeeded in establishing it and how we see it helping to shape the future of lesbian and gay psychology.

After the destruction of the early homosexual emancipation movement by the Second World War, there was very little European psychological research offering positive images of lesbians or gay men until the 1960s – and then there were only scattered instances (for example, Hopkins, 1969). In the late 1970s and early 1980s, two psychologists, John Hart and Diane Richardson, published some important work covering a range of topics in lesbian and gay psychology including therapy (Richardson and Hart, 1980), parenting (Richardson, 1978) and theories about the causation and implications of homosexuality (Hart and Richardson, 1981) – including one article (on the differences between homosexual men and women) in the official journal of the British Psychological Society – then called the *Bulletin* (Hart and Richardson, 1980; see also Furnell, 1986). This work fitted well with developments in British sociology at the time (for example, Plummer, 1981; Weeks, 1981) and, in her subsequent writing, Richardson addressed sociological and women's studies readerships rather than a psychological audience (for example, Richardson, 1996). This early British work by Hart and Richardson, however, laid some of the groundwork for Kitzinger's research on lesbianism which addressed a specifically psychological audience and was published during the mid 1980s (Kitzinger and Stainton Rogers, 1985; Kitzinger, 1987). This was followed by an article on 'heterosexism in psychology' (Kitzinger, 1990) published in *The Psychologist* (as the official journal of the BPS had been retitled). By the early 1990s, lesbian and gay psychology was also establishing a foothold in mainland Europe. A European Association of Lesbian, Gay and Bisexual Psychologists was founded in 1992 (and had symposia accepted for subsequent European Congresses of Psychology) and, in 1993, homosexuality was removed from the World Health Organization's *International Classification of Diseases*, the diagnostic handbook generally used outside North America.

Despite these developments, however, and despite a general sense that both the world in general and psychology in particular were in some ways becoming more 'liberal' and accepting of lesbianism and of male homosexuality, by the beginning of the 1990s, the campaigners for the Section were very aware of the need both for social and political change and for radical challenges to psychology's continued assumption of heterosexuality as the default option – the normal and natural way for (most) people to be. In the last decade of the twentieth century, there was still (and continues to be) a massive amount of discrimination. Lesbians, gay men and other non-heterosexuals are discriminated against and oppressed to varying degrees by laws and social policies across the world (Ellis, 1999). Same-sex sexual acts are still illegal in more than 70 countries and are punishable with prison sentences (for example, in Bermuda, Nigeria and Romania); beatings (for example, in India and Pakistan); and execution (for example, in Iran, Kuwait and Saudi Arabia) (Amnesty International, 1997). In the USA, where one survey found 54 per cent of the population stating that homosexuality was a 'sin' (Peyser, 1998), crimes of violence and harassment against lesbians and gay men are endemic (Herek and Berrill, 1992). A US national survey of males aged 15–19 found that few (12 per cent) felt they could have a gay friend and that most (89 per cent) considered sex between males to be 'disgusting' (Marsiglio, 1993). Large scale surveys in Britain also indicate continued negative attitudes towards lesbians and gay men (Wellings *et al.*, 1994; Jowell *et al.*, 1996). Attempts were (and are) still being made to convert homosexuals into heterosexuals (Leland and Miller, 1998). In most countries, lesbians and gay men also face widespread discrimination in education, in the workplace and in health care, and (at the time of writing) in no country in the world do same-sex relationships have the same legal and social status as heterosexual marriage (Amnesty International, 1997, 1999).

Meanwhile, psychology as a discipline – while (on the whole) no longer actively collaborating in the oppression of lesbians and gay men – did not actively seek to challenge this oppression. By the 1990s, it had become apparent that, while the British Medical Association and other professional bodies were increasingly willing to make public statements aimed at policy makers on lesbian and gay issues, the British Psychological Society remained conspicuously silent. Public debates on lesbian and gay issues in education, adoption and fostering and lesbian insemination rights passed by with virtually no formal and official comment from psychologists. There was still nothing of substance taught about lesbians and gay men in undergraduate psychology courses and on educational, clinical and occupational psychology programs (see Pilkington and Cantor, 1996, and Long, 1996, for a review of the situation in the USA). Newly-qualified psychologists were practising within their fields without any specialist training on the issues facing lesbian and gay children or the children of lesbian and gay parents in the classroom; without any specialist training which might help them to treat successfully the relationship problems which lesbians or gay men might bring into therapy; and without any expert knowledge of lesbian and gay equal opportunity issues in the workplace. There was, still, very little British lesbian and gay psychological research, in part because students wanting to do undergraduate projects or doctoral dissertations were warned off researching lesbian and gay topics on the (probably accurate) grounds that the stigma associated with carrying out such work would be detrimental to their careers. Without formal recognition by the BPS of lesbian and gay psychology as a legitimate area of the discipline, it was hard for those of us working in the field to be seen as legitimate psychologists (in the same sense as developmental psychologists or health psychologists, for example) and our work was not supported financially or administratively by the BPS in the same way as work in other areas. We had no newsletter or journal, no symposia at BPS conferences, no conferences of our own and no formal right to input into the BPS committees which determine issues of the psychology curriculum, professional training and accreditation, policy statements and so on. Those of us who had previously been involved in the BPS Psychology of Women Section (PoWS) Committee (notably Sue Wilkinson, a founder member and the first elected Chair of PoWS and Celia Kitzinger, a member of the PoWS committee) had experienced at first hand the concrete benefits that accrue to areas of psychology that become formally recognized as Sections within the BPS. We wanted that for lesbian and gay psychology.

The first attempts to gain formal recognition for lesbian and gay psychology in the UK were launched in 1990 by four lesbians (no gay men were, at that time, forthcoming). Two academic psychologists (Celia Kitzinger and Sue Wilkinson), a clinical psychologist (Rachel Perkins) and an educational psychologist (Louise Comely) formed the steering group 'Lesbians in Psychology Sisterhood' (LIPS) which spent many evenings over pizza and wine in Louise's flat planning tactics, drafting documents and stuffing envelopes for mailings (see Wilkinson, 1999, for a history of the development of the Section). The aim was to generate a 'climate' conducive to submitting a Section proposal for formal approval within the BPS. This included mailing hundreds of letters, seeking expressions of support and interest and organizing and participating in conferences. Our first Section proposal – for a Psychology of Lesbianism Section – was rejected by the BPS Scientific Affairs Board (SAB) in April 1991 and by the BPS Council the following October, thereby halting the process. At this time, LIPS members received some abusive mail from BPS members (for example, one correspondent suggested that 'lesbians do not need psychology, they need a good stiff all-round talking to').

This first proposal also precipitated a major split within PoWS, of which all four of LIPS were members. The PoWS Committee refused to support the proposal (Ussher, 1991) on the grounds that lesbian concerns could be dealt with by PoWS under the remit of 'women's' issues, and also refused LIPS permission to address PoWS members at their Annual Conference. In protest, LIPS and its supporters staged a disruption. Wearing t-shirts emblazoned with the words 'Visible Lesbian', a group of lesbians invaded the platform after the conference keynote address, releasing balloons and delivering a rehearsed performance to dramatize our complaints. A change of Chair finally led to this decision being reversed (Beloff, 1993) but PoWS's support was too little and too late and the proposal submitted to the BPS in 1993 was again turned down, both by SAB and by Council. In psychology, as in activism more generally, there has been insufficient recognition of the intersection of oppressions and this incident offers an illustration of the extent to which attempts are sometimes made to advance women's liberation at the expense of lesbians (and there are many instances, of course, in which efforts are made to advance gay liberation at the expense of women: see Kitzinger, 1996).

The following year saw a major change in strategy, as gay men joined lesbians in the struggle for a Section. Six of us (Marc Burke, Adrian Coyle, Rob Flynn, Celia Kitzinger, Rachel Perkins and Sue Wilkinson) submitted a revised proposal – now for a 'Lesbian and Gay Psychology Section' (Ian Rivers stepped in to replace Marc Burke at the end of 1994). The proposal was endorsed by SAB but was rejected by the BPS Council by just one vote. Following this disappointment, we continued to publish strategically in Society journals, including a review article on lesbian and gay relationships in *The Psychologist* (Kitzinger and Coyle, 1995), which was followed by two virulently heterosexist letters published under the headline 'Are you normal?' (Davis, 1995; Hamilton, 1995). Previously 'neutral' members of the Society were galvanized into supporting us by these letters. This led to a debate both about homosexuality in general and about the wisdom of creating a new Section, which spanned the June, July and September issues of *The Psychologist* that year. A revised version of the proposal – submitted by Celia Kitzinger, Adrian Coyle, Sue Wilkinson and Martin Milton – quickly obtained overwhelming support both at SAB and at Council in 1997–8. The tide of opinion had finally turned.

However, we still faced two final major hurdles – a requirement to obtain statements of intention to join the Section (should it be established) from one per cent of the BPS membership (i.e., from 230 individuals), followed by a ballot of the entire membership. The four of us spent from March to May 1998 mailing, by hand, not only our personal contacts but the entire Register of Chartered Psychologists (i.e., some 9 000 people) with information about the proposed Section and requests to support us. Subsequent abusive mail from Society members (for example, 'don't solicit, bitch'; 'your lot disgusts me'; 'keep to yourselves'; 'this reflects my disgust'), which we publicized, brought in more supporters. However, although we easily obtained the required 230 statements of intent to join, the amount of abusive mail left us uncertain about the outcome of the membership ballot. *The Psychologist* scheduled publication of an article on lesbian and gay psychology (Kitzinger *et al.*, 1998) to coincide with the date of the ballot and the result was announced on 5th December 1998: 1 988 members voted in favour, 1 623 voted against – the biggest 'anti' vote in any comparable ballot in the history of the BPS. But a simple majority was all we needed – and so later that month, the Section was born.

The formation of the Section has already brought many of the positive gains for lesbians and gay men that we hoped for, although as we write it is only two years since its formation. In particular, we have been successful in encouraging research developments through providing a forum for members to disseminate their research findings and engage in theoretical debate in the Section *Newsletter* (which was retitled *Lesbian & Gay Psychology Review* in 2000 to reflect more accurately the nature of its journal-standard, peer-reviewed articles); in special issues of journals (such as the special issue of the *Journal of Community & Applied Social Psychology* on 'Social psychological perspectives on lesbian and gay issues in Europe' – Coyle and Wilkinson, forthcoming); in Section Annual Conferences; and in Section symposia at BPS Annual and London Conferences (on lesbians, gay men and the family, lesbian and gay affirmative therapy, research perspectives in lesbian and gay psychology and gay men's behavioural responses to HIV/AIDS). Mindful of the need to encourage new researchers in the domain, the Section instituted a postgraduate prize in 2000 for original research in lesbian and gay psychology undertaken by Section members on postgraduate courses: the inaugural prize was won by Victoria Clarke (who has contributed a chapter to this volume) for her work on the psychology and politics of lesbian and gay parenting. The Section has acted as a channel for the dissemination of psychological expertise on issues related to lesbian and gay lives and, since its inception, has responded to many requests for advice and information from individuals, groups and organizations, thereby contributing to the shaping of public policy. For example, in May 2000, Fiona Tasker – who was a member of the inaugural Section committee – responded to an invitation from the Solicitors' Family Law Association and ran a workshop for this organization on same-sex parenting (to find out more about her ideas on this topic, see Chapter 5). The Section also prepared a statement on the age of consent for gay men – an issue which has been keenly debated in the UK parliament – concluding that, on the basis of psychological research, creating parity in the age of consent for gay men and heterosexuals would be psychologically beneficial for young gay men. Links have also been created with our sister organization, Division 44 of the APA, and officers of both organizations have contributed to each others' publications (Coyle, 1999; James, 2000). Although informal groups of lesbian and gay psychologists exist in

other countries, the BPS and the APA are the only national psychological societies that have formal subsystems devoted to lesbian and gay
psychology (although some attempts are being made in New Zealand:
see Lapsley and Paulin, 1994).

Current contributions: developing lesbian and gay psychology

This book, which was made possible by the formation of the Section, is
the first British-edited and authored collection on lesbian and gay psychology and offers a snapshot of the state of British lesbian and gay
psychology at the turn of the twenty-first century. The 14 chapters
reflect the current wide range and diversity of this psychological
domain in Britain. Despite the recurrent suggestions encountered
when we were campaigning to establish the Section that it should be
called the 'Psychology of Sexuality' Section, it is clear from the contents
of this book that the field of lesbian and gay psychology is not limited
to research on 'sex' or 'sexuality' but embraces a broad range of psychosocial issues. Ironically, the psychology of lesbian and gay *sexuality*
is only touched on in this book (although the psychology of gay male
sexuality has been partly addressed in the substantial literature on
HIV/AIDS) and this is one omission we would like to see rectified in
future research. The chapters address key issues across a variety of
mainstream areas of the discipline, including developmental psychology (the chapters by Ian Rivers; Laura A. Markowe; and Fiona Tasker),
health psychology (Sue Wilkinson; Ian Warwick and Peter Aggleton),
clinical, psychotherapeutic and counselling psychology (Gary Taylor;
Martin Milton, Adrian Coyle and Charles Legg; Maeve Malley and
Damian McCann), social, discursive and feminist psychology (Christine Griffin; Victoria Clarke; Sue Wilkinson; Brendan Gough), the
psychology of identity (Christine Griffin; Laura A. Markowe; Gary
Taylor), the psychology of close relationships (Christine Griffin) and
the psychology of rights, moral reasoning, attitudes and attitude
change (Sonja J. Ellis; Elizabeth Peel).

It is unfortunate that 'mainstream' psychology has, so far, generally
not seen lesbian and gay psychology as having anything of value to
offer in these areas. As various contributors to this volume point out,
lesbian and gay psychology has been pretty much ignored by mainstream psychological research or sidelined into token footnotes or final
paragraphs on 'diversity' (see Kitzinger, 1996; Coyle *et al.*, 1999). For
example, in a 20 year period, just 0.006 per cent of articles in marriage
and family therapy journals focused on gay, bisexual or lesbian issues
(Clarke and Serovich, 1987). Leaving lesbians, gay men and bisexuals
out of psychological research on core topics of psychology means that
we have a psychology of heterosexuals only – just as surely as the

exclusion of women and black people resulted in the development of a 'male' psychology and a 'white' psychology. As Christine Griffin points out in Chapter 3, for example, the widespread presumption of heterosexuality has biased youth research and our understanding of 'friendship' and, as Fiona Tasker illustrates in Chapter 5, theories of sexuality and gender development have been predicated upon the nuclear family. Feminist psychology and anti-racist psychology have demonstrated that 'adding in' a group of people who have been systematically excluded often entails major theoretical reconceptualization – a task which is just beginning. Heterosexual assumptions have often been built into the theories (for example, of adolescent development, of marriage and the family, of health services delivery) of basic and applied psychology and erasing them may mean fundamentally altering the theory itself, as Martin Milton, Adrian Coyle and Charles Legg point out in relation to the possibility of creating 'lesbian and gay affirmative' versions of psychotherapeutic theories in Chapter 10, for example. Here, we will introduce the specific contents of this volume by focusing on three major issues that are attended to in the chapters, i.e., theory, therapy and oppression.

Theory

In terms of theory, the 14 chapters span a broad range of approaches, from a clearly positivist or 'essentialist' perspective (Ian Rivers; Fiona Tasker; Sonja J. Ellis) to a broadly social constructionist perspective (Christine Griffin; Victoria Clarke; Brendan Gough). The research methods used reflect this theoretical divide: the 'essentialist' contributions rely mostly on quantitative data such as data collected using traditional psychological scales – or adaptations of them – to measure, for example, post traumatic stress disorder (Ian Rivers), psychological adjustment (Fiona Tasker) and support for lesbian and gay human rights (Sonja J. Ellis). Where essentialist researchers have collected qualitative data (through interviews or open-ended questions on written questionnaires), these are analysed using standardized coding schemes (Fiona Tasker) or content analysis (Sonja J. Ellis). Qualitative methods of data collection and analysis – such as individual or focus group interview data analysed using a thematic form of content analysis (Laura A. Markowe), discourse analysis (Victoria Clarke), grounded theory (Martin Milton, Adrian Coyle and Charles Legg) or a combination of the latter two (Brendan Gough) – tend to be associated with a more 'social' or social constructionist theoretical approach. Several of the authors here also reflect upon the methods that they use in terms of their commitment to an anti-heterosexist psychology (Victoria Clarke; Brendan Gough; see also Braun, 2000).

  The social constructionist/essentialist debate has been described as the 'hottest' philosophical controversy to hit psychology in years

(Weinrich, 1987) and it is a controversy in which lesbian and gay psychology has been deeply enmeshed (Dickins, 1999; Kitzinger, 1999; O'Dell and Worrell, 1999; Parker, 1999; Rahman, 1999a, 1999b; Rivers and Tasker, 1999; see Kitzinger, 1995, for an overview). In this volume, two chapters in particular offer paradigmatic examples of the difference it makes to take an essentialist compared with a social constructionist perspective on a single topic. The chapters by Fiona Tasker (Chapter 5) and Victoria Clarke (Chapter 6) both deal with lesbian and gay parenting – Tasker from an essentialist and Clarke from a (feminist) social constructionist position. It is sometimes difficult for people to see research of the type reported by Tasker as 'essentialist' because it is simply good psychology as it is usually done – albeit here with a positive and pro-lesbian theme. Its essentialism is signalled first of all in its aim: 'empirically to evaluate the basis on which lesbian mothers were commonly refused custody', i.e., to compare children from lesbian families with children from heterosexual mother families in relation to four key areas – family relationships, mental health, peer relationships and psychosexual development. In effect, then, the questions Tasker addresses are whether or not the children of lesbians have worse family relationships, suffer from more mental health problems, have to endure bullying and are more likely to be lesbian or gay themselves – these being factors that are often cited as reasons for denying custody to lesbian mothers. In seeking to answer these questions, Tasker uses standardized coding of interview data and standardized questionnaire data to measure depression and anxiety. What the young people who were interviewed say is treated (with the usual cautions about self-report data) as offering more or less reliable evidence about the actual experiences of children in both types of family. Care is taken to ensure, for example, that the answers given by interviewees are not 'superficial' or 'contradictory'. The findings of the study are reported as offering new 'facts' about family life: for example, that 'the quality of family relationships is more important than family structure in terms of the child's psychological well-being'.

The contrast with Clarke's chapter is striking. Whereas Tasker's work *contributes* to 'positive' representations of lesbian parenting, Clarke's research *interrogates* these representations and does so not from the 'neutral' position of the scientist but from a politically-engaged, feminist perspective. Whereas Tasker's chapter is concerned with scientific evidence as to whether or not the children of lesbian families grow up psychologically healthy and well-adjusted, Clarke asks about the political *effects* of making this kind of argument. Rather than asking about the truth value of claims made in support of lesbian and gay families (i.e., whether they are empirically true or false), she explores the strategies people use to defend lesbian and gay parenting and discusses the political costs and benefits of these different strategies. So, for example, where Tasker claims, on the basis of her research, that the quality of family relationships is more important than whether the family is composed of same-sex or other-sex parents, Clarke represents this kind of claim as a 'discourse' which 'emphasizes the importance of love, security and stability over any particular family structure…According to this representation of family life, families can assume any shape or form as long as they are loving and stable environments'. Clarke's assessment of this 'discourse' is not in terms of its truth value but rather in terms of its rhetorical uses: 'such talk is rhetorically robust in an argumentative context' but also – she argues – it runs the risk of being 'defensive' and judging lesbian and gay families in accordance with 'heterosexual norms and expectations'. In sum, whereas Tasker is aiming to uncover something approximating to 'truths' about lesbian and gay parenting, Clarke treats these truth claims as 'discourses' to be assessed not in terms of their facticity but in terms of their rhetorical force and political implications.

As argued elsewhere (Kitzinger, 1995), neither essentialism nor social constructionism is intrinsically best suited to be the theoretical precursor to lesbian and gay liberation. *Both* have been used successfully by lesbians and gay men; *both* have led their proponents to political positions which they, or other activists, find uncomfortable or downright offensive. The oppression of lesbians and gay men can be effected by both essentialism and social constructionism alike; and equally, the struggle against that oppression can make use of both (albeit logically incompatible) perspectives. It can only be a sign of the vitality of lesbian and gay psychology as a field and of its potential for making a continuing contribution to lesbian and gay politics that research and practice continue within both traditions.

Therapy

Although factors and situations which may exert adverse effects upon the psychological well-being of lesbians and gay men are frequently attended to throughout the book, three chapters focus specifically on issues related to this and to psychotherapeutic practice with lesbian and gay clients. In Chapter 9, Gary Taylor examines the link between psychopathology and the social and historical construction of gay male identities. In more specific terms, he considers how the identities and psychological difficulties of gay men are socially constructed and represent the products of social and historical forces and processes. His broad-ranging, critical analysis goes beyond identifying the usual 'villains' of church, state and medicine/psychiatry and examines the implications of representations of homosexuality found in popular culture and in modern gay cultures, including a consideration of the impact of HIV/AIDS upon these representations. To some, Taylor's chapter (like Clarke's) may appear to resemble a sociological, cultural or political analysis more than a psychological one. However, we would contend that psychology routinely operates in an historical vacuum and frequently fails to engage in a concerted way with social factors, thereby producing individualized, decontextualized analyses which overlook the often considerable impact of social and historical dimensions upon its subject matter. An analysis which attends to social and historical dimensions in a concerted way offers a much-needed antidote to the often impoverished analyses arising from more traditional, narrow understandings of 'the psychological'. We hope that this form of thoroughly contextual analysis will be taken up by others working within lesbian and gay psychology in order to challenge and extend what is regarded as legitimately 'psychological'.

In his chapter, Taylor briefly attends to the implications of his analysis for therapeutic practice with gay men. However, therapeutic practice is addressed in a more concerted way in Chapters 10 and 11. In Chapter 10, Martin Milton, Adrian Coyle and Charles Legg present key findings from their qualitative, grounded theory exploration of what is meant by 'lesbian and gay affirmative therapy'. Much has been written about this approach to therapeutic practice but this literature tends to focus on identifying and elaborating some fundamental principles, which means that affirmative practice remains rather poorly elaborated, especially in empirical terms. Milton and colleagues set out to rectify this by interviewing therapists who claimed to be working from a lesbian and gay affirmative position and clients who had received affirmative therapy; the interviews explored their ideas about the nature, implications and challenges of affirmative practice. The resultant analysis constitutes a valuable, empirically-grounded elaboration of this therapeutic stance. In Chapter 11, Maeve Malley and Damian McCann examine the potential of one particular therapeutic approach, i.e., family (and systemic) therapy, to offer a beneficial and respectful therapeutic experience to lesbian and gay clients. With its focus upon human relationships, this approach is favoured by many therapists who wish to base their practice upon a more thoroughly social and contextualized level of analysis than that which tends to be favoured by the individualizing mainstream of therapeutic theory. With its emphasis on analyses of power (including power within the therapeutic context), family therapy can also be seen as welcoming the political into the therapeutic arena – although some commentators maintain that therapy can only ever accommodate a narrow and debased version of the political (Kitzinger and Perkins, 1993). Both of these chapters present challenges to therapeutic theory, practice and training. If these challenges were to be addressed in a concerted way, this would facilitate the development not only of lesbian and gay affirmative therapy but also of therapy *per se*.

Oppression

Finally, virtually every chapter in this book illustrates the continuing problem of anti-lesbian and anti-gay prejudice in Britain, and shows how lesbian and gay lives are shaped by this heterosexist social context. In Chapter 2, Ian Rivers demonstrates – through his own research in the UK and through reviewing the work of others both in the UK and in the USA – that young lesbians, gay men and bisexual people routinely experience oppression and discrimination during childhood and adolescence, including verbal and physical abuse from parents and peers, rejection from their families and other forms of victimization and harassment which lead to self-harm, suicidal behaviour and other mental health problems. Both Christine Griffin and Laura A. Markowe (in Chapters 3 and 4 respectively) illustrate some of the same problems for young women who may be isolated from their peers after coming out as lesbian and who, in Markowe's research, described feeling 'frightened' and 'lonely' – which is not surprising when fewer than a quarter of her heterosexual participants responded positively to the hypothetical situation of a daughter or son coming out to them. Prejudice affects lesbians' and gay men's experience of parenting (Fiona Tasker; Victoria Clarke), and of health care (Sue Wilkinson; Ian Warwick and Peter Aggleton). Whereas these chapters view lesbians' and gay men's problems as a consequence of heterosexism, the final three chapters focus on heterosexual attitudes themselves as the problem. In Chapter 12, Brendan Gough explores the role of homophobia in the production of heterosexual masculinity by British male university students and in Chapter 13, Sonja J. Ellis reports on her large scale questionnaire study of over 600 British university students' attitudes to lesbians and gay men and support for lesbian and gay human rights. She shows that not only is support for lesbian and gay rights rather more limited than one might expect from students but also that even those who do express support for lesbian and gay human rights are unwilling to see the protection of those rights as their responsibility and are unlikely to do anything practical or proactive to ensure that lesbian and gay rights are protected. Finally, in Chapter 14, Elizabeth Peel draws on her interviews with British lesbians and gay men involved in awareness training to consider some of the dilemmas which underlie education designed to challenge negative attitudes and beliefs.

Until recently, heterosexist legislation and social discrimination were justified and excused with reference to psychological research demonstrating homosexual pathology. Lesbian and gay psychology is now using its disciplinary tools to challenge oppression instead of reinforcing it. Psychology as a discipline can gain in theoretical sophistication and explanatory power by routinely incorporating the experiences of lesbians and gay men in its theories and methods and by considering the effects of heterosexism – whatever the research topic. An understanding of heterosexism and the insights of lesbian and gay psychology are relevant even in research in which there are (so far as is known) no lesbian, gay or bisexual participants (see the chapters by Christine Griffin and Brendan Gough).

In conclusion, this book presents lesbian and gay psychology as a 'work in progress', reviewing what has been achieved but also pointing to the considerable work which remains to be done. Our hope is that it will invigorate, inspire and guide those who have been working in lesbian and gay psychology for some time, those who are relatively new to the field and those who are thinking of adopting lesbian and gay psychology as their specialist area. We believe that this book takes both lesbian and gay psychology and mainstream psychology forward into the twenty-first century and contributes to the building of a profession – and a social world – in which the rights and freedoms not just of lesbians and gay men but of all of us can be assured. The contributors to the book have outlined the task ahead: the question now is – how will you respond?

Note

1. Unless otherwise indicated, the historical information in this section is derived from Adam (1987) and Blumenfeld and Raymond (1993).

References

ADAM, B.D. (1987) *The Rise of a Gay and Lesbian Movement.* Boston, MA: Twayne Publishers.

ADAMS, S. (1992) A Section too far [letter]. *The Psychologist, 5,* 500.

AMNESTY INTERNATIONAL (1997) *Breaking the Silence: Human Rights Violations Based on Sexual Orientation.* London: Amnesty International.

AMNESTY INTERNATIONAL (1999) *'The Louder We Will Sing': Campaigning for Lesbian and Gay Human Rights.* London: Amnesty International.

ANNESLEY, P. and COYLE, A. (1995) Clinical psychologists' attitudes to lesbians. *Journal of Community & Applied Social Psychology, 5,* 327–331.

ANNESLEY, P. and COYLE, A. (1998) Dykes and psychs: Lesbian women's experiences of clinical psychology services. *Changes: An International Journal of Psychology and Psychotherapy, 16,* 247–258.

BELOFF, H. (1993) Progress on the BPS Psychology of Lesbianism front. *Feminism & Psychology, 3,* 282–283.

BOHAN, J. (1996) *The Psychology of Sexual Orientation.* New York: Routledge.

BRAUN, V. (2000) Heterosexism in focus group research: Collusion and challenge. *Feminism & Psychology, 10,* 133–140.

BLUMENFELD, W.J. and RAYMOND, D. (1993) *Looking at Gay and Lesbian Life.* Boston, MA: Beacon Press.

BURCH, B. (1982) Psychological merger in lesbian couples: A joint ego psychological and systems approach. *Family Therapy, 1,* 201–208.

CARPENTER, E. (1908) *The Intermediate Sex: A Study of Some Transitional Types of Men and Women.* London: S. Sonnenschein.

CHERNIN, J., HOLDEN, J.M. and CHANDLER, C. (1997) Bias in psychological assessment: Heterosexism. *Measurement and Evaluation in Counseling and Development, 30,* 68–76.

CLARKE, W.M. and SEROVICH, J.M. (1997) Twenty years and still in the dark? Content analysis of articles pertaining to gay, lesbian and bisexual issues in marriage and family therapy journals. *Journal of Marital & Family Therapy, 23,* 239–253.

CLUNIS, D.M. and GREEN, G.D. (1988) *Lesbian Couples.* Seattle, WA: Seal Press.

COLEMAN, E. (1981/1982) Bisexual and gay men in heterosexual marriages: Conflicts and resolutions in therapy. *Journal of Homosexuality, 7(2/3),* 93–103.

COLEMAN, E. (1985) Bisexual women in marriages. *Journal of Homosexuality 11(1–2),* 87–99.

CORY, D.W. (1951) *The Homosexual in America: A Subjective Approach.* New York: Greenberg.

COYLE, A. (1999) Qualitative research and lesbian, gay, and bisexual psychology: Reflections from the British scene. *Newsletter of Division 44 (the Society for the Psychological Study of Lesbian, Gay, and Bisexual Issues) of the American Psychological Association, Fall,* 14–16.

COYLE, A., MILTON, M. and ANNESLEY, P. (1999) The silencing of lesbian and gay voices in psychotherapeutic texts and training. *Changes: An International Journal of Psychology and Psychotherapy, 17,* 132–143.

COYLE, A. and RAFALIN, D. (2000) Jewish gay men's accounts of negotiating cultural, religious, and sexual identity: A qualitative study. *Journal of Psychology and Human Sexuality, 12(4),* 21–48.

COYLE, A. and WILKINSON, S. (Eds) (forthcoming) Social psychological perspectives on lesbian and gay issues in Europe: The state of the art. A special issue of the *Journal of Community & Applied Social Psychology.*

DAVIS, M. (1995) Are you normal? [letter] *The Psychologist, 8,* 151–152.

D'AUGELLI, A.R. and PATTERSON, C.J. (Eds) (1995) *Lesbian, Gay, and Bisexual Identities Over the Lifespan: Psychological Perspectives.* New York: Oxford University Press.

D'AUGELLI, A.R. and PATTERSON, C.J. (Eds) (2001) *Lesbian, Gay, and Bisexual Identities and Youth: Psychological Perspectives.* New York: Oxford University Press.

DICKINS, T. (1999) Lesbians, gays and social constructionism [letter]. *The Psychologist, 12,* 113.

ELLIS, H. (1897) *Sexual Inversion.* London: Wilson and Macmillan.

ELLIS, S.J. (1999) Lesbian and gay issues are human rights issues: The need for a human rights approach to lesbian and gay psychology. *BPS Lesbian & Gay Psychology Section Newsletter, issue 3,* 9–14.

FIRESTEIN, B. (Ed.) (1996) *Bisexuality:The Psychology and Politics of an Invisible Minority.* London: Sage.

FOX, R.C. (1995) Bisexual identities. In A.R. D'Augelli and C.J. Patterson (Eds) *Lesbian, Gay, and Bisexual Identities Over the Lifespan: Psychological Perspectives.* New York: Oxford University Press.

FURNELL, P.J. (1986) Lesbian and gay psychology: A neglected area of British research. *Bulletin of the British Psychological Society, 39,* 41–47.

GARNETS, L., HANCOCK, K.A., COCHRAN, S.D., GOODCHILDS, J. and PEPLAU, L.A. (1991) Issues in psychotherapy with lesbians and gay men: A survey of psychologists. *American Psychologist, 46*, 964–972.

GARNETS, L.D. and KIMMEL, D.C. (Eds) (1993) *Psychological Perspectives on Lesbian and Gay Male Experiences.* New York: Columbia University Press.

GRAY, D. and ISENSEE, R. (1996) Balancing autonomy and intimacy in lesbian and gay relationships. In C.J. Alexander (Ed.) *Gay and Lesbian Mental Health: A Sourcebook for Practitioners.* New York: Harrington Park Press.

GREENE, B. (Ed.) (1997) *Ethnic and Cultural Diversity among Lesbians and Gay Men.* Thousand Oaks, CA: Sage.

GREENE, B. and HEREK, G.M. (Eds) (1994) *Lesbian and Gay Psychology: Theory, Research, and Clinical Applications.* Thousand Oaks, CA: Sage.

GREENE, B. and CROOM, G.L. (Eds) (2000) *Education, Research, and Practice in Lesbian, Gay, Bisexual, and Transgendered Psychology: A Resource Manual.* Thousand Oaks, CA: Sage.

HALL, M. (1985) *The Lavender Couch.* Boston, MA: Alyson Press.

HALL, R. (1928) *The Well of Loneliness.* London: Jonathan Cape.

HAMILTON, V. (1995) Are you normal? [letter] *The Psychologist, 8*, 151.

HART, J. and RICHARDSON, D. (1980) The differences between homosexual men and women. *Bulletin of the British Psychological Society, 33*, 451–454.

HART, J. and RICHARDSON, D. (1981) *The Theory and Practice of Homosexuality.* London: Routledge and Kegan Paul.

HEGARTY, P. and CHASE, C. (2000) Intersex activism, feminism and psychology: Opening a dialogue on theory, research and clinical practice. *Feminism & Psychology, 10*, 117–132.

HEREK, G.M. (Ed.) (1998) *Stigma and Sexual Orientation: Understanding Prejudice Against Lesbians, Gay Men, and Bisexuals.* Thousand Oaks, CA: Sage.

HEREK, G.M. and BERRILL, K.T. (Eds) (1992) *Hate Crimes: Confronting Violence Against Lesbians and Gay Men.* Newbury Park, CA: Sage.

HEREK, G.M. and GREENE, B. (Eds) (1995) *AIDS, Identity, and Community: The HIV Epidemic and Lesbians and Gay Men.* Thousand Oaks, CA: Sage.

HOOKER, E. (1957/1992) The adjustment of the male overt homosexual. In W.R. Dynes and S. Donaldson (Eds) *Studies In Homosexuality: Homosexuality And Psychology, Psychiatry and Counseling.* New York: Garland.

HOPKINS, J.H. (1969) The lesbian personality. *British Journal of Psychiatry, 115*, 1433–1436.

JAMES, S.E. (2000) Lesbian and gay adoptions: An introduction to emerging clinical and ethical issues. *Lesbian & Gay Psychology Review, 1*, 4–10.

JOWELL, R., CURTICE, J., PARK, A., BROOK, L. and THOMSON, K. (Eds) (1996) *British Social Attitudes: The 13th Report.* Aldershot: Dartmouth.

KITZINGER, C. (1987) *The Social Construction of Lesbianism.* London: Sage.

KITZINGER, C. (1990) Heterosexism in psychology. *The Psychologist, 3*, 391–392.

KITZINGER, C. (1993) Teaching psychology of lesbianism: Reviewing the literature. *Psychology Teaching Review, 2*, 59–61.

KITZINGER, C. (1995) Social constructionism: Implications for lesbian and gay psychology. In A.R. D'Augelli and C.J. Patterson (Eds) *Lesbian, Gay, and Bisexual Identities Over the Lifespan: Psychological Perspectives.* New York: Oxford University Press.

KITZINGER, C. (1996) The token lesbian chapter. In S. Wilkinson (Ed.) *Feminist Social Psychologies: International Perspectives.* Buckingham: Open University Press.

KITZINGER, C. (1999) Lesbians, gays and social constructionism [letter]. *The Psychologist, 12,* 113.

KITZINGER, C. (2000) Women with androgen insensitivity syndrome. In J. Ussher (Ed.) *Women's Health: An International Reader.* Leicester: BPS Books.

KITZINGER, C. (2001) Sexualities. In R.K. Unger (Ed.) *Handbook of Psychology of Women/Gender.* New York: Wiley.

KITZINGER, C. and COYLE, A. (1995) Lesbian and gay couples: Speaking of difference. *The Psychologist, 8,* 64–69.

KITZINGER, C., COYLE, A., WILKINSON, S. and MILTON, M. (1998) Towards lesbian and gay psychology. *The Psychologist, 11,* 529–533.

KITZINGER, C. and PERKINS, R. (1993) *Changing Our Minds: Lesbian Feminism and Psychology.* London: Onlywomen Press.

KITZINGER, C. and STAINTON ROGERS, R. (1985) A Q methodological study of lesbian identities. *European Journal of Social Psychology, 15,* 167–187.

KITZINGER, C. and WILKINSON, S. (1995) Transitions from heterosexuality to lesbianism: The discursive construction of lesbian identities. *Developmental Psychology, 31,* 95–104.

KLINKENBERG, D. and ROSE, S. (1994) Dating scripts of gay men and lesbians. *Journal of Homosexuality, 26(4),* 23–25.

KRESTAN, J. and BEPKO, C.S. (1980) The problem of fusion in the lesbian relationship. *Family Process, 19,* 277–289.

LAPSLEY, H. and PAULIN, K. (1994) Lesbians in psychology. *Bulletin of the New Zealand Psychological Society, 80,* 24–26.

LELAND, J. and MILLER, M. (1998) Can gays 'convert'? *Newsweek, August 17th,* 47–50.

LONG, J.K. (1996) Working with lesbians, gays, and bisexuals: Addressing heterosexism in supervision. *Family Process, 35,* 377–388.

MACKAY, T. (2000) Speaking out on public issues. *The Psychologist, 13,* 539.

MARSIGLIO, W. (1993) Attitudes toward homosexual activity and gays as friends: A national survey of 15–19 year old males. *Journal of Sex Research, 30,* 12–17.

MARTIN, B.H. (1995) Sectional misapprehensions [letter]. *The Psychologist, 8,* 392.

MILTON, M. and COYLE, A. (1998) Psychotherapy with lesbian and gay clients. *The Psychologist, 11,* 73–76.

MOON, L. (2000) Lesbian and Gay Section inaugural annual conference report. *Counselling Psychology Review, 15(4),* 34–35.

MORIN, S.F. (1977) Heterosexual bias in psychological research on lesbianism and male homosexuality. *American Psychologist, 19,* 629–637.

MORIN, S.F. and ROTHBLUM, E. (1991) Removing the stigma: Fifteen years of progress. *American Psychologist, 44,* 947–949.

O'DELL, L. and WORRELL, M. (1999) Are we abandoning science? [letter] *The Psychologist, 12,* 224–225.

PARKER, I. (1999) Are we abandoning science? [letter] *The Psychologist, 12,* 224.

PARKER, R. and CACERES, C. (Eds) (1999) Alternative sexualities and changing identities among Latin American men. A special issue of *Culture, Health & Sexuality, 1,* 201–299.

PATTERSON, C.J. and D'AUGELLI, A.R. (Eds) (1998) *Lesbian, Gay, and Bisexual Identities in Familes: Psychological Perspectives.* New York: Oxford University Press.

PERLMAN, S.F. (1989) Distancing and connectedness: Impact on couple formation and lesbian relationships. *Women & Therapy, 8,* 77–88.

PEYSER, M. (1998) Battling backlash. *Newsweek, August 17th,* 50–52.

PHELLAS, C.N. (1998) *Sexual and Ethnic Identities of Anglo-Cypriot Men Resident in London who have Sex with Men.* Unpublished PhD thesis, University of Essex.

PILKINGTON, N.W. and CANTOR, J.M. (1996) Perceptions of heterosexual bias in professional psychology programs: A survey of graduate students. *Professional Psychology: Research and Practice, 27,* 604–612.

PLUMMER, K. (1981) *The Making of the Modern Homosexual.* London: Hutchinson.

RAHMAN, Q. (1999a) Making lesbian and gays invisible [letter]. *The Psychologist, 12,* 8–9.

RAHMAN, Q. (1999b) Intellectual imperialism? [letter]. *The Psychologist, 12,* 329.

REYES, E.E. and YEP, G.A. (1997) Challenging complexities: Strategies with Asian Americans in Southern California against (heterosex)isms. In J.T. Sears and W.L. Williams (Eds) *Overcoming Heterosexism and Homophobia: Strategies that Work.* New York: Columbia University Press.

RHUE, S. and RHUE, T. (1997) Reducing homophobia in African American communities. In J.T. Sears and W.L. Williams (Eds) *Overcoming Heterosexism and Homophobia: Strategies that Work.* New York: Columbia University Press.

RICHARDSON, D. (1978) Do lesbians make good parents? *Community Care, 224,* 16–17.

RICHARDSON, D. (Ed.) (1996) *Theorising Heterosexuality: Telling It Straight.* Buckingham: Open University Press.

RICHARDSON, D. and HART, J. (1981) Gays in therapy: Getting it right. *New Forum: The Journal of the Psychology and Psychotherapy Association, 6,* 58–60.

RIVERS, I. and TASKER, F. (1999) Are we abandoning science? [letter] *The Psychologist, 12,* 225.

ROSARIO, V. (Ed.) (1997) *Science and Homosexualities.* London: Routledge.

ROTHBLUM, E. and BOND, L. (Eds) (1996) *Preventing Heterosexism and Homophobia.* Thousand Oaks, CA: Sage.

SAVIN-WILLIAMS, R.C. and COHEN, K.M. (Eds) (1996) *The Lives of Lesbians, Gays, and Bisexuals: Children to Adults.* Fort Worth, TX: Harcourt Brace.

SILVERA, M. (Ed.) (1991) *Piece of my Heart: A Lesbian of Colour Anthology.* Toronto: Sister Vision Press.

SIMONI, J.M (1996) Confronting heterosexism in the teaching of psychology. *Teaching of Psychology, 23,* 220–226.

USSHER, J. (1991) Letter to Chair of BPS Scientific Affairs Board, May 21st, reprinted in *The British Psychological Society Psychology of Women Newsletter, issue 8,* 66.

WEEKS, J. (1977) *Coming Out: Homosexual Politics in Britain from the Nineteenth Century to the Present.* London: Quartet.

WEEKS, J. (1981) *Sex, Politics and Society: The Regulation of Sexuality since 1800.* London: Longman.

WEEKS, J. (2000) *Making Sexual History.* Cambridge: Polity Press.

WEINDICH, J.D. (1987) *Sexual Landscapes: Why We Are What We Are, Why We Love Who We Love.* New York: Charles Scribners' Sons. [Chapter 5 reprinted in Stein, E. (Ed.) (1990) *Forms of Desire: Sexual Orientation and the Social Con-*

structionist Controversy. New York: Routledge]

WELLINGS, K., FIELD, J., JOHNSON, A.M. and WADSWORTH, J. (1994) *Sexual Behaviour in Britain: The National Survey of Sexual Attitudes and Lifestyles.* London: Penguin.

WILKINSON, S. (1999) The struggle to found the Lesbian and Gay Psychology Section. *BPS Lesbian & Gay Psychology Section Newsletter, issue 2*, 3–5.

WILKINSON, S. and KITZINGER, C. (Eds) (1993) *Heterosexuality: A 'Feminism & Psychology' Reader.* London: Sage.

Chapter 2

Developmental Issues for Lesbian and Gay Youth

Ian Rivers

The scientific study of lesbian and gay developmental psychology is a relatively new phenomenon. While, in the past, researchers have proposed and tested a number of theories relating to the development of lesbian and gay identities, these studies have tended to use adult samples, asking participants to reflect upon their experiences and to draw conclusions from them. More recently, with the establishment of community organizations and support groups catering for young people who are lesbian, gay or, indeed, bisexual, it has been possible for developmental researchers to work collaboratively with these bodies to gain a better understanding of the process of growing up lesbian, gay or bisexual in a heterosexual world.

According to D'Augelli (1994), it has been impossible to offer insights into the so-called 'normal' development of lesbian, gay and bisexual youth because, as he points out, in a world where lesbians and gay men regularly face discrimination, there are few young people who have grown up 'normally', i.e., free from harassment and fear of intolerance. Furthermore, little data have been available concerning the prevalence of homosexuality and bisexuality within the general population. The popularly held belief that ten per cent of the population is lesbian or gay is based upon the aggregation of data collected by Alfred Kinsey and his colleagues in the United States between 1938 and 1953 (Kinsey *et al.*, 1948, 1953) but more recent estimates suggest a figure of between one and four per cent (Nevid *et al.*, 1995) – although such estimates are invariably problematic as they tend to be based on unacknowledged assumptions about the nature of sexual orientation. For example, demographic evidence on the incidence of homosexuality among young people collected through a survey of 35 000 young people in the state of Minnesota (Remafedi *et al.*, 1992) found that only 1.1 per cent of participants identified themselves as lesbian, gay or bisexual. The same survey found, however, that 11 per cent of participants reported 'questioning' their sexual orientation. One of the difficulties with this and numerous other surveys of lesbian, gay and bisexual youth has been the fact that researchers have often relied upon participants self-identifying as lesbian, gay or bisexual, although research on sexual behaviour suggests that self-identified orientation and actual sexual behaviour do not necessarily correlate (Isay 1988). Indeed, many young people growing up in an atmosphere of fear and mistrust may be actively deterred from self-identifying as lesbian, gay or bisexual (hence Remafedi *et al.*'s high percentage of 'questioning' youth). The effects of growing up lesbian, gay or bisexual in a hetero-sexual world have been charted by various researchers who have suggested that, like racist or sexist discrimination (to which the same young people may also be subject), discrimination on the grounds of sexual orientation is positively associated with school failure, poor psychological well-being and an increased likelihood of self-harming behaviour (see Rivers, 1997a, for an overview).

The causes of sexual orientation

One of the questions numerous researchers have sought to answer relates to the causes of homosexuality and, by implication, bisexuality and heterosexuality in the individual. Unfortunately, much of the research that has focused upon the development of sexual orientation has tended to be polarized, with those interested in the subject asking the question 'Is homosexuality the result of biological or genetic processes or is it the result of free choice?'. Interestingly, those who most strongly advocate the biological or genetic antecedents of homo-sexuality have received the support of many gay and (to a lesser extent) lesbian activist groups because biological determinism appears to provide an answer that might end discrimination: if a person is born lesbian or gay, she or he should not be discriminated against because she or he 'cannot help it'. However, as feminist researchers have point-ed out (for example, Kitzinger, 1995), being born female or Black or disabled has never guaranteed protection against discrimination and some lesbian feminists have argued in favour of lesbianism as a choice that any woman can make. Nonetheless, many of those who are most opposed to the recognition of homosexuality as a valid alternative to heterosexuality have tended to base their arguments on the free choice model: they contend that a person who chooses to be lesbian or gay should not receive equal treatment because she or he has actively decided to behave in ways that run counter to the conventions of soci-ety. In the United Kingdom, such arguments have been used with great effect in the debates surrounding the repeal of Section 28 of the 1988 Local Government Act (which prohibits the promotion of the accept-ability of homosexuality as 'a pretended family relationship' by any local authority) and the reduction of the age of consent for gay men to bring it into line with the heterosexual age of consent (see Rivers and Hardcastle, 2000). Indeed, as D'Augelli (1994) points out, much of the legislative debate surrounding the issue of equality for lesbians, gay men and bisexual men and women has revolved around the issue of causation. Yet studies that have sought to advance either the nature or 'free choice' explanations of human sexual orientation have tended to ignore the arguments and theories of the other perspective and it has often been left up to the 'interactionists' to make sense of this research and attempt to draw conclusions from it (Storms, 1981).

Since the early 1970s, much of the research on the causes of homosexuality has focused upon its possible biological origins. Early research on the endocrinology of homosexuality has recently been superceded by researchers working in the biomedical sciences who have suggested that a genetic link exists between male homosexuality and a particular marker on the X chromosome, specifically Xq 28 (Hamer *et al.*, 1993). Hamer *et al.*'s analysis of the genetic tissue of 40 pairs of gay male twins resulted in the claim that they had 'produced evidence that one form of male homosexuality is preferentially transmitted through the maternal side and is genetically linked to chromosomal region Xq28'; however, they also acknowledged that the locus or loci for sexual orientation lie(s) 'approximately within 4 million base pairs of DNA on the tip of the long arm of the X chromosome' (p. 325).

By way of contrast to biological and genetic theories of homosexuality, social-developmental theories have not received much attention. One of the reasons for this disparity in interest is undoubtedly the fact that social-developmental theories have yet to be tested 'scientifically'. For example, Storms (1981) suggested that homosexuality is the result of an interaction between biological and social influences. However, the exact nature of this possible interaction was not clearly delineated by the author. Storms argued that since sexual development in adolescence coincides with a significant shift in social development with the emergence of opposite-sex rather than solely same-sex friendships, then the earlier puberty begins, the more likely it is that homosexual attraction will occur. Although Storms' argument can be supported by research looking at the self-reported times of puberty onset among samples of lesbians and gay men, it is worth noting that this theory does not adequately explain the presence of bisexuality as an alternative to either heterosexuality or homosexuality (Rivers, 1997b). A further difficulty with this theory is the fact that young people who identify as either lesbian or gay often find themselves isolated from their same-sex peers and thus by implication their social development may be inhibited.

According to Bem (1996), the development of sexual orientation is not so much grounded in the social interactions in which young people engage but in their identification with one gender group. This theory, which Bem described as 'Exotic Becomes Erotic', suggests that we are all romantically or erotically attracted to those people who are unfamiliar or dissimilar to ourselves. Heterosexual young people form erotic or romantic attachments to individuals of a different gender because they are attracted to the mystery surrounding the other gender. Lesbians and gay men form erotic or romantic attachments to individuals of the same gender because, according to this theory, they have always identified with others of the same gender.

Such theories – which tend to be used selectively and strategically by those wishing to advance one particular political argument or belief – are complex and it remains true to say that sexual orientation is something which cannot be easily understood in terms of a single causative factor (for example, a link between claimed biological 'causes' and female homosexuality is tenuous at best), and, as Kitzinger (1995) indicates, from a social constructionist perspective, the issue of sexual orientation cannot always be reduced to a series of scientific 'facts' or universal 'truths'. Much of what we understand sexual orientation to be is determined by the social, political, cultural and historical context in which it features. To take as an example Bem's theory of erotic orientation, this has been challenged because it attempts to link sexual orientation to gender identification and thus, by implication, gender dysphoria – and this is not supported by empirical evidence.

Growing up lesbian, gay or bisexual

As D'Augelli (1994) has pointed out, young people who identify as lesbian, gay or bisexual have to consider how their choices and decisions will impact upon the quality of their lives, those of their families and, indeed, those of their friends (see Chapter 3 for a discussion of the impact of sexual identities on friendship formation among girls). Young people must also consider how their sexual orientation will impact upon their relationships with parents, siblings, extended family members, friends and current or future partners. Concomitantly, they must also be aware of the social, political and legal implications of living as lesbians, as gay men and, to a lesser extent, as bisexuals in a heterosexual world. D'Augelli (1994) has suggested that it is only when they have weighed up many (if not all) of the pros and cons of living as a lesbian, gay man or bisexual man or woman that the process of identity formation and, ultimately, disclosure can begin.

The decision to disclose or 'come out' to other people is not one taken by all lesbians, gay men and bisexuals and the reasons underpinning this decision are often linked to social, familial or cultural attitudes towards homosexuality. In the following sections of this chapter, the implications of growing up as a young lesbian, gay man or bisexual man or woman are considered with respect to home and family issues, education and mental health respectively.

Home and family

Parental attitudes towards homosexuality and bisexuality are often shaped by stereotypical representations of the 'homosexual lifestyle' which are reinforced by society, education and the media. The way in which a young lesbian, gay man or openly bisexual man or woman is perceived by their family influences how the family copes with the child's or sibling's sexual orientation. For example, in a survey of 500 young lesbians, gay men and bisexual men and women who sought the support of the Hetrick-Martin Institute in New York (an educational and support facility for sexual minority youth), Hunter (1990) found that not only had nearly half (46 per cent) experienced a violent assault perpetrated against them because of their sexual orientation but, of that group, 61 per cent said that it had occurred within the home. According to Pilkington and D'Augelli (1995), of the 194 youths who took part in their survey, 36 per cent had either been insulted or otherwise degraded by a member of their immediate family. When these results were analysed further, they found that 22 per cent of young women and 14 per cent of young men had been verbally abused and that 18 per cent and 8 per cent respectively had been physically assaulted by a member of their immediate family. The authors then asked participants to identify the perpetrators of such behaviour and it was found that mothers (22 per cent) were more likely to be abusive to their children than fathers (14 per cent), brothers (16 per cent) or sisters (9 per cent). However, it was also found that mothers tended to be far more protective towards their lesbian, gay or bisexual child (25 per cent) than fathers (13 per cent), brothers (11 per cent) or sisters (10 per cent).

In the United Kingdom, as elsewhere, parental reactions to a child's homosexuality have been found to vary considerably. While some parents have been entirely accepting of their child's sexual orientation, others have reacted with verbal taunts and physical violence (Albert Kennedy Trust, 1995). It has been suggested that one of the reasons why mothers in particular are more likely to be abusive towards their lesbian, gay or bisexual children relates to the fact that they may face a great deal more social condemnation than fathers or siblings because they are viewed as having been responsible for their child's upbringing (Rivers, 1997a). Any perceived variation in their child's development is likely to be attributed to poor parenting skills rather than to any genetic, biological or social-developmental factor outside parental control. In addition, it has also been suggested that parents use more covert and insidious forms of rejection when they find out that their child is lesbian, gay or bisexual. For example, parents may distance themselves from their children through the withdrawal of affection or through their exclusion from recreational activities such as family meals, outings and holidays (see Rivers, 1997a). Voluntary agencies have also reported that while parents may react positively when their child 'comes out', in the face of mounting criticism from others, such reactions can turn sour:

> When they found out they said they didn't mind. Then after a few months my dad started saying things like, 'When you're 17 you can piss off and do anything you like with those other poofters.' (Albert Kennedy Trust, 1995, p. 11)

In some cases, young lesbians, gay men and bisexual men and women have been forced to leave their home either as a result of their family's inability to deal with their homosexuality/bisexuality or as a result of the mounting pressure parents and siblings face from 'friends' and extended family members to distance themselves from their son/daughter or brother/sister.

According to Rivers and D'Augelli (2001), for many young lesbians, gay men and bisexual men and women, family rejection has resulted in them leaving home and relocating to large metropolitan areas where there are visible lesbian and gay communities. For the most part, those young people who are forced out of their homes leave with the intention of finding both shelter and employment. However, as both Kruks (1991) in the United States and Gibson (1995) in the United Kingdom have shown, such intentions are rarely realized and, for some, prostitution may be the only means of survival. As one 24–year-old man recalled:

> It was a nightmare for me every time someone picked me up. Although I needed the money, weeks went by when I didn't do a punter and didn't have a penny to my name. It was literally a case of sleeping wherever, and getting food wherever I could; out of bins, backs of restaurants, wherever. (Gibson, 1995, p. 129)

In his study of lesbian and gay street youth in California, Kruks (1991) demonstrated that experiences such as those recounted above are not out of the ordinary. According to Kruks, while 'the street' can provide a degree of peer acceptance and support from like-minded homeless people, those young men and women who hope to find 'love' or a caring partnership to replace the family they have lost are at risk of falling into a series of short-term exploitative relationships which, as he has argued, ultimately end in rejection and a return to the streets. Indeed, of those homeless youths who sought the help of the Los Angeles Gay and Lesbian Community Services Center, Kruks found that this cycle of sexual exploitation and rejection had resulted in 53 per cent attempting suicide on at least one occasion, and 47 per cent attempting suicide more than once.

Of course, not all young lesbians and gay men are forced to leave their family home when they decide to 'come out' and many young people have reported being fully supported by parents and siblings who have challenged the way in which others perceive them and their families. However, as noted earlier, having a lesbian, gay or (to a lesser extent) bisexual young person in the home brings with it a number of reappraisals for the family, which includes getting used to the idea of a son/daughter exploring their sexuality as might any other adolescent but with a partner of the same gender (Owens, 1998).

Education

In addition to the challenges faced by family members in the home when coming to terms with a child's or sibling's sexual orientation, challenges may also appear when a young person comes out at school or at college. Peer victimization and a lack of understanding by teachers and local education authorities can bring a number of additional stresses for a young person and, by implication, her or his family. For example, one of the first studies specifically to address the experiences of lesbian, gay and bisexual youth in secondary school contexts was conducted in the United Kingdom by the London Gay Teenage Group for the Inner London Education Authority. Over the course of a year, some 416 young lesbians, gay men and bisexual men and women completed detailed questionnaires about their experiences of growing up which were published in three separate reports during 1984 (see Trenchard, 1984; Trenchard and Warren, 1984; Warren, 1984). Warren (1984) found that 39 per cent of participants (N=164) had experienced 'problems at school' which included bullying or pressure to conform because of their gender atypical behaviour. Of the 154 participants (115 gay or bisexual young men and 39 lesbian or bisexual young women) who had specified the nature of the 'problems' they had encountered, 25 per cent said they felt isolated at school and had nothing in common with their peers; 21 per cent reported having been called names or otherwise verbally abused; 13 per cent said they had been teased; 12 per cent said they had been physically assaulted; a further 7 per cent recalled being ostracized (deliberately) by their peers; and another 7 per cent said that they had been pressured by peers to change their behaviour.

In a more recent study conducted in the United Kingdom, Rivers (1999a) reported that, of the 190 lesbians, gay men and bisexual men and women surveyed who had been bullied at school, the most common form of victimization experienced was name-calling (82 per cent) and being ridiculed in front of others (71 per cent). Teasing was also reported by a large number of participants (58 per cent) while slightly more (60 per cent) reported being hit or kicked at school. Forty-nine per cent recalled having their belongings stolen by their tormentors as a form of harassment. Indirect or relational harassment was also frequently reported by participants. In total, 59 per cent said that rumours had been spread about them while 52 per cent said they were often frightened by the way in which a particular person looked or stared at them. Twenty-seven per cent reported being isolated by their peers and 11 per cent said they had been sexually assaulted either by peers or by teachers while at school.

In the United States, several empirical investigations have been undertaken, often with the support of the state or national legislature, investigating the experiences of young lesbians, gay men and bisexual men and women at school. For example, in their study of anti-lesbian and anti-gay abuse in schools across the state of Pennsylvania (with a sample of 461 gay men and 260 lesbians), Gross *et al.* (1988) noted that 50 per cent of the gay men and 12 per cent of the lesbians who were surveyed had experienced some form of victimization in junior high school (12–14 years), rising to 59 per cent for gay men and 21 per cent for lesbians in high school (14–18 years). According to Berrill (1992), from the evidence collected by various state and national task forces and coalitions at the time, estimates of the prevalence of school-based victimization for lesbian, gay and bisexual youth resident in the USA ranged from 33 per cent to 49 per cent.

Pilkington and D'Augelli (1995), in their survey of 194 lesbian, gay and bisexual young people, found that 30 per cent of gay and bisexual young men and 35 per cent of lesbian and bisexual young women had experienced some form of harassment or verbal abuse in school because of their sexual orientation. In terms of physical assault, 22 per cent of young men and 29 per cent of young women reported having been hurt by someone of the same age: white students were far more likely to be attacked (27 per cent) than those from other cultural groups (19 per cent). In terms of social support, the researchers found that 43 per cent of the young men and 54 per cent of the young women surveyed has lost at least one friend as a result of their actual or perceived sexual orientation while a further 36 per cent and 27 per cent respectively feared they would lose their friends if they were 'open' about their sexual orientation. In the United Kingdom, research suggests that pupils who are bullied at school because of their actual or perceived sexual orientation are much more likely to report having few friends and spending much more time alone in the school yard or playground during lunch or break times (Rivers, 1999b).

Similar results have been found in a series of small-scale studies. For example, Sears (1991) reported that, of the 36 young lesbians, gay men and bisexual men and women he questioned, 35 recalled their class-mates having negative attitudes towards homosexuality or bisexuality and most feared being victimized or harassed if they 'came out' in high school. This is a view shared by participants in Pilkington and D'Augelli's (1995) study: 28 per cent of young men and 19 per cent of young women indicated that their degree of openness about their sexual orientation was influenced by their fear of physical violence being directed against them. However, as Fricke (1981) pointed out in his autobiography, it is not just physical violence with which lesbian, gay and bisexual pupils have to contend:

> One day while sitting in a science class, I happened to glance around the room and detect a fellow classmate glaring at me. I overlooked it at first, but ten minutes later I noticed he was still staring. His name was Bill Quillar. He must have been a quiet student because I had hardly ever taken notice of him before. I never saw him fraternizing with anyone else. He was a small student, not intimidating in size, but the look in his eyes was petrifying. He stared at me with an uninterrupted gaze that could melt steel. It was a look of complete disgust. I ignored him but the next day he was staring again and the next...and the next...and the next. (pp. 28–29)

Although much of the research cited in this chapter has focused upon victimization perpetrated by peers, Pilkington and D'Augelli (1995) also found that 7 per cent of their total sample reported being hurt by a teacher, especially the young women (11 per cent). They also found that those students who were from ethnic minority groups were more likely to report abusive behaviour by teachers than white students (10 per cent and 6 per cent respectively). In the United Kingdom, both Warren (1984) and Mac an Ghaill (1994) have reported that, although teachers may not actively engage in any form of physical, verbal or emotional abuse, they had ridiculed pupils who exhibited 'gender inappropriate behaviour' and, on occasions, had been less than supportive when approached for help as the following excerpts illustrate:

> The Head of Sixth Form, who warned that I might get expelled, enquired if I had been dropped on my head as a baby. (Warren, 1984, p. 17)

> I went to a teacher and told him that I thought I might be gay. He said, no I mustn't think like that, it was just a phase all boys went through. (Mac an Ghaill, 1994, p. 168)

Overall, Pilkington and D'Augelli's (1995) study, together with those of organizations such as the National Gay and Lesbian Task Force (1984), converge with Warren's (1984) findings to suggest that approximately one third of young people who are lesbian, gay or bisexual are victimized or bullied at school because of their sexual orientation.

In addition to the physical and emotional trauma caused by the experience or fear of intimidation, evidence is beginning to emerge suggesting that lesbians, gay men and bisexual young men and women are also more likely to leave school with fewer academic qualifications than their heterosexual or 'closeted' peers. For example, in one study, Rivers (2000a) charted the implications of social exclusion at school for 116 lesbians, gay men and bisexual men and women. Comparisons were made between those who reported a great deal of absenteeism at school with those who did not. The results showed that those participants who reported a history of absenteeism at school were more likely to recall victimization that was relational or verbal rather than physical in expression. In addition, absentees reported obtaining fewer pass grades at 'A' level than non-absentees.

As much of the research conducted with lesbian, gay and bisexual youth has often included young women and men up to the age of 21 years, it has also been possible to chart the experiences of undergraduates as they pass through college and university. In his review of data collected from three cross-sectional studies undertaken at American universities, Comstock (1991) found that 22 per cent of lesbian and gay students surveyed reported having been followed or chased by other undergraduates; 15 per cent said they had had objects thrown at them; 11 per cent indicated that they had been the victims of arson or acts of vandalism; a further 4 per cent had been physically assaulted; 3 per cent had been spat upon; and 1 per cent had been assaulted with a weapon. Based upon this data, Comstock estimated that students from sexual minority groups were four times more likely to be victims of assault or harassment than any other group on a university or college campus.

Qualitative research conducted by Taulke-Johnson and Rivers (1999) has similarly suggested that young lesbians and gay men face a number of challenges when they enter university, especially when they move into halls of residence (dormitories) or other forms of shared living arrangments with people whom they have never met before. Under these circumstances, they face a range of potential reactions if and when they disclose their sexual orientation to others and some of those reactions may not be positive. As one young man suggested:

> I wouldn't let onto anyone that you were lesbian, gay or bisexual until you'd sussed out your flat mates...Don't tell them until you feel confident and until you're sure they won't beat you up. (p. 81)

Self-harm and mental health

Deliberate self-harming behaviour
In one study conducted in the United States, Hershberger and D'Augelli (1995) found that 42 per cent of their sample of 194 lesbian, gay and bisexual youth had attempted suicide on at least one occasion as a result of being victimized or otherwise alienated by peers, family or community members. In the United Kingdom, Warren (1984) found that 20 per cent of the lesbian, gay and bisexual teenagers in his study had contemplated or attempted suicide because of their sexual orientation. More alarming figures have been reported among those who

were bullied at school because of their sexual orientation. In a three year study of the nature and long-term implications of school bullying, over 50 per cent of participants reported having contemplated self-harm or suicide when they were at school, with 40 per cent reporting one or more actual attempts (Rivers, 1997b). While there remains a great deal of debate concerning whether or not teenagers are generally more prone to engage in self-destructive behaviours such as self mutilation and suicide (see Meuhrer, 1995), according to Bagley and Tremblay (1997), suicidal ideation is considerably higher among sexual minority groups compared to its incidence within the general population. Based upon a random sample of 750 males (identified via census data) aged 18–27 years living in Calgary, Canada, Bagley and Tremblay (1997) found that gay and bisexual males (N= 115) accounted for more than half (62.5 per cent) of all attempted suicides and self-harming behaviours reported by participants. Based upon these results, Bagley and Tremblay estimated that gay and bisexual men are nearly 14 times more likely to attempt suicide than heterosexual men.

Although, in their study, Hershberger and D'Augelli (1995) were cautious about making a direct link between attempted suicides and peer, family and community intolerance, they found that the best predictor of mental health among the young lesbians, gay men and bisexual men and women whom they surveyed was self-acceptance. However, they also found that self-acceptance was related to family support – but only for those who had experienced low levels of victimization. For those who had experienced high levels of victimization, support from family members did not protect against the onset of mental health problems or, indeed, thoughts of suicide.

Mental health

In their study of suicidality and mental health among 194 lesbian, gay and bisexual young people, Hershberger and D'Augelli (1995) suggested that the combined effects of familial as well as societal homophobia were also likely to have a contributory influence upon participants' predisposition toward self-destructive behaviours, and while an episode of harassment may have precipitated an episode of self-destructive behaviour, there may have also been a number of underlying factors (including internalized homophobia or self-loathing) which may have had an impact upon participants' affective state at the time.

In a comparable British study, Rivers (1999b) examined the histories of 119 lesbians, gay men and bisexual men and women who had experienced a great deal of harassment at school and had completed an extensive battery of measures relating to their life experiences since leaving education. In terms of those factors that may mitigate against adult psychopathology, it was found that issues such as the nature, frequency and duration of victimization experienced at school were

generally unrelated to participants' reports of suicidal ideation in adolescence, negative affect in adulthood, relationship status and
internalized homophobia. However, those who were exposed to indirect methods of victimization (i.e., rumour-mongering and social
isolation) were found to have higher scores on a measure of post-trau-
matic stress disorder (PTSD) than did those who were exposed to
direct methods. This suggested that those participants who primarily
experienced direct aggression fared better than those who experienced
indirect aggression, perhaps because they were better able to retaliate.
Overall, 17 per cent of participants in this study met the criteria for
PTSD and these participants were also more likely to suffer from
depression than their non-PTSD peers. An additional 40 per cent
reported the regular occurrence ('often' or 'always') of one or more secondary symptoms associated with the disorder which suggested that a
number of participants were hidden from medical and psychiatric services and were living with the effects of their experiences of
victimization and harassment on a daily basis. Interestingly, and somewhat contrary to Hershberger and D'Augelli's (1995) findings, it was
also found that participants who were supported to some degree by
friends, family members or teachers fared better in terms of their affective state than those who were not 'out' as lesbian, gay or bisexual or
who recalled receiving little, if any, support when they were at school.
Furthermore, those who had not disclosed their sexual orientation
were also found to be more uncomfortable about being lesbian, gay or
bisexual than those who had disclosed and they expressed greater discomfort at the possibility of disclosing to another person. Indeed, the
data suggested that those who had not disclosed their sexual orientation were more likely to suffer from symptoms associated with PTSD
than those who were 'open'.

Surprisingly, in terms of self-esteem and comfort with sexual orientation, lesbian, gay and bisexual young people who experienced a
great deal of harassment at school were more likely to be accepting of
their own homosexuality in the long-term than those who were able to
hide their sexual orientation (Rivers, 2000b). Constant reinforcement
by peers of their 'different' status may result in those who are victimized having to come to terms personally and ideologically with the
idea that they are lesbian, gay or bisexual very early on in their social
development. However, this does not necessarily mean that they are
any more willing to be 'open' about their sexual orientation as this may
have serious consequences for their relationships with members of
their family, friends and peers at school.

Implications

In sum, young lesbians, gay men and bisexual men and women face a
great many challenges as they grow up. The gradual processes of

recognizing one's sexual orientation and 'coming out' (described in more detail in Chapters 3 and 4) mark key transitional stages in the formation of an identity that is often challenged by society. Research has suggested that the combined effects of social opprobrium, whether at home or at school, can have long-term and debilitating effects upon young people. School failure, poor psychological well-being and deliberate self-harm have been found to be issues of particular relevance to young lesbians, gay men and bisexual men and women. Furthermore, inequalities resulting from the disparity in the age of consent for gay men and heterosexual men (only rectified late in 2000) and the maintenance (at the time of writing) of Section 28 of the 1988 Local Government Act have only resulted in the alienation of another generation of young people. In the United Kingdom, developmental research with lesbian, gay and bisexual young people is still very much in its infancy but the evidence is mounting which suggests that there is a need for proactive strategies that challenge intolerance and discrimination and that offer effective support to those who have experienced it.

References

ALBERT KENNEDY TRUST (1995) *General Information Guide*. Manchester: Albert Kennedy Trust.

BAGLEY, C. and TREMBLAY, P. (1997) Suicidal behaviors in homosexual and bisexual males. *Crisis, 18*, 24–34.

BEM, D.J. (1996) Exotic becomes erotic: A developmental theory of sexual orientation. *Psychological Review, 103*, 320–335.

BERRILL, K.T. (1992) Anti-gay violence and victimization in the United States: An overview. In G.M. Herek and K.T. Berrill (Eds) *Hate Crimes: Confronting Violence Against Lesbians and Gay Men*. Newbury Park, CA: Sage.

COMSTOCK, G.D. (1991) *Violence Against Lesbians and Gay Men*. New York: Columbia University Press.

D'AUGELLI, A.R. (1994) Identity development and sexual orientation: Toward a model of lesbian, gay, and bisexual development. In E.J. Trickett, R.J. Watts and D. Birman (Eds) *Human Diversity: Perpsectives on People in Context*. San Francisco, CA: Jossey-Bass.

FRICKE, A. (1981) *Confessions of a Rock Lobster*. Boston, MA: Alyson.

GIBSON, B. (1995) *Male Order: Life Stories From Boys Who Sell Sex*. London: Cassell.

GROSS, L., AURAND, S. and ADDESSA, R. (1988) *Violence and Discrimination Against Lesbian and Gay People in Philadelphia and the Commonwealth of Pennsylvania*. Unpublished Report: Philadelphia Lesbian and Gay Task Force.

HAMER, D.H., HU, S., MAGNUSON, V.L., HU, N. and PATTATUCCI, A.M.L. (1993) A linkage between DNA markers on the X chromosome and male sexual orientation. *Science, 261*, 321–327.

HERSHBERGER, S.L. and D'AUGELLI, A.R. (1995) The impact of victimization on the mental health and suicidality of lesbian, gay, and bisexual youths. *Developmental Psychology, 31*, 65–74.

HUNTER, J. (1990) Violence against lesbian and gay male youths. *Journal of Interpersonal Violence, 5,* 295–300.

ISAY, R.A. (1988) Homosexuality in heterosexual and homosexual men. *Psychiatric Annals, 18,* 43–46.

KINSEY, A.C., POMEROY, W.B. and MARTIN, C.E. (1948) *Sexual Behavior in the Human Male.* Philadelphia, PA: Saunders.

KINSEY, A.C., POMEROY, W.B., MARTIN, C.E. and GEBHARD, P.H. (1953) *Sexual Behavior in the Human Female.* Philadelphia, PA: Saunders.

KITZINGER, C. (1995) Social constructionism: Implications for lesbian and gay psychology. In A.R. D'Augelli and C.J. Patterson (Eds) *Lesbian, Gay, and Bisexual Identities Over the Lifespan: Psychological Perspectives.* New York: Oxford University Press.

KRUKS, G. (1991) Gay and lesbian homeless street youth: Special issues and concerns. *Journal of Adolescent Health, 12,* 515–518.

MAC AN GHAILL, M. (1994) *The Making of Men: Masculinities, Sexualities and Schooling.* Buckingham: Open University Press.

McKNIGHT, J. (1997) *Straight Science? Homosexuality, Evolution and Adaptation.* London: Routledge.

MUEHRER, P. (1995) Suicide and sexual orientation: A critical summary of recent research and directions for future research. *Suicide and Life Threatening Behavior, 25,* 72–81.

NATIONAL LESBIAN AND GAY TASK FORCE (1984) *Anti-Gay/Lesbian Victimization: A Study by the National Gay Task Force in Cooperation with Gay and Lesbian Organizations in Eight U.S. Cities.* Washington, DC: National Gay and Lesbian Task Force.

NEVID, J.S., FICHNER-RATHUS, L. and RATHUS, S.A. (1995) *Human Sexuality in a World of Diversity.* Boston, MA: Allyn and Bacon.

OWENS, R.E. (1998) *Queer Kids: The Challenges and Promise for Lesbian, Gay, and Bisexual Youth.* New York: Harrington Park Press.

PILKINGTON, N.W. and D'AUGELLI, A.R. (1995) Victimization of lesbian, gay and bisexual youth in community settings. *Journal of Community Psychology, 23,* 33–56.

REMAFEDI, G., RESNICK, M., BLUM, R. and HARRIS, L. (1992) Demography of sexual orientation in adolescents. *Pediatrics, 89,* 714–721.

RIVERS, I. (1997a) Violence against lesbian and gay youth and its impact. In M.S. Schneider (Ed.) *Pride and Prejudice: Working with Lesbian, Gay, and Bisexual Youth.* Toronto: Central Toronto Youth Services.

RIVERS, I. (1997b) Lesbian, gay and bisexual development: Theory, research and social issues. *Journal of Community & Applied Social Psychology, 7,* 329–343.

RIVERS, I. (1999a) The impact of homophobia at school over the lifespan. Paper presented at the 107th Annual Convention of the American Psychological Association, Boston, Massachusetts, 20th -24th August.

RIVERS, I. (1999b) *The Psycho-Social Correlates and Long-Term Implications of Bullying at School for Lesbians, Gay Men and Bisexual Men and Women* (Vols. I and II). Unpublished PhD thesis, Roehampton Institute London.

RIVERS, I. (2000a) School exclusion, absenteeism and sexual minority youth. *Support for Learning 15,* 13–19.

RIVERS, I (2000b) Lesbian, gay and bisexual youth: The challenges of education. Paper presented at the 7th Biennial Conference of the European Association for Research on Adolescence, Jena, Germany, 31st May – 4th June.

RIVERS, I. and D'AUGELLI, A.R. (2001) The victimization of lesbian, gay, and bisexual youths: Implications for intervention. In A.R. D'Augelli and C.J. Patterson (Eds) *Lesbian, Gay, and Bisexual Identities and Youth: Psychological Perspectives*. New York: Oxford University Press.

RIVERS, I. and HARDCASTLE, H. (2000) The representation and misrepresentation of research: Homosexuality and the House of Lords Debates 1998–2000. Paper presented at the Inaugural Conference of the Lesbian and Gay Psychology Section of the British Psychological Society, University of Surrey, 18th July.

SEARS, J.T. (1991) *Growing Up Gay in the South: Race, Gender, and Journeys of the Spirit*. New York: Harrington Park Press.

STORMS, M.J. (1981) A theory of erotic orientation. *Journal of Personality and Social Psychology, 38*, 783–792.

TAULKE-JOHNSON, R.A. and RIVERS, I. (1999) Providing a safe environment for lesbian, gay and bisexual students living in university accommodation. *Youth and Policy, 64*, 74–89.

TRENCHARD, L. (1984) *Talking About Young Lesbians*. London: London Gay Teenage Group.

TRENCHARD, L. and WARREN, H. (1984) *Something to Tell You…The Experiences and Needs of Young Lesbians and Gay Men in London*. London: London Gay Teenage Group.

WARREN, H. (1984) *Talking About School*. London: London Gay Teenage Group.

Chapter 3

Girls' Friendships and the Formation of Sexual Identities

Christine Griffin

In the early 1990s, I wrote a critical review of youth studies in Britain and the USA which involved a comprehensive analysis of mainstream and radical research during the 1980s on many aspects of young people's lives across a range of academic disciplines including psychology (Griffin, 1993). In the concluding chapter I reviewed the position of radical youth research in the period after Thatcher and Reagan, arguing that a

> ...notable absence in radical youth research has been the lack of work concerned with the lives of young lesbians, gay men and bisexuals, who still remain relatively invisible in the radical literature...The growing international literature on young women's friendship groups, for example, still tends to assume that all young women are heterosexual unless specified otherwise, and it stops short of examining the processes through which the transition to heterosexuality is policed in the arena of friendships between young women. (p. 212)

As I write almost ten years later, reviewing more recent research concerned with the lives of young lesbians and gay men, the picture has changed remarkably little, although there are a number of positive signs. A few recent research studies with a focus on young lesbians and gay men in psychology, cultural studies, education, sociology and the new cultural geography have expanded the field a little, as has the new wave of studies from the emerging area of lesbian and gay psychology (for example, Greene and Herek, 1994; Khayatt, 1994). However, in most mainstream and radical youth research, the picture remains depressingly static. The primary focus remains on young (white, working class, able-bodied) heterosexual males, and the presumption of heterosexuality as the 'normal' and 'natural' form of mature sexuality is still pervasive (see Epstein and Johnson, 1998, for a review). There are, however, a few recent studies in feminist youth research which have examined the social, psychological and cultural processes through which traditional heterosexuality is maintained as compulsory (for example, Griffin, 1985; Lees, 1993; Holland *et al.*, 1998). The two research literatures on young women's entry to hetero-sexuality and on the lives of young lesbians remain relatively distinct, so there is little sense of how young women might move between these two worlds. In this chapter, I will be considering recent research which has focused on the lives of young lesbians, but it is important to remember that such studies continue to form only a small proportion of the extensive research literature on young people in contemporary western societies[1].

For those with an interest in the psychological and social welfare of lesbians, gay men and bisexuals, the teenage years signify a period of particular importance, some aspects of which are discussed in Chapter 2 in this volume. There is evidence from research involving gay men that 'adolescence' is a particularly salient period for the formation of sexual identities (for example, Savin-Williams, 1988; Troiden, 1988). There are a number of studies which have argued that the process of self-identification as lesbian may occur after the teenage years for many lesbians (for example, Cass, 1984; Schneider, 1989; Kitzinger and Wilkinson, 1995; Epstein and Johnson, 1998). To some degree, however, young lesbians and gay men appear at first glance to be little different from other groups of young people, for whom peer relation-ships of all kinds provide an important arena in which the processes of sexual identification are negotiated (Kehily and Nayak, 1997). It is for this reason that young women's friendships are an important focus for understanding the formation of sexual identification and same-sex desire. Whilst some other researchers might see such processes as a consequence of the 'natural' hormonal turmoil of adolescence, I would argue that wider social and political structures/forces – especially relating to the institutions of marriage and family life – produce the conditions in which sexuality takes on such a heightened salience for young people themselves and for representations of youth and adoles-cence (Epstein and Johnson, 1998). I want to begin with a brief examination of the treatment of same-sex and cross-sex friendships in the mainstream social psychology research literature before returning to take a more critical look at the construction of adolescence as a cru-cial period for the formation of lesbian identities.

Mainstream social psychology research on same-sex and cross-sex friendships

Traditionally, social psychology research has tended to differentiate friendship from two other types of close personal relationships: those between relatives and those involving romantic love and sexual intimacy. Relationships based on friendship are therefore defined as (a) voluntary and (b) platonic (Franzoi, 1996). However, one of the consequences of this distinction is that it carries the assumption that platonic friendships and sexual relationships differ in specific and fairly fundamental ways. This assumption appears to map neatly onto common (though by no means universal) patterns of close personal relationships in Western societies in which intimate heterosexual relationships and platonic same-sex friendships are viewed as distinctively different (Franzoi, 1996; Baron and Byrne, 2000). Most traditional social psychology research on friendship has operated according to an implicit heterosexual norm – what Epstein and Johnson (1994) term the 'presumption of heterosexuality'. That is, most respondents tend to be – or are presumed to be – heterosexual and no other groups of potential respondents are assumed to exist. Where lesbian and gay relationships are acknowledged, they tend to be covered in little depth and frequently in a stereotyped manner (for example, Baron and Byrne, 2000).

In addition, mainstream social psychology researchers have argued that women's (platonic) friendships 'tend to be more intimate and involve more emotional sharing' than men's, to quote one American undergraduate text book on social psychology (Franzoi, 1996, p. 351). So researchers tell us that men's friendships tend to revolve around shared activities, whereas women are more likely to spend time talking about intimate personal matters (see Franzoi, 1996, for a review). However, other recent research challenges this over-simplistic distinction, arguing that both women and men frequently meet to talk and that women are just as likely as men to engage in shared activities in their friendships (Duck and Wright, 1993). Franzoi's (1996) social psychology textbook emphasizes that the above research findings on differences between patterns of women's and men's same-sex friendships refer primarily to group averages and that there will always be a considerable degree of within-group variation. In general, the traditional social psychology research literature gives us a relatively detailed picture concerning patterns of close personal relationships (sexual and otherwise) amongst (predominantly white, Western) heterosexuals but very little information about other groups and scant indication that alternative patterns of close personal relationships exist.

Lesbian, gay and feminist psychology research on same-sex and cross-sex friendships

There has been some research on same-sex and cross-sex friendships which has avoided the prevailing norm of heterosexuality found in most mainstream psychology studies. Researchers in this area have been informed by the work of feminists and lesbian and gay psychologists (Greene and Herek, 1994; Kitzinger, 1997). Partly as a consequence of the critical perspective on gender relations which emerged from feminist analyses, in more recent years a number of researchers have taken a closer look at same-sex (platonic) male friendships, viewing men as gendered beings who operate in specific social, historical and political contexts. Recent critical research on masculinity has begun to argue that the avoidance of intimacy in many male friendships – at least in contemporary Western societies – is actually specific to (or most marked amongst) heterosexual males. Peter Nardi and Drury Sherrod (1994) argued, following the work of Gregory Herek (1987), that the avoidance of emotional expressiveness and intimacy is a consequence of men being socialized to value heterosexual masculinity. This system associates emotional expressiveness with femininity and therefore with homosexuality in males. In contemporary western societies, if men are emotionally close to other men outside of a few specific contexts (for example, playing sport, being drunk, fighting), this tends to be associated with being gay or 'not a real man'. So notions of gender and sexuality are intimately intertwined.

Nardi and Sherrod (1994) proposed that the 'stigma' associated with this avoidance of emotional intimacy may be most relevant to heterosexual men. As they argue, why should gay men worry about being seen as gay if they show affection for other men – providing they are in a situation in which they feel safe? In addition, many families of lesbians and gay men are unsupportive or reject them because of their sexuality, so friendships (sexual or otherwise) can be viewed as a form of family relationship, according to Nardi (1992). Nardi and Sherrod's (1994) questionnaire study with lesbians and gay men in the USA indicates that there are no differences in reported levels of openness, self-disclosure and satisfaction in the close personal same-sex friendships of lesbians and gay men. This implies that the gender differences in levels of intimacy within the same-sex friendships of women and men reported in mainstream psychology research may apply primarily to heterosexuals.

There also appear to be differences in the nature of sexual relationships amongst gay men and lesbians compared to heterosexual men and women respectively. Lesbians and gay men are more likely to report that they remain friends *after* a sexual relationship has ended, whereas for cross-sex relationships between heterosexuals, sexual intimacy typically *ends* a friendship. For lesbians and gay men, sex is more likely to *lead to* (continuing) friendship (Nardi, 1992). There remains relatively little research in this area and most studies are from the USA but they indicate that the distinction between platonic friendships and sexual relationships simply does not operate in the same way for lesbians and gay men compared to their heterosexual peers. No equivalent research information is available for those identifying as bisexual but what literature there is suggests that the platonic and sexual relationships of bisexual women and men with both sexes are likely to be closer to the pattern for lesbians and gay men than for heterosexuals, although not necessarily identical (George, 1993; Storr, 1999).

It is worth noting here that the above discussion implies a sharp divide between the social worlds of people identifying as heterosexual and those identifying as lesbian, gay or bisexual, and there is considerable historical evidence that this is not the case in practice (Faderman, 1992). In general, heterosexual women and men do occupy different psychological and social worlds compared to many lesbians and gay men, especially with regard to the spheres of domestic life and leisure (Greene and Herek, 1994). This does not mean that there is not considerable scope for overlap and social contact between these 'two worlds', however. For example, many lesbians and gay men 'pass' as straight, living in married (and apparently heterosexual) couples with spouses or partners and children who may often be unaware of their sexuality. There are also many documented examples of women and men who grow up identifying as heterosexual, only to 'shift' to lesbian, gay or bisexual identity later in life – and some others move in the opposite direction (Faderman, 1992; Kitzinger and Wilkinson, 1995; Menasche, 1998). It is also important to note that most undergraduate social psychology texts which cover intimate personal relationships – as many of them do – fail to mention differences in patterns of same-sex and cross-sex relationships for heterosexual women and men as compared to lesbians and gay men at all. I have quoted the text by Franzoi (1996) but this remains a relatively unusual example.

What evidence that is available from mainstream social psychology research on personal relationships implies that the existing conceptualization of this area is based on a set of assumptions which is primarily appropriate to heterosexuals in contemporary Western cultures. Despite this, the dominant approach continues to be applied to non-Western contexts with minimal success (Kofune, 1999) and clearly is of limited value for understanding the friendships and sexual relationships of lesbians and gay men – and also bisexuals. It is in this context that I want to consider research which has concentrated on friendships amongst girls and young women.

Overlooking the possibility of same-sex desire in friendships between girls and young women

A similar presumption of heterosexuality operates in research on young women's friendships as in studies of youth and of friendships more generally. There are relatively few studies that have taken young women's friendships seriously – and most of these have been undertaken by feminist researchers. The latter have also tended to presume that their respondents are heterosexual and have had little to say about the possibility of same-sex desire between young women. As I have argued elsewhere, if research overlooks the possibility of same-sex female desire, it also marginalizes lesbian (and bisexual) existence, thereby assuming that young women are always already heterosexual by default (Griffin, 2000). Young women's sexual identities are usually taken for granted in most research on female friendship groups, rather than examining the role of young women's friendships and pressures to 'get a man' in the *construction* of female sexualities, whether lesbian, heterosexual or bisexual.

Most radical youth research on subcultures has been dominated by what I have termed the 'gang of lads' model and this has resulted in a male norm against which the experiences and friendship patterns of young women have been compared (Griffin, 1987). This male norm was challenged by the emergence of feminist youth research during the 1970s (for example, McRobbie and Garber, 1975). Although young women do participate in mixed-sex friendship groups and larger gang-type social structures, young women's friendship groups tend to be smaller, more intimate and intense and they can be long-standing compared to the gang model favoured by some (though not all) of their male peers (Lees, 1993; Hey, 1997). Young women's friendships are sometimes characterized by the dyad or close 'best friend' relationship between two girls, although there is some evidence to suggest that it may be more useful to think in terms of 'shifting pairs' or 'parallel friendships' amongst young women (Griffin, 2000).

Much of this feminist youth research examined intersections between gender and class in young women's lives, with only a few studies looking at the impact of 'race', ethnicity and racism and/or the experiences of young African Caribbean, Asian and mixed parentage women in the UK (see Amos and Parmar, 1981, for a critique). The 1990s saw a few more pieces of research concerned with the lives of young Black women, although most of these have concentrated on education and the job market rather than friendships, sexuality or leisure (for example, Phoenix, 1990; Bhavnani, 1991; Mirza, 1992; Tizard and Phoenix, 1993; Basit, 1997; Haw, 1998). It is now more common for feminist research in this area to include more diverse groups of young women (for example, Griffiths, 1988; Holland *et al.*, 1998), although the Anglo-centric perspective has far from disappeared (see McLean Taylor *et al.*, 1995). It is regrettably still the case that few studies which concentrate on the lives of young white women consider them as racialized beings (see Fine *et al.*, 1997, for some recent exceptions). As a consequence, we still know relatively little about the patterns of friendship between young women from a full range of ethnic and class locations (Griffin, 2000).

Feminist research on young women's friendships does not deny the existence of young lesbian (or bisexual) women but it frequently overlooks the *possibility* of same-sex desire between young women, regardless of their sexual identification. Same-sex desire – and therefore the possibility of lesbian identification – lurks in the background of *all* young women's friendship groups, although only a few studies have reflected the way that this can operate in practice (for example, Hey, 1997). Most research has tended to treat young lesbians as already different and distinctive from their heterosexual peers and young bisexual women are scarcely mentioned at all. What is lacking in the feminist youth research literature is a sense of the *process* of movement into (and out of and between) such categories of sexual identity and a sense of the *instability* as well as the stability of such categories as young women's sexualities are produced in practice. As a consequence, we have one set of studies about the lives of young heterosexual women and another (much smaller) group of studies that focus on young lesbians and fewer still with young women who identify as queer and/or bisexual (George, 1993; Rose and Stevens, 1996).

In her book *Sugar and Spice*, British feminist Sue Lees (1993) reviewed research on different aspects of young women's lives alongside her own research. The book is subtitled 'Sexuality and Adolescent Girls' and is unusual in devoting a whole chapter to the subject of 'friendship'. As a feminist sociologist, Lees' research has primarily involved the use of ethnographic observation and informal semi-structured interviews with respondents and her work has considerable relevance for social psychological analyses of young women's friendships. Lees challenges the prevailing assumption that women's same-sex friendships are less significant than men's and examines attempts by academic researchers to render women's same-sex friendships invisible, giving priority to (heterosexual) women's supposedly greater interest in competing with each other for male attention.

Drawing on her own research, Lees discusses the differences she observed between young women's and men's same-sex and cross-sex friendships, many of which mirror the findings of the social psychological studies on friendship mentioned earlier in this chapter. She argues that young women's friendship networks are wide, involving all-female and mixed-sex groups as well as pairs of female 'best friends'. Much of Lees' chapter on friendship is taken up with discussion of the relative importance of heterosexual girls' same-sex friendships and their relationships with boyfriends, as well as issues of secrecy and bitchiness between girls. Lees does address some questions which are generally overlooked in such studies, one being platonic relationships between young men and young women. She argues that for young men to 'hang around with girls' is to acknowledge their similarity and such boys are frequently assumed to be gay, especially by other boys (Lees, 1993, p. 90). Simply by having (non-sexual) contact with girls, boys are seen to be getting 'too close' to femininity and this carries the connotation of homosexuality.

At the very end of Lees' chapter on friendship she mentions the possibility of same-sex desire between women and of lesbianism (p. 102), with reference to Adrienne Rich's (1981) notion of the system of compulsory heterosexuality and the lesbian continuum. So Lees acknowledges the role of peer friendships in policing young women's sexuality and especially the path to heterosexuality and the prevalence of challenges to women's same-sex friendships via the everyday practices of homophobia and anti-lesbianism between young women. Like much of the feminist literature on youth cultures, Lees' work tells us much about the social, psychological and cultural processes through which heterosexuality is established and maintained as a prevailing norm amongst young women but less about how they might become lesbian or bisexual. To find research on the latter processes, we have to look elsewhere.

In a British study of girls' friendships, Valerie Hey (1997) demonstrates the inadequacies of most approaches to the study of 'youth' when it comes to appreciating the relatively secret world of girls' friendships. The latter, she argues, have also been overlooked by the focus on youth cultural styles and forms of female resistance in sociology research and cultural studies (for example, McRobbie, 1978) and by the emphasis on the 'authentic' voices of girls in the Harvard Project (Brown and Gilligan, 1992; McLean Taylor *et al.*, 1995)[2]. Hey looks at the various ways in which the young, white, middle and working class women in her study resisted the pressures of traditional patriarchal heterosexual femininity, resisted relationships with boys 'taking over' female friendships and negotiated the 'accusations' of lesbianism which hover around close female friendships. Hey's study draws on the work of previous feminist youth researchers to consider how same-sex female friendships are negotiated and policed through the use of terms like 'lesbian' and 'slag' and the importance placed on young women's sexual reputations (see Lees, 1986; Holland *et al.*, 1998). However, Hey's study is unusual because, without assuming that these young women are necessarily lesbian (or heterosexual), she argues that they "*do* experience their relations with each other as a passion" (1997, p. 114, emphasis in original) and that this gives the term 'lesbian' greater power to control girls' relationships with one another (and with boys). Hey (1997) considers some of the notes that passed between the girls in school. In her consideration of one extremely lengthy note, which she terms a 'transgressive text', Hey argues that these young women adopt a 'textual flirtation with lesbian positioning' (p. 83) but manage this by projecting any 'deviant' possibilities onto other young women:

'Sally responds to Jude's remarks:

Yeah, I like a little bit of both [oral sex with both sexes]. Know what I mean?

... Jude writes to Sally:

Well that's fine with me just as long as you don't pick on me. I mean you can pick on Princess or Jocelyn because I think they're a bit like that. They never let go of each other. Mind you the way we go on kissing each other on the cheek, people give us funny looks.

... Sally's response:

Well, there's nothing wrong with that. We all know we like boys and that's as far as it goes.

... Jude signs off:

I know as long as we know that [ie. that we only like boys], that's OK, but I'm not so sure about Princess and Jocelyn you know'

(Hey, 1997, pp. 82–83)

Hey's analysis of the above extract examines Jude and Sally's construction of themselves as heterosexual subjects ('We all know we like boys...') in contrast to Princess and Jocelyn, who are represented as 'a bit like that', without the girls ever having to specify precisely what 'that' might entail. When Jude goes on to describe herself and Sally as 'kissing each other on the cheek', they both locate one another as 'OK'. Jude and Sally are here shown to be negotiating the blurred line between heterosexuality (constructed as acceptable) and lesbianism (constructed as unacceptable), taking care to distinguish between same-sex physical practices which can only be represented as acceptable if they are associated with heterosexual identities.

To some extent, what Hey's analysis is pointing to here is *not* that all girls are intrinsically lesbian or heterosexual but that girls themselves (as well as boys and adults, including parents) use the label 'lesbian' to police and limit the erotic possibilities of girls' (and women's) relationships with one another. Heterosexual femininity, in all its complexity, is formed partly in reaction to the 'spectre' of lesbianism and the implied 'threat' posed by the possibility of lesbian existence (Khayatt, 1994). Feminism and women's identification as feminists have been shaped by similar pressures (Griffin, 1989; Lees, 1993). In a related but rather different way, heterosexual masculinity is formed partly in reaction to the implied 'threat' of men being (seen as) gay (Connell, 1995; see also Chapter 12 in this volume).

The role of same-sex friendship in the formation of young lesbian lives

In the British context, some of the key texts in research concerned with the lives of young lesbians (and gay men) have emerged from outside of mainstream academia. Trenchard and Warren's classic 1984 text *Something To Tell You* was funded and published by the London Gay Teenage Group and illustrated some of the pressures faced by young lesbians and gay men in their daily lives in school, family life, leisure and the job market. Trenchard and Warren paid particular attention to the difficulties young lesbians and gay men reported in coming out to parents, teachers and friends but had less to say about the formation of lesbian and gay identities *per se*. The social and psychological implications of adopting a lesbian identity and 'coming out' are explored by Laura A. Markowe in Chapter 4 in this volume.

There is now an extensive and traditionally academic literature on lesbian and gay identity formation, especially in the USA – most notably the various stage theories of 'homosexual identity formation' which locate the primary moment of 'choice' concerning 'sexual orientation' as occurring during adolescence (for example, Kourany, 1988; see Coyle, 1992, for a review). Richard Troiden's (1988) four-stage 'ideal-typical' model for the 'attainment of gay identity' is rather more radical, rejecting both the notion of gay identification as either a passing phase or a fixed sexual orientation and the argument that gay identity should necessarily begin or occur during adolescence. In addition, Adrian Coyle (1992) has emphasized the role of subcultural narratives and identity processes in the formation of gay identity such that the latter is viewed in terms of telling a story rather than having a specific and relatively static identity (see also Plummer, 1995). Only a few models of 'homosexual identity development' have acknowledged the specific experiences of young lesbians as distinct from young gay men, and these have been more prevalent in the small literature on 'lesbian identity development' (for example, Schneider, 1989; see Markowe, 1996, for a review). The latter are more likely to draw on feminist analyses and to deconstruct the notion of 'identity' and of specifically 'homosexual' or lesbian identity than their male counterparts (for example, Cass, 1984; Chapman and Brannock, 1987; see

Griffin, 1993, for a discussion). Chapman and Brannock (1987), for example, use the term 'lesbian self-labelling' in order to avoid the representation of lesbianism as a disease or a perversion, which has been so prevalent in mainstream psychology (Kitzinger, 1997). They also emphasize the diversity of lesbian experiences. However, much of this work has been Anglo-centric in approach and only a few studies have focused on the lives of young lesbians and gay men of colour, to use the US terminology (for example, Gerstel *et al.*, 1989; Phellas, 1998).

Valerie Hey's (1997) text *The Company She Keeps* is an important book in the small, disjointed, but persistent history of research around young women's friendships. As in many other feminist youth research texts, however, I am still left wondering how any young women ever come to identify as lesbian – or bisexual. We still know relatively little about the untold story of young women like Princess and Jocelyn from Hey's study. Such young women do exist but they seem to remain invisible (or in the closet) to most youth researchers, unless the study explicitly focuses on the lives of young lesbians. One exception is an analysis by Didi Khayatt (1994), who reports on an interview study with 12 young lesbians in their mid-teens in Toronto, Canada. This research was carried out in 1991 as part of a larger study of barriers to quality education for lesbian and gay youth. As self-identified lesbians, all these young women spoke retrospectively of the 'coming-out' process and of their experiences of the relative invisibility of lesbianism (and gay male sexuality) in the school system[3].

As in the earlier UK study by Trenchard and Warren (1984) – and other similar studies – a significant proportion (one third) of Khayatt's respondents reported at least one attempt to kill themselves as a consequence of the pressures involved in trying to live as a young lesbian. Khayatt and her colleague, George Smith, drew on ethnographic methods to investigate 'a "section" of the social world from the standpoint of the organisation of the practices and activities of those who, in various ways, are involved with its production' (Khayatt, 1994, p. 48). This technique, she argued, enabled the researchers to 'comprehend how lesbians and gay youth are rendered invisible' (*ibid.*), thus making it extremely difficult for lesbian and gay students to 'break the relative silence which envelops their lives at school' (*ibid.*).

Khayatt (1994) mentions a number of instances in which friendship played a role in her respondents' lives – or rather the impact of the lack of supportive friendships for young lesbians. She notes that several of her respondents experienced discrimination at school in terms of 'a general climate of rejection of lesbians and gays' (p. 50) and a negativity which forced some of them into self-imposed isolation. She also mentioned two of her respondents who were relatively unusual in being 'out' as lesbians at school and who felt that their isolation from other students was a consequence of having come out, since other students began to avoid them from that time. The overwhelming theme of Khayatt's study is the damage associated with the officially sanctioned silence around the topic of homosexuality in schools, set alongside the everyday practices of homophobic abuse and bullying which pervaded the general (ie., heterosexual) school culture (see Kehily and Nayak, 1997; Epstein and Johnson, 1998). All of the above points are confirmed by Ian Rivers in Chapter 2 and Laura A. Markowe in Chapter 4.

Perhaps Khayatt's study provides an indication of one possible reason for the relative separation between research on young heterosexual women and studies of young lesbians. That is, girls and young women who are out as lesbians, those who self-identify as lesbians but dare not come out and possibly also those identified by other girls as 'lezzies' are all either isolated from girls' friendship groups or develop a form of self-imposed isolation as a strategy of self-protection. These are the girls and young women who have been rendered relatively invisible in school cultures due to the pervasive nature of homophobic and anti-lesbian abuse, pressures to present themselves as heterosexual and the officially-sanctioned silence around homosexuality. They appear to have been equally invisible to some researchers, including feminist researchers. There is as yet no evidence to confirm or refute this argument and it would provide an important focus for future research.

One of the very few studies to examine the role of same-sex friendships in the formation of young lesbian subjectivities/identities (albeit relatively briefly) is reported in the book *Schooling Sexualities* by Debbie Epstein and Richard Johnson (1998). This text presents an analysis of the accounts of lesbians and gay men who were involved in the British school system during the 1980s as pupils, teachers or parents of school pupils. Epstein and Johnson present a forceful argument that 'sexuality is intrinsic to the formation of individual and group identities in school and that schools are sites for the active making of such identities and meanings around sexuality' (p. 9). *Schooling Sexualities* is unusual in that Epstein and Johnson examine the ways in which sexualities are (re)produced in racialized, gender- and class-specific forms. The book considers the pressures of compulsory heterosexuality, the operation of a prevailing presumption of heterosexuality and the impact of homophobia and anti-lesbianism on lesbians and gay men in schools whether as students, teachers or parents. The book offers a few glimpses of possible connections between young women's friendships and accounts of coming out – or rather 'realising that I was a lesbian', as female respondents framed this process (p. 153).

Epstein and Johnson (1998) devote some attention to the processes involved in identifying as lesbian or gay for young people (and for teachers and parents) in schools. Their analysis is based on 50 interviews with lesbians and gay men about their experiences in school, including retrospective accounts of adults recalling their school years.

The authors argue that the narratives of gay men differed from those of lesbians in several respects (see also de Monteflores and Schultz, 1978; Cass, 1984; Schneider, 1989). Firstly, adult gay men spoke of early same-sex 'experimentation' and said they 'knew' they were gay from puberty or earlier. Most of the adult women they interviewed spoke about identifying as lesbians much later, often after spending 15 or 20 years in heterosexual relationships (see also Kitzinger and Wilkinson, 1995). Epstein and Johnson's female respondents constructed their move from heterosexuality to lesbianism not in terms of 'becoming a lesbian' but 'realising that I was a lesbian', which carries the implication that they constructed themselves as having always been lesbian, without necessarily recognizing this. Epstein and Johnson explain this difference between the retrospective accounts of gay men and lesbians with reference to:

> the dominant discourses of (hetero)sexuality current in contemporary British society which tend to render female sexuality passive, with women as objects of the male gaze rather than active, desiring agents – or, if they are desirous sexual objects, they become immediately dangerous. Given common-sense perceptions of lesbian and gay sexualities as being only about sex, about 'what you do in bed', identification as lesbian or gay involves a discursive assertion of sexuality. This makes the ability to identify against the heterosexual grain in this way much more readily available to men than to women. (pp. 153–154)

Epstein and Johnson (1998) reinforce the arguments of Khayatt (1994) when they quote Rogers' (1994) thesis that 'young lesbians are subject to a triple invisibility' (p. 35), i.e., as children in an adult world, as women in a male-dominated world and as lesbians in a gay world. Epstein and Johnson add to this the possibility of other parallel invisibilities for different groups of young women around race/ethnicity and social class. Issues of silence around lesbianism are also reflected in their analysis of their female respondents' accounts of growing up and only identifying as lesbian after they had left school. As one woman put it, 'all you talked about was boys' and so the possibility of lesbian existence was not even considered.

Epstein and Johnson are unusual in mentioning the role of women's friendships, academic success and single-sex schools in the formation of lesbian identities for young women. They argue that single-sex schools are 'somewhat more friendly places for those who identify as lesbians than boys-only schools are for boys perceived as gay or than co-educational schools are for either' (p. 157). This does not mean that single-sex girls' schools are havens for lesbians, free of anti-lesbian bullying and pressure to be heterosexual. It does imply that such schools can be more sympathetic to close female friendships. Epstein and Johnson quote one of their adult respondents speaking about one such friendship between girls in a single-sex school, in which the boundary between platonic and sexual intimacy dissolved:

> 'Maxine: There's a lot of feelings between young women in schoolgirl books and schoolgirl stories about how much they cared for each other and stuff. And in that situation you *do* care for people because you live with them at school...You really do form very, very close friendships...And so you know, we got up to a lot of things and certainly, from about age 10 onwards we'd all piss around and sort of, like, kiss each other and *pretend* that we were practising for when we met a man. D'you know what I mean?
>
> DE: [Laughs]
>
> Maxine: Um, but that was the justification for a lot of the girls, where it never was for me. But I kept my gob shut about it, 'cos I, I understood that what I felt was good and I really liked it, um, and I definitely fell in love with, um, a, a, another girl at the age of 10 who was the same age as me. Um, but I also knew that I shouldn't tell *anybody* about how I was feeling'.
>
> (Epstein and Johnson, 1998, p. 158, emphases in original)

In this extract we again see the familiar theme of lesbian invisibility and the taboo on acknowledging same-sex female desire. This is one of very few instances in which researchers mention the involvement of *all* young women in same-sex erotic practices and hence point to a degree of blurring between categories of heterosexuality and lesbianism for young women. The implication of Maxine's account is that what marks out young heterosexual women from young lesbians is not sexual practices or erotic desires but young women's different discursive constructions of such practices in relation to the formation of their sexual identities/subjectivities. Drawing on a narrative approach, one could argue that young women who identify (or come to identify) as lesbian or bisexual are likely to tell different stories about same-sex sexual practices than those who identify as heterosexual. Maxine's account implies that most young women 'justified' kissing other girls with recourse to a narrative about a future which was presumed as heterosexual – practising for what was constructed as 'the real thing'. For Maxine, no such 'justification' was necessary, since the practice was presented as sufficient in itself and was associated with the romanticized moment of falling in love with another girl, rather than a mythical heterosexual future. Maxine's account also implies that she maintained a silence about these taboo events. For Maxine and her friends, it appears that the boundary between platonic friendships and sexual intimacy was somewhat blurred and did not follow the neat association between same-sex platonic relationships and cross-sex sexual intimacy which is assumed in most of the mainstream social psychology research on friendships.

Conclusion

What does all of this research tell us about the role of girls' friendships in the formation of lesbian (and heterosexual and bisexual) identities? In summary, this chapter makes a number of points about the importance of female friendships for girls and young women and the role of female friendships in the construction of lesbian (and heterosexual and bisexual) identities. Firstly, most research on friendship in mainstream social psychology is primarily relevant to the relationship patterns of heterosexual women and men and especially those in Western industrialized societies. Evidence from the emerging field of lesbian and gay psychology indicates that same-sex and cross-sex friendships are not so differentiated by gender amongst lesbians and gay men compared to their heterosexual peers. Secondly, close female friendships are important to all young women as part of the process of sexual identification and negotiation. However, radical youth research – including much feminist work – has paid more attention to the role of female friendships in policing the transition to heterosexuality than to the possibility of same-sex desire between girls and young women. This makes it especially difficult to understand the psychological, social and cultural processes involved in girls' and young women's identification as lesbians. Finally, there is a small and relatively distinct research literature which focuses on the lives of young lesbians and which indicates that female friendships can be a source of support, intimacy, longing and abuse for young lesbians. A number of young lesbians report adopting strategies of social isolation as a means of self-protection from homophobic and anti-lesbian abuse, whilst others report being isolated by their heterosexual peers after coming out as lesbian (Khayatt, 1994; Epstein and Johnson, 1998). Overall, the picture is one of relative silence and invisibility for most young lesbians, both in schools and in youth cultural groups. Radical youth research, including some (although not all) feminist work, has not always challenged this invisibility. A great deal more research remains to be carried out if we are to appreciate the diverse experiences of young lesbians and to be able to offer them meaningful support.

Notes

1. In 1999, the ESRC (Economic and Social Research Council) – which is the main British independent government institution funding social science research – launched its third major research programme on young people since the late 1970s. This research programme, entitled 'Youth, Citizenship and Social Change', includes as one of the 15 funded studies a project which features young lesbians and gay men as half of its sample of respondents; the other half is made up of young people with hearing impairments. This project is the only one in the programme to focus on 'vulnerable youth' and

is directed by Dr Gill Valentine, a social geographer at the University of Sheffield.

2. The Harvard Project on Women's Psychology and Girls' Development is a series of collaborative studies through which feminist researchers 'set out to learn from girls about girls' experiences and to explore the psychology of becoming girls in North America at the end of the 20th century' (McLean Taylor *et al.*, 1995, p. 6).

3. Khayatt's study is one of many to illustrate some of the damaging consequences of this officially sanctioned silence around homosexuality in schools. Despite a growing literature in this area, there remains a substantial climate of popular opinion in British society which is opposed to the repeal of Section 28 of the 1988 Local Government Act. This is a clause which forbids local authorities from funding activities that 'promote homosexuality as a pretended family unit'. This was repealed by the Scottish parliament in 2000 but remains on the statute book in England and Wales at the time of writing.

References

AMOS, V. and PARMAR, P. (1981) Resistances and responses: The experiences of Black girls in Britain. In A. McRobbie and T. McCabe (Eds) *Feminism for Girls: An Adventure Story*. London: Routledge and Kegan Paul.

BARON, R.A. and BYRNE, D. (2000) *Social Psychology*, 9th ed. Boston, MA: Allyn and Bacon.

BASIT, T. (1997) *Eastern Values, Western Milieu: Identities and Aspirations of Adolescent British Muslim Girls*. Aldershot: Ashgate.

BHAVNANI, K.-K. (1991) *Talking Politics: A Psychological Framing for Views from Youth in Britain*. Cambridge: Cambridge University Press.

BROWN, L.M. and GILLIGAN, C. (1992) *Meeting at the Crossroads: Women's Psychology and Girls' Development*. Cambridge, MA: Harvard University Press.

CASS, V.C. (1984) Homosexual identity: A concept in need of definition. *Journal of Homosexuality, 9(2/3)*, 105–126.

CHAPMAN, B.E. and BRANNOCK, J. (1987) Proposed model of lesbian identity development: An empirical investigation. *Journal of Homosexuality, 14(3/4)*, 17–32.

CONNELL, R.W. (1995) *Masculinities*. Cambridge: Polity Press.

COYLE, A. (1992) 'My own special creation'? The construction of gay identity. In G.M. Breakwell (Ed.) *Social Psychology of Identity and the Self Concept*. London: Surrey University Press/Academic Press.

de MONTEFLORES, C. and SCHULTZ, S.J. (1978) Coming out: Similarities and differences for lesbians and gay men. *Journal of Social Issues, 34(3)*, 59–72.

DUCK, S. and WRIGHT, P.H. (1993) Reexamining gender differences in same-gender friendships: A close look at two kinds of data. *Sex Roles, 28*, 709–727.

EPSTEIN, D. and JOHNSON, R. (1994) On the straight and narrow: The heterosexual presumption, homophobia and schools. In D. Epstein (Ed.) *Challenging Lesbian and Gay Inequalities in Education*. Buckingham: Open University Press.

EPSTEIN, D. and JOHNSON, R. (1998) *Schooling Sexualities*. Buckingham: Open University Press.

FADERMAN, L. (1992) *Odd Girls and Twilight Lovers: A History of Lesbian Life in Twentieth-Century America*. New York: Penguin Books.

FINE, M., WEIS, L., POWELL, L. and MUN WONG, L. (Eds) (1997) *Off White: Readings on Race, Power and Society*. New York: Routledge.

FRANZOI, S.L. (1996) *Social Psychology*. Dubuque, IA: Brown and Benchmark.

GEORGE, S. (1993) *Women and Bisexuality*. London: Scarlet Press.

GERSTEL, C.J., FERAIOS, A.J. and HERDT, G. (1989) Widening circles: An ethnographic profile of a youth group. *Journal of Homosexuality*, 17(1/2), 75–92.

GREENE, B. and HEREK, G.M. (Eds) (1994) *Lesbian and Gay Psychology: Theory, Research, and Clinical Applications*. Thousand Oaks, CA: Sage.

GRIFFIN, C. (1985) *Typical Girls: Young Women from School to the Job Market*. London: Routledge and Kegan Paul.

GRIFFIN, C. (1987) Youth research: Young women and the 'gang of lads' model. In J. Hazekamp, W. Meeus and Y. te Poel (Eds) *European Contributions to Youth Research*. Amsterdam: Free University Press.

GRIFFIN, C. (1989) 'I'm not a women's libber, but…': Feminist consciousness and gender identity. In S. Skevington and D. Baker (Eds) *The Social Identity of Women*. London: Sage.

GRIFFIN, C. (1993) *Representations of Youth: The Study of Youth and Adolescence in Britain and America*. Cambridge: Polity Press.

GRIFFIN, C. (2000) Absences that matter: Constructions of sexuality in studies of young women's friendship groups. *Feminism & Psychology*, 10, 227–245.

GRIFFITHS, V. (1988) From 'playing out' to 'dossing out': Young women and leisure. In E. Wimbush and M. Talbot (Eds) *Relative Freedoms: Women and Leisure*. Milton Keynes: Open University Press.

HAW, K. (1998) *Educating Muslim Girls: Shifting Discourses*. Buckingham: Open University Press.

HEREK, G.M. (1987) On heterosexual masculinity: Some psychical consequences of the social construction of gender and sexuality. In M.S. Kimmel (Ed.) *Changing Men: New Directions in Research on Men and Masculinity*. Newbury Park, CA: Sage.

HEY, V. (1997) *The Company She Keeps: An Ethnography of Girls' Friendships*. Buckingham: Open University Press.

HOLLAND, J., RAMAZANOGLU, C., SHARPE, S. and THOMSON, R. (1998) *The Male in the Head: Young People, Heterosexuality and Power*. London: The Tufnell Press.

KEHILY, M. and NAYAK. N. (1997) 'Lads and laughter': Humour and the production of heterosexual hierarchies. *Gender and Education*, 9, 69–88.

KHAYATT, D. (1994) Surviving school as a lesbian student. *Gender and Education*, 6, 47–62.

KITZINGER, C. (1997) Lesbian and gay psychology: A critical analysis. In D. Fox and I. Prilleltensky (Eds) *Critical Psychology: An Introduction*. Thousand Oaks, CA: Sage.

KITZINGER, C. and WILKINSON, S. (1995) Transitions from heterosexuality to lesbianism: The discursive production of lesbian identities. *Developmental Psychology*, 31, 95–104.

KOFUNE, S. (1999) *Love Styles and Attachment Styles among Japanese Young Adults*. Unpublished BSc dissertation, University of Birmingham.

KOURANY, R. (1988) Gay and lesbian youth and the resolution of sexual identity. *Journal of Adolescent Health Care*, 9, 114–122.

LEES, S. (1986) *Losing Out: Sexuality and Adolescent Girls*. London: Hutchinson.

LEES, S. (1993) *Sugar and Spice: Sexuality and Adolescent Girls*. London: Penguin.

MARKOWE, L.A. (1996) *Redefining the Self: Coming Out as Lesbian*. Cambridge: Polity Press.

McLEAN TAYLOR, J., GILLIGAN, C. and SULLIVAN, A.M. (1995) *Between Voice and Silence: Women and Girls, Race and Relationship*. Cambridge, MA: Harvard University Press.

McROBBIE, A. (1978) Working class girls and the culture of femininity. In Women's Studies Group (Ed.) *Women Take Issue: Aspects of Women's Subordination*. London: Hutchinson.

McROBBIE, A. and GARBER, J. (1975) Girls and subcultures: An exploration. In S. Hall and T. Jefferson (Eds) *Resistance Through Rituals: Youth Sub-cultures in Post-war Britain*. London: Hutchinson.

MENASCHE, A.E. (1998) *Leaving the Life: Lesbians, Ex-lesbians and the Heterosexual Imperative*. London: Onlywomen Press.

MIRZA, H.S. (1992) *Young, Female and Black*. London: Routledge.

NARDI, P.M. (Ed.) (1992) *Men's Friendships*. Newbury Park, CA: Sage.

NARDI, P.M. and SHERROD, D. (1994) Friendship in the lives of gay men and lesbians. *Journal of Social and Personal Relationships*, 11, 185–199.

PHELLAS, C.N. (1998) *Sexual and Ethnic Identities of Anglo-Cypriot Men Resident in London who have Sex with Men*. Unpublished PhD thesis: University of Essex.

PHOENIX, A. (1990) *Young Mothers?* Oxford: Polity Press.

PLUMMER, K. (1989) Lesbian and gay youth in England. *Journal of Homosexuality*, 17(3/4), 38–45.

PLUMMER, K. (1995) *Telling Sexual Stories: Power, Change and Social Worlds*. London: Routledge.

RICH, A. (1981) Compulsory heterosexuality and lesbian existence [pamphlet]. London: Onlywomen Press.

ROSE, S. and STEVENS, C. (THE OFF PINK COLLECTIVE) (Eds) (1996) *Bisexual Horizons: Politics, Histories, Lives*. London: Lawrence & Wishart.

SAVIN-WILLIAMS, R.C. (1988) Theoretical perspectives accounting for adolescent homosexuality. *Journal of Adolescent Health Care*, 9, 95–104.

SCHNEIDER, M. (1989) Sappho was a right-on adolescent: Growing up lesbian. *Journal of Homosexuality*, 17(1/2), 111–130.

STORR, M. (Ed.) (1999) *Bisexuality: A Critical Reader*. London: Routledge.

TIZARD B. and PHOENIX, A. (1993) *Black, White or Mixed Race? Race and Racism in the Lives of Young People of Mixed Parentage*. London: Routledge.

TRENCHARD, L. (1984). *Talking About Young Lesbians*. London: London Gay Teenage Group.

TRENCHARD, L. and WARREN, H. (1984) *Something to Tell You…The Experiences and Needs of Young Lesbians and Gay Men in London*. London: London Gay Teenage Group.

TROIDEN, R.R. (1988) Homosexual identity development. *Journal of Adolescent Health Care*, 9, 105–113.

Chapter 4

Coming Out as Lesbian

Laura A. Markowe

If we lived in a society in which same sex relationships were as acceptable, as positively valued and as 'normal' as opposite sex relationships, 'coming out' as lesbian would not be an issue. Coming out – in the sense of coming to identify oneself as lesbian and the disclosure of this information to others – must be seen in the context of the discrimination that lesbians and gay men experience within a predominantly heterosexual society. This chapter focuses on some of the major underlying themes that define coming out as lesbian, drawing on research that investigated lesbians' perceptions and heterosexual men's and women's attitudes (Markowe, 1996). The analysis grounds the process of coming out within a social psychological framework. It also highlights how we can usefully understand both the experience of coming out and the development of lesbian identity within what remains a largely heterosexual society.

Towards a social psychological framework: resources for understanding coming out

Coming out needs to be examined not simply from the perspective of the individual and interpersonal relations but also from intergroup and cultural/societal viewpoints, i.e., the four levels of analysis proposed by Doise (1986). The framework suggested here to encompass coming out links social theories of self (Mead, 1934; Giddens, 1991) with theories of self disclosure (Derlega *et al.*, 1993) and coping with threat to identity (Breakwell, 1986), social identity theory (Tajfel, 1981) and social representations theory (Moscovici, 1984). An integral feminist perspective also emphasizes issues of gender.

Underlying this analysis of coming out is a thoroughly social understanding of self. The self is seen – as suggested by Mead (1934) – as originating and being maintained within social interaction. It is seen as historically situated and as reflecting the cultural context. Giddens (1991) discussed how self-identity is both shaped by and shapes institutions of modernity – the institutions and ways of behaving that have become established during the twentieth century – '"self" and "society" are interrelated in a global milieu' (p. 32).

Social identity theory allows consideration of coming out from the perspective of group membership. Tajfel (1981) defined social identity as 'that *part* of an individual's self-concept which derives from his [sic] knowledge of his membership of a social group (or groups) together with the value and emotional significance attached to that membership' (p. 255, emphasis in original). Comparisons made with other groups and salience of group membership are important, and the theory permits analysis of power relations.

The cultural/ideological level of analysis is vital to an understanding of coming out. The theory of social representations (Moscovici, 1984) provides a link to this level. Social representations are described by Moscovici and Hewstone (1983) as 'cognitive matrices co-ordinating ideas, words, images and perceptions that are all interlinked. They are common-sense "theories" about key aspects of society' (p. 115). Common-sense knowledge consisting of images, metaphors, etc., is shared. Social representations have two roles: they conventionalize persons or events, putting them into categories, and they are prescriptive. Their purpose is to make the unfamiliar, familiar. Their functions include allowing communication between individuals or groups and guiding social action and socialization of individuals (Moscovici and Hewstone, 1983; Moscovici, 1984). Thus, social representations lie 'beyond' stereotypes and attitudes; they 'restrain' attitudes and perceptions; stereotypes and attitudes can be seen as 'symptoms' of a social representation (Moscovici and Hewstone, 1983). Social representations of gender (Lloyd and Duveen, 1992) and of human nature (Moscovici and Hewstone, 1983) are especially relevant to coming out. These latter, Moscovici and Hewstone, (1983) suggested, consist of biological, psychological and religious elements, with, for example, views on 'normality'.

Within our culture, social representations both create and reflect particular understandings of gender and 'normality'. Our society continues to maintain gender boundaries and power differences between women and men. Bem (1993) pointed to three 'lenses of gender' – androcentrism, gender polarization and biological essentialism – forming hidden assumptions within culture, social institutions and individual psyches. These gender lenses contribute to defining what is 'normal' or 'natural'.

The perspective of coping with threat to identity provides a further useful way of examining coming out. Breakwell (1986, 1996) proposed a model (termed 'identity process theory') in which the identity processes of assimilation-accommodation and evaluation are guided by identity principles such as continuity, distinctiveness, self-esteem and self-efficacy, in maintaining identity structure. A threat to identity is defined by Breakwell (1986) as arising when the identity processes cannot comply with the identity principles. Thus, threat arises when one or more of the identity principles is challenged. Coping strategies described by Breakwell include those at intra-psychic, interpersonal and intergroup levels. In these terms, it is fair to say that women may experience threat to identity in coming out to self and others, with some or all of the identity principles being challenged by the demands of assimilating-accommodating a lesbian identity that carries a negative social evaluation.

If there are different types of lesbian identity as suggested in previous studies (for example, Ettorre, 1980; Golden, 1987; Kitzinger, 1987), coming out experiences and perceptions would vary: women defining themselves as lesbian for political reasons would experience coming out differently to others, for example. Indeed, women's multiple social identities (Frable, 1997) must influence coming out. Ethnic background is also pertinent (Chan, 1995, 1997; Alquijay, 1997; Dworkin, 1997; Fygetakis, 1997); lesbians with disabilities would have further issues to be considered (Appleby, 1994). Coming out also needs to be understood within social and historical context (see Chapter 9 in this volume).

The theoretical considerations described are to be used to inform an analysis of data derived from a study of coming out among lesbian women (Markowe, 1996). This mainly qualitative study was designed to explore issues of coming out as lesbian from both lesbian and heterosexual perspectives (my own perspective is lesbian). It was expected that coming out to self would be generally gradual and emotionally based. It was thought that decisions on coming out to others would be influenced by perceptions of risks and possible gains and perceptions of others' likely reactions. Reactions were expected to be influenced by personal understandings of what homosexuality means, societal attitudes and stereotyping.

Method

Forty lesbians (mean age 35.2 years; standard deviation 10.9; range 21–63 years) and thirty heterosexual women and men (15 males and 15 females: mean age 34 years; standard deviation 11.8; range 18–60 years) participated in the study. Lesbian participants were mainly from one London group. This group, open to any lesbians, met weekly in the upstairs room of a pub for social evenings, talks or discussions. Of the heterosexual participants, approximately half were students. Each took part in an individual semi-structured interview. For the lesbian sample, interviews focused on how women had come to identify themselves as lesbian and their experiences of coming out (or choosing not to come out) to family, heterosexual friends and work colleagues. Interviews with heterosexual participants looked at perceptions of attitudes towards lesbians and gay men and feelings about the hypothetical situation of a friend or family member coming out. The heterosexual interview schedule corresponded where possible to the lesbian interview schedule. Examples of questions are shown in Boxes 4.1 and 4.2.

Box 4.1: Sample questions from the interview schedule for lesbian participants

Can you remember when you first started feeling that you might be a lesbian?

Do you think there are any reasons why some women are lesbian and some women are heterosexual?

How have you dealt with 'coming out', or not 'coming out', to your family?

Have you 'come out' to your friends?

Box 4.2: Sample questions from the interview schedule for heterosexual participants

How do you think most heterosexual people feel about lesbians and gay men?

Do you think there are any reasons why some people are homosexual and some people are heterosexual?

How do you think you would feel if your sister told you that she were gay?

Content analysis of the interview material focused on recurrent themes (Krippendorf, 1980; Weber, 1985). In the quotations that are cited in subsequent sections, empty square brackets indicate where material has been omitted; material that has been added for clarification appears within square brackets; and words in upper case lettering convey emphasis. Pseudonyms are used to indicate the sources of the quotations.

The social context

The social context is revealed through attitudes towards homosexuality, perceptions and ideas about lesbianism and shared definitions and stereotypes: these can be seen as indicators of underlying social representations of human nature and gender/sexuality. Large scale surveys suggest that attitudes towards lesbians and gay men in Britain remain rather negative (Wellings *et al.*, 1994; Jowell *et al.*, 1996). Negative attitudes reported in this study were often linked with notions of threat and abnormality:

> I think in some ways [heterosexual people] don't understand [homosexuality]. It's something beyond their comprehension and in some ways they feel threatened by it because it's something they can't understand. (Lynn, heterosexual group)

In the interviews, lesbians were asked 'Do you remember what you thought lesbians might be like before you met others?' and heterosexual participants were asked 'How do you think most people might describe a typical lesbian?'. A stereotype of lesbians as masculine, abnormal, aggressive and unattractive was found; as Felicity (heterosexual group) said, 'lesbian women are seen as non-feminine women'. This contrasted with a stereotype of heterosexual women as normal, attractive and feminine. There was also some evidence of a feminine lesbian stereotype. Recently, the media has focused on new images of lesbians (so-called 'lesbian chic') – images in which lesbian identity disappears, sometimes through transformation into heterosexual identity (Cottingham, 1996). This raises issues to be addressed in future studies, including how lesbians perceive themselves and wish to be portrayed.

Lesbian and heterosexual participants defined lesbianism differently. For the heterosexual participants, lesbianism was simply sex between women. For the lesbian participants, lesbianism referred to more than sex: it was about love and emotion, so that it was seen as possible to be lesbian and celibate. For some, politics were important. Furthermore, while lesbians perceived others as androgynous, heterosexual participants perceived lesbians as masculine.

Lesbian 'invisibility' can be a problem and was indicated in a variety of ways. Lesbian participants often described having felt very alone in coming out to self and not knowing any other lesbians. This isolation was especially clear among those who had come to perceive themselves as lesbian during their teenage years. There was little evidence of contact with lesbians among most heterosexual participants. As Brian (heterosexual group) put it, 'I have no associations with lesbians that I know of'.

For many women, on initially coming out, media images of lesbians had been few, and those presented were sometimes hard to relate to. Heterosexual participants reported little experience of seeing lesbians on television or reading about them in newspapers or books. In recent years, there has been an increasing media presence, with lesbian characters appearing in UK soap operas and programmes. There is potential too for an increase in visibility from technological advances: the internet opens up possibilities that may ease coming out for some (McKenna and Bargh, 1998). Increased visibility is a positive step forward, although *how* lesbians are portrayed will need to be monitored.

Gossip and rumour form another aspect of the social context. In everyday conversation, with friends, at work, in school, for example, people may joke about homosexuality and may gossip and speculate about whether others are lesbian or gay. For a woman who perceives herself as lesbian but is not out to others, this can be difficult to deal with. This type of conversation can be seen as reinforcing heterosexual norms, defining boundaries, specifying who are the 'insiders' and who are the 'outsiders'. Indeed, a primary function may be to assert and maintain heterosexual identity. From the perspective of social identity theory, effects may include raising self-esteem for heterosexual group members, reinforcing group boundaries and excluding lesbians and gay men from the ingroup.

Often, there is ambiguity or uncertainty about whether someone is lesbian or gay. Heterosexual participants described learning that someone was lesbian or gay through someone else mentioning it or it having been 'obvious' from the way the person behaved or simply that they had assumed this was so. Direct self-disclosure by a lesbian or gay person was not the way that most came to know someone was lesbian or gay. In general conversation, discussions arose on homosexuality. Heterosexual participants recalled jokes, comments, derogatory slights and speculations about people being lesbian or gay. Many mentioned the topic arising in conversations at work.

Recalling schooldays, rumour was a recurring theme within both lesbian and heterosexual accounts:

> From the age of ten, I think, there was all this chitter-chatter in the playground [ ] Everyone picking up on words and terms and not knowing what they were talking about. (Dawn, lesbian group)

> I think there were always rumours [ ] all those things like gym teachers. (Linda, lesbian group)

There was the gossip and the rumours and the use of the word but never in a factual [sense] – it was used in that immature rather paranoiac sense [ ] It's very much a sort of dirty-joke type word all through that school period. (Susan, heterosexual group)

There are always rumours about teachers, aren't there? [ ] At seven we were actually discussing the fact that they were [lesbians] [ ] I don't think we realized completely what we were talking about. (Lynn, heterosexual group)

For those who identify themselves as lesbian, this background of rumour and gossip can be threatening. At the very least, it is probably embarrassing. Goffman (1956) described how embarrassment relates to social organization and has a social function. More seriously, this kind of situation may isolate, impede coming out, encompass bullying and, at the most damaging extreme, contribute to suicidal thoughts or attempts. There is evidence of the distress that teasing or being called 'names' can cause young children (Crozier and Dimmock, 1999) and of the impact of bullying on lesbian and gay teenagers (Rivers, 1995a, 1995b; see also Chapter 2). The context of rumour and gossip described here may have its origins in the school playground but clearly occurs within the adult world too. Even where such conversation is not direct-ed specifically towards an individual, it is nonetheless an uncomfortable and isolating experience for any who perceive them-selves as lesbian or gay.

Coming out to self and others

How do women come to identify themselves as lesbian and what impact does this have on their relationships with others? For most of this sample, coming out to self was experienced in relative isola-tion: it included only three women who came to identify as lesbian through involvement with feminism. While the experiences of some women may correspond to those suggested by stage theories of lesbian (and gay) identity (for example, Cass, 1979), many women's experiences do not. Considering coming out from differ-ent levels of analysis helps in understanding some of the complexities.

Relevant social representations reflect the cultural context. These relate to both gender and human nature and underlie the attitudes, stereotypes, etc. described. On the intergroup level, 'lesbians' may be viewed as a negatively valued group initially but, on defining self as lesbian and coming out to other lesbians, perceptions of the group are likely to become more positive. Individuals perceive themselves as belonging to a number of different groups (for example, gender, ethnic and occupational groups). Particular categorizations become salient under certain conditions (Oakes, 1987). In coming out to self, a woman needs to be aware of the existence of lesbians and perceive herself as possessing the characteristics associated with the category: stereotypical notions can impede this. In coming out to others, categorization as lesbian may obscure other identities and become a dominant identity status that overshadows all other identity possibilities in the eyes of others.

At an individual level, if we consider the self as originating in and being maintained through social interaction, the influence of the predominantly heterosexual world is highlighted. Obviously, the vast majority of women who identify as lesbian interact with numerous heterosexual others as family members, work colleagues, friends and acquaintances on a daily basis. They read newspapers, books and magazines, watch television and see films created by, and reflecting, this heterosexual society. If the social context of representations and that created within interpersonal interactions reflect negative images – or perhaps no images – of lesbian existence, this will be reflected in women's self-perceptions.

One aspect of identity is reflected in perceptions of whether lesbian identity is a choice. While some women in the study perceived themselves as having had a choice, others did not. Exemplifying the latter stance, Melanie (lesbian group) said 'No, I think that it's me and I didn't really choose – it just happened'. Some suggested there was no choice regarding feelings but there was a choice of behaviour. For over half, lesbian identity was perceived as, to some extent, *not* a choice. Such perceptions become interwoven with an emotional basis, notions of authenticity and the need to be understood within the social context, as will become clear.

Most importantly, coming out to self as lesbian is based on strong emotional feelings for women. As we noted earlier, lesbian women defined the word 'lesbian' in terms of love and emotion. They recalled falling in love with or having crushes on other girls or women as their first lesbian feelings, whether or not these were labelled as such at the time. Strong positive feelings towards other women (rather than negative feelings towards men) formed the basis for identifying as lesbian. This emotional basis is consistent with Wolff's (1973) notion of lesbians as 'homoemotional' rather than 'homosexual' and Faderman's (1981) historical perspective of lesbian identity based on romantic friendship. Emotion may be understood as social, i.e., based on a social notion of self, arising within social interaction, influenced by the cultural context (Averill, 1985; Parkinson, 1996), and linked to our understandings of gender (Fischer, 2000). In order for women to identify as lesbian, there needed to be awareness of lesbianism as an identity option and a level of emotional acceptance of homosexuality as well as emotional feelings for women. A social context of perceived invisibility, stereotyping and negative attitudes does not encourage either awareness or acceptance.

There were varied experiences in coming out to self. Some women recalled feelings from early childhood that they later interpreted as relating to lesbian identity. Many identified as lesbian in their teens or early twenties but a quarter were aged thirty or more. Many, whatever their age, recalled negative or conflicting feelings, fear and isolation, often associated with others' attitudes. As Melanie (lesbian group) put it, 'I wasn't particularly happy at that time. Lonely – I felt very, very lonely'. Feelings were said to have become more positive as the women accepted themselves as lesbian.

Coming out to self was often gradual, sometimes covering years. Meeting other lesbians for the first time often required taking positive steps like telephoning a helpline and going along to meetings or bars. Within the context of invisibility and negative attitudes, it is not surprising that this could be difficult: 'I was very frightened to go into the Gateways [lesbian club] and very frightened ringing the Switchboard' (June, lesbian group). However, actually meeting others for the first time was usually experienced very positively – not least, with the discovery that lesbians were 'just like any ordinary women'. As Melanie (lesbian group) remarked, 'I'm a lot happier now that I've actually got some gay friends'. This could provide a supportive background for coming out to heterosexual friends or family (although it is important to remember that lesbian – and gay – community contexts are not always characterized by an open, accepting attitude towards all those who seek support there).

There is a choice in deciding whether or not to talk to family, heterosexual friends, work colleagues or others about one's lesbian identity. There are both risks and potential benefits. Reasons given for not coming out were protecting others, lack of necessity to tell particular people, negative attitudes and feeling afraid. Where decisions were made to tell, it was often for support or not wanting to be assumed to be heterosexual or simply expecting that others would not mind. Underlying these decision-making concerns are societal notions of 'normality'. Heterosexuality is seen as 'natural' and 'normal' within society: if homosexuality were regarded similarly, disclosure as lesbian or gay would not require consideration. It was usual to tell others in a direct manner but sometimes women chose indirect approaches, including not hiding a relationship or even just assuming that people 'knew'. However, even with direct approaches, how others interpret information varies as it may be re-constructed and re-interpreted over time. For example, they may 'not believe it', think it is 'just a phase', think it is a 'one-off' or gradually 'come to terms with it'.

Lesbian participants were more likely to come out to their mothers than their fathers and to their sisters than their brothers. Of those who had been or still were married, some had come out to husbands; others had not. Participants who had children tended to be out to older/adult children but not to younger ones. Many women had told heterosexual friends about themselves but almost a quarter were out to few or none. Nearly a third had not come out at work. Reported reactions to coming out ranged from understanding, interest and support, through to shock, upset, disapproval, disbelief or more extreme responses and were often a mixture. The majority of lesbians and just over half the heterosexual participants described some kind of positive reaction. However, less than a quarter of heterosexual participants responded positively regarding the hypothetical situation of a teenage/adult daughter or son coming out to them. As Darren (heterosexual group) put it, 'I'd be upset, to put it mildly'. The majority of lesbian and heterosexual participants described negative reactions in a variety of situations, with lesbians more likely to mention extreme negative reactions and rejection. These reactions again need to be understood within the context of societal notions of gender and 'normality'.

There is no doubt that feeling unable to talk to others and feeling it necessary to hide such a fundamental aspect of oneself and one's life are very stressful. Self-disclosure is important for one's health and general relationships with others (Jourard, 1971; Derlega and Berg, 1987; Derlega *et al.*, 1993). While there may be occasions or situations where coming out to others is unnecessary or inappropriate and there are real risks of negative reactions, overall, coming out is often very beneficial, ultimately strengthening relationships and affirming lesbian identity. As Brenda (lesbian group) remarked, 'Overall I'm the happiest I have ever been'. The majority of lesbian participants perceived the main benefit of coming out in terms of 'being yourself', being true to yourself or authentic and being a whole person. Once again, it is important to view this from the perspective of the societal and cultural context – a context in which the self is understood in essentialist terms, in which heterosexuality is the norm and homosexuality discouraged.

In coming out to others, contrasts between lesbian and heterosexual perspectives are particularly pertinent. Dissimilarities in perceptions may contribute to misunderstandings, difficulties in communication and negative attitudes. Differing beliefs may influence what occurs when a lesbian tells a heterosexual person about herself, the reactions that are elicited and how relations develop thereafter.

Coming out and threat to identity

Within the current social context, it is not surprising that women experience threat to identity – in the sense described by Breakwell's (1986, 1996) identity process theory – on coming out. Threats varied in type and intensity and women had coped using various intra-personal, interpersonal and intergroup strategies.

Some women perceived themselves as 'always' having been lesbian. For these women considerable threat was indicated during the teenage years and the early twenties, not because coming out had disrupted continuity of identity (and thereby hindered the assimilation-accommodation of lesbian identity within their overall identity structure). Instead, the evaluative dimension of identity was the major concern – but in terms of social evaluation (i.e., other people's attitudes towards their lesbian identity) rather than self-evaluation. Intra-psychic strategies for coping with this tended to take the form of simply accepting lesbian identity. A need for authenticity or integrity was clearly evident as a driving force in these women's accounts of developing a lesbian identity (see below).

Accounts from women who described previous heterosexual experience but had perceived themselves as possibly lesbian at the time indicated some continuity of lesbian feelings over time, although approximately half the accounts reflected perceptions of initial repression or denial of lesbian feelings. Relationships with men were often viewed as unsatisfactory. There was also some evidence of threat to identity on coming out to self in some accounts. 'Being yourself' (which can be interpreted as another expression of the need for authenticity) was perceived as a main benefit of coming out.

For most of the lesbian women who had identified themselves as heterosexual in the past, some continuity of lesbian feelings was indicated. Lesbianism had often been viewed as negatively distinctive and about half these accounts reflected initial repression, suppression or denial. While some indicated considerable threat on becoming aware of self as lesbian, others showed greater threat from external sources (such as conflict with marriage) and little internal threat. Like the other groups, the majority described being oneself/not having to pretend as a main benefit of coming out.

As can be seen, Breakwell's (1986, 1996) identity process theory provided a useful structure for examining coming out, with the addition of two further identity principles that appeared particularly pertinent to this group, one relating to authenticity/integrity and the second, to affiliation (Markowe, 1996).

The need for authenticity/integrity

A need for authenticity or integrity was reflected in both coming out to self and others. In the latter case, there was a concern not to be assumed to be heterosexual, not to have to hide an important part of oneself and to be open to others about oneself. At both levels, the need for authenticity can be seen as fundamentally social, involving a social self and interaction with others.

This desire for authenticity or integrity permeated many of the lesbian women's accounts. It was especially evident within women's perceptions of why some women were lesbian and some women heterosexual and whether lesbianism was a choice, in terms of the emphasis on lesbian identity as 'a state of being', 'something in the person', 'the way you are'. It was also an issue when women described how they felt about their lesbian identity. Furthermore, it was a major consideration in deciding to tell family or friends and even a reason for women wishing to be out at work. Most strikingly, three quarters of the sample mentioned 'being yourself' as a main benefit of coming out.

In the following discussion, Lucy's account represents the perspective of a woman (25 years old) who perceived herself as 'always' having been lesbian; Gail (33 years old) represents a woman who had had heterosexual relationships but perceived herself as lesbian at that time; and Harriet (56 years old) provides an example of a lesbian who identified as heterosexual in the past. Both Lucy and Gail traced lesbian feelings back to an early age, as a basic aspect of identity:

> It's a cliché, you know, 'I always knew I was different' sort of thing, but I didn't know why – you don't really know when you are five [ ] I find it hard to understand people that suddenly realize that they're gay when they're about 40. I mean what – why do you not know? It's such a major part of you. How could you misunderstand yourself so much all those years – know yourself so little? [ ] I always was a potential lesbian [ ] when you're five [ ] nothing to do with sex – more the way you look at things and the way you respond to things even then. I always knew I wasn't going to get married. (Lucy)

> I went on – even though I was seeing men – being attracted to women. I'm sort of what they call a born lesbian. (Gail)

Gail is making a distinction here between lesbian identity and her behaviour which was not in accordance with the identity. For Harriet, however, there was no tracing back of lesbian feelings to childhood:

> I considered myself straight until I fell in love [with another woman].

Considering why some women are lesbian and some heterosexual, Lucy re-emphasizes her views of lesbianism as a core aspect of identity:

> Yes because they are basically [ ] I don't have a lot of patience with people dithering about whether they are/they aren't – I mean if you are, you KNOW [ ] like you know you're right or left handed – you are or you're not.

Perceptions of choice further illuminate notions of authenticity and integrity. For Lucy, there is no choice:

> I think it's in you and the choice is whether or not you acknowledge it and do something about it. I just don't see how you can choose.

Similarly, Gail argues:

> It is a choice now because I've actually sat down and made a choice. But then I think of a choice as related to my personality – if I choose to be this it must be because I feel the urge anyway [ ] [If] people weren't prejudiced against homosexuality and lesbians there would have been no question of a choice because I would have naturally fallen into that [ ] I still don't think that I've made a choice. I think it's something that I've come to because it's ME.

Gail has provided the explanation here for the incongruence between her heterosexual behaviour and lesbian identity. For Harriet, the perspective is a little different but very obviously involves issues of authenticity and demonstrates how these are bound up with emotional feelings:

> Yes, I would think it is a choice for people like me [ ] There is a choice – yes – because I could have actually ignored it and even now if I wanted to turn my back on the pain of being in love, I could ditch the whole lot and say I will not be emotionally involved with anybody again.

The theme of an authentic/integral self recurred throughout these and the majority of the other accounts, particularly for those who perceived themselves as 'always' lesbian but also for many lesbians with heterosexual backgrounds. Discussing the women's movement and considering women who say they could not have come out without it, Lucy remarked 'I don't understand it because the women's movement is external and your inner make up is inside you'. Gail, talking about her coming out experiences, commented 'The very core of one's being is there whereas before when I was just sort of a shell, [it was] a shallow sort of existence – trying to be what you really are not'. Gail's feelings about being lesbian further reflected this notion of self when she commented: 'I've always been positive [ ] It's always been there – it's me. I can't be negative about myself'. For Harriet too, feelings about being lesbian reflected integrity of self: 'I'm glad I am what I am. I'm glad I'm honest enough to realize it'. Finally, considering the main benefit of coming out, Lucy emphasized 'acknowledging to yourself what you are'; and for Gail, it was 'finding out "this is me"'. Only a few women did not perceive their lesbian identity in these terms.

How are we to understand this reported need for authenticity? For Giddens (1991), authenticity guides self-actualization and forms its moral basis. He suggested that a 'pure relationship' which is focused internally on satisfaction within the relationship rather than externally is dependent on trust. Trust in the relationship becomes linked with authenticity. Lack of external connections makes such relationships limiting. However, Giddens put forward the idea of life politics – a politics of self-actualization. Within this context, he suggested, self identity is

linked reflexively to local and global influences, and moral and existential questions are raised: the opportunity is provided for a 'remoralising'
of social life. Gergen (1991) has suggested that with 'social saturation'
and a multiplicity of relationships, there is fragmentation of self-concep-
tions and the concept of an 'authentic self' disappears. However, as
Smith (1994) has pointed out, Giddens' conceptualization of the self and
life politics provides a more positive contribution than the postmodern
relativism of Gergen. Particularly if we consider lesbian identity as feminist, Giddens' ideas form a useful framework.

Taylor (1991) argued for a deeper understanding of the notion of
authenticity as a moral ideal. He pointed out that, while authenticity
may be seen as involving creative aspects and discovery, originality
and sometimes opposition to societal rules, our understanding must
also recognize context – 'horizons of significance' (p. 66) – and the way
the self is defined in dialogue. Postmodern, deconstructionist perspectives – Taylor pointed out – neglect these latter requirements. Lesbian
identity can only be understood within its social context.

Ideas of an authentic self and sexuality as a core part of this identity must be understood as arising from our social representations and
cultural understanding of human nature. For lesbians, authenticity
and integrity link with the emotional base of identity. Together, these
form a strong foundation for lesbian identity – a firm basis on which to
construct and re-construct one's sense of self and relationships with
others. Understanding the self as originating from and being maintained within social interaction and understanding individual and
cultural levels linking within a context of social representations allow
us to perceive these aspects of lesbian identity as reflexively linked to
our society and culture.

The need for affiliation

Also clearly shown within the lesbian women's accounts was an
underlying need for attachment or affiliation. In coming out to self, this
need for friendship or family attachments could conflict with the need
for identification and distinctiveness as lesbian, with implications too
for self-esteem. In coming out to others, the need for attachment or
affiliation was evident in a number of ways. Underlying the move from
the isolation of perceiving oneself as lesbian but knowing no others to
taking the first positive steps towards meeting others was the basic
need for belonging and relationship in the broadest sense. In general,
decisions taken either to come out to another – or not to – may be seen
as underpinned by the need for attachment or affiliation.

Fear of losing family or friends stopped some women from coming
out. Kim thought college friends 'would probably be very shocked and
wouldn't talk to me any more'. Social interactions and relationships
became limited and impoverished. As Stella put it, 'I was beginning to

cut my family out of my life because there was so much I couldn't tell'. Jean felt she had 'never really formed any lasting friendships through work' because such friends might 'ask about my private life, you know "What do you do at weekends?"'. Melanie did not want to 'lie' to her family: 'They said "Get a boyfriend. When are you going to get a boyfriend?" [and I responded] "I have to go now", "Too busy"'. Stella, however, eventually talked to her family about herself: for her the main benefit of coming out was being 'back in my family'. Thus, women chose to tell others about themselves with the aim of maintaining or improving friendships and family or work relationships and they chose not to reveal their lesbian identity in order to avoid endangering or damaging these relationships.

Conclusions

The focus of this study has been on lesbians' perceptions and experiences of coming out. The theoretical framework linked a social understanding of self with group identity and social representations of gender and human nature. While this study focused on lesbians, some of the findings may be relevant to gay men's experiences of coming out. However, gender inequalities within our society mean that men's experiences may well differ from women's. Indeed it has been noted that the development of sexual identity is different for lesbians and gay men – and also varies across cultural groups too (de Monteflores and Schultz, 1978; Greene, 1997; Coyle, 1998). As this study was focused on one London-based group, care should be taken when applying its findings to lesbian women in other settings. Care is also needed in light of the retrospective nature of the data, as retrospective accounts may involve re-interpretation of the past through the lens of the present, thereby decreasing the likelihood that they constitute an accurate representation of the events and experiences which they describe (the same argument is made in analyses of similar retrospective data reported by Kitzinger and Wilkinson, 1995). However, there exists research evidence to suggest that retrospective reports and autobiographical memory are not necessarily and inevitably inaccurate and unstable (for example, Brewin *et al.*, 1993; Neisser, 1994; Blane, 1996). Despite this, longitudinal investigations – as well as studies of friendship of the kind suggested by Christine Griffin (2000; also see Chapter 3) – would be a valuable addition to the literature.

With these caveats in mind, the accounts offered by the women in this study provide some insights into their perceptions and experiences. Underlying coming out as lesbian were societal attitudes and understandings of sexuality and differing lesbian and heterosexual perspectives. The social context included 'invisibility' of lesbians, stereotyping, and a background of rumour and gossip. Coming out to self had a strong emotional basis. Fundamental to many women's experiences of coming out were notions of authenticity or integrity and the need for affiliation. Coming out to others involved risks and potential benefits and sometimes mixed feelings, ambiguity or uncertainty.

The issues presented here need to be understood as historically and culturally specific. They present a picture of coming out as lesbian for one group of women in Britain during the latter part of the twentieth century. How the situation may change during the twenty-first century is hard to predict. If attitudes were to become more positive, gender boundaries more flexible and conceptualizations of human nature more open to diversity, coming out as lesbian would become easier. While some of these trends can now be discerned within society, it is fair to say that there is still a long way to go.

Acknowledgement

I wish to thank Dr. Jan Stockdale for advice and support throughout this research. The chapter draws on work funded by ESRC award no. A00428624071.

References

ALQUIJAY, M.A. (1997) The relationships among self-esteem, acculturation, and lesbian identity formation in Latina lesbians. In B. Greene (Ed.) *Ethnic and Cultural Diversity Among Lesbians and Gay Men*. Thousand Oaks, CA: Sage.

APPLEBY, Y. (1994) Out in the margins. *Disability & Society, 9*, 19–32.

AVERILL, J.R. (1985) The social construction of emotion: With special reference to love. In K.J. Gergen and K.E. Davis (Eds) *The Social Construction of the Person*. New York: Springer-Verlag.

BEM, S.L. (1993) *The Lenses of Gender: Transforming the Debate on Sexual Inequality*. New Haven: Yale University Press.

BLANE, D.B. (1996) Collecting retrospective data: Development of a reliable method and a pilot study of its use. *Social Science & Medicine, 42*, 751–757.

BREAKWELL, G.M. (1986) *Coping with Threatened Identities*. London: Methuen.

BREAKWELL, G.M. (1996) Identity processes and social changes. In G.M. Breakwell and E. Lyons (Eds) *Changing European Identities: Social Psychological Analyses of Social Change*. Oxford: Butterworth Heinemann.

BREWIN, C.R., ANDREWS, B. and GOTLIB, I.H. (1993) Psychopathology and early experience: A reappraisal of retrospective reports. *Psychological Bulletin, 113*, 82–98.

CASS, V.C. (1979) Homosexual identity formation: A theoretical model. *Journal of Homosexuality, 4(3)*, 219–235.

CHAN, C.S. (1995) Issues of sexual identity in an ethnic minority: The case of Chinese American lesbians, gay men, and bisexual people. In A.R. D'Augelli and C.J. Patterson (Eds) *Lesbian, Gay, and Bisexual Identities Over the Lifespan: Psychological Perspectives*. New York: Oxford University Press.

CHAN, C.S. (1997) Don't ask, don't tell, don't know: The formation of a homosexual identity and sexual expression among Asian American lesbians. In B.

Greene (Ed.) *Ethnic and Cultural Diversity Among Lesbians and Gay Men*. Thousand Oaks, CA: Sage.

COTTINGHAM, L. (1996) *Lesbians Are So Chic...That We Are Not Really Lesbians At All*. London: Cassell.

COYLE, A. (1998) Developing lesbian and gay identity in adolescence. In J. Coleman and D. Roker (Eds) *Teenage Sexuality: Health, Risk and Education*. London: Harwood Academic.

CROZIER, W.R. and DIMMOCK, P.S. (1999) Name-calling and nicknames in a sample of primary school children. *British Journal of Educational Psychology, 69*, 505–516.

de MONTEFLORES, C. and SCHULTZ, S.J. (1978) Coming out: Similarities and differences for lesbians and gay men. *Journal of Social Issues, 34(3)*, 59–72.

DERLEGA, V.J. and BERG, J.H. (Eds) (1987) *Self-Disclosure: Theory, Research and Therapy*. New York: Plenum Press.

DERLEGA, V.J., METTS, S., PETRONIO, S. and MARGULIS, S.T. (1993) *Self-Disclosure*. Newbury Park, CA: Sage.

DOISE, W. (1986) *Levels of Explanation in Social Psychology*. Cambridge: Cambridge University Press.

DWORKIN, S.H. (1997) Female, lesbian, and Jewish: Complex and invisible. In B. Greene (Ed.) *Ethnic and Cultural Diversity Among Lesbians and Gay Men*. Thousand Oaks, CA: Sage.

ETTORRE, E.M. (1980) *Lesbians, Women and Society*. London: Routledge and Kegan Paul.

FADERMAN, L. (1981) *Surpassing the Love of Men*. London: Junction Books.

FISCHER, A.H. (Ed.) (2000) *Gender and Emotion: Social Psychological Perspectives*. Cambridge: Cambridge University Press.

FRABLE, D.E.S. (1997) Gender, racial, ethnic, sexual, and class identities. *Annual Review of Psychology, 48*, 139–62.

FYGETAKIS, L.M. (1997) Greek American lesbians: Identity odysseys of honorable good girls. In B. Greene (Ed.) *Ethnic and Cultural Diversity Among Lesbians and Gay Men*. Thousand Oaks, CA: Sage.

GERGEN, K.J. (1991) *The Saturated Self: Dilemmas of Identity in Contemporary Life*. New York: Basic Books.

GIDDENS, A. (1991) *Modernity and Self-Identity: Self and Society in the Late Modern Age*. Cambridge: Polity Press.

GOFFMAN, E. (1956) Embarrassment and social organization. *American Journal of Sociology, 62*, 264–271.

GOLDEN, C. (1987) Diversity and variability in women's sexual identities. In Boston Lesbian Psychologies Collective (Ed.) *Lesbian Psychologies: Explorations and Challenges*. Chicago, IL: University of Illinois Press.

GREENE, B. (Ed.) (1997) *Ethnic and Cultural Diversity Among Lesbians and Gay Men*. Thousand Oaks, CA: Sage.

GRIFFIN, C. (2000) Absences that matter: Constructions of sexuality in studies of young women's friendships. *Feminism & Psychology, 10*, 227–245.

JOURARD, S.M. (1971) *The Transparent Self*. New York: Van Nostrand Reinhold.

JOWELL, R., CURTICE, J., PARK, A., BROOK, L. and THOMSON, K. (Eds) (1996) *British Social Attitudes: The 13th Report*. Aldershot: Dartmouth.

KITZINGER, C. (1987) *The Social Construction of Lesbianism*. London: Sage.

KITZINGER, C. and WILKINSON, S. (1995) Transitions from heterosexuality to lesbianism: The discursive production of lesbian identities. *Developmental Psychology, 31*, 95–104.

KRIPPENDORF, K. (1980) *Content Analysis: An Introduction to its Methodology.* Beverly Hills, CA: Sage.

LLOYD, B. and DUVEEN, G. (1992) *Gender Identities and Education: The Impact of Starting School.* London: Harvester Wheatsheaf.

MARKOWE, L.A. (1996) *Redefining the Self: Coming Out as Lesbian.* Cambridge: Polity Press.

McKENNA, K.Y.A. and BARGH, J.A. (1998) Coming out in the age of the internet: Identity 'demarginalization' through virtual group participation. *Journal of Personality and Social Psychology, 75,* 681–694.

MEAD, G.H. (1934) *Mind, Self and Society: From the Standpoint of a Social Behaviorist.* Chicago, IL: University of Chicago Press.

MOSCOVICI, S. (1984) The phenomenon of social representations. In R.M. Farr and S. Moscovici (Eds) *Social Representations.* Cambridge: Cambridge University Press.

MOSCOVICI, S. and HEWSTONE, M. (1983) Social representations and social explanations: From the 'naïve' to the 'amateur' scientist. In M. Hewstone (Ed.) *Attribution Theory: Social and Functional Extensions.* Oxford: Basil Blackwell.

NEISSER, U. (1994) Self narratives: True and false. In U. Neisser and R. Fivush (Eds) *The Remembering Self: Construction and Accuracy in the Self-Narrative.* New York: Cambridge University Press.

OAKES, P.J. (1987) The salience of social categories. In J.C. Turner, M.A. Hogg, P.J. Oakes, S.D. Reicher and M. Wetherell *Rediscovering the Social Group: A Self-Categorization Theory.* Oxford: Basil Blackwell.

PARKINSON, B. (1996) Emotions are social. *British Journal of Psychology, 87,* 663–683.

RIVERS, I. (1995a) The victimization of gay teenagers in schools: Homophobia in education. *Pastoral Care in Education, 13,* 35–41.

RIVERS, I. (1995b) Mental health issues among young lesbians and gay men bullied in school. *Health and Social Care in the Community, 3,* 380–383.

SMITH, M.B. (1994) Selfhood at risk: Postmodern perils and the perils of postmodernism. *American Psychologist, 49,* 405–411.

TAJFEL, H. (1981) *Human Groups and Social Categories.* Cambridge: Cambridge University Press.

TAYLOR, C. (1991) *The Ethics of Authenticity.* Cambridge, MA: Harvard University Press.

WEBER, R.P. (1985) *Basic Content Analysis.* Beverly Hills, CA: Sage.

WELLINGS, K., FIELD, J., JOHNSON, A.M. and WADSWORTH, J. (1994) *Sexual Behaviour in Britain: The National Survey of Sexual Attitudes and Lifestyles.* London: Penguin.

WOLFF, C. (1973) *Love Between Women.* London: Duckworth.

Chapter 5

Lesbian and Gay Parenting

Fiona Tasker

One of the first British studies to be published on the well-being of children in lesbian mother families was the landmark paper by Golombok *et al.* (1983) entitled 'Children in lesbian and single parent households: Psychosexual and psychiatric appraisal'. Since then, research interest in lesbian and gay parenting has blossomed across the social sciences in Britain, Europe and the USA.

As yet, no British surveys have attempted to ascertain either the number of children who have lesbian or gay parents or how many lesbians and gay men are involved in parenting. Large scale surveys of lesbian and gay communities in the USA find that approximately one in five lesbians identify as mothers and about one in ten gay men identify as fathers (Bryant and Demian, 1994). However, it seems likely that many more lesbians and gay men are involved in parenting in some capacity. While impressive efforts have been made to survey widely within lesbian and gay communities, the proportion of lesbian, gay and bisexual people who respond to these surveys cannot be estimated with any accuracy and surveys may not pick up the wide variety of parenting involvement that lesbians and gay men have reported in smaller scale studies that have used semi-structured interviews to explore family connections and responsibilities. When lesbians and gay men define their 'families of choice' – as opposed to household membership or blood relatives – wider networks of care-giving responsibilities become apparent (Weeks *et al.*, 1996). When considering a broader definition of parenting, it seems that many lesbians and gay men may have made regular commitments to caring for children who do not live with them and who are not biologically related to them.

There is a variety of different parenting arrangements in families led by a lesbian, gay or bisexual parent or parents and probably a greater variety of family constellations than in families led by a heterosexual parent or heterosexual couple. One of the main sources of diversity is the origin of the parenting relationship with the child. Many lesbian, gay and bisexual parents are involved in parenting children from previous or current heterosexual relationships. Family relationships for both parents and children in these families involve the challenge of finding ways to acknowledge the sometimes complex web of both opposite-gender and same-gender past and present relationships.

In recent years the number of children with lesbian and gay parents has increased, with more lesbians and gay men having children in the context of a lesbian or gay lifestyle (i.e., in planned lesbian mother or gay father families). There is a growing group of lesbian mothers in Britain who have had children through donor insemination at a clinic or through self-insemination using donor sperm. Some gay fathers have become parents through surrogacy arrangements, although voluntary surrogacy arrangements can be extremely difficult to organize and paid surrogacy arrangements are not legal in Britain. Many more gay men have become involved in co-parenting arrangements with lesbian mothers: some of them have been sperm donors for lesbians achieving motherhood through self-insemination but others have no biological connection with the child whom they parent. Lesbians and gay men also may become parents through adoption or fostering.

Research on lesbian and gay parenting has considered children in a variety of different families. Most importantly, psychologists have accumulated an impressive array of empirical evidence stating that children are not influenced by their parent's sexual orientation on the key developmental outcomes assessed. While the link between research and policy change is never translucent, nevertheless research – particularly on children's well-being in lesbian-led families – has been cited both in Britain and abroad in relation to campaigns for legal recognition of lesbian and gay parenting (Barlow et al., 1999). In particular, the position of lesbian mothers with children from a previous marital relationship has changed. Back in the 1970s, if a lesbian mother decided to end her marriage, she was unlikely to be able to continue to live with her child if the child's father contested custody and made the mother's lesbian identity known to the court. In some cases, even visiting arrangements between the lesbian mother and her children were burdened with conditions, for example, preventing the children from meeting the mother's partner (Rights of Women Lesbian Custody Group, 1986). Nowadays lesbian mothers have been more successful in winning legal cases and many have been awarded care and control of their children (Harne and Rights of Women Lesbian Custody Group, 1997).

Children raised by lesbian or gay parents after parental divorce or separation

The first studies of lesbian and gay parenting began to be published in the early 1980s. These papers focused on evaluating the psychological well-being of school-aged children of lesbian mothers (Hoeffer, 1981;

Kirkpatrick *et al.*, 1981; Golombok *et al.*, 1983; Green *et al.*, 1986). These mothers had initially brought up their children within a heterosexual relationship but later identified as lesbian, separated from the child's father and managed to retain custody of their child (in spite of the hostility often encountered in the legal systems at that time). Little is known about the likely distress felt by both children and their lesbian or gay parent if a previously close relationship is lost after parental separation.

One of the reasons for conducting research in the area was empirically to evaluate the basis on which lesbian mothers were commonly refused custody. Until then, it was commonly assumed that the children would have difficulties in four developmental areas: family relationships, psychological adjustment, psychosexual development and peer relationships. In particular, it was argued that the daughters and sons of lesbian mothers would themselves become lesbian and gay, with the generally unchallenged problematic assumption that this would be a negative outcome.

Assumptions that parents of each gender play a crucial role in children's psychosocial development echo the ideas expressed within major theories of children's development. Consequently, studying the development of children raised by lesbian and gay parents also provides an empirical test of some of the theoretical questions at the heart of developmental psychology.

Two main theoretical schools argue that the child's home environment plays an important role in children's psychosexual development. Exponents of these theories also often assume that adequate psychological adjustment depends partly upon the resolution of psychosexual development so that gender identification and gender role behaviour congruent with both biological sex and heterosexual development are seen as markers of good psychological health. Psychoanalytic theories suggest that the balance of influence between the mother and father is important for the heterosexual resolution of the Oedipal conflict and gender identification with the same gender parent and is crucial to psychological health (Fine, 1987), although some psychoanalysts have contested these claims (Isay, 1989; O'Connor and Ryan, 1993). According to social learning theories, modelling the behaviours of others and reinforcement by others are the two processes through which psychological development occurs. The model of behaviour provided by a parent of the same gender has been seen as particularly important in both psychological adjustment and psychosexual development. Nevertheless, other adults and peers may also serve as role models and reinforcers of behaviour. Later versions of social learning theory are less mechanistic, suggesting that the child evaluates information in relation to cultural stereotypes rather than simply 'copying' observed behaviour that is rewarded (Bandura, 1986, 1989).

Other major theories of gender and sexual identity development, however, would not regard the immediate home environment as an important influence on children's development. Cognitive developmental theories of gender development regard children as active constructors of information gleaned from the gendered world around them from which they adopt behaviours and characteristics they perceive as consistent with their own gender (Kohlberg, 1966; Stagnor and Ruble, 1987). Others have argued that social construction is the key to understanding identity and that gender and sexual identity are cultural creations (Kitzinger, 1995). Finally, some theories suggest that psychosexual development is largely governed by biological processes and that social factors make a minimal contribution (Bailey, 1995).

As we noted at the start of this chapter, the first published British study of children of lesbian mothers was undertaken by Susan Golombok and colleagues at the Institute of Psychiatry (Golombok *et al.*, 1983). In common with the North American studies on children in lesbian mother families published in the 1980s, the British study recruited a relatively small volunteer sample of lesbian mothers who had their school-aged children from a previous heterosexual relationship living at home with them. The study compared 37 children living in lesbian mother families – where some of the mothers were living with their new female partner – with a comparable group of children brought up by single heterosexual mothers. The mean age of the children at the time of data collection was 9.5 years (range – 4 to 18 years). Both groups of children therefore were growing up in female-headed households, enabling the research to distinguish the particular influence of growing up in a lesbian-led family aside from any possible influences arising from father absence. Furthermore, both groups of children had experienced their mother and father's separation, thus controlling for any general effects of parental divorce. A semi-structured interview with a standardized coding scheme was used to gather data from the mothers. Children were briefly interviewed to ascertain information on gender role behaviour. In each family, the mother completed the Rutter A Scale (a frequently-used checklist of behavioural and emotional indicators found to be predictive of clinical diagnosis) to provide a standardized assessment of the child's psychological adjustment. An independent assessment of any emotional or behavioural difficulties that the child might have was also provided by the child's class teacher who completed the parallel Rutter B Scale (Rutter *et al.*, 1975).

Findings from the study revealed no statistically significant differences between the children in the lesbian and heterosexual mother families on any of the interview or questionnaire measures of psychological adjustment. Furthermore, the rates of difficulties for children in the lesbian mother group were within the normal range reported for children in heterosexual two parent families on the Rutter A and B Scales. Both lesbian mothers and single heterosexual mothers reported generally good parenting relationships with their children. However, children from lesbian mother families were more likely than children from single heterosexual mother families to have regular contact with their non-resident father.

None of the children in the lesbian mother group or single heterosexual mother group were confused about their gender identity. Furthermore, no differences in gender role behaviour were found between the children in the two types of family. Sons and daughters from either family background tended to show quite traditional gender-typed preferences for toys, activities and friendships. The children with lesbian mothers also seemed to have similar peer relationships to the children in the heterosexual single mother families, with only a small number of children in either group experiencing difficulties.

The findings from this British study were similar to those reported by other researchers in the field (Hoeffer, 1981; Kirkpatrick *et al.*, 1981; Green *et al.*, 1986). On the basis of these studies, a number of review papers were published which concluded that children with lesbian mothers were not developmentally disadvantaged by growing up in a lesbian-led household (Knight, 1983; Kirkpatrick, 1987; Falk, 1989; Gibbs, 1989; Patterson, 1992, 1995; Golombok and Tasker, 1994; Parks, 1998; Tasker, 1999). Nevertheless, the early work on developmental outcomes for children in lesbian mother families still left questions on longer-term developmental outcomes unanswered. Only a minority of the children in any of the research samples had entered adolescence, so a systematic assessment of long-term sexual development was not possible in the majority of cases. Furthermore, while younger children might be relatively protected against peer stigma, teasing or bullying about family background (or indeed the young person's own emerging sexuality) might become more of a problem during adolescence. Finally, in the early studies of lesbian mother families, the children themselves had not been asked about their perceptions of growing up in a lesbian-led family. Other than the limited information from clinical cases (for example, Lewis, 1980; Jarvaid, 1983), little was known of what the sons and daughters of lesbian mothers thought about their families.

In order to examine some of these remaining questions, a follow-up study was conducted in 1991–1992 with the children who had taken part in the original study conducted by Susan Golombok and colleagues (Tasker and Golombok, 1997). A major strength of the British Longitudinal Study of Lesbian Mother Families is the use of prospective data gathered from interviews with mothers prior to long-term outcomes being known. The young adults interviewed did not select themselves into the sampling frame for the study but were invited to participate because of their earlier inclusion as children. However, as in most longitudinal studies, there was some attrition of the original sample as only 62 per cent of the children were interviewed at follow-up. Data from the previous interviews with mothers in the first phase of the study were used to compare the young people who participated at follow-up and those who did not. There were no differences in the quality of the mother's relationship with her child, the child's peer relationships, the child's gender role or psychological adjustment. However, in the lesbian-led family group, children were less likely to participate at follow-up if their mothers originally reported that their child did not know about her lesbian relationship or reported more conflict in her relationship with her lesbian partner. These findings suggest that children who participated at follow-up might have experienced better family relationships during childhood compared with non-participants but that, in other respects, the sample composition remained unaffected.

A total of 25 young adults from lesbian mother families (8 men and 17 women) and 21 young adults from heterosexual mother families (12 men and 9 women) were interviewed in the follow-up study (mean age at follow up – 23.5 years). These young people were interviewed using a semi-structured interview schedule with a standardized coding scheme that covered long-term developmental outcomes in the four key areas outlined previously: family relationships, mental health, peer relationships and psychosexual development. This methodology provided quantitative data for comparisons between children from the two types of family and qualitative data to illuminate their experiences, particularly of children in the lesbian mother group. The interviews lasted on average two and a half hours and this enabled full exploration of any initially superficial or apparently contradictory answers.

During the course of the interview, all the young people in both types of families were asked about their health and contacts with health care professionals. Young adults from the lesbian mother group were no more likely than young people from the heterosexual mother group to have received help for mental health problems; likewise they did not report higher levels of anxiety or depression on the standard questionnaires (the State-Trait Anxiety Inventory and the Beck Depression Inventory) that each young person completed during the follow-up interview (Spielberger, 1983; Beck and Steer, 1987).

In the follow-up interviews, the young people from lesbian mother families and heterosexual mother families generally reported good relationships with their mother and their non-resident father. However, since the lesbian and single heterosexual mothers were interviewed in the first phase of the study, family relationships had changed in many cases. In particular 85 per cent of the single heterosexual mothers had cohabited with a new male partner or remarried, while 88 per cent of the lesbian mothers had lived with a female partner. Therefore, most of the sons and daughters in both types of family had experienced growing up in a stepfamily. Findings in this area are particularly interesting because the wider literature on stepfamilies concentrates on heterosexual stepfamilies without consideration of how parental sexual identity may influence new partnerships.

When interviewed about their relationship with their step-parent, those from lesbian mother families reported more positive relationships with their mother's female partner compared with the young people from heterosexual mother families. From the descriptions of family life given during interviews, the young people from lesbian mother families described a greater flexibility in the way that the lesbian partner joined the family compared with the pattern seen in the heterosexual stepfamilies. In many cases, lesbian partners were accepted into the family as an additional family member, often with a role constructed by the young person as a second mother, a big sister or a very close family friend. In contrast, stepfathers in the heterosexual family group were more likely to be regarded by the young person with some hostility as a competitor to their absent father, especially if they tried to move beyond being the mother's partner and attempted to take an active role in parenting.

Data from the interviews with the sons and daughters also suggested that a new lesbian partner was less likely than a new heterosexual partner to have a clearly articulated role in the child's life when initially moving into the family home. This lack of definition sometimes presented difficulties for the children of lesbian mothers when describing their relationship with their mother's female partner to those outside the family. However, it often meant that the relationship between the child and the mother's partner could evolve in the ways that family members wanted and at a pace that allowed for any resulting transitions to be accepted. Thus the lack of prescriptive roles in lesbian-led families may help to accommodate additional family members. These findings contrast with findings from studies examining heterosexual stepfamilies where it is often concluded that stepfathers – and in particular stepmothers – have difficulty finding a step-parent role (Smith, 1990; Gorell Barnes *et al.*, 1997).

The young people interviewed in the British Longitudinal Study of Lesbian Mother Families also were asked how they felt about their mother's identity currently and how they remembered feeling during their secondary school years. The two groups of young people did not differ in whether they recollected positive or negative feelings during adolescence about their mother's identity. As young adults, however, those who had been brought up by lesbian mothers were significantly more likely to be proud of their mother's sexual identity compared with young adults raised by heterosexual mothers.

Children may be victimized for all sorts of reasons but the follow-up study showed that young people from lesbian mother families were no more likely than those from heterosexual backgrounds to report general bullying or vicious teasing during their time at school. In addition, all the young people in the study were asked whether they had been teased about their mother or about their family background. Again, young people with lesbian mothers were no more likely to experience this than were young people in the comparison group. However, there was a non-significant trend indicating that young people with lesbian mothers were more likely than those with heterosexual mothers to remember having been teased about their own sexuality. These recollections were particularly discernible in the interviews with young men from lesbian-led families. This may reflect the fact that children from lesbian families are indeed more likely to be teased about being lesbian or gay themselves or it may be that they are more aware of homophobic bullying at school and so remember examples of this because it resonates with their family background.

Most lesbian mothers were alert to the possibility of homophobia and helped their children to avoid experiencing prejudice by helping the young person to decide when it was safe to be 'out' about having a lesbian mother. Over half of the young people from lesbian-led families were able to inform at least one close friend about their family relationships who did not react negatively. In other cases, friends were not aware of the young person's lesbian family background but this did not inhibit the young person's social life, for example, by preventing the young person bringing friends home.

The last part of the follow-up study interview took a detailed psychosexual history from each of the young people interviewed. No differences were found between the proportions of young adults from lesbian and heterosexual family backgrounds who reported having felt attraction towards someone of the same gender. However, those who had grown up in a lesbian family were more likely to consider the possibility of having lesbian or gay relationships and five young women and one young man from the lesbian mother family group who had experienced same gender attractions also reported a same gender relationship. These relationships varied from an evening spent holding hands and kissing to setting up a home together. However, all of the children in lesbian-led families had also experienced heterosexual relationships and the vast majority of young adults brought up by a lesbian mother identified as heterosexual (only two young women identified as lesbian and none of the young men identified as gay or bisexual).

Neither the closeness of the mother-daughter relationship nor the closeness of the mother-son relationship was associated with the young adult's expressed interest in same-gender sexual relationships. Young people from lesbian-led families who were most likely to show an interest in same-gender relationships were those whose mothers had earlier reported in the first round of interviews that they were more open at home about having lesbian relationships or that they had no preference about their child's future sexual orientation (Golombok and Tasker, 1996). In the follow-up study interviews, many of these young people from lesbian-led families felt that they could make more informed choices about heterosexual as well as lesbian or gay relationships because of greater openness and acceptance in their family (Tasker and Golombok, 1997). This seemed to be particularly the case among the young women from lesbian family backgrounds.

Results from the British Longitudinal Study of Lesbian Mother Families and from North American studies that have surveyed lesbian and gay parents on the sexual orientation of their sons and daughters suggest that the vast majority of children of lesbian and gay parents grow up to be heterosexual young adults (Bailey and Dawood, 1998). Results from the British study do not lend support to either psychoanalytic theories or social learning theories suggesting that lesbian parenting may have a direct influence on the child's later sexual orientation. However they do suggest that parental attitudes are important in broadening the child's consideration of sexual identity possibilities.

Children raised in lesbian-led families

Since the 1990s, studies have been published on children raised in planned lesbian-led families, where a single lesbian mother or a lesbian couple had a child through anonymous donor insemination at a fertility clinic, self-insemination with donor sperm or, in a few cases, heterosexual intercourse. Most of these studies have evaluated the well-being of primary school-aged children of lesbian mothers using controlled comparisons with children from heterosexual mother families. Studies in Britain (Golombok *et al.*, 1997), the Netherlands (Brewaeys *et al.*, 1997) and the United States (Chan *et al.*, 1998) all found that the children with lesbian mothers generally had good psychological adjustment and were no more likely than children with heterosexual mothers to show either psychological difficulties at home or signs of emotional or behavioural problems at school. One study of children aged around seven years old conceived by donor insemination to single or two-parent, lesbian or heterosexual families found that neither family structure nor parental sexual orientation influenced children's psychological adjustment (Chan *et al.*, 1998). However, in all types of families, increased levels of parenting stress, parental conflict and relationship dissatisfaction were associated with increased behavioural problems among the children concerned. These findings suggest that the quality of family relationships is more important than family structure in terms of the child's psychological well-being.

The British study by Golombok and colleagues also considered the family relationships of children in single and two-parent lesbian mother families, families headed by a single never-married heterosexual mother and families headed by a heterosexual couple. This research design enabled two main types of comparisons to be made. First, it was possible to look at the mother-child relationships in families led by a single lesbian mother or lesbian couple in relation to parent-child relationships in two-parent heterosexual families or in single heterosexual mother families (Golombok *et al.*, 1997). Second, it enabled comparison of the role of non-biological mothers in lesbian-led families in relation to the role of fathers in two-parent heterosexual families where the child had been conceived through donor insemination through a fertility clinic (Tasker and Golombok, 1998). Semi-structured interviews were administered to birth mothers in all family types to collect data on family relationships. Non-biological mothers in lesbian-led families were also interviewed about family relationships.

The main findings from the British study of children in planned lesbian-led families were that children in both lesbian and single heterosexual mother households benefited from closer relationships with their birth mother compared with children in two parent heterosexual families, as assessed through interviews with mothers in each type of family. Furthermore, children from both lesbian-led and single heterosexual mother families scored higher on an attachment-related assessment than children whose father lived with them, suggesting that the children had more secure attachment relationships with their mothers (Golombok *et al.*, 1997).

Comparisons between children in two-parent lesbian-led families and children who were conceived via donor insemination to heterosexual couples or conceived by heterosexual couples without the aid of fertility treatment were used to assess the involvement of the non-biological parent in the child's life. The interview data indicated that non-biological mothers in lesbian-led families played a more active role in daily care-giving than did most fathers in heterosexual families, although this difference was often less pronounced in heterosexual families where the child had been conceived by donor insemination. Other results from both the birth mothers' interview data and the children's own reports of the closeness of co-mother or father-child relationships on the Family Relations Test (Bene and Anthony, 1985) showed that family relationships were equally warm and affectionate across all three types of family (Tasker and Golombok, 1998). Other British research has found that many non-biological mothers in two-parent lesbian-led families were very involved in care-giving and that lesbian couples tended to want to share parenting equally and find a more equitable balance to the work-home equation than most heterosexual couples with children (Dunne, 1998).

Gay men as parents

Until recently, the main topic of interest in this area – both in Britain and internationally – has been lesbian parenting. Just as heterosexual motherhood has been the major focus in developmental research on parenting, so lesbian motherhood has been 'scrutinized' more than gay fatherhood. Can gay men be effective parents? Currently, research is limited to the reports of gay men who had children from previous relationships who have volunteered for surveys. The largest group of men surveyed in the recent British Gay and Bisexual Parenting Survey were biological parents, most of whom were parenting children from previous heterosexual relationships (Barrett and Tasker, 2001). The men surveyed reported that older children were more likely than younger children to be aware of their gay or bisexual parent's identity. Respondents also suggested that daughters rather than sons were more likely to respond with greater understanding to their parent 'coming out' about his sexual identity. However, as yet the sons and daughters of gay fathers have not been interviewed so conclusions may only be drawn from the reports of gay parents.

Other research evidence suggests that gay men's parenting is in most respects similar to the parenting of heterosexual fathers in similar circumstances. One North American study found that gay and heterosexual non-resident fathers parenting children after divorce reported similar relationships with their children, except that gay fathers tended to be less indulgent and more authoritative in their parenting (Bigner and Jacobsen, 1989). However, gay fathers often have to deal with a double dose of marginalization. On the one hand, their parental responsibilities often leave gay fathers feeling excluded by other gay men. On the other hand, they may feel stigmatized because of their sexual identity in mainstream, i.e., heterosexual, society. Prejudice directed at gay men's parenting often arises from the confusion of paedophilia and homosexuality – a misconception that is not supported by legal or research evidence (Schofield, 1965; Strasser, 1997). One North American survey found that many gay fathers were worried that their child could be stigmatized at school because of having a gay father; however, only a fifth of fathers reported that any of their children had actually experienced any problems (Wyers, 1987). It seems likely that gay fathers and their children are mostly successful in using a variety of strategies to deal with or avoid the possibility of encountering homophobia.

Findings from two studies appear to suggest that for post-divorce gay parenting, a key factor is the presence and quality of the new gay partnership. In the Gay and Bisexual Parenting Survey, parents with male partners – particularly men who lived with their lover – rated themselves as being more successful at managing a variety of common parenting challenges compared with single gay male parents (Barrett and Tasker, 2001). Findings from a North American study of gay male stepfamilies indicate that for the divorced gay father, his adolescent son or daughter and his male partner, the factor most associated with family satisfaction was the degree to which the new gay partner had become integrated into family life (Crosbie-Burnett and Helmbrecht, 1993).

As yet, little research exists on planned gay father families. However, the most recent British survey of gay men's parenting suggests that there is a growing number of gay men who have become involved in parenting as openly gay men or who are planning to become parents (Dunne, 1999). Case histories and review articles detailing the experiences of lesbians and gay men who apply to adopt or foster children have highlighted the particular hurdles placed in the path of gay men who make applications to local authorities or agencies (Hicks and McDermott, 1999; James, 2000; McCann and Tasker, 2000). Other routes to parenthood for gay men through surrogacy or co-parenting arrangements may also be difficult to finance or negotiate (Martin, 1993). Nevertheless, successful case histories have been reported and the field awaits systematic investigation.

Lesbian and gay parenting pioneers at the vanguard of parenting research

Why is it important to research lesbian and gay parenting arrangements and developmental outcomes for children raised by lesbian mothers or gay fathers? The recognition that lesbian mothers gained during the 1970s and 1980s is still to be achieved by gay fathers. Gay fathers who have children from previous heterosexual relationships still find that their access to their children is curtailed if the child's mother contests the case (Powell, 1997). Research has yet to examine systematically the developmental outcomes for children of gay fathers.

While lesbian mothers have been more successful in keeping care and control of their children after separating from the child's father, lesbian parents and their children still face discrimination and homophobia. The most recent generation of lesbian mothers in Britain who have had children through donor insemination at a clinic or through self-insemination with donor sperm are still establishing parenting rights. There are a number of advantages to self-insemination, including being able to have a known donor who may or may not have contact with the child (Saffron, 1994). However, donor insemination via a clinic offers access to rigorous screening of sperm samples for known health conditions and exemption from legislation governing the actions of the Child Support Agency (a government agency which – at the time of writing – endeavours to trace 'absent' fathers and compel them to contribute financially towards their children's maintenance). Trying to access donor insemination services from a clinic often involves difficult negotiations and many clinics do not offer services to lesbians or unmarried heterosexual women. In Britain, after the Warnock Report on the regulation of new reproductive technology, it was left to the discretion of individual clinics whether they were willing to provide donor insemination for lesbians or single heterosexual women (Committee of Inquiry into Human Fertilisation and Embryology, 1984). However, the Human Fertilisation and Embryology Act of 1990 states that clinics should assess the future welfare of any child resulting from treatment, including the need of that child for a father and this has meant that many lesbians are reluctant to apply to clinics.

The non-biological mother in a lesbian couple and the non-biological father in a gay relationship also have limited parenting rights in law. There is no legal recognition of the non-biological parent unless the couple apply for a residence order under the 1989 Children Act. This means that the non-biological parent cannot take legal or medical decisions on the part of the child. For this reason alone, many non-biological parents feel marginalized or unrecognized in their parental role. Findings on the role of non-biological parents in families led by a lesbian or gay couple begin to suggest that successful parenting skills are not governed by biology but further research in this area would help to establish this.

Lesbians and gay men are also seeking to become parents by fostering or adopting children (James, 2000; McCann and Tasker, 2000). In the UK, the law does not prohibit lesbians or gay men from fostering or adopting but legally only one parent in a lesbian or gay couple can be recognized as the carer. Existing research on children with lesbian or gay parents may not apply to the unique situations of adopted or fostered children.

Research interest within psychology has mainly concentrated on developmental outcomes for children but less is known about the *experience* of lesbian and gay parenting. Research that focused on lesbian and gay parents would help to establish how sexual identity interacts with parenting and begin to unpack the concepts of 'motherhood' and 'fatherhood' that have so far only been addressed in relation to heterosexual parents.

Most of the published studies have relied on data from a relatively small number of families who selected themselves into the sampling frame. Only a couple of studies – one in the United States (Chan *et al.*, 1998) and one in the Netherlands (Brewaeys *et al.*, 1998) – have used clinic records to contact a sample; however, even clinic records may be selective. Research studies need to explore ways of increasing the representativeness of their samples. In particular, there is a need for research to examine the cultural diversity of different lesbian and gay parenting contexts. The major research projects on lesbian parenting in Britain, the Netherlands and the United States have all sampled mainly white, middle class parents. Only one published research study begins to examine how culture, racism and sexual identity influence the lives of African American lesbian mothers (Hill, 1987). Both cultural variation in the way that families organize parenting and differing cultural beliefs about non-heterosexual relationships are likely to be major influences on whether and when lesbian and gay parenting is stigmatized.

As more lesbians and gay men come out as parents, research on lesbian and gay parenting is also booming. Research in Britain and elsewhere has been influential in showing that children from lesbian-led families are not developmentally disadvantaged. Yet there is still a long way to go, especially in addressing public misconceptions and discrimination. The foundations have been laid but new research is needed to fortify our limited knowledge of the circumstances and processes that make lesbian and gay parenting similar to, or different from, the heterosexual parenting circumstances upon which many of the research conclusions in developmental psychology rest.

References

BAILEY, J.M. (1995) Biological perspectives on sexual orientation. In A.R. D'Augelli and C.J. Patterson (Eds) *Lesbian, Gay, and Bisexual Identities Over the Lifespan: Psychological Perspectives*. New York: Oxford University Press.

BAILEY, J.M and DAWOOD, K. (1998) Behavioral genetics, sexual orientation, and the family. In C.J. Patterson and A.R. D'Augelli (Eds) *Lesbian, Gay, and Bisexual Identities in Families: Psychological Perspectives*. New York: Oxford University Press.

BARLOW, A., BOWLEY, M., BUTLER, G., COX, L., DAVIES, M., GRYK, W., HAMILTON, A., SMITH, P. and WATSON, M. (1999) *Advising Gay and Lesbian Clients: A Guide for Lawyers*. London: Butterworths.

BANDURA, A. (1986) *Social Foundations of Adult Thought and Action: A Social Cognitive Theory*. Englewood Cliffs, NJ: Prentice-Hall.

BANDURA, A. (1989) Social cognitive theory. *Annals of Child Development, 6,* 1–60.

BARRETT, H. and TASKER, F. (2001) Growing up with a gay parent: Views of 101 gay fathers on their sons' and daughters' experiences. *Educational and Child Psychology, 18,* 62–77.

BECK, A.T. and STEER, R.A. (1987) *Manual for the Beck Depression Inventory*. San Antonio, TX: The Psychological Corporation.

BENE, E. and ANTHONY, J. (1985) *Manual for the Family Relations Test*. Windsor: NFER-Nelson.

BIGNER, J.J. and JACOBSEN, R.B. (1989) Parenting behaviors of homosexual and heterosexual fathers. In F.W. Bozett (Ed.) *Homosexuality and the Family*. New York: Harrington Park Press.

BREWAEYS, A., PONJAERT, I., VAN HALL, E.V. and GOLOMBOK, S. (1997) Donor insemination: Child development and family functioning in lesbian mother families with 4–8 year old children. *Human Reproduction, 12,* 1349–1359.

BRYANT, A.S. and DEMIAN (1994) Relationship characteristics of American gay and lesbian couples: Findings from a national survey. *Journal of Gay and Lesbian Social Services, 1,* 101–117.

CHAN, R.W., RABOY, B. and PATTERSON, C.J. (1998) Psychosocial adjustment among children conceived via donor insemination by lesbian and heterosexual mothers. *Child Development, 69,* 443–457.

COMMITTEE OF INQUIRY INTO HUMAN FERTILISATION AND EMBRYOLOGY (1984) *Report of the Committee of Inquiry into Human Fertilisation and Embryology (Cmnd 9314).* London: HMSO.

CROSBIE-BURNETT, M. and HELMBRECHT, L. (1993) A descriptive empirical study of gay male stepfamilies. *Family Relations, 42,* 256–262.

DUNNE, G.A. (1998) Introduction: Add sexuality and stir: Towards a broad understanding of the gender dynamics of work and family life. *Journal of Lesbian Studies, 2,* 1–8.

DUNNE, G.A. (1999) The different dimensions of gay fatherhood: Report to the Economic and Social Research Council. Retrieved June 29th 2000 from the world wide web: http://www.lse.ac.uk/Depts/GENDER/esrcgay.htm#esrcgay

FALK, P.J. (1989) Lesbian mothers: Psychosocial assumptions in family law. *American Psychologist, 44,* 941–947.

FINE, R. (1987) Psychoanalytic theory. In L. Diamant (Ed.) *Male and Female Homosexuality: Psychological Approaches.* London: Hemisphere.

GIBBS, E.D. (1989) Psychosocial development of children raised by lesbian mothers: A review of research. *Women & Therapy, 8,* 65–75.

GOLOMBOK, S., SPENCER, A. and RUTTER, M. (1983) Children in lesbian and single parent households: Psychosexual and psychiatric appraisal. *Journal of Child Psychology & Psychiatry, 24,* 551–572.

GOLOMBOK, S. and TASKER, F. (1994) Children in lesbian and gay families: Theories and evidence. *Annual Review of Sex Research, 5,* 73–100.

GOLOMBOK, S. and TASKER, F. (1996) Do parents influence the sexual orientation of their children? Findings from a longitudinal study of lesbian families. *Developmental Psychology, 32,* 3–11.

GOLOMBOK, S. TASKER, F. and MURRAY, C. (1997). Children raised in fatherless families from infancy: Family relationships and the socioemotional development of children of lesbian and single heterosexual mothers. *Journal of Child Psychology & Psychiatry, 38,* 783–791.

GORELL BARNES, G., THOMPSON, P., DANIEL, G. and BURCHARDT, N. (1997) *Growing Up in Stepfamilies.* Oxford: Clarendon.

GREEN, R., MANDEL, J.B., HOTVEDT, M.E., GRAY, J. and SMITH, L. (1986) Lesbian mothers and their children: A comparison with solo parent heterosexual mothers and their children. *Archives of Sexual Behavior, 15,* 167–184.

HARNE, L. and RIGHTS OF WOMEN LESBIAN CUSTODY GROUP (1997) *Valued Families: The Lesbian Mothers' Legal Handbook,* 2nd ed. London: The Women's Press.

HICKS, S. and McDERMOTT, J. (1999) Editorial essay. In S. Hicks and J. McDermott (Eds) *Lesbian and Gay Fostering and Adoption: Extraordinary Yet Ordinary.* London: Jessica Kingsley.

HILL, M. (1987) Child-rearing attitudes of black lesbian mothers. In Boston Lesbian Psychologies Collective (Ed.) *Lesbian Psychologies: Explorations and Challenges.* Chicago, IL: University of Illinois Press.

HOEFFER, B. (1981) Children's acquisition of sex-role behavior in lesbian-mother families. *American Journal of Orthopsychiatry, 5,* 536–544.

ISAY, R.A. (1989) *Being Homosexual: Gay Men and their Development.* London: Penguin.

JAMES, S.E. (2000) Lesbian and gay adoptions: An introduction to emerging clinical and ethical issues. *Lesbian & Gay Psychology Review, 1*, 4–10.

JARVAID, G.A. (1983) The sexual development of the adolescent daughter of a homosexual mother. *Journal of the American Academy of Child Psychiatry, 22*, 196–201.

KIRKPATRICK, M. (1987) Clinical implications of the lesbian mother studies. *Journal of Homosexuality, 14 (1/2)*, 201–211.

KIRKPATRICK, M., SMITH, C. and ROY, R. (1981) Lesbian mothers and their children: A comparative survey. *American Journal of Orthopsychiatry, 51*, 545–551.

KITZINGER, C. (1995) Social constructionism: Implications for lesbian and gay psychology. In A.R. D'Augelli and C.J. Patterson (Eds) *Lesbian, Gay, and Bisexual Identities Over the Lifespan: Psychological Perspectives*. New York: Oxford University Press.

KNIGHT, R.G. (1983) Female homosexuality and the custody of children. *New Zealand Journal of Psychology, 12*, 23–27.

KOHLBERG, L. (1966) A cognitive-developmental analysis of children's sex-role concepts and attitudes. In E.E. Maccoby (Ed.) *The Development of Sex Differences*. Stanford, CA: Stanford University Press.

LEWIS, K.G. (1980) Children of lesbians: Their point of view. *Social Work, 25*, 198–203.

MARTIN, A. (1993) *The Guide to Lesbian and Gay Parenting*. London: Pandora.

McCANN, D. and TASKER, F. (2000) Lesbian and gay parents as foster carers and adoptive parents. In A. Treacher and I. Katz (Eds) *The Dynamics of Adoption: Social and Personal Perspectives*. London: Jessica Kingsley.

O'CONNOR, N. and RYAN, J. (1993) *Wild Desires and Mistaken Identities: Lesbianism and Psychoanalysis*. London: Virago.

PARKS, C.A. (1998) Lesbian parenthood: A review of the literature. *American Journal of Orthopsychiatry, 68*, 376–389.

PATTERSON, C.J. (1992) Children of lesbian and gay parents. *Child Development, 63*, 1025–1042.

PATTERSON, C.J. (1995) Lesbian mothers, gay fathers, and their children. In A.R. D'Augelli & C.J. Patterson (Eds) *Lesbian, Gay, and Bisexual Identities Over the Lifespan: Psychological Perspectives*. New York: Oxford University Press.

POWELL, V. (1997) Fighting fathers' corner. *Gay Times, No. 225*, 12–14.

RIGHTS OF WOMEN LESBIAN CUSTODY GROUP (1986) *Lesbian Mothers' Legal Handbook*. London: Women's Press.

RUTTER, M., COX, A., TUPLING, C., BERGER, M. and YULE, W. (1975) Attainment and adjustment in two geographical areas: The prevalence of psychiatric disorder. *British Journal of Psychiatry, 126*, 493–541.

SAFFRON, L. (1994) *Challenging Conceptions: Planning a Family by Self-Insemination*. London: Cassell.

SCHOFIELD, M. (1965) *Sociological Aspects of Homosexuality*. London: Longmans.

SMITH, D. (1990) *Stepmothering*. London: Harvester Wheatsheaf.

SPIELBERGER, C.D. (1983) *Manual for the State-Trait Anxiety Inventory*. Palo Alto, CA: Consulting Psychologists Press.

STAGNOR, C. and RUBLE, D.N. (1987) Development of gender role knowledge and constancy. In L.S. Liben and M. L. Signorella (Eds) *New Directions for Child Development: No. 38. Children's Gender Schemata*. San Francisco, CA: Jossey-Bass.

STRASSER, M. (1997) Fit to be tied: On custody, discretion, and sexual orientation. *American University Law Review 46*, 841–895.

TASKER, F. (1999) Children in lesbian-led families: A review. *Clinicial Child Psychology and Psychiatry, 4*, 153–166.

TASKER, F. and GOLOMBOK, S. (1997) *Growing Up in a Lesbian Family: Effects on Child Development*. New York: The Guilford Press.

TASKER, F. and GOLOMBOK, S. (1998) The role of co-mothers in planned lesbian-led families. *Journal of Lesbian Studies, 2*, 49–68.

WEEKS, J., DONOVAN, C. and HEAPHY, B. (1996) *Families of Choice: Patterns of Non-Heterosexual Relationships*. London: South Bank University School of Education, Politics and Social Science Research Report No. 2.

WYERS, N. L. (1987) Homosexuality in the family: Lesbian and gay spouses. *Social Work 32*, 143–148.

Chapter 6

Resistance and Normalization in the Construction of Lesbian and Gay Families: A Discursive Analysis

Victoria Clarke

Lesbian and gay parenting appears to be among the most controversial of lesbian and gay rights issues. While many people are willing to support the extension of basic civil rights to individual lesbians and gay men, lesbians and gay men raising children is simply, in some views, taking lesbian and gay rights 'too far'. Arguments used to oppose lesbian and gay parenting are familiar and well-rehearsed: lesbian and gay parenting is abnormal, unnatural and against God's will; the 'gay lifestyle' is incompatible with raising children; children need a mother *and* a father – not two mothers or two fathers – to develop into 'normal' (i.e., heterosexual) individuals; and children in lesbian and gay households suffer the stigma of 'difference' (Clarke, 1999). These arguments draw on common sense notions of the 'natural' family and taken-for-granted wisdom about the formation of gender and sexuality. However, numerous studies have repeatedly claimed that they have 'no basis in reality' (DiLapi, 1989) and rely on stereotyped notions of lesbian and gay existence (Raymond, 1992; Alldred, 1998). In this chapter, I focus on 'positive' representations of lesbian and gay parenting in the public sphere. I explore how these representations often attend to and attempt to address arguments commonly used to undermine lesbian and gay parenting, such as those identified above.

As Kath Weston (1991) notes, the emergence of lesbian and gay families represents a major historical shift, 'particularly when viewed against the prevalent assumption that claiming a lesbian or gay identity must mean leaving blood relatives behind and foregoing any possibility of establishing a family of one's own' (p. 196). Discussions about family within the lesbian and gay community have often focused on whether laying claim to kinship will move the lesbian and gay rights movement in a politically conservative or radical direction: whether lesbian and gay families are 'inherently assimilationist or inherently progressive' (Weston, 1991, p. 198). I will not try to adjudicate on this issue in this chapter. Rather, I am interested in the social construction of lesbian and gay parenting – how we, as a community, as individual lesbians and gay men and as supporters of lesbian and gay rights, represent and portray lesbian and gay families. To this end, I employ a feminist social constructionist perspective (Kitzinger, 1987, 1995) to examine the construction of lesbian and gay parenting in a variety of different data including talk shows, documentaries and newspaper articles, as well as focus groups and interviews with lesbian and gay parents, university students and others[1]. The media data constitute a serendipitous sample on the topic of lesbian and gay parenting. The interviews and focus groups were conducted by the author and involved questions about the meaning of family in contemporary life and attitudes towards (for non-lesbian and gay parent groups) and experiences of (for lesbian and gay parent groups) lesbian and gay parenting. The data were transcribed orthographically (including all false starts and hesitations) and emphasize readability.

The most prevalent construction of lesbian and gay parenting (perhaps especially within 'gay friendly' contexts) draws on a discourse of sameness, highlighting the similarities between lesbian and gay and heterosexual families. This construction (often) 'normalizes' lesbian and gay families – denying or downplaying 'gayness' or difference and emphasizing the ways in which lesbian and gay parenting is 'no different' from the heterosexual norm. Repeated readings of the data revealed a number of normalizing strategies commonly used to represent lesbian and gay families in the 'public' domain, especially in contexts where there was opposition to lesbian and gay parenting. I have organized these strategies into themes and will demonstrate and critically discuss four key ones here. These four strategies (or resources) construct lesbian and gay parenting as 'just like' heterosexual parenting through (i) emphasizing love and security; (ii) explicit parallelism; (iii) emphasizing ordinariness; and (iv) highlighting the methods whereby children of lesbian and gay parents can be compensated for the supposed deficits of their family structure.

I will demonstrate that these strategies are often produced as direct counters to negative depictions of lesbian and gay parenting. On talk shows, for example, lesbian and gay parents are called upon to defend themselves and their parenting against the arguments of the 'opposition'. However, these strategies are also produced in 'lesbian and gay friendly' contexts (such as in an interview with a lesbian researcher), thereby demonstrating lesbians' and gay men's almost constant orientation to the anti-lesbian and anti-gay agenda.

I discuss each of these four strategies in turn and then examine why it is that lesbians, gay men and our supporters so often use these normalizing strategies to defend our parenting. I evaluate the costs and benefits of these strategies and their political implications for lesbian and gay rights and identify some radical alternatives to portraying lesbian and gay families in this way. First, however, I will briefly discuss the methodology employed in the study reported in this chapter.

Social constructionism and discourse analysis

There is a growing interest in constructionist and discursive approaches within lesbian and gay psychology, usually discussed in opposition to essentialist or positivist approaches (see Kitzinger, 1995). Many feminists have also found these approaches compelling (Gavey, 1989; Kitzinger and Wilkinson, 1995a). Lesbian and gay and feminist psychologists have used social constructionism and discourse analysis to study a range of topics including sexual harassment (Kitzinger and Thomas, 1995), the 'attitudes' of the police towards lesbians and gay men (Praat and Tuffin, 1996) and the relationship between masculinity and homophobia (Gough, 1998; see also Chapter 12 in this volume).

Broadly speaking, constructionism is an overarching framework for a range of approaches that prioritize the study of language and meaning in historically and culturally specific contexts. From a constructionist perspective, language (or discourse) is held to play a central role in the constitution of social life. The particular method I employ in this chapter is discourse analysis (Kitzinger and Wilkinson, 1995b; McCreanor, 1996; Coyle, 2000). Discourse analysis takes discourse (talk and text) as its topic rather than using it as a basis for inferring the content of people's internal psychological make-up, such as their beliefs or attitudes. The concern is with how people use talk to perform specific actions and construct versions of the social world. There are several different 'styles' of discourse analysis; in this chapter, I use an approach which locates discursive patterns within their wider political context and focuses on their broader ideological consequences, as well as their functions at the level of localized discursive context (Wetherell and Potter, 1988; see Edwards and Potter, 1992, for an alternative approach).

Strategies of normalization

(i) Emphasizing love and security

The first strategy through which lesbian and gay parenting is normalized is by 'emphasizing love and security'. This discourse emphasizes the importance of love, security and stability over any particular family structure:

Extract 1[2]

> The nuclear family as we know it is evolving. The emphasis should not be on a father and a mother, but on loving, nurturing parents, whether that be a single mother or a gay couple in a committed relationship.
> (Barry Drewitt, gay parent, quoted in 'The Times', Thursday 28th October 1999)

Extract 2

> The important thing...this business about the ideal of the family, the important thing...is that, the ideal, well, the ideal is love, care, support. If you've got love, care, and support, whether, you know, for whatever reason, you're brought up by just the mum, and the dad's disappeared off the face of the earth, who knows. If you've got the love, the care, and the support...that's what really matters.
> (Rev Mervyn Roberts, 'Living Issues', January 1998)

Extract 3

> I think at the end of the day it doesn't really matter what anyone else thinks, and it's – at the end of the day like, if those, if those two...men or women love the child and that's what's important.
> (Kelly, heterosexual, student focus group, October 1998)

This is perhaps the most common (and one of the most powerful) ways in which lesbian and gay parenting is defended and portrayed both in the wider world and within the lesbian and gay community. It is often used to counter the claims that lesbian and gay parenting is deviant, against God's will and generally bad for children. This talk constructs 'love' as the essence of family life: note the use of phrases that signal the over-riding importance of what is being said, such as 'the important thing' and 'what really matters' (extract 2) and 'at the end of the day...that's what's important' (extract 3). According to this representation of family life, families can assume any shape or form as long as they are loving and stable environments. Other similar qualities emphasized here include 'care' (extract 2), 'support' (extract 2), 'commitment' (extract 1) and 'nurture' (extract 1) – all qualities which can be easily depicted as unrelated to sexuality or gender and ones which most people recognize as the building blocks of the family. Such talk is rhetorically robust in an argumentative context: it is difficult to suggest, without appearing callous or cruel or rigidly adherent to bigoted values, that such qualities are not at the centre of family life.[3] Talk about love is often related to the changing nature of the family: in extract 1, for example, Barry Drewitt, a gay father, suggests that the traditional nuclear family is outdated and, as a society, we now recognize the pivotal importance of love. Comparisons are often drawn between un-loving heterosexual families and loving lesbian and gay families, with the latter heralded as a better environment for a child. For example, on the American talk show *Leeza* in 1998, the host asked an opponent of lesbian and gay parenting 'Isn't it better to have two loving parents who get along, than heterosexual parents that don't get along?'. According to Diane Raymond (1992), 'to argue that we must tolerate...gay parents because we have no better options' and 'to suggest that some arrangements could be much worse' is to 'damn gays and lesbians with faint praise, if it is to praise at all' (p. 127). 'Emphasizing love and security' normalizes lesbian and gay families by highlighting the universal values that all families share. It holds that lesbian and gay families are not fundamentally different from heterosexual families because, 'at the end of the day', all families are about love.

(ii) Explicit parallelism

In talk about lesbian and gay parenting, comparisons are often made between lesbian and gay and heterosexual family structures. The strategy of 'explicit parallelism' emphasizes the *similarities* between lesbian and gay and heterosexual families. Consider the following examples:

Extract 4
> Vanessa: ...Do you think you'll be providing your children with everything a child could want in life?
> Dawn: Yeah, 'cos there's loads of single mums out there, those children grow up without father figures, so what's the difference?
> (Dawn Whiting, lesbian parent, interviewed by host Vanessa Feltz on 'The Big Breakfast', August 1997)

Extract 5
> How many single mothers out there raise their own children? What difference because I'm gay?
> (Tamara, lesbian, 'Ricki Lake', April 1998)

Extract 6
> Kate and I have been together for six years, and Dominic's ten, so in – in effect we're as, er, the same as a sort of step-family in a heterosexual sense... [Kate] does virtually 50 per cent of the slog of – of being a parent.
> (Karen, lesbian parent, 'You Decide', August 1997)

In highlighting the qualities that lesbian and gay families and heterosexual families (such as single parent families and step-families) often share in common, this strategy downplays the significance of parental sexuality and is often used to defend lesbians' and gay men's parental rights (see extract 5) and to answer potential criticism of lesbian and gay families (see extract 4). As these examples of 'explicit parallelism' (especially extracts 4 and 5) illustrate, this strategy is often used to address concerns about the lack of appropriate role models in lesbian and gay families. For example, in extract 4, when responding to Vanessa's question about providing a child with everything they could want in life, Dawn addresses the implied criticism about lesbian and gay parents, one that she understands to be about an absence of suitable role models. Dawn emphasizes the large number of single mothers raising children in society and highlights a key similarity between them and her family – the lack of a 'father figure'. Extract 5 is almost identical in this respect: both Dawn and Tamara challenge opponents of lesbian and gay parenting to identify differences between their families and single parent families. Although often maligned in other contexts (Radford, 1991), single parents (and step-parents) are constructed as 'adequate' parents and as favourable points of comparison for lesbian and gay families in this context. This strategy is sometimes also used to emphasize that lesbian and gay families are 'families' and to make them recognizable as such to a wider audience, particularly in a context where lesbian and gay relationships are described in law (at the time of writing) as 'pretended family relationships' (see Section 28 of the 1988 Local Government Act: Reinhold, 1994). For example, in extract 6, Kate argues that, by virtue of the length of time she and her lover have been partners and the effort her lover, Kate, puts into raising her son, together they are the 'same' as a heterosexual step-family. The strategy of 'explicit parallelism' suggests that lesbian and gay families are no different to heterosexual families. In doing so, it shifts the focus of attention away from parental sexuality and onto the safer – albeit still precarious – ground of gender and 'role models' (i.e., children in lesbian and gay families are often thought to be short of 'correct' role models because they only have a parent/parents of one sex – see strategy iv below).

(iii) Emphasizing ordinariness

The third normalizing strategy commonly found in discourse about lesbian and gay parenting is 'emphasizing ordinariness'. This strategy highlights the similarities between the everyday lives of lesbian and gay families and heterosexual families:

Extract 7
> He does the dishes, I do dishes...we do everything like everybody else does. We're just the family next door.
> (Don Harrelson, gay father, 'Oprah', 1990)

Extract 8
> Erm, can I just say, this gentleman just said that we're not a family, erm,

we get up at seven o'clock every morning, make packed lunches, make breakfast...we go through the same things that every other family goes through, as boring, as exciting, anything you like, as any other family. We are a family.

(Kate, lesbian parent, 'You Decide', 1997)

Extract 9

We watch Sesame Street every morning. We eat pancakes together on the weekends. We go for walks in the woods, swim in the summertime, read books, visit our friends, just like heterosexual families.

(Bonnie Zellers, lesbian parent, quoted in 'Love Makes a Family' by Kaeser and Gillespie, 1999, p. 36)

This strategy focuses on the mundane aspects of family life such as doing the dishes (extract 7), making breakfast (extract 8), and reading books (extract 9). It suggests that lesbian and gay families are essentially normal because they share with heterosexual families the ubiquitous qualities associated with the day-to-day reality of family life. It makes lesbian and gay families comprehensible to a potentially hostile audience and normalizes them, constructing them as no different to heterosexual families. This strategy is often used to accord lesbian and gay families status as family (see extract 8) and to address concerns about the (much maligned) gay lifestyle. As I indicated earlier, opponents of lesbian and gay parenting often point to the incompatibility of this lifestyle with raising children. The 'ordinariness' strategy provides a powerful contrast to the stereotype of lesbian and gay life as exotic and different and organized around an insatiable sexual appetite. This strategy propounds that lesbian and gay parents help their children with their homework, do the dishes, go shopping, make packed lunches, argue about their children's bed time – all recognizable components of normal family life. Documenting a large number of everyday tasks demonstrates their generality and is used to convince a sceptical audience that lesbian and gay families do everything that everybody else does. In fact, discourse and conversation analysts have demonstrated that lists (particularly three-part lists, as evident in extract 8: 'as boring, as exciting, anything you like') can be used to indicate the commonality, and thus normality, of something (Potter, 1996).

(iv) Highlighting compensations for 'deficits': role models

The final normalizing strategy I demonstrate is 'highlighting compensations for "deficits"'.[4] Lesbian and gay parenting is often undermined through reference to the supposed deficits of lesbian and gay families. One of the deficits that children brought up in lesbian and gay households are often thought to suffer is a lack of appropriate role models.

For example, in extract 10, taken from an early morning show, *The Big Breakfast*, one of the hosts, Vanessa Feltz, articulates what 'lots of people at home will be thinking'. The 'highlighting compensations' strategy is used to address such criticism:

Extract 10

Vanessa: Lots of people will be thinking watching this, you know, a baby needs a mother and a father, a male role model, and a female role model, a couple of lesbians are not gonna give this little girl the right start in life, would you agree with them or not?

Dawn: No not really, because there are loads of male roles in her life, there's my father, there's Lisa's father, there's my brother, erm, there's my uncles, you know, loads of our – of our friends are male, and they're always around her.

(Dawn Whiting, lesbian parent, interviewed by host Vanessa Feltz on 'The Big Breakfast', August 1997)

Extract 11

The thing is Molly has men in her life, we've always gone out of our way to involve men, like her grandfather, her uncles, friends...And because we're not living on planet lesbian, that means Molly meets boys and men and she sees men in cars and men on the street and the postman delivers the post and there's boy children at the child minders and her – her life is just as full of men as any other child's is, except that there doesn't happen to be one living at home with her. She has two parents living at home with her and they are both women.

(Brenda, lesbian parent, 'Modern Times – Pink Parents', November 1998)

Extract 12

[Mrs Bellamy] said there would be no question the children would lack female influences in their lives just because their parents were both men. 'Children all through their lives need certain role models and I know they are going to have the right kind of role models. They have lots of aunts in their families, lots of grandmothers and they are also going to know who I am and who the egg donor is, so they are definitely going to be having roles models as women.'

(Rosalind Bellamy, surrogate mother for a gay couple, quoted in 'The Independent', September 1999)

This strategy addresses fears about the (normal) development of children's gender and sexuality. Both lesbian and gay parents are the subject of these fears. When challenged to explain how they will manage the lack of appropriate role models in their children's lives, lesbian and gay parents and their supporters often proceed to list the many 'right kind of role models' (extract 12) children will have – be they male (see extracts 10 and 11) or female (extract 12) role models. One particular response to arguments about supposed deficits involves highlighting the inevitable presence of men (or women) in the world and, in doing so, orienting to implicit fears that children in lesbian families live on 'planet lesbian' (extract 11) (or children in gay families live on 'planet gay'). In extract 11, for example, Brenda, a participant in a documentary about lesbian and gay parenting, addresses the concern that her daughter will only interact with lesbians and as such will have an 'unbalanced' existence. The idea of living on 'planet lesbian' is extreme and ironic and parodies the idea that children in lesbian families only encounter lesbians. Brenda emphasizes both the effort she and her partner make to include men in their daughter's life ('we've always gone out of our way') and the existence of men in the wider world, using very mundane examples to do so such as the postman and boy children at the child-minders. This strategy is hard to undermine without denying the presence of men in the world. Brenda also comments on the incidental nature of Molly's gendered family life – that there doesn't 'happen' to be a man living at home suggests that Molly's family 'just is' rather than being a calculated attempt on her mothers' part to exclude men from her life. These lesbian and gay parents and supporters of lesbian and gay parenting accept that a lack of role models is a deficit and they illustrate how children will be compensated. They rarely, if ever, challenge the assumption underlying questions such as the question Vanessa asks Dawn in extract 10 – that children need two opposite-sex parents to develop 'normally'. Instead, they emphasize how children 'won't miss out' and, as such, how lesbian and gay families are just the same as heterosexual families.

Evaluating normalizing as a political strategy

I have demonstrated four strategies used to normalize lesbian and gay parenting. In emphasizing ordinariness and love and security through explicit parallelism and highlighting compensations, lesbians and gay men and their supporters portray lesbian and gay parenting as no different from heterosexual parenting. This construction of lesbian and gay parenting is in widespread use. The psychological literature on lesbian and gay parenting, for example, engages in normalizing practices by constructing lesbian and gay families as just like heterosexual families through a process of normative comparison. Much of this research compares lesbian and gay families to a heterosexual 'control' group (see Chapter 5). For instance, numerous studies have compared lesbian mothers with single heterosexual mothers (Golombok *et al.*, 1983; Huggins, 1989; Chan *et al.*, 1998). Explicit parallelism is evident in the conclusions drawn from this research. For example, Harris and Turner (1985) suggest that 'gay parents are little different from heterosexual parents except in their sexual orientation' (p. 104). Similarly McLeod and Crawford (1998) argue that 'gay parents and their children do not differ significantly from the norm' (p. 211). The strategy of 'empha-sizing love and security' maps onto psychological arguments about children's well-being and how it relates to parental sexuality. For example, Chan *et al.* (1998) suggest that 'children's well-being is more a function of parenting and relationship processes within the family (i.e., family interactions and processes) than it is a function of house-hold composition or demographic factors (i.e., family structure)' (p. 454). In a similar vein, Basile (1974, p. 18, quoted in Allen and Burrell, 1996, pp. 30–31) argues that 'the best interests of the child lay with a loving parent, not with a heterosexual parent or a homosexual parent'.

These arguments have been used successfully by psychologists to support lesbians and gay men in custody hearings, in their demands for fostering and adoption rights and in legal battles concerning the rights of lesbian and gay co-parents (Harne and Rights of Women Les-bian Custody Group, 1997). The use of similar arguments in both academic and 'lay' contexts demonstrates the reciprocal relationship between psychology and common sense. As Pam Alldred (1996) observes, 'each informs the other and the two cannot be completely disentangled from each other' (p. 152). Convergences of psychological knowledge and lay wisdom can be seen in the types of questions that psychological research asks and in the answers it generates to these questions (Alldred, 1996).

Theoretically, it is possible to portray lesbian and gay families as fundamentally different from or the same as heterosexual families (Clarke, 2000). From a social constructionist perspective, neither rep-resentation is any less 'true' than the other. However, each has different political ramifications. In presenting lesbian and gay fami-lies as just like heterosexual families, it could be argued that we transform hegemonic understandings of family life and relation-ships. Indeed, I am not using the concept of 'normalizing' in a pejorative sense but I think of it as a strategy of representation which has the potential to be both politically conservative and politically transformative in its uses and ramifications. As I discuss below, from a lesbian feminist perspective, constructing lesbian and gay parent-ing as just like heterosexual parenting is a politically reactionary move. However, I do not wish merely to critique this construction of lesbian and gay families but to evaluate its possibilities as a way of advancing lesbian and gay rights in the public domain. I now identi-fy a number of benefits that adhere to normalizing discourse, as well as a number of costs. I also discuss lesbian feminist constructions of lesbian and gay families as 'radical' and the costs and benefits of this alternative discourse of difference.

The political benefits of normalizing strategies

Employed as a political strategy, normalizing lesbian and gay families is often a very persuasive way of representing lesbian and gay experience in the wider world. Strategies such as the ones I have highlighted above are effective precisely because they do not question common-sense wisdom about family life and relationships. In fact, these strategies demonstrate how lesbian and gay families conform to such norms. For example, gay fathers highlight the number of female role models their children have rather than question the assumptions underlying concerns about a lack of 'appropriate' role models. In assimilating to a heterosexual norm, rather than attempting to undermine or challenge it, normalizing strategies allow lesbian and gay parents and supporters of lesbian and gay rights to participate (often successfully) in public debates about lesbian and gay parenting. These strategies enable us to address fears about lesbian and gay parenting and its effect on children. They allow engagement with mainstream concerns, rather than simply dismissing them as 'heterosexist' or 'homophobic' and not worthy of our attention. Dominant attitudes towards lesbian and gay parenting clearly have an overwhelming impact on our families and not to engage with them may be a politically regressive move.

Normalizing strategies also make lesbian and gay families recognizable (as families) to potentially hostile or unknowing heterosexuals. Strategies such as 'emphasizing ordinariness' and 'emphasizing love and security' foreground values which our society acknowledges as being central to family life and they allow heterosexuals to identify commonalities between their families and lesbian and gay families. These are potentially powerful ways of combating prejudice towards lesbian and gay families, which often relies on stereotyped notions of lesbian and gay existence and the idea that lesbians and gay men are (somehow) fundamentally different. One of the lesbian parents I interviewed, who was co-parenting her children with her partner and the children's donor-father, commented that 'We think one of the reasons why so many straights are quite keen on us is 'cos we've got a man, we've got a father for our children, so it kind of normalizes – it seems to reassure people in some way'. This woman identified the presence of a father in her family as 'reassuring' for their heterosexual friends and acquaintances.

Normalizing constructions of lesbian and gay parenting are also 'safe' and, unlike more radical constructions of lesbian and gay families, do not kindle the fears of (extremist) opponents of lesbian and gay rights. Right wing literature, for example, often pulls out quotations from lesbian and gay manifestos and lesbian and gay literature about 'destroying the family' as evidence for the belief that the advancement of lesbian and gay rights poses a threat to traditional family values. For example, Burtoft (1994), a key right wing author, describes gay author,

Michael Swift's, critique of the violence and hypocrisy of the traditional family as 'vitriolic, anti-family rhetoric' and Swift and others like him as 'aggressively seeking to "de-construct" the family' (p. 59). Swift's critique is taken as evidence for the view that any extension of lesbian and gay rights will undermine the family. In sum, normalizing strategies may extend our rights within the world as it is but, in the long term, offer no challenges to the system and institutions of hetero-patriarchy which oppress us.

The political costs of normalizing strategies

From a feminist perspective, strategies such as 'emphasizing ordinariness' and 'highlighting compensations for deficits' reinforce heterosexual norms rather than trying to transform or resist them. They represent another example of the phenomenon whereby lesbians and gay men are compelled to demonstrate the extent to which they are just like heterosexuals in order to be considered normal (Epstein and Steinberg, 1998). Furthermore, normalizing strategies reinforce the pre-eminence of heterosexual families (in whatever shape or form they assume) as the ideal environments in which to raise a child, providing implicit support for normative constructions of gender and sexuality and pandering to fears about children's failure to develop into normal boys and girls in lesbian and gay families. They offer no resistance to the notion that every child needs a mother and a father nor to the place of men and women in the (traditional) family. The lesbian parents quoted here accept the idea that children need male role models or a father figure, rather than offering a critique of men's contribution to family life. Similar costs are evident in relation to the psychological literature on lesbian and gay parenting. With the weight of 'science' behind them, psychological studies – such as those outlined above – provide tacit support for an array of norms concerning gender and sexuality. Normalizing also reinforces psychology's power to define normal and psychologically 'healthy' behaviour.

The tone of normative discourses is fundamentally defensive: rather than celebrating lesbian and gay families, they apologise for our existence, emphasizing the qualities that make our families similar to heterosexual families (Raymond, 1992). The diversity and unique strengths of lesbian and gay families are hidden behind a cloud of comparison (and other attempts to highlight our similarities), although virtually all lesbians and gay men can recite how their life is forced into difference by homophobia (Raymond, 1992) and 'the lack of acknowledgement' (Nelson, 1996, p. 132) of lesbian and gay families. These strategies ignore the diversity in the structure of many lesbian and gay families and the variety of different relationships they encompass. For example, one lesbian mother whom I interviewed said that she wanted 'to do something different' and have 'two mummies and a daddy' for her children, rather than 'try and reproduce the existing model of the nuclear family' (Lisa).

The use of normalizing strategies in public debates 'makes us once more invisible, and obscures the radical alternative lesbian lives can model' (Pollack, 1992, p. 316); they also 'negate the healthy and positive characteristics unique to lesbian parenting' (*ibid.*). These strategies encourage us to shy away from the labels 'gay father' or 'lesbian mother' rather than have pride in them. In fact, Pollack (1992) argues that the discourse of sameness replaces one problematic assumption – 'lesbians are not mothers' – with another – 'lesbians are not different'. In downplaying the importance of prejudice, normalizing strategies do not enable lesbian and gay parents to discuss the impact of oppression on their daily lives.

Although normalizing strategies permit engagement with mainstream discussion, they do not allow us to set our own (political) agendas and talk about lesbian and gay parenting on our own terms. For example, the lesbian and gay literature on lesbian and gay parenting addresses issues such as whether gay fathers are guilty of 'de-gaying gayness' (Bersani, quoted in Faderman, 1997, p. 63) and whether lesbians should become mothers because if they do they will be 'fulfilling a male-defined role of feminity and Motherhood' (Jo, 1988/1984, p. 316).

Furthermore, the use of these resources in public debate suggests that traditional concerns are valid and worthy of being taken seriously rather than, say, dismissing them out of hand as unsound and born out of ignorance and prejudice. Likewise, research on lesbian and gay parenting (such as that discussed above) would appear to find a place for lesbian and gay families inside psychology, adding lesbians and gay men into the framework of mainstream psychology without disrupting it. In a similar fashion to what has been dubbed the 'just add women and stir' approach in feminist psychology (see Crawford and Marecek, 1992), normalizing strategies allow lesbian and gay families to be acceptable as 'alternative families' but do not fully integrate them into psychological theories and frameworks. However, as Tasker and Golombok (1997) point out, if we accept the conclusion that lesbian parents are little different from heterosexual parents, this necessitates a fundamental re-working of the way we conceive of child development within psychology – parental influence (particularly on the development of gender and sexuality) is less significant than previously thought. Despite this, lesbian and gay families remain the subject of the 'token chapter' (Kitzinger, 1996) in both feminist and mainstream texts about parenting and the family, tucked away under such headings as 'diversity' (Cole and Knowles, 1990) and 'differing family circumstances' (Woollett and Phoenix, 1991). This kind of psychological research is conducted in response to mainstream agendas and not in response to our interests as lesbians and gay men.

Some more radical alternatives

The discourse of sameness is informed by liberal humanism – the ideological framework that guides much contemporary discussion of lesbian and gay issues (Kitzinger, 1987; see also Chapter 14 in this volume). Kitzinger and Coyle (1995) suggest that liberalism is characterized by 'a rejection of the concept of homosexuality as a central organizing principle of the personality in favour of recognizing the diversity and variety of lesbians and gay men as individuals' (p. 64). It holds that lesbians and gay men should be 'accepted as part of humanity in all its rich variety' (Kitzinger, 1989, p. 85). The prevalence of the liberal humanist framework within lesbian and gay psychology has led to a heavy emphasis on the similarities between lesbians and gay men (Kitzinger and Coyle, 1995) and, consequently, the denial of our differences (Kitzinger, 1989). More radical constructions of lesbian and gay parenting are rarely articulated or, at least, do not get a hearing in the public arena. Many lesbian feminists have argued that lesbian families[5] pose a fundamental challenge to traditional family values. Gillian Dunne (2000), for example, argues that the prioritization of egalitarian ideals in lesbian families represents 'a fundamental challenge to the foundation of the gender order' (p. 33). Likewise, Baba Copper (1987) asserts that 'radical lesbian mothering' – unlike 'patriarchal-' or 'hetero-mothering' – 'embodies a remarkable chance to redesign women's primary biologically-based role in the service of women-chosen goals' (p. 240). And, according to Jess Wells (1997):

> Lesbian households are raising a new generation of men who will be significantly different from their counterparts in ˙ patriarchal families...Patriarchal families teach girls what they cannot do and teach boys what they cannot feel...Lesbian families teach their sons to embrace the full range of their emotions. No one in a lesbian household says, 'Take it like a man' or 'Big boys don't cry'. (pp. x-xi)

Wells (1997) argues that lesbian parents should focus on 'acknowledging the beautiful, inherent differences in the children we bring into the world' (p. x). Obviously, this construction of lesbian parenting as radical is no more or less *true* than the construction of lesbian and gay families as being just like heterosexual families. However, it is a less apologetic and defensive portrayal of our parenting. Radical constructions acknowledge and celebrate our differences from the 'norm' instead of denying them. As Nancy Polikoff (1987) has pointed out, in mainstream society (for example, in custody cases) by positioning themselves 'as close to the...norm as possible – the spitting image of [their] ideal heterosexual counterpart', lesbian parents are 'forced to deny any pride in [their] lesbianism, any solidarity with other lesbians' (pp. 325–326). These constructions also subvert traditional notions of gender and sexuality and expose the sexism underlying the claim that children need male role models (Pollack, 1992).

Conclusion

In conclusion, I have identified four resources that are used to construct lesbian and gay families as just like heterosexual families and that provide a compelling means of representing lesbian and gay families in mainstream society. They directly address concerns about lesbian and gay parenting, providing reassurance that lesbian and gay families are, in fact, no different from the heterosexual norm. Viewed from a lesbian feminist perspective, however, normalizing strategies provide ideological support for the institution of the family as it exists now and as it has existed throughout history: a site of oppression, violence and abusive relationships for many women and gay men. Moreover, these strategies do not celebrate lesbian and gay families on their own terms – in the sameness discourse, lesbian and gay families only have validity and a presence in mainstream society if they conform to heterosexual norms and expectations.

Although normalizing is a politically useful strategy, we should also give thought to the (politically conservative) consequences of employing it in the public sphere. We must fight for a space for more radical constructions of lesbian and gay parenting within mainstream discourse on the family. There is room for multiple constructions of lesbian and gay families within contemporary society: we should celebrate and have pride in our differences as well as appealing to the mainstream.

Notes

1. The data are drawn from a larger project on lesbian and gay parenting which explores the social construction of lesbian and gay parenting, focusing on the various arguments deployed to undermine or uphold lesbians' and gay men's parental rights and the differing constructions of lesbian and gay families which emerge from debates about lesbian and gay parenting.
2. Where possible, I have indicated the following information about the data: the name – or, in the case of interview data, the pseudonym – of the speaker or speakers; their status as a speaker (for example, 'lesbian parent', 'host'); the source of the data; and – in the case of media data – the date on which it appeared or was broadcast. In addition, three dots indicate where material has been omitted from the original text.

3. It is interesting to consider how opponents of lesbian and gay parenting respond to such talk, for example, on talk shows. Apart from avoiding confronting this talk altogether, opponents tend to preface any comments about the importance of male and female role models with concessions such as 'I am not saying that you don't love your child' or 'Of course care is important'. These concessions display the robustness of talk about love: it would appear to be very difficult to challenge the claim that a parent loves or cares for their children.
4. This strategy is used to answer specific criticism about a lack of role models – unlike the other three strategies I have discussed which also have more general functions and are used to respond to a range of criticism.
5. These arguments are rarely applied to gay families.

Acknowledgements

With thanks to Virginia Braun, Sonja J. Ellis, Celia Kitzinger, Elizabeth Peel and Susan Speer for their feedback on an earlier version of this chapter and to Celia Kitzinger and Jonathan Potter for their supervision of the PhD research from which the work reported here is drawn. This research was supported by ESRC postgraduate training award R00429734421.

References

ALLDRED, P. (1996) 'Fit to parent'? Developmental psychology and 'non-traditional' families. In E. Burman, P. Alldred, C. Bewley, B. Goldberg, C. Heenan, D. Marks, J. Marshall, K. Taylor, R. Ullah and S. Warner *Challenging Women: Psychology's Exclusions, Feminist Possibilities*. Buckingham: Open University Press.

ALLDRED, P. (1998) Making a mockery of family life? Lesbian mothers in the British media. *Journal of Lesbian Studies, 2*, 9–21.

ALLEN, M. and BURRELL, N. (1996) Comparing the impact of homosexual and heterosexual parents on children: Meta-analysis of existing research. *Journal of Homosexuality, 32(2)*, 19–35.

BURTOFT, L.F. (1994) *Setting the Record Straight: What Research Really Says About the Social Consequences of Homosexuality*. Colorado Springs, CO: Focus on the Family Public Policy Division.

CHAN, R.W., RABOY, B. and PATTERSON, C.J. (1998) Psychosocial adjustment among children conceived via donor insemination by lesbian and heterosexual mothers. *Child Development, 69*, 443–57.

CLARKE, V. (1999) 'God made Adam and Eve, not Adam and Steve': Lesbian and gay parenting on talk shows. *The British Psychological Society Lesbian and Gay Psychology Section Newsletter, issue 1*, 7–17.

CLARKE, V. (2000) Lesbian mothers: Sameness and difference. *Feminism & Psychology, 10*, 273–278.

COLE, E. and KNOWLES, J.P. (Eds) (1990) Motherhood: A feminist perspective. *Women and Therapy*, 10(1/2).

COPPER, B. (1987) The radical potential in lesbian mothering of daughters. In S. Pollack and J. Vaughn (Eds) *Politics of the Heart: A Lesbian Parenting Anthology*. Ithaca, NY: Firebrand Books.

COYLE, A. (2000). Discourse analysis. In G.M. Breakwell, S. Hammond & C. Fife-Schaw (Eds) *Research Methods in Psychology*, 2nd ed. London: Sage.

CRAWFORD, M. and MARACEK, J. (1992) Psychology reconstructs the female, 1968–1988. In J.S. Bohan (Ed.) *Seldom Seen, Rarely Heard: Women's Place in Psychology*. Boulder, CO: Westview Press.

DILAPI, E.M. (1989) Lesbian mothers and the motherhood hierarchy. *Journal of Homosexuality*, 18(1/2), 101–21.

DUNNE, G.A. (2000) Opting into motherhood: Lesbians blurring the boundaries and transforming the meaning of parenthood and kinship. *Gender & Society*, 14, 11–35.

EDWARDS, D. and POTTER, J. (1992) *Discursive Psychology*. London: Sage.

EPSTEIN, D. and STEINBERG, D.L. (1998) American dreamin': Discoursing liberally on *The Oprah Winfrey Show*. *Women's Studies International Forum*, 21(1), 77–94.

FADERMAN, L. (1997) Outside the inside. In J. Wells (Ed.) *Lesbians Raising Sons: An Anthology*. Los Angeles, CA: Alyson Books.

GAVEY, N. (1989) Feminist poststructuralism and discourse analysis: Contributions to feminist psychology. *Psychology of Women Quarterly*, 13, 459–475.

GOLOMBOK, S., SPENCER, A. and RUTTER, M. (1983) Children in lesbian and single parent households: Psychosexual and psychiatric appraisal. *Journal of Child Psychology & Psychiatry*, 24, 551–572.

GOUGH, B. (1998) Projecting the gay other: Men, masculinity and the discursive reproduction of homophobia. In R. Forrester and C. Percy (Eds) *Proceedings of the International Conference on Discourse & the Social Order*. Birmingham: Aston Business School.

HARNE, L. and RIGHTS OF WOMEN LESBIAN CUSTODY GROUP (1997) *Valued Families: The Lesbian Mothers' Legal Handbook*, 2nd ed. London: The Women's Press.

HARRIS, M.B. and TURNER, P.H. (1985) Gay and lesbian parents. *Journal of Homosexuality*, 12(2), 101–113.

HUGGINS, S.L. (1989) A comparative study of self-esteem of adolescent children of divorced lesbian mothers and divorced heterosexual mothers. *Journal of Homosexuality*, 18(1/2), 123–135.

JO, B. (1988) For women who call themselves lesbians – are you thinking of getting pregnant? In S. Lucia-Hoagland and J. Penelope (Eds) *For Lesbians Only: A Separatist Anthology*. London: Onlywomen Press [originally published in 1984].

KAESER, G. and GILLESPIE, P. (1999) *Love Makes a Family: Portraits of Lesbian, Gay, Bisexual, and Transgender Parents and their Families*. Amherst, MA: University of Massachusetts Press.

KITZINGER, C. (1987) *The Social Construction of Lesbianism*. London: Sage.

KITZINGER, C. (1989) Liberal humanism as an ideology of social control: The regulation of lesbian identities. In J. Shotter and K.J. Gergen (Eds) *Texts of Identity*. London: Sage.

KITZINGER, C. (1995) Social constructionism: Implications for lesbian and gay psychology. In A.R. D'Augelli and C.J. Patterson (Eds) *Lesbian, Gay, and Bisexual Identities Over the Lifespan: Psychological Perspectives.* New York: Oxford University Press.

KITZINGER, C. (1996) The token lesbian chapter. In S. Wilkinson (Ed.) *Feminist Social Psychologies: International Perspectives.* Buckingham: Open University Press.

KITZINGER, C. and COYLE, A. (1995) Lesbian and gay couples: Speaking of difference. *The Psychologist, 8,* 64–69.

KITZINGER, C. and THOMAS, A. (1995) Sexual harassment: A discursive approach. In C. Kitzinger and S. Wilkinson (Eds) *Feminism and Discourse: Psychological Perspectives.* London: Sage.

KITZINGER, C. and WILKINSON, S. (Eds) (1995a) *Feminism and Discourse: Psychological Perspectives.* London: Sage.

KITZINGER, C. and WILKINSON, S. (1995b) Transitions from heterosexuality to lesbianism: The discursive production of lesbian identities. *Developmental Psychology, 31,* 95–104.

McCLOUD, A. and CRAWFORD, I. (1998) The postmodern family: An examination of the psychosocial and legal perspectives of gay and lesbian parenting. In G.M. Herek (Ed.) *Stigma and Sexual Orientation: Understanding Prejudice Against Lesbians, Gay Men, and Bisexuals.* Thousand Oaks, CA: Sage.

McCREANOR, T. (1996) 'Why strengthen the city wall when the enemy has poisoned the well?' An assay of anti-homosexual discourse in New Zealand. *Journal of Homosexuality, 31(4),* 74–105.

NELSON, F. (1996) *Lesbian Motherhood: An Exploration of Canadian Lesbian Families.* Toronto: University of Toronto Press.

POLIKOFF, N.D. (1987) Lesbian mothers, lesbian families: Legal obstacles, legal challenges. In S. Pollack and J. Vaughn (Eds) *Politics of the Heart: A Lesbian Parenting Anthology.* Ithaca, NY: Firebrand Books.

POLLACK, S (1992) Lesbian mothers: A lesbian-feminist perspective on research. In D.J. Maggiore (Ed.) *Lesbians and Child Custody: A Casebook.* New York: Garland.

POTTER, J. (1996) *Representing Reality: Discourse, Rhetoric and Social Construction.* London: Sage.

PRAAT, A.C. & TUFFIN, K.F. (1996) Police discourses of homosexual men in New Zealand. *Journal of Homosexuality, 31(4),* 57–73.

RADFORD, J. (1991) Immaculate conceptions. *Trouble & Strife, 21,* 8–12.

RAYMOND, D. (1992) 'In the best interests of the child': Thoughts on homophobia and parenting. In W.J. Blumenfeld (Ed.) *Homophobia: How We All Pay the Price.* Boston, MA: Beacon Press.

REINHOLD, S. (1994) Through the parliamentary looking glass: 'Real' and 'pretend' families in contemporary politics. *Feminist Review, 48,* 61–79.

TASKER, F. and GOLOMBOK, S. (1997) *Growing Up in a Lesbian Family: Effects on Child Development.* New York: The Guilford Press.

WELLS, J. (1997) Introduction. In J. Wells (Ed.) *Lesbians Raising Sons: An Anthology.* Los Angeles, CA: Alyson Books.

WESTON, K. (1991) *Families We Choose: Lesbians, Gays, Kinship.* New York: Columbia University Press.

WETHERELL, M. and POTTER, J. (1988) Discourse analysis and the identification of interpretative repertoires. In C. Antaki (Ed.) *Analysing Everyday Explanations: A Casebook of Methods.* London: Sage.

WOOLLETT, A. and PHOENIX, A. (1991) Afterword: Issues related to motherhood. In A. Phoenix, A. Woollett and E. Lloyd (Eds) *Motherhood: Meanings, Practices and Ideologies*. London: Sage.

Chapter 7

Lesbian Health

Sue Wilkinson

Lesbian health issues first appeared as a distinctive area in the 1970s in the USA with the beginnings of 'second wave' feminism and the early attempt to reclaim women's bodies (and minds) from the male-dominated medical professions (for example, see the first edition of The Boston Women's Health Book Collective's *Our Bodies, Ourselves*, 1971). Lesbian-specific, grassroots-produced, single-issue pamphlets – particularly around reproductive issues (for example, how to find a sperm donor, how to self-inseminate) – were widely distributed, as was the booklet *Lesbian Health Matters!* (O'Donnell *et al.*, 1979), published by the Santa Cruz Women's Health Center and spanning a range of lesbian health issues, including gynaecological examinations, dealing with alcoholism and choosing an appropriate therapist. A decade later, this was succeeded by the now-classic *Alive and Well: A Lesbian Health Guide* (Hepburn and Gutierrez, 1988).

The 1990s saw a surge in the number of books devoted exclusively to lesbian health and covering a broad range of issues (for example, Stern, 1992; McClure and Vespry, 1994; White and Martinez, 1997; Ponticelli, 1998; Solarz, 1999), including the first British one, *Good for You: A Handbook of Lesbian Health and Wellbeing* (Wilton, 1997); there are now also many more lesbian-specific health books on single issues, most commonly sexual health, reproduction and parenting (for example, O'Sullivan and Parmar, 1992; Saffron, 1994; Arnup, 1995). There have been two journal special issues on lesbian health – *Health Care for Women International* (Stern, 1992) and the *Journal of Lesbian Studies* (Ponticelli, 1998) – and even mainstream women's health books now routinely address lesbian health issues and/or include a lesbian health chapter. In this chapter, I will first sketch out the (largely) North American context for the field and then highlight two contrasting British studies: a large scale national survey of lesbian health and a small scale qualitative project on lesbians and breast cancer. These two studies are among the first specifically on lesbian health to be conducted by psychologists in Britain.

The lesbian health research literature is heavily dominated by North American studies. The field has developed dramatically since the mid-1990s as a result of successful campaigns by lesbian health activists in lobbying the (US) Department of Health and Human Services (Plumb, 1997). These campaigns have produced a number of federal initiatives, including supplemental funding from the National Institute of Health to include lesbians in ongoing studies and a major workshop held by the Institute of Medicine to make recommendations regarding future research on lesbian health (Solarz, 1999). This trend continues: in May 2000, representatives of big-city health departments across the USA met to consider the health issues (other than HIV/AIDS) facing 'sexual minorities'. Their agenda included reviewing research on 'special risks for victimization by anti-gay violence, suicide, depression, smoking and alcohol/drug abuse, and breast and cervical cancer among lesbians' and identifying public health campaigns 'that could make a difference, such as encouraging lesbians to perform regular breast self-examinations or obtain mammograms' (http://www.planetout.com/news/search.html?related=l&search=news_articles.2000/05/17/3).

To date, the research agenda on lesbian health has been dominated by two main types of study: studies of health care experiences – most frequently from a nursing perspective – and demographic surveys, both large and small-scale. Sometimes demographic surveys have included questions about health care experiences.

Studies of lesbians' health care experiences have generally been undertaken to examine the difficulties lesbians face in accessing appropriate and effective health care. In virtually all studies published to date, lesbians have reported experiencing hostility, intimidation and sometimes humiliation from health care providers. In reviewing these studies, Stevens (1992) suggests that the greatest barrier to obtaining good health care is the routine presumption of heterosexuality. One Nicaraguan-American lesbian told the following story of her experiences in getting a lump in her breast checked out:

> I called my HMO [Health Maintenance Organization] and they made me talk to the advice nurse. So I am on the phone describing this lump to her and she says, 'Are you sexually active?' I said yes. 'What kind of birth control do you use?' I said I don't use any. Then she gets excited. 'You don't use birth control? Don't you realize you could get pregnant?' So I said I was a lesbian. She says, 'Oh.' I figured, fine, she wrote it down. Then I went into the HMO like she told me to. And this nurse comes in. The first question she asks, with the clipboard in her hand, is 'Are you sexually active?' 'Yes.' 'Are you on the pill?' 'No.' 'What kind of birth control do you use?' 'I don't use any. I'm a lesbian.' There is no change in her voice, so I figured, okay, fine, she wrote it down in my chart, no problem. Then the doctor comes in and she says, 'Are you sexually active?' I thought, not again. So I said, 'Yes. And I am a les-

bian. Frankly, this is the third time that I have been asked. I don't like it that you all keep assuming I am straight.' Why did I have to answer to this again and again when what I needed to hear about was the lump in my breast? (Stevens, 1996a, p. 174)

The presumption of heterosexuality not only makes lesbians feel invisible, uncomfortable and vulnerable – it typically leads to insensitive questions, irrelevant information and inadequate treatment. Misdiagnosis is not uncommon. At least half the lesbians in these studies of lesbians' health care experiences express reluctance to 'come out' to health care professionals – and some say they would lie about their sexual orientation if asked directly (Dardick and Grady, 1980). The situation may be even worse for lesbians from ethnic minorities (Cochran and Mays, 1988; Mays and Cochran, 1988).

Among those lesbians who do 'come out' (like the woman above), a substantial number report negative responses – including embarrassment, shock, withdrawal, excessive curiosity, insulting remarks and breaches of confidentiality (Stevens, 1992). One African-American participant in a study of lesbians' experiences of cancer support recounts the following experience of 'coming out' to a physician:

I wouldn't have said that I was lesbian if it wasn't that I was having female problems. I really expected him to have a little more professionalism. When his face turned red and he couldn't look me in the eye, he had totally lost control. He left the room and didn't come back in. He sent a nurse in after that. [I thought] Am I the first lesbian to walk through this door? (Matthews, 1998, p. 196)

Not surprisingly, then, lesbians have also been found to avoid routine check-ups, to delay seeking medical help and to turn to lesbian friends for advice, rather than to medical professionals (Smith *et al.*, 1985; Stevens and Hall, 1988; Deevy, 1990; Zeidenstein, 1990; Trippett and Bain, 1992). A range of further studies has documented blatantly anti-lesbian attitudes among a variety of health care providers (for example, Douglas *et al.*, 1985; Mathews *et al.*, 1986; Randall, 1989; Eliason and Randall, 1991; O'Hanlan, 1996; Peterson and Bricker, 1996; Schwanberg, 1996; Stevens, 1996b; Eliason, 1998).

Demographic surveys have been popular because so little is known about the lesbian population. Such surveys have aimed primarily to assess the status of lesbian health as a precursor to identifying lesbians' particular health care needs. One of the largest, most comprehensive and most frequently cited is Bradford and Ryan's (1988) *National Lesbian Health Care Survey*. This is based on a nationwide sample of 1 917 lesbians in the USA, with questions ranging across general health and health care; obstetrics and gynaecology; sexually transmitted diseases; mental health; paying for treatment; self-care; experiences of physical abuse, sexual attack and incest; use of alcohol, drugs and other substances; eating disorders; community and social life; 'outness'; and experiences with anti-gay discrimination. However, although the final report of the survey is readily available from its authors or the sponsoring body (The National Lesbian and Gay Health Foundation), to date only the data relating to mental health have been published in an academic journal (Bradford *et al.*, 1994). Bradford and Ryan's (1988) survey served – to some extent – as a model for the UK survey reported in this chapter and has also informed surveys of lesbian health recently completed in New Zealand (Saphira and Glover, 1999) and proposed in Australia and Italy. Other USA surveys include Johnson *et al.*'s (1987) large survey of 1 921 geographically-diverse lesbians attending women's music festivals in 1980; and smaller-scale surveys in Iowa City (Johnson *et al.*, 1981), Southern California (Saunders *et al.*, 1988), Michigan (Bybee, 1991), New York state (Buenting, 1992) and Boston (Roberts *et al.*, 1997–8).

A useful synopsis of the main findings of the early USA surveys – including Bradford and Ryan's – is provided by Haas (1994). Despite lesbians' often-negative experiences of health care, these surveys suggest a generally positive picture of lesbian health overall and no health problems specifically linked to lesbianism (Johnson *et al.*, 1981). However, the surveys do identify high levels of stress among lesbians, exacerbated by limited social support networks (particularly among those living alone and/or in rural settings) and manifested in stress-related illnesses, depression, suicidal tendencies and alcohol abuse. Any discussion of such findings must acknowledge the considerable methodological problems inherent in these surveys, particularly in relation to sampling issues. For example, it is likely that the frequency of alcohol problems among lesbians has been overestimated by using samples drawn disproportionately from lesbian and gay bars. Most surveys have relied exclusively on volunteer respondents and have made little or no attempt to be representative of the lesbian population; few have included heterosexual controls; and there is huge variability in their definitions of 'lesbian'. However, given the near-impossibility of population-based probability sampling in a lesbian context (Solarz, 1999), combining multiple methods of non-probability sampling may be a more fruitful strategy (Fish, 1999, 2000) – this is the technique used in the first of the two British studies described below.

The (UK) Lesbians and Health Care Survey

Although there has been a number of small, unpublished British surveys of lesbian health needs (for example, Farquhar, undated; SHADY, 1996; Sheffield Health Steering Group, 1996; Mantle, 1998; Mugglestone, 1999), the Lesbians and Health Care Survey – the basis for doctoral research by Julie Fish at Loughborough University – was the first large-scale national survey of lesbian health and health care in

Britain. The Lesbians and Health Care Survey focused particularly on screening for cervical cancer and breast cancer and consisted of a semi-structured questionnaire, divided into four broad sections. The first section included questions on attendance for cervical screening, good and bad experiences of smear tests and perceived risk of developing cervical cancer. The second section asked about the practice of breast self-examination and the reasons for performing or not performing it. The third section asked about attendance for breast screening, good and bad experiences of mammograms and perceived risk of develop-ing breast cancer. The final section recorded demographic information. One of the particular strengths of the survey was that the design of the questionnaire allowed for both quantitative and qualitative responses throughout – asking, for example, about the frequency of attendance for smear tests *and* for explanations of attendance or non-attendance.

Another strength of the survey was the widespread geographical distribution of its respondents – covering 117 of the 122 postal districts in the UK. This was achieved via a multi-dimensional sampling strate-gy (Fish, 1999). The research was publicized in the lesbian press (at local, regional and national levels) and via a wide range of groups across the country (for example, lesbian switchboards, women's cen-tres, health groups, lesbian and women's organizations). Questionnaires were distributed through a broad spectrum of lesbian venues and at specific events ranging from Pride festivals to parties, as well as through snowballing techniques and offers from specific indi-viduals to utilize their networks and groups. Approximately 3 600 questionnaires were distributed and 1 066 returned – a response rate of 30 per cent (broadly comparable with other surveys of lesbian com-munities: see Morris and Rothblum, 1999). I will concentrate here on the main results obtained in relation to cervical cancer and screening for cervical cancer (see Fish and Wilkinson, 2000a, 2000b for more detailed presentation and discussion of these findings).

Cervical cancer has been little studied in relation to lesbians because it is widely believed that lesbians are at little or no risk of contracting it (Burns, 1992; Haas, 1994; O'Hanlan, 1996; Price *et al.*, 1996) – despite the fact that the causes of cervical cancer are not known, nor is it clear exactly how the disease is contracted (Singleton and Michael, 1993). However, cervical cancer does appear to be associated with (hetero)sexual activity – and the biggest risk factor for women seems to be having penetrative sex with men (McPherson and Austoker, 1995). Genital wart virus (strongly linked to cervical cancer) can be passed on through semen; sperm bonding to cervical cells can interfere with their function; and smegma (the substance which collects under the foreskin of an uncircumcised penis) has also been implicated in the develop-ment of cervical cancer (see Szarewski, 1994). It has frequently been reported that nuns (i.e., women assumed not to have had sex with men) have lower rates of cervical cancer (for example, Hulka, 1982;

Cancer Research Campaign, 1990; Walsh *et al.*, 1995) – and lesbians (equated with nuns and/or virgins) have also typically been assumed to be at lower risk than heterosexual women (for example, Rosser, 1993; Simkin, 1993; Haas, 1994). However, lesbians are not a unitary group (for example, some will previously have had sex with men and some will continue to do so: Rankow and Tessaro, 1998) and any woman who has – or has had – sex with men is potentially at risk. There is also some (limited) evidence for cervical abnormalities in lesbians who report no experience of heterosex (Edwards and Thin, 1990; Ferris *et al.*, 1996). In addition, any woman (lesbian or heterosexual) may be subject to the other suggested risk factors for cervical cancer: for example smoking, childbirth or a dirty workplace (see Chomet and Chomet, 1989).

Cervical cancer is unusual in that it has a 'warning' stage in which abnormal, pre-cancerous cells are present for several years before cancer develops; this makes it a good candidate for screening (the aim of which is the early detection of pre-cancerous cells). The failure to detect cervical cancer at an early stage – by means of regular screening – has therefore been characterized as a risk factor in its own right (Duncan, 1992). A national screening programme is in operation in many countries, including in the UK, where women are called for a cervical smear test every three years. Approximately 15 per cent of all women do not attend for screening in the UK. It is a government priority to investigate women's reasons for non-attendance, with a view to increasing their uptake of screening (Department of Health, 1999). Lesbians' non-attendance for cervical screening has largely been ignored, although some reports suggest that lesbians may think they do not need smear tests (Sheffield Health Steering Group, 1996; Bailey *et al.*, 2000) and others note that lesbians may explicitly be told this by health care providers (Das and Farquhar, 1996; SHADY, 1996; Mantle, 1998).

The Lesbians and Health Care Survey asked respondents whether they currently have cervical smears on a regular basis and/or whether they have ever had them in the past. In addition, respondents were invited to explain why they do or do not attend for screening. Over half the total sample (54 per cent; N=573) said they currently have smears on a regular basis; around a third (31 per cent; N=327) reported having had at least one smear test in the past; and 15 per cent (N=165) reported never having had a smear test. Excluding the 37 women who were too young to be called for screening (i.e., under the age of 20), this represents 12 per cent (N=128) of those lesbians eligible for a smear test who said they have never attended for screening. In other words, the non-attendance rate among lesbians in this survey was very similar to the government's published non-attendance rate for all women.

Lesbians' explanations for non-attendance fell largely into three broad categories: 'not needing' a smear test (40 per cent); negative aspects of the screening procedure (38 per cent); and problems with time management (20 per cent). Most frequently, lesbians mentioned not having sex with men as (self-evidently) the reason for 'not needing' a smear test: 'I have never had sexual contact with a man'; 'never been penetrated by a man'; 'never slept with men'. They also commonly reported health professionals' advice that they did not need a smear test: 'the nurse said as I was a lesbian I didn't need one'; 'the GP said I was technically a virgin'. The most frequently-specified negative aspects of the screening procedure were the anticipation of pain and the expectation of embarrassment or humiliation. Other concerns centred around the perceived invasiveness or intrusiveness of the procedure: 'I don't want to be tampered with'; 'invasion of privacy'; 'I don't want a man poking around in my body'. Only a few respondents specifically raised anxieties around experiences or expectations of heterosexism in medical encounters (for example, 'I was worried that my sexuality would be questioned...coupled with feeling uneasy about their response to lesbianism'). Finally, some women explained their non-attendance for screening in terms of being 'horribly busy' or 'hopelessly disorganized'.

Unusually, the Lesbians and Health Care Survey also asked respondents who said they *did* attend for cervical screening to explain why this was the case. The 54 per cent of the sample who reported having smear tests on a regular basis gave some 566 different explanations (responses were open-ended and some respondents gave more than one explanation). These explanations can be grouped into four broad categories: 'early detection' (40 per cent); 'prompted by the service' (22 per cent); 'sexual experiences' (17 per cent); and 'experiences of abnormal smears' (10 per cent). The most frequently-cited explanation for having regular smears was an acknowledgement of the role of screening in the early detection of cervical cancer: 'am concerned that any irregularities in the cervix are picked up early'; 'cervical cancer is relatively simple to cure if caught early enough'. Attendance for screening was also described as actively participating in health care: 'I value my health and take every possible step to maintain and/or improve it'; 'I feel it is taking responsibility for my health'. The simplest explanation given for regular screening was 'being called for': 'my surgery issues [a] letter when I am due for a test'; 'I go when the computer tells me to' – in this category, lesbians' attendance is a response to prompting by the screening service. In the category 'sexual experiences', lesbians explained their screening attendance *both* in terms of a history of heterosex ('I used to have sex with men so understand there is still a risk') *and* in terms of current – lesbian – sexual practices ('even if I don't sleep with men I'm still sexually active'). They described assessing their own risk, sometimes not basing this on medical advice: 'my GP did say that as I was lesbian I didn't really need tests but I've gone anyway'. Finally, a substantial minority of respondents offered previous experience of an 'abnormal' smear – their own or that of a friend/partner – as an explanation for regular screening.

Lesbians and breast cancer

Like cervical cancer, breast cancer has also been little studied in relation to lesbians. This is surprising because it is widely believed that lesbians are *more* at risk of contracting breast cancer than are heterosexual women (Bybee, 1991; Lucas, 1992; Rankow, 1995). In the early 1990s, the claim that one in three lesbians – compared with one in eight heterosexual women (in the USA) – will develop breast cancer was widely reported in both the feminist and lesbian and gay media (for example, Gates, quoted in Douglas, 1993; Gessen, 1993) and in the mainstream press (for example, Campbell, 1993; Selvin, 1993). The one-in-three statistic became something of a 'myth' in the lesbian community and beyond – at least in the USA. Although there may be strategic value in making such a claim in order to mobilize health care activists (see Winnow, 1993) or to lobby for increased funding for breast cancer projects (see Kaufert, 1998), there is little evidence to support it. And, of course, subsequent debunkings of the 'myth' (for example, Love with Lindsay, 1995; Yadlon, 1997) – including those in the lesbian press (for example, Smedman and Tryggvason, 1998) – are unlikely to attract comparable attention.

It is a salutary exercise to unpick the basis of the original media reports – particularly given that *no* studies have yet been done specifically on lesbians and breast cancer risk. The one-in-three statistic is typically referenced – if it is referenced at all – to one (or occasionally both) of two sources: Bradford and Ryan's (1988) *National Lesbian Health Care Survey*; and an unpublished conference paper delivered at the 1992 Lesbian and Gay Health Conference in Los Angeles by epidemiologist, Suzanne Haynes, then at the (USA) National Cancer Institute. In fact, Bradford and Ryan's survey did not include questions which would have enabled them to determine lesbians' cancer risk, nor did they find a higher breast cancer rate among lesbians. Furthermore, they caution against generalizing their findings to all lesbians (and against using them to make unwarranted comparisons between lesbians and heterosexual women). However, Haynes subsequently extrapolated from Bradford and Ryan's data (and the data of others) to suggest five general 'lifestyle' reasons why lesbians' risk might be higher than heterosexual women's: less likelihood of having children, higher alcoholism rate, higher body mass, fewer gynaecological exams and fewer breast cancer screenings. In broader epidemiological surveys, all of these factors have been shown statistically to be associated with higher rates of breast cancer. This extrapolation, in turn, appears to have led to the widespread, but unjustified, implication that lesbianism is itself a risk factor for developing breast cancer.

Prior to the media spate of 'scare stories' in the 1990s, it appears that the possibility of lesbians' greater susceptibility to breast cancer was first raised by O'Donnell *et al.* (1979) in relation to childless lesbians and was subsequently reiterated by Johnson *et al.* (1981) and Hepburn and Gutierrez (1988). Subsequent discussions have also focused on differences in breast health care between lesbians and heterosexual women: for example, it appears that lesbians are less likely to practise breast self-examination than are heterosexual women (Rankow, 1995; Ellingson and Yarber, 1997) and that they delay in seeking treatment (Trippet and Bain, 1992; White and Dull, 1997). Such differences would have implications for mortality (rather than morbidity) rates: if these findings are robust, then lesbians would be at greater risk of dying from breast cancer rather than of developing it in the first place because, in this case, breast cancer would not be detected – and therefore not treated – sufficiently early. Early treatment is a crucial factor in reducing the risk of breast cancer mortality (see Love with Lindsay, 1995).

Lesbians – particularly lesbian feminists – have been at the forefront of breast cancer activism, especially in the USA. Jackie Winnow, who died of breast cancer in 1991, described herself both as an AIDS activist and as a cancer activist. Indeed, she explicitly used the comparison between the (relatively small) number of women/lesbians with AIDS and the (relatively large) number of women/lesbians with breast cancer in campaigning for better resources and services for breast cancer survivors (Winnow, 1993). Winnow founded the Women's Cancer Resource Center in Berkeley, California, which, together with similar organizations in San Francisco, Boston, Washington and Chicago, was one of the first grassroots community cancer projects in the USA. Susan Love's work embodies a very different kind of activism: working within – rather than outside or against – the medical profession and the political establishment as an 'out' lesbian medical doctor and breast surgeon. Love's work has included writing an accessible handbook (Love with Lindsay, 1995) on breast cancer, in which heterosexuality is not assumed and lesbian experience is made visible; establishing a state-of-the-art breast cancer treatment program at a leading Oncology Center; co-founding the (US) National Breast Cancer Coalition (which co-ordinates the pressure-group activities of several hundred breast cancer organizations); and using the Coalition to advocate and campaign at government level for increased funding for breast cancer research and improved health care (see Kaufert, 1998).

A few lesbians – including feminists and cancer activists – have also written movingly about their personal experiences of breast cancer (see Lorde, 1985; Butler and Rosenblum, 1994; and the lesbian 'voices' included in the anthologies edited by Brady, 1991; Stocker, 1993; Kahane, 1995; Duncker and Wilson, 1996). Audre Lorde's *The Cancer Journals*, published in Britain in 1985, is perhaps the most widely-cited volume to span the personal and the political. Writing explicitly as a

Black lesbian feminist, Lorde's stated intentions are to break through the silence and isolation experienced by women with breast cancer and to encourage other women also to speak out and to act against all preventable cancers. Her – still radical – decision not to wear a prosthesis (artificial breast) to disguise her mastectomy and her early exposé of so-called breast 'reconstruction' are powerful statements against the 'false values' which control and subjugate women and the profit economy of the plastic surgery industry. Audre Lorde died of her cancer in 1992. Sandra Butler and Barbara Rosenblum's joint memoir, *Cancer in Two Voices* (1994), related their experiences of life with and Barbara's death from breast cancer from their perspective as a Jewish lesbian couple; the book is both a love story and a celebration of the strength of lesbian community. Their diary entries document Barbara's three-year struggle with breast cancer and how she was sustained and supported both by her central relationship with Sandra and by their circle of lesbian and gay friends, family and colleagues, who also supported Barbara after Sandra's death.

Apart from these autobiographical accounts, very little is known about lesbians' experiences of breast cancer. Although surveys of lesbian health may include the topic of breast cancer, it rarely merits more than a (closed) question or two, while (qualitative and quantitative) studies of breast cancer seldom explicitly include lesbians and almost none are explicitly lesbian-focused. I am currently conducting a small-scale study using focus groups and interviews to explore this neglected area. The study includes lesbians who have had a breast cancer diagnosis themselves and the partners, friends and families of those who have experienced breast cancer. It is designed, in some respects, to parallel a larger focus group study of heterosexual women's experiences of breast cancer (see Wilkinson, 1998, 1999, 2000a, 2000b, 2000c; Wilkinson and Kitzinger, 2000). Focus groups have been a popular method in the field of community health, including lesbian health (see Loevy and O'Brien, 1994; Stevens, 1996a; Chiu and Knight, 1999; Farquhar with Das, 1999; Mugglestone, 1999). The study is in its early stages and here I simply document some preliminary observations and highlight some of the issues the study has raised so far. First, as one might expect, in the context of facing a life-threatening illness, many of the issues raised by lesbians are very similar to those raised by heterosexual women. Lesbians with breast cancer are just as concerned as heterosexual women about whether they will live or die, how they will cope with their illness and what effects it will have on their lives and the lives of those around them. Matthews (1998) makes this point in relation to lesbians' experience of cancer more generally. The concerns of lesbians who attended her cancer support groups included: 'anxiety and depression following diagnosis; changes in self-perception and wellness; pressures to return to premorbid functioning; relationship issues; fear of coping with recurrence; mortality issues; treatment side-effects; uncertainty about the future; and coping with chronic illness and pain' (Matthews, 1998, p. 195).

However, there are also some important differences. Although lesbians with breast cancer may suffer just as much anxiety, fear, and pain as do heterosexual women, they do so in a context in which the *expectations* they face are very different. The literature on breast cancer is suffused with heterosexist assumptions (see Wilkinson and Kitzinger, 1993, for a feminist critique): women are assumed to be obsessed with their personal appearance and sexual attractiveness, to feel 'unfeminine' and unattractive to men after breast surgery and to want to look 'feminine' and attractive again as quickly as possible. Equally, lesbians (and older heterosexual women) are assumed *not* to care about their physical appearance and, it seems, are even told by some surgeons that they do not 'need' their breasts – presumably, because breasts are primarily for attracting men and for satisfying them sexually (and maybe occasionally for breastfeeding babies). As one focus group participant said, 'it's very easy for them to just whip it off and think it doesn't matter'. But, of course, lesbians' breasts also have a sexual role (and sometimes a maternal one too) and the appearance, touch and feel of breasts are often central to lesbians' sex lives, as many of my research participants emphasized: 'I really like my breasts a lot and I have a really erotic relationship to them'; 'I just love [my partner's] breasts and they do turn me on'; 'I think sexually my nipples are very sensitive; when that's the most exciting part of sex, I get so bloody turned on it can drive me up the wall'; 'I must say I think breasts are, you know, one of the most attractive parts of a woman's body'; 'I love my breasts'; 'they're erotic'. Not surprisingly, then, the loss of a breast was also described by many lesbians as 'devastating'. One lesbian who had had a mastectomy told me: 'I thought, "Well, you know, this is the end of life as I know it", and I actually, I sort of mourned for the loss of my breast...I was really very disturbed and distressed about it'. Another woman, whose lover had developed breast cancer, found it extremely difficult to come to terms with her lover's appearance after her mastectomy: 'I thought it was horrific what the body looks like without a breast...she looked like she'd been butchered...the fact she was flat-chested wasn't the issue, it's the scars'. Lesbians contemplating the possibility of mastectomy said 'I would just feel so mutilated'; 'it's something that is sexual'; 'in my sex life I would miss it'; 'it's not just your breasts, it's your whole body image – it's the way you feel about your body as a whole afterwards'. There was no suggestion at all that breasts are unimportant or irrelevant to lesbians or that the loss of a breast (or breasts) would be anything other than traumatic.

Another assumption faced by lesbians with breast cancer is that their partners will be supportive and empathetic, simply because they are women and that is how women are supposed to be (perhaps also because they too have the experience of having breasts). But many of my research participants explicitly countered this assumption (suggesting, for example, that factors such as age and personal health experiences are much more important in determining how partners respond). Others expressed the opinion that a woman may find it *harder* to cope with her female partner's breast cancer because it raises the possibility of the same thing happening to her, evoking her own vulnerability and mortality. Two participants spoke at length of partners who simply could not cope. One had a lover whose mother had died of breast cancer when she was eight, leaving her 'pathologically frightened' that she would develop breast cancer herself. This woman said that her lover had enlisted in various clinical trials to increase the level of professional monitoring of her breasts and described how her anxiety mounted to an 'almost pathological obsession' before every hospital visit:

> It's always, you know, 'You examine my breasts, can you feel anything?' And, er, we work ourselves up to it as the weeks go by, for probably, for about two months before the examination. And everything is, 'Do they look normal? Do they look normal?'

She described their relationship as 'very fraught'. The other participant whose lover could not cope had, in fact, broken off their relationship soon after her (the participant's) breast cancer diagnosis. Her lover had had a benign breast lump (described as 'a false alarm') removed shortly before the participant's own diagnosis. The lover was reportedly very shocked to encounter 'the real thing' and subjected the relationship to 'huge *sturm und drang*'. When the participant in my research found her own lump, her lover denied that it was suspicious ('"Don't be ridiculous, it's just your period, it will go away"'); reportedly accused her of using visits to the cancer specialist as a screen for an illicit affair; and 'had to leave the room to throw up' when the cancer was confirmed. Despite the fact that this research participant had supported her lover through a breast cancer 'false alarm', it seemed that her lover was completely unable to reciprocate this support.

These preliminary findings suggest how urgently lesbian-centred research is needed in order to challenge the heterosexist assumptions that pervade the diagnosis, treatment and subsequent support of women with breast cancer and to provide health services and support facilities that are better attuned to the specific needs and concerns of lesbians.

Towards the future

The breast cancer literature is not substantially different from most of the literature on women's health (see Wilkinson, 2000a). Feminists have critiqued mainstream health research for often using only male participants; for inappropriately generalizing findings from male participants to women; and for under-researching (at least until recently) health conditions which affect only, or predominantly, women (for example, Stanton and Gallant, 1995). In medical schools, the 'paradigm patient' is a 70–kilogram man and medical students learn how to treat his allergies, appendicitis, diahorrea and urinary problems, computing medication doses based on his weight (Tavris, 1992). When women's health is studied, it is likely to be the health of women who are (or who are assumed to be) middle-class, middle-aged, white, heterosexual, non-disabled women, with vaginas and ovaries; there has been little attention to diversity among women and its effects on their health (Dan, 1994; Chrisler and Hemstreet, 1995). For example, Kitzinger (2000) has recently pointed out that for women with Androgen Insensitivity Syndrome (born with XY chromosomes and testes) – many of whom are lesbian – no research has been done on health issues, including (but not limited to) breast cancer. It is highly unlikely that the hormone-based treatments routinely given to women with breast cancer would work in the same way for a woman who is insensitive to androgens. Lesbians (and other minorities) are generally either ignored or invisible – or, if studied at all, their health experiences are typically misunderstood or misrepresented. In addition, lesbian health has sometimes been subsumed under the rubric of 'lesbian and gay health', leading to a disproportionate focus on sexual health, particularly in relation to HIV/AIDS – which affects very few lesbians directly. This makes the separate focus on lesbian health issues and gay male health issues (see Chapter 8) in this text very welcome.

There is a need both to disaggregate 'lesbian and gay health' and to expand and diversify the study of women's health in order to identify the full range of health needs and concerns of a wide variety of lesbians. Both large and small-scale quantitative and qualitative research projects are necessary for the future development of the field. More attention needs to be given to operational definitions, sampling issues and methods of analyzing and reporting data. The task of developing a comprehensive and representative psychology of lesbian health has barely begun. The studies of cervical screening and breast cancer reported here are just a small step towards that goal.

References

ARNUP, K. (1995) *Lesbian Parenting: Living with Pride and Prejudice*. San Francisco, CA: Gynergy Books.

BAILEY, J.V., KAVANAGH, J., OWEN, C., McLEAN, K.A. and SKINNER, C.J. (2000) Lesbians and cervical screening. *British Journal of General Practice*, 50(455), 481–482.

BOSTON WOMEN'S HEALTH BOOK COLLECTIVE (1971) *Our Bodies, Ourselves*. Boston, MA: The Boston Women's Health Collective, Inc.

BRADFORD, J. and RYAN, C. (1988) *The National Lesbian Health Care Survey:*

Final Report. Washington, DC: National Lesbian and Gay Health Foundation.

BRADFORD, J., RYAN, C. and ROTHBLUM, E. (1994) The National Lesbian Health Care Survey: Implications for mental health care. *Journal of Consulting and Clinical Psychology, 62*, 228–242.

BRADY, J. (Ed.) (1991) *1 in 3: Women With Cancer Confront an Epidemic*. Pittsburgh, PA: Cleis Press.

BUENTING, J.A. (1992) Health life-styles of lesbian and heterosexual women. *Health Care for Women International, 13*, 165–171.

BURNS, J. (1992) The psychology of lesbian health care. In P. Nicolson and J. Ussher (Eds) *The Psychology of Women's Health Care*. Basingstoke: Macmillan.

BUTLER, S. and ROSENBLUM, B. (1994) *Cancer in Two Voices*. London: The Women's Press.

BYBEE, D. (1991) *The Michigan Lesbian Health Survey*. Lansing, MI: Michigan Organization for Human Rights.

CAMPBELL, K. (1993) One in three lesbians may get breast cancer, expert theorizes. *The Washington Blade, 2nd October*, 23–24.

CANCER RESEARCH CAMPAIGN (1990) *Factsheet 12: Cancer of the Cervix Uteri*. London: Cancer Research Campaign.

CHIU, L.-F. and KNIGHT, D. (1999) How useful are focus groups for obtaining the views of minority groups? In R.S. Barbour and J. Kitzinger (Eds) *Developing Focus Group Research: Politics, Theory and Practice*. London: Sage.

CHOMET, J. and CHOMET, J. (1989) *Smear Tests: Cervical Cancer, Its Prevention and Treatment*. London: Thorsons.

CHRISLER, J.C. and HEMSTREET, A.H. (1995) The diversity of women's health needs. In J.C. Chrisler and A.H. Hemstreet (Eds) *Variations on a Theme: Diversity and the Psychology of Women*. Albany, NY: State University of New York Press.

COCHRAN, S.D. and MAYS, V.M. (1988) Disclosure of sexual preference to physicians by black lesbian and bisexual women. *Western Journal of Medicine, 149*, 616–619.

DAN, A.J. (Ed.) (1994) *Reframing Women's Health: Multidisciplinary Research and Practice*. Thousand Oaks, CA: Sage.

DARDICK, L. and GRADY, K.E. (1980) Openness between gay persons and health professionals. *Annals of Internal Medicine, 93*, 115–119.

DAS, R. and FARQUHAR, C. (1996) Lesbians' conceptualisations of health and well-being. Paper presented at a conference on 'Teaching to Promote Women's Health', Women's College Hospital, University of Toronto, June.

DEEVY, S. (1990) Older lesbian women: An invisible minority. *Journal of Gerontological Nursing, 16*, 35–39.

DEPARTMENT OF HEALTH (1999) Cervical screening programme, England: 1997–98. Available on the world wide web from http://www.doh.gov.uk/public/cervscr.htm

DOUGLAS, C.A. (1993) The Mautner Project: Lesbians unite vs. cancer. *off our backs, March*, 12.

DOUGLAS, C.J., KALMAN, C.M. and KALMAN, T.P. (1985) Homophobia among physicians and nurses: An empirical study. *Hospital and Community Psychiatry, 36*, 1309–1311.

DUNCAN, I. (1992) *Guidelines for Clinical Practice and Programme Management*. Oxford: National Co-ordinating Network – National Cervical Screening Programme.

DUNCKER, P. and WILSON, V. (Eds) (1996) *Cancer Through the Eyes of Ten Women*. London: Pandora.

EDWARDS, A. and THIN, R.N. (1990) Sexually transmitted diseases in lesbians. *International Journal of STD and AIDS, 1*, 178–181.

ELIASON, M.J. (1998) Correlates of prejudice in nursing students. *Journal of Nursing Education, 37*, 27–29.

ELIASON, M.J. and RANDALL, C.E. (1991) Lesbian phobia in nursing students. *Western Journal of Nursing Research, 13*, 363–374.

ELLINGSON, L.A. and YARBER, W. (1997) Breast self-examination, the Health Belief Model, and sexual orientation in women. *Journal of Sex Education and Therapy, 22(3)*, 19–24.

FARQUHAR, C. (undated) 'Coming out' in sexual health care: An effective sexual health promotion strategy for lesbians? Unpublished MS.

FARQUHAR, C. with DAS, R. (1999) Are focus groups suitable for 'sensitive' topics? In R.S. Barbour and J. Kitzinger (Eds) *Developing Focus Group Research: Politics, Theory and Practice*. London: Sage.

FERRIS, D.G., BATISH, S., WRIGHT, T.C., CUSHING, C. and SCOTT, E.H. (1996) A neglected lesbian health concern: Cervical neoplasia. *The Journal of Family Practice, 43*, 581–584.

FISH, J. (1999) Sampling lesbians: How to get 1000 lesbians to complete a questionnaire. *Feminism & Psychology, 9*, 229–238.

FISH, J. (2000) Sampling issues in lesbian and gay psychology: Challenges in achieving diversity. *Lesbian & Gay Psychology Review, 1*, 32–38.

FISH, J. and WILKINSON, S. (2000a) Cervical screening. In J.M. Ussher (Ed.) *Women's Health: International Perspectives*. Leicester: BPS Books.

FISH, J. and WILKINSON, S. (2000b) Lesbians and cervical screening: Preliminary results from a UK survey of lesbian health. *Psychology of Women Section Review, 2*, 45–68.

GESSEN, M. (1993) Lesbians and breast cancer. *The Advocate, No. 62 (9th February)*, 45–48.

HAAS, A.P. (1994) Lesbian health issues: An overview. In A.J. Dan (Ed.) *Reframing Women's Health: Multidisciplinary Research and Practice*. Thousand Oaks, CA: Sage.

HAYNES, S. (1992) Are lesbians at high risk of breast cancer? Paper presented at the 14th National Gay and Lesbian Health Foundation Conference, Los Angeles, CA, 9–10 July.

HEPBURN, C. and GUTIERREZ, B. (1988) *Alive and Well: A Lesbian Health Guide*. Freedom, CA: The Crossing Press.

HULKA, B. (1982) Risk factors for cervical cancer. *Journal of Chronic Diseases, 35*, 3–11.

JOHNSON, S.R., GUENTHER, S.M., LAUBE, D.W. and KEETTEL, W.C. (1981) Factors influencing lesbian gynaecological care: A preliminary study. *American Journal of Obstetrics and Gynaecology, 140*, 20–28.

JOHNSON, S.R., SMITH, E.M. and GUENTHER, S.M. (1987) Comparison of gynaecologic health care problems between lesbians and bisexual women. *Journal of Reproductive Medicine, 32*, 198–200.

KAHANE, D.H. (Ed.) (1995) *No Less a Woman: Femininity, Sexuality and Breast Cancer*, 2nd ed. Alameda, CA: Hunter House.

KAUFERT, P.A. (1998) Women, resistance, and the breast cancer movement. In M. Lock and P.A. Kaufert (Eds) *Pragmatic Women and Body Politics*. Cambridge: Cambridge University Press.

KITZINGER, C. (2000) Women with Androgen Insensitivity Syndrome. In J.M. Ussher (Ed.) *Women's Health: International Perspectives*. Leicester: BPS Books.

LOEVY, S.S. and O'BRIEN, M.U. (1994) Community-based research: The case for focus groups. In A.J. Dan (Ed.) *Reframing Women's Health: Multidisciplinary Research and Practice*. Thousand Oaks, CA: Sage.

LORDE, A. (1985) *The Cancer Journals*. London: Sheba Feminist Publishers.

LOVE, S.M. with LINDSAY, K. (1995) *Dr Susan Love's Breast Book*, 2nd ed. Reading, MA: Addison-Wesley.

LUCAS, V.A. (1992) An investigation into the health care preferences of the lesbian population. *Health Care for Women International, 13*, 221–228.

MANTLE, J. (1998) *A Survey of Lesbian Health in Manchester: 1995–1998*. Manchester: Mancunian Health Promotion Specialist Service. [Available from: Mancunian Health Promotion Specialist Service, Withington Hospital, Nell Lane, West Didsbury, Manchester M20 2LR]

MATHEWS, W.C., BOOTH, M.W., TURNER, J.D. and KESSLER. L. (1986) Physicians' attitudes toward homosexuality: Survey of a California county medical society. *Western Journal of Medicine, 144*, 106–110.

MATTHEWS, A.K. (1998) Lesbians and support: Clinical issues for cancer patients. *Health Care for Women International, 19*, 193–203.

MAYS, V.M. and COCHRAN, S.D. (1988) The black women's relationship project: A national survey of black lesbians. In M. Shernoff and W. Scott (Eds) *The Sourcebook on Lesbian/Gay Health Care*. Washington, DC: National Gay and Lesbian Health Foundation.

McCLURE, R. and VESPRY, A. (Eds) (1994) *The Lesbian Health Guide*. Toronto: Queer Press.

McPHERSON, A. and AUSTOKER, J. (1995) Cervical cytology. In A. McPherson (Ed.) *Women's Problems in General Practice*. Oxford: Oxford University Press.

MORRIS, J. and ROTHBLUM, E. (1999) Who fills out a lesbian questionnaire? The interrelationship of sexual orientation, sexual experience with women, and participation in the lesbian community. *Psychology of Women Quarterly, 23*, 537–557.

MUGGLESTONE, J. (1999) *Report of the Bolton and Wigan Lesbian Health Needs Assessment*. Bolton: Bolton Specialist Health Promotion Service (Bolton NHS Trust Community Health Care). [Available from: Bolton Specialist Health Promotion Service, Lever Chambers Centre for Health, Ashburner Street, Bolton BL1 1SQ]

O'DONNELL, M., LEOFFLER, V., POLLOCK, K. and SAUNDERS, Z. (1979) *Lesbian Health Matters!* Santa Cruz, CA: Santa Cruz Women's Health Center.

O'HANLAN, K.A. (1996) Homophobia and the health psychology of lesbians. In P.M. Kato and T. Mann (Eds) *Handbook of Diversity Issues in Health Psychology*. New York: Plenum Press.

O'SULLIVAN, S. and PARMAR, P. (1992) *Lesbians Talk Safer Sex*. London: Scarlet Press.

PETERSON, K.J. and BRICKER, J.M. (1996) Lesbians and the health care system. In K.J. Peterson (Ed.) *Health Care for Lesbians and Gay Men: Confronting Homophobia and Heterosexism*. New York: Harrington Park Press.

PLUMB, M. (1997) *Statement of the Gay and Lesbian Medical Association to the Institute of Medicine Committee on Lesbian Health Research Priorities Regarding Community Perspective*. Washington, DC: Gay and Lesbian Medical Association.

PONTICELLI, C.M. (Ed.) (1988) Gateways to improving lesbian health and health care. Special Issue of *The Journal of Lesbian Studies, 2(1)*.

PRICE, J.H., EASTON, A.N., TELLJOHANN, S.K. and WALLACE, P.B. (1996) Perceptions of cervical cancer and pap smear screening behavior by women's sexual orientation. *Journal of Community Health, 21(2)*, 89–105.

RANDALL, C.E. (1989) Lesbian phobia among BSN educators: A survey. *Journal of Nursing Education, 28*, 302–306.

RANKOW, E.J. (1995) Breast and cervical cancer among lesbians. *Women's Health Issues, 5(3)*, 123–129.

RANKOW, E. and TESSARO, I. (1998) Cervical cancer risk and papanicolaou screening in a sample of lesbian and bisexual women. *Journal of Family Practice, 47*, 139–143.

ROBERTS, S.J., PATSDAUGHTER, C.A., GRINDEL, C.G. and TARMINA, M.S. (1997–8) *Boston Lesbian Health Project*. Boston, MA: Northeastern University.

ROSSER, S. (1993) Overlooked or subsumed: Research on lesbian health and health care. *National Women's Studies Association Journal, 5(2)*, 183–203.

SAFFRON, L. (1994) *Challenging Conceptions: Planning a Family by Self-Insemination*. London: Cassell.

SAPHIRA, M. and GLOVER, M. (1999) *National Lesbian Health Survey*. Auckland: Papers Inc.

SAUNDERS, J.M., TUPAC, J.D., and MacCULLOCH, D. (1988) *A Lesbian Profile: A Survey of 1000 Lesbians*. West Hollywood, CA: Southern California Women for Understanding.

SCHWANBERG, S.L. (1996) Health care professionals' attitudes toward lesbian women and gay men. *Journal of Homosexuality, 31(3)*, 71–83.

SELVIN, B. (1993) One in three lesbians risks death from breast cancer. *The Guardian, 6th February*, 11.

SHADY (1996) *Final report of the Research on the Sexual Health Needs of Lesbians, Bisexuals and Women Who Have Sex With Women in Merseyside*. Liverpool: SHADY. [Available from: SHADY, MASG PO Box 11, Liverpool L69 1SN]

SHEFFIELD HEALTH STEERING GROUP (1996) *Lesbian Health Needs Assessment*. Sheffield: Department of Health Promotion. [Available from: Department of Health Promotion, 5, Old Fulwood Road, Sheffield, S10 3TG]

SIMKIN, R. (1993) Unique health concerns of lesbians. *Canadian Journal of Obstetrics/Gynaecology and Women's Health Care, 5*, 516–522.

SINGLETON. V. and MICHAEL, M. (1993) Actor networks and ambivalence: General practitioners in the UK cervical screening programme. *Social Studies of Science, 23*, 227–264.

SMEDMAN, L. and TRYGGVASON, N.K. (1998) Dykes in danger. *Girlfriends (Special Breast Cancer Issue), October*, 23 and 42.

SMITH, E.M., JOHNSON, S.R. and GUENTHER, S.M. (1985) Health care attitudes and experiences during gynaecological care among lesbians and bisexuals. *American Journal of Public Health, 75*, 1085–1087.

SOLARZ, A.L. (Ed.) (1999) *Lesbian Health: Current Assessment and Directions for the Future*. Washington, DC: National Academy Press.

STANTON, A.L. and GALLANT, S.J. (Eds) (1995) *The Psychology of Women's Health*. Washington, DC: American Psychological Association.

STERN, P.N. (Ed.) (1992) Lesbian health: What are the issues? Special Issue of *Health Care for Women International, 13(2)*.

STEVENS, P.E. (1992) Lesbian health care research: A review of literature from 1970 to 1990. *Health Care for Women International, 13*, 91–120.

STEVENS, P.E. (1996a) Focus groups: Collecting aggregate-level data to understand community health phenomena. *Public Health Nursing, 13(3),* 170–176.

STEVENS, P.E. (1996b) Lesbians and doctors: Experiences of solidarity and domination in health care settings. *Gender & Society, 10,* 24–41.

STEVENS, P.E. and HALL, J.M. (1988) Stigma, health beliefs and experiences with health care in lesbian women. *Image: Journal of Nursing Scholarship, 20,* 69–73.

STOCKER, M. (Ed.) (1993) *Confronting Cancer, Constructing Change: New Perspectives on Women and Cancer.* Chicago, IL: Third Side Press.

SZAREWSKI, A. (1994) *A Women's Guide to the Cervical Smear Test.* London: Optima.

TAVRIS, C. (1992) *The Mismeasure of Woman.* New York: Touchstone/Simon and Schuster.

TRIPPET, S.E. and BAIN, J. (1992) Reasons American lesbians fail to seek traditional health care. *Health Care for Women International, 13,* 145–153.

WALSH, C., KAY, E. and LEADER, M. (1995) The pathology of cervical cancer. *Journal of Obstetrics and Gynaecology, 38,* 653–661.

WHITE, J.C. and DULL, V.T. (1997) Health risk factors and health-seeking behavior in lesbians. *Journal of Women's Health, 6,* 103–112.

WHITE, J. and MARTINEZ, M.C. (Eds) (1997) *The Lesbian Health Book: Caring for Ourselves.* Seattle, WA: Seal Press.

WILKINSON, S. (1998) Focus groups in health research: Exploring the meanings of health and illness. *Journal of Health Psychology, 3,* 329–348.

WILKINSON, S. (1999) Focus groups: A feminist method. *Psychology of Women Quarterly, 23,* 221–244.

WILKINSON, S. (2000a) Feminist research traditions in health psychology: Breast cancer research. *Journal of Health Psychology, 5,* 353–366.

WILKINSON, S. (2000b) Breast cancer: A feminist perspective. In J.M. Ussher (Ed.) *Women's Health: International Perspectives.* Leicester: BPS Books.

WILKINSON, S. (2000c) Women with breast cancer talking causes: Comparing content, biographical and discursive analyses. *Feminism & Psychology, 10,* 431–460.

WILKINSON, S. and KITZINGER, C. (1993) Whose breast is it anyway? A feminist consideration of advice and 'treatment' for breast cancer. *Women's Studies International Forum, 16,* 229–238.

WILKINSON, S. and KITZINGER, C. (2000) Thinking differently about thinking positive: A discursive approach to cancer patients' talk. *Social Science & Medicine, 50,* 797–811.

WILTON, T. (1997) *Good For You: A Handbook of Lesbian Health and Wellbeing.* London: Cassell.

WINNOW, J. (1993) The politics of cancer. In M. Stocker (Ed.) *Confronting Cancer, Constructing Change: New Perspectives on Women and Cancer.* Chicago, IL: Third Side Press.

YADLON, S. (1997) Skinny women and good mothers: The rhetoric of risk, control and culpability in the production of knowledge about breast cancer. *Feminist Studies, 23,* 645–677.

ZEIDENSTEIN, L. (1990) Gynecological and childbearing needs of lesbians. *Journal of Nurse-Midwifery, 35(1),* 10–18.

Chapter 8

Gay Men's Physical and Emotional Well-being: Re-orienting Research and Health Promotion

Ian Warwick and Peter Aggleton

A vast amount of nonsensical research continues to be conducted into 'the gay lifestyle' by people who would presumably scoff at the notion that all heterosexuals share an identical way of life. In reality, gay men experience sex in as many ways as everyone else, ways which change over time...It must be recognised that bad research conducted by social scientists causes real harm, both by delaying the implementation of the type of work that leads to more effective social policies, and more simply, by squandering precious resources, human and financial.
(Watney, 1991, cited in Watney, 1994, p. 239)

Towards the end of the 1970s, in parts of Europe and the USA, it might have seemed as if there was never a better time to be gay. Arising from the momentum that had been created over the last century by various progressive social and political (and scientific) campaigns, movements and organizations (including feminism and 'gay liberation') (see Chapter 1 in this volume), new and more positive images of gay men were being created. Taboos against public displays of same sex affection were to some extent breaking down and, with the growing commercialization of gay culture and the idea of a per-fectible masculine body, 'straight-looking' and 'straight-acting' gay men gave one kind of legitimacy to a new type of homosexual (but see Gary Taylor's critical analysis of some of these processes in Chapter 9). This new more *macho* style challenged heterosexuals – and probably some gay men too – to consider that perhaps 'homosexual' did not necessarily mean 'ineffectual' after all.

It was not only appearances that were being re-made. Gay men's emotions and indeed their very souls were also the objects of scrutiny in projects of reformation. Self-help manuals sought to inform and educate gay men about the ways in which they might best live their lives. Self-esteem was to be raised, coming out performed well and friendships made and sustained (see, for example, Sanderson, 1986). To assist them with these endeavours, calls were made and guidelines offered for the development of a (lesbian and) gay 'affirmative' form of therapy (see Chapter 10). A new gay affirmative religiosity was also taking hold (for example, see Perry and Lucas, 1987; Balka and Rose, 1989). By acting as 'prophets of a sex positive truth', Uhrig (1986) suggested that gay men could become a 'source of human healing and a place of divine revelation' (p. 9).

The Joy of Gay Sex (Silverstein and White, 1977) was, for many men, a guide to ideas and practices associated with this new lust for a lifestyle. Matters of the physical body were addressed alongside those of a more emotional and social nature. Replete with fuzzy pencil drawings conjuring up images as much of romance as of raunch, this 'intimate guide' for gay men introduced readers to 'the pleasures of a gay lifestyle'. From bars to blow-jobs, from crabs to cruising, from jealousy to jerk-off buddies, from mental health to money matters, here, in easy-to-read prose, were the essentials of a new way of living. Perhaps the most startling thing about the book, given its publication over 20 years ago, was its breadth of coverage and the matter-of-fact way it engaged with topics such as venereal and other diseases, as well as tenderness and self-esteem – issues which many today can find difficult to discuss.

Of course, the practicality, evangelism and gay positivity that characterized the 1970s and early 1980s arose in reaction to earlier portrayals of 'homosexuality' as sin, crime and sickness (Stevens, 1992; Morgan and Nerison, 1993). From the 13th and 14th century onwards and throughout much of the Western world, Judaeo-Christian philosophy encouraged an understanding of 'homosexuality' as both chosen and sinful (see King and Bartlett, 1999). This perspective in turn informed medical and early sexological understandings of same sex relationships (the pathologization of gay sexuality is examined in more detail from an historical perspective in Chapter 9). Once homosexuality had been constituted as a symptom rather than a pathological entity in and of itself, the authority of the scientific gaze and its attendant methods for revealing truth could be brought to bear in discovering its causes (see Foucault, 1979).

The biomedical, the psychological and their consequences

Wherever in the scientific mind there is cause and negative effect, there will also be 'treatments' that seek to break this link. In the field of medicine and with respect to male homosexuality, these interventions have included cold baths, castration and lobotomy. Psychological treatments for homosexuality have included hypnosis, electroshock and psycho-analysis, as well as abstinence training and conditioning through aversion therapy (Morgan and Nerison, 1993). The aspirations of the 'psy professionals' (Rose, 1999) were not realized in the results they achieved. Indeed, in retrospect, such interventions can be seen as not simply ineffective but positively harmful, not infrequently resulting in depression, psychosis and death (Morgan and Nerison, 1993; King and Bartlett, 1999).

Lack of effectiveness was not, however, the main reason why these practices became less common. Inter-disciplinary rivalry between psychoanalysts and behaviourists led to heated arguments about which methods were most effective in excising homosexual desire. However, as therapists argued about how best to understand the phenomena they claimed to be able to treat, their authority for doing so was also challenged by those to whom they owed a profes-sional and ethical responsibility – namely, gay men themselves. In 1970, gay activists disrupted the American Psychiatric Association's (APA) meetings to demand that psychiatry develop a more positive stance towards homosexuality and, by the end of 1973, the APA had voted to remove homosexuality from the *Diagnostic and Statistical Manual of Mental Disorders*, so ending the classification of homosex-uality as a psychiatric illness in the USA (Morgan and Nerison, 1993). In the UK, however, psychiatrists generally follow the *International Classification of Diseases* and homosexuality was not removed as a disorder from this glossary until the production of the fourth edition in 1992.

It is important to recognize that these earlier ways of thinking equated sexual health not with the joy of sex nor with the security of loving relationships but with the absence of all things negative – health being here understood not as a resource for everyday living but as the absence of disease (see Katz and Peberdy, 1992). Through largely bio-medical interventions, the causes of disease were to be detected and malfunctions treated with drugs or removed from the body. Far from being a neutral activity, this 'curative, individualistic and interventionist' approach turned people into patients, objectified them and denied 'their status as social beings' (Doyal and Pennell, 1979, p. 30).

By the early 1980s, a number of new influences came to affect the construction of and responses to male homosexuality. In both Britain and North America – and under the influence of New Right political agendas – major cultural and political shifts were under way. What many had hitherto seen as intensely private matters were now brought into public view. Anti-gay crusades in the USA were watched ner-vously from the UK where the gay liberation movement had more or less exhausted itself (see Weeks, 2000). Under Ronald Reagan and

Margaret Thatcher, both US and UK Governments aspired to roll back the state, cut spending on health and education and bolster what were promoted as 'traditional' forms of family life. Gay men and lesbians became easy targets for victimization and vilification. Yet paradoxically and in these same countries, the 1980s also saw the emergence of new social and sexual networks, helped by the growth of commercial gay venues and a burgeoning gay press. And there was, of course, a new illness among gay men, most noticeably in the USA, the nature and origins of which baffled scientists.

From gay men's health to AIDS

As with homosexuality, a number of social forces colluded to construct the 'problem' of AIDS. From the earliest days, it was organized linguistically via the languages of medicine and stigma (Plummer, 1988). The medical model claimed AIDS as an organic problem of individual bodies. Knowledge about it was to be accrued through scientific methods, the causes of the problem were to be explained in terms of germ theory and its management achieved through clinical practice. Stigma-based models, on the other hand, focused more on lifestyles, with AIDS being conceptualized as a moral, political or theological problem. Here, knowledge of the condition was constructed in relation to evil, sin and individual choice and responsibility. Management of AIDS was to be achieved chiefly through processes of segregation, discrimination and exclusion.

However, even before the logics of bio-medicine, public health and stigma took hold and most certainly before a viral cause for AIDS had been identified, gay men had invented safer sex (Callen, 1983) and had initiated what might now be called peer-led education (Patton, 1987; Scott, 1997). Perhaps one of the reasons why safer sex education became so popular among gay men was its development within and from existing community networks (Altman, 1986; King, 1993; Scott, 1997). As King (1993) notes:

> The peer endorsement of safer sex, reinforced by educational interventions by groups recognised as part of that community and by the gay press, played a key role in helping gay men put factual information about safer sex into practice. Contrary to popular wisdom, this unprecedented mass behaviour change owed little or nothing to the actions of governments or others outside the gay community, or to HIV-antibody testing, or to the application of theory-based health educational models. (p. 75)

By way of contrast, official versions of events most usually promote the idea that government and public health departments 'acted rationally, on the best medical and epidemiological advice' to secure these changes (Scott, 1997, p. 308). This downplays the role of self-help among gay men, discounts the fact that gay men's needs were largely ignored by governments and public HIV prevention agencies – in the early days at least – and fails to recognize the political obstacles put in the way of safer sex education (Scott, 1997). In essence, AIDS was from the start 'de-gayed' (King, 1993) – the active involvement and participation of gay men (the people most affected by AIDS in the industrialized West) being of little importance to professional understandings of what the problem was or how its impact could be ameliorated.

While initial responses to AIDS emerged from within the communities most affected, as national authorities began to respond, resources became available to buy technology, to fund health education and to pay for staff. Welcome as this no doubt was, by 1987 authors were already warning against the 'creeping professionalisation' (Aggleton and Homans, 1987, p. 32) of those working to combat AIDS. Patton (1989) went further to describe the construction of an AIDS industry with its attendant 'experts', 'volunteers' and 'victims'. These processes imbued the field with a degree of respectability, a 'scientific' evidence base and services geared to the needs of users, clients and patients – all supposedly undertaken with objectivity by a relatively autonomous workforce.

In retrospect, however, the problem of AIDS was dealt with in much the same way as the problem of homosexuality. The expert medical gaze and rational-legal authority came to replace the action-oriented response of the individuals concerned and the communities most affected. Of course, public health's involvement was not uninformed. Its actions were guided by theories of a kind – importantly not those of education, self-empowerment or social change but rather those which emphasized the importance of rationality, communication and individual behaviour change (Aggleton, 1996). Behind these theories were epistemological assumptions about how best to generate knowledge and what was ultimately to count as 'truth'.

A very positivist endeavour

Kitzinger (1997) – among others – has highlighted the extent to which lesbian and gay psychology has adopted a positivist-empiricist and individualistic stance. While critical of such an approach, she highlights the authority inherent in such a position, its contribution to processes of professionalization, and its capacity to mystify:

> From the perspective of critical psychology, this adherence to mainstream values accounts not only for the notable successes of lesbian and gay psychology, but also for its notable failures. In pursuit of short-term gains, it reinforces the power of psychology as an oppressive institution, doing little more than tinkering with diagnostic criteria but leaving

intact the whole rotten apparatus of diagnosis, control and domination. (p. 216)

More generally, one of the key features of professional practice is the fact that it is guided by a body of technical or specialist knowledge beyond the reach of lay people (Hoyle and John, 1995). Only specific forms of knowledge count in this respect, with special emphasis being given to those forms of understanding constructed and made valid through scientific method. The authority of positivism has therefore been stamped on research both within the fields of homosexuality and HIV/AIDS, leading human beings and science to be neatly aligned (see also Patton, 1990).

This process has not occurred because contrasting ideas about research and HIV-related health promotion were simply unavailable. In fact, the first official guidance on HIV/AIDS-related health promotion in the UK contrasted *four different* models of, or approaches to, education about AIDS (Aggleton and Homans, 1987). Prepared for the then National Health Service Training Authority, this review stressed the importance of taking into account people's lay beliefs about health and illness, HIV and AIDS. It also offered a critique of behaviour change models of health education, highlighting the advantages and disadvantages of self-empowerment and community oriented models and outlining a more social transformatory model of AIDS education. This latter model argued for the need to de-mystify medical knowledge, promote individual and social rights and address stigma. Other writers at the time, most notably Simon Watney (1989), also argued for the importance of building on the indigenous AIDS-related meanings and practices current among gay men.

Growing professionalization

Somewhat paradoxically, and in the UK at least, the growing professionalization of AIDS work has provided new opportunities for gay men, sometimes employed not because of their expertise in health education or promotion but because of their gay identity (Deverell, 1997). The assumed familiarity of these workers with gay culture and gay community was intended to ensure that projects and interventions were more securely rooted in felt or expressed needs. However, as Oppenheimer (1997) has noted, the early activism which marked gay men's responses to AIDS decreased significantly as greater access was gained to public health and mainstream political processes. In retrospect, it seems clear that the intensely personal experiences that many gay workers brought to their jobs failed to provide the breadth of vision necessary to ensure that HIV-related prevention remained relevant and appropriate to diverse groups of homosexually-active men. Still less did such work lead to a more developed appreciation of what health promotion among gay men might be like – engaging with a broader set of physical health issues and mental health concerns.

In retrospect, it is possible to see how professional boundaries, failure to address the often homophobic assumptions of employing authorities and lack of training in project planning and management impacted negatively on the ability of many health promotion workers to build upon the meanings and practices of communities of gay men themselves. While there was often encouragement to carry out needs assessments, for example, those working in the health service and in voluntary groups tended to fall back on common sense and traditionally 'scientific' understandings of what had to be done – such as the analysis of responses to questionnaires consisting of narrow and relatively closed questions (Warwick *et al.*, 1995). A significant opportunity for expanding an understanding of gay men's health needs was thereby lost.

A further difficulty arose from the lack of accountability between the health service 'purchasers' of prevention services and the client groups whose interests they often claimed to represent. Despite the promise of evidence-based approaches to health promotion (popular in Britain throughout the 1990s) which putatively aimed to ground practice in the researched needs of populations, the popularity of these approaches has perhaps been more closely linked to the rationing of resources and issues of control (see Harrison, 1998) than providing what was needed. Meanwhile, the actions of health and local authorities have continued to be policed by the vitriolic and homophobic 'rampant sensationalism of the mass media' (Watney, 1992, cited in Watney, 1994, p. 254).

Throughout the 1980s and 1990s, therefore, a number of factors aligned gay men's health more or less exclusively with HIV and AIDS. The language of bio-medicine and stigma linked homosexuality to AIDS and reinforced the belief that health equates to the absence of pathology. Rather than seeking to reinforce protective factors in gay men's lives, interventions therefore sought to eliminate risk factors and the causes of HIV transmission. The authority of positivism inhibited forms of enquiry that could generate new understandings of gay men's lives and the importance of context, culture and community within these. The belief that health promotion equated to individual behaviour change downplayed the importance of complementary actions in the field of public policy which were needed to achieve health gain. Finally, the professionalization of HIV prevention patronized gay men's activism and community-based organizing, bringing it under institutional control. Resources henceforth were to be directed towards HIV and AIDS prevention rather than sexual, or HIV-related, health promotion. As a result, the broader health needs of gay and other homosexually-active men have come to be marginalized and/or ignored.

Some broader considerations

There is clear evidence that physicians and other health care workers not infrequently express discomfort and anxiety when providing care to lesbians and gay men (American Medical Association Council on Scientific Affairs, 1996; see also Chapter 7). This can discourage gay and bisexual men from attending primary health care services, resulting in significant mental and physical morbidity (Robertson, 1998; King and Bartlett, 1999; Ungvarski and Grossman, 1999).

The lack of attention paid to the needs of gay men, both in research and practice, is well documented. For example, marriage and family therapy may have much to offer gay men by providing opportunities to discuss dyadic relationships and how best to address the disclosure of homosexuality in a family, as well as parenting issues (see Chapter 11). Yet in a twenty year period, just 0.006 per cent of articles in marriage and family therapy journals focused on gay, bisexual or lesbian issues (Clark and Serovich, 1997). More generally, up to one third of mental health professionals in a recent review were reported as holding negative attitudes towards lesbians and gay men (cited in Morgan and Nerison, 1993; see also Garnets *et al.*, 1991; Proctor, 1994; Annesley and Coyle, 1995, 1998; Golding, 1997; McFarlane, 1998; Milton and Coyle, 1998). There is an urgent need, therefore, for professionals to examine all aspects of their practice, from initial assessment through to service provision and from advocacy for gay men to the training of colleagues (Faria, 1997). Unhelpfully, there remains too little teaching about sexuality on training courses for health and other professionals (Harrison and Silenzio, 1996; Coyle *et al.*, 1999). While new texts and approaches are being developed (see, for example, Wilton 2000), what should by now be commonsense is still presented as exceptional.

Beyond the issues already highlighted, gay men can face violence and intimidation in their everyday lives, and this can be a particular problem for younger gay men (Warwick *et al.*, 2000). In conjunction with such violence, feeling bad about one's own sexuality – or 'internalized homophobia' as some authors term it (see Williamson, 2000, for a critical review) – appears to contribute to elevated rates of suicidal ideation and completed suicide, particularly among young gay men (Warwick *et al.*, 2000) and gay men from Black and minority ethnic communities (Harrison and Silenzio, 1996). There is also some evidence to suggest that gay men may be more dissatisfied with their bodies than heterosexual men, leading to eating disorders (Harrison and Silenzio, 1996), especially bulimia nervosa (Carlat *et al.*, 1997) and occasionally the misuse of steroids (Dillon *et al.*, 1999).

In the USA, substance misuse among lesbians and gay men is said to range from 28 per cent to 35 per cent, compared with 10 per cent to 12 per cent among sampled heterosexual populations (American Medical Association Council on Scientific Affairs, 1996). Ungvarski and Grossman (1999) suggest that gay men appear to be at increased risk for lung and heart disease and cite studies that estimate rates of smoking among gay men to be 35 per cent, compared to 27 per cent of men in the general population. There is some debate whether the misuse of alcohol is higher among gay men when compared to heterosexual men, although alcohol use among gay men does not appear to reduce with age as it does with heterosexual men (Bickelhaupt, 1995; Bergmark, 1999). In a review of incidence studies, it was suggested that 20–30 per cent of gay men and lesbians may have problems with alcohol use (Bickelhaupt, 1995). Concern about alcoholism among gay men has led to the setting up of specialized forms of support, including special interest groups of Alcoholics Anonymous (Kus and Latcovich, 1995).

While care should be taken in extrapolating from research on the problematic use of alcohol and other recreational drugs – as some authors have noted that samples of lesbians and gay men tend to be drawn from commercial venues such as bars and clubs where a higher prevalence of substance use might be expected (American Medical Association Council on Scientific Affairs, 1996) – the fact that such high levels of tobacco and alcohol use are reported is a subject for concern.

While some studies, especially in the USA, have linked drug and substance use to the practice of unsafe sex ('unsafe' in the sense of there being a possibility of transmission of HIV: see, for example, American Medical Association Council on Scientific Affairs, 1996; Stall *et al.*, 1999; Ryan *et al.*, 2000), studies conducted in other countries have suggested that those gay men who have consumed alcohol are no more likely to have unsafe sex than those who have not consumed it (Weatherburn *et al.*, 1993). Ultimately, sexual practices seem to be influenced by the type of substance use, the meanings attached to substance use and the context within which it occurs. Even if 35 per cent of lesbians and gay men do occasionally use recreational drugs, many may do so functionally with minimal negative impact on their personal and professional lives. Nevertheless, where there are drug-related problems, gay men should feel able to access treatment and other services without concerns about discrimination related to their sexuality.

While we have already noted that young gay men may have specific mental health issues, other groups of gay men are also reported to be more vulnerable to mental health problems. In particular, there is a concern that gay men from minority ethnic groups – particularly African-Caribbean gay men – have higher reported levels of depressive distress than their gay white or heterosexual black peers (Cochran and Mays, 1994). Gay male members of minority ethnic groups must manage both racism and heterosexism. While families can be sources of support in relation to ethnic background, they can be unsupportive and indeed discriminatory when required to address issues related to sexual orientation. And while lesbian and gay communities can provide support in relation to sexual orientation, being dominantly culturally white, they may be as implicated in racism as white heterosexual people (Greene, 1994).

Many more gay men – and at an earlier age than might otherwise be expected – are facing bereavement through the deaths of partners from AIDS-related illnesses. This can be especially distressing when the couple are not 'out' to others about their sexuality (Seabold, 1997). Neither colleagues at work nor family members may know of the bereavement, leaving the surviving partner without adequate forms of support (Wright and Coyle, 1996), possibly contributing to a traumatic stress reaction (Shernoff, 1997). Even where informal sources of support are available, gay 'widowers' may need assistance from mental health or other professionals. This, again, highlights the importance of gay men feeling able to access psychological and mental health services. Specialized community-based bereavement groups for gay men have indeed been set up. The future challenge for them is to ensure that they provide support to men other than those who have lost a partner due to an AIDS-related illness (Shernoff, 1997).

Income and social status appear to be among the most important determinants of health (Department of Health, 1999). While it is often popularly believed that all gay men are middle class or have above average income, this is challenged by a major survey conducted in the USA which suggests that both gay men's personal and mean household incomes are lower than those of heterosexual men (cited in Ryan *et al.*, 2000). Notwithstanding the difficulties associated with measuring class, it appears that lower social class has been associated with a higher incidence of HIV and higher rates of unprotected anal intercourse in France, Germany and the UK (Bochow, 2000). Protection against homophobic discrimination in employment or – especially for younger people – in educational settings, has been called for (Douglas *et al.*, 1997; Ryan *et al.*, 2000).

Much current insight into the health problems and needs of gay and other homosexually-active men derives from studies conducted in the USA and, currently, little is known about the specific health promotion needs of gay men in the UK. Of particular concern is the absence of other than largely anecdotal data on mental health and emotional well-being. Qualitative information from well-designed studies is badly needed to help dispel popular myths about homosexual men leading unhappy lives and to shed light on the mental health problems that do exist. Furthermore, both quantitative data and qualitative information are needed to guide the development of new forms of service provision which are being adopted by HIV/AIDS agencies as they broaden out their work from HIV prevention to gay men's health promotion.

A way forward

In this chapter, we have tried to highlight a number of what might be termed 'disorienting tendencies' in contemporary work with gay and other homosexually-active men. First, and in common with many other fields, there has been a tendency to view health negatively, as the absence of pathology and disease, rather than more positively as an affirmative state of being – a palpable presence characterized by qualities such as wholeness and well-being. Second, and perhaps not unrelated to the above, positivist assumptions as opposed to those placing greater emphasis on subjective perceptions and felt needs have achieved pre-eminence in health promotion and research. This has meant something of an under-emphasis upon those realms of gay men's experience that are not amenable to 'capture' and 'explanation' by way of methods associated with positivist understandings of science. Issues of stigma (both felt and enacted), discrimination and subjective well-being have been downplayed in favour of those more amenable to rapid diagnosis – for example, sexually transmitted infections and serious mental illness. Third, there has been a clear tendency over the past two decades to link understanding of gay men's needs to issues of HIV and AIDS. This elision has, in our view, reinforced stigma and discrimination – both against those living with HIV disease and those who are gay. It has, moreover, enabled a substantial part of the population to deny that HIV/AIDS has personal relevance to them, with serious and as yet unrealized consequences. Finally, professional practice with gay men in the domain of HIV/AIDS has, we believe, focused too much on 'risk groups' and 'risk behaviours' and on 'relapse' and 'recidivism'. There has been a corresponding under-emphasis on eroticism and sex as it is lived – the joys of sex and the joys of life – and on the contextuality of sexual practice and desire. Given these tendencies, it is perhaps timely to consider what actions can be taken to re-orient health promotion work with and for gay men.

A framework for understanding

As a number of authors have pointed out, health promotion properly involves complementary and commensurate activities at a number of levels. The Ottawa Charter for Health Promotion, for example, identifies five key areas for work: the building of healthy public policy, the creation of supportive environments, the development of personal skills through information and education, the strengthening of community action and the re-orientation of health services towards prevention and health promotion (World Health Organization *et al.*, 1986). The subsequent Jakarta Declaration points to five key principles of health promotion, i.e., promoting social responsibility for health, increasing investment for health development, consolidating and expanding partnerships for health, increasing community capacity and empowering individuals and securing an infrastructure for health promotion (World Health Organization and Ministry of Health, Republic of Indonesia, 1997). While there is some evidence of these principles influencing work in HIV education and prevention (Peterson and Carballo-Diéguez, 2000; Ross and Kelly, 2000), there is little evidence as yet of their acceptance more generally in relation to gay men's health.

A necessary broadening of perspective

Just as there are complementary areas of action for health promotion, so are there corresponding domains of analysis in research (Sapsford, 1998). Professionals working in each field need to consider how best to coordinate their efforts to promote gay men's health in a rather more holistic way than has hitherto been the case. Future research should, in our view, aim to move beyond the individual to address interpersonal, group, community, organizational and societal issues and concerns. The overall social context within which gay men live their lives, the setting within which particular health risks emerge, the situated activities in which individuals engage both with other gay men and with others, as well as self understanding, are all worthy of closer scrutiny, both synchronically and diachronically (Cohen and Hubert, 1997; Wright, 1998).

From the pathogenic to the salutory

A pathogenic orientation has suffused much Western medical thinking and has tended to influence those working in health to view what they do as either curative or preventive (Antonovsky, 1996). This has led to an undue focus on the elimination or reduction of pathogens and risk factors. Far better, Antonovsky (1996) argues, is a re-orientation of work towards a consideration of salutary or health promoting factors. Adopting such a perspective might enable not only the identification of influences which help people move towards health but might help those working in health promotion to develop a distinct area of expertise and authority (albeit in partnership with curative and preventive medicine) with a clear focus on health-producing rather than health destructive factors (Bennett and Murphy, 1997; Frochlich and Potvin, 1999).

For example, social policy has a major impact on constituting heterosexuality as both 'natural' and a 'normal set of relations' (Carabine, 1997, p. 58). Much more could be done to protect men and women from homophobic discrimination in, among other settings, the workplace and schools. As noted, the environments in which gay men find themselves can be particularly challenging, whether these be associated with work, with leisure or with family life. The bar and club cultures within which many gay men feel safe to socialize may have contradictory elements with regard to gay men's physical and emotional well-being (Rofes, 1998). On the one hand they can provide opportunities for social support, while on the other hand – as we noted earlier – they can contribute to problematic levels of alcohol, tobacco and other drug use (Kus and Smith, 1995). There may be much to learn from initiatives in health promotion that have looked to create 'healthy settings'. Although these initiatives have focused on cities, workplaces, schools, hospitals and prisons, there is little to prevent those concerned with gay men's health working to identify how best – in partnership with managers of gay commercial venues – to improve the overall well-being of customers and workers within them.

There is not and never has been one single gay community. Like heterosexuals, gay men's relationships are structured by, at least, class, ethnicity and age. The ways in which degrees of solidarity and social support are achieved within and across these areas needs to be identified and built upon. Furthermore, despite gay men in general facing discrimination, what is it that enables some men not only to cope with this but also to enhance their life-skills in the process? Identifying the interpersonal and individual factors that act as protective agents may enable service providers to re-orient what they do so as to assist gay men in exercising greater control over their environments.

Changing dominant understandings of gay men

Efforts are also needed to help change the perceptions people hold about gay men. Overcoming a long history of prejudice and discrimination will, however, be difficult. Those working in health promotion hold both personal and professional opinions about gay men. As we noted earlier, some of these may be less than accurate and/or less than positive. Efforts need to be made through training and professional development to encourage critical re-appraisal of these beliefs as part of broader efforts to promote greater equity in health (see World Health Organization Europe, 1998). Rather than viewing gay men as subjects, users, clients or consumers, notions of (sexual) citizenship may offer a more productive way forward. Linked to this are concepts of rights, participation, democracy and more direct engagement with political processes (see Watney, 1990, cited in Watney, 1994; Brown, 1997; Burrington, 1998; see also Chapter 13).

The active engagement of gay men as citizens in health promotion and research could well shift professional practice from exclusivity to involvement. Certainly, much early AIDS-related work has been distinguished by the activism and participation of gay men themselves, even if it is open to question how well this has been sustained. At the heart of the Ottawa Charter, for example, are notions of participation and empowerment. The challenge for health promotion lies in making such empowerment real and avoiding the dangers of social regulation highlighted by Lupton (1995), among others, who said:

> within the context of a bureaucratic structure that is funded by the state and conforms to its own set objectives...Every individual is now involved in observing, imposing and enforcing the regulations of public health particularly through the techniques of self-surveillance and bodily control encouraged by the imperatives of health promotion. (p. 76)

Re-evaluating some key assumptions

This is not some kind of simplistic argument for 'doing away with the state' nor for the abandonment of more narrowly focused efforts in prevention as the struggle for a more encompassing health promotion takes place. Rather, it is to recognize that the dimensions along which health promotion is constructed need constantly to be re-examined. Where there are calls for the involvement and empowerment of individuals and communities in health promotion, these too need critical interrogation (Sarantakos, 1998). As Lupton (1995) has put it:

> A critical approach to health promotion should involve an explicit questioning of whose voices are being heard and privileged, the alliances and conflicts involved, what body of expertise is cited in support, 'what counts as knowledge', how it is organized, controlled, authenticated and disseminated, who has access to knowledge and how this knowledge is taken up, justified and used by health promotion practitioners. (p. 49)

It would be naive to suggest that action is not required to address the health-related needs of gay men but there can be no return to the late 1970s. Notwithstanding some gay men's continued pursuit of a perfectible body or the expanding commercialization of gay culture, there have been marked changes to the political and cultural landscape. Responses to HIV/AIDS have created divisions between some and alliances and solidarity among others. Work around HIV/AIDS has provided new insights into the limits as well as the strengths of different approaches to health promotion and research. Recent policy change has asserted the importance of equity, rights and citizenship as a cornerstone of health for all.

To some extent, this may be what has brought about the shifts of perspective discernible in two noteworthy European collections of essays by Van Campenhoudt *et al.* (1997) and Moatti *et al.* (2000). While not focusing exclusively upon gay men, both share a concern to bring a social and interpersonal dimension to an analysis and understanding of, *inter alia,* HIV prevention, adherence to drug regimes, sexuality and sexual interactions and familial responses to AIDS. Learning from this work may provide more fruitful future perspectives on gay men's health. Key areas for future enquiry include income and social status, culture, gender, social settings (such as those related to employment, education, leisure and family life), social and community networks, personal health practices and coping skills, biological and genetic endowment, as well as service provision (see Ryan *et al.,* 2000).

In our view, a primary purpose of future research should not be to 'explain' social life, predict events and 'discover' universal laws (as a positivist approach might encourage); nor indeed to interpret and 'understand' social life (as an interpretivist perspective might advocate). Rather, it should be to change social understanding and social reality by addressing issues of prejudice, discrimination, deliberate 'mis-understanding', inequality and power. Only by having this kind of strategic aspiration (Dean, 1999; Rose, 1999) can we facilitate movement towards greater equity in health (World Health Organization Europe, 1998). By seeking in this way to foster health promotion that is properly inclusive of gay men, the values underpinning research and practice would be made explicit, the political nature of the endeavour evident, the ethical base transparent and the action-oriented frame of reference deliberate.

References

AGGLETON, P.J. (1996) Global priorities for HIV/AIDS intervention research. *International Journal of STD/AIDS, 7 (suppl 2),* 13–16.

AGGLETON, P. and HOMANS, H. (1987) *Education about AIDS. A Discussion Document for Health Education Officers, Community Physicians, Health Advisers and Others with a Responsibility for Effective Education about AIDS.* Bristol: NHS Training Authority.

ALTMAN, D. (1986) *AIDS and the New Puritanism.* London: Pluto Press.

AMERICAN MEDICAL ASSOCIATION COUNCIL ON SCIENTIFIC AFFAIRS (1996) Health care needs of gay men and lesbians in the United States. *Journal of the American Medical Association, 275,* 1354–1359.

ANNESLEY, P. and COYLE, A. (1995) Clinical psychologists' attitudes to lesbians. *Journal of Community & Applied Social Psychology, 5,* 327–331.

ANNESLEY, P. and COYLE, A. (1998) Dykes and psychs: Lesbian women's experiences of clinical psychology services. *Changes: An International Journal of Psychology and Psychotherapy, 16,* 247–258.

ANTONOVSKY, A. (1996) The salutogenic model as a theory to guide health promotion. *Health Promotion International, 11,* 11–26.

BALKA, C. and ROSE, A. (Eds) (1989) *Twice Blessed: On Being Lesbian or Gay and Jewish.* Boston, MA: Beacon Press.

BENNETT, P. and MURPHY, S. (1997) *Psychology and Health Promotion.* Buckingham: Open University Press.

BERGMARK, K.H. (1999) Drinking in the Swedish gay and lesbian community. *Drug and Alcohol Dependence, 56*, 133–143.

BICKELHAUPT, E.E. (1995) Alcoholism and drug abuse in gay and lesbian
persons: A review of incidence studies. In R.J. Kus (Ed.) *Addiction and Recovery in Gay and Lesbian Persons*. London: Harrington Press.

BOCHOW, M. (2000) Socio-economic status and HIV prevalence among gay
men in Germany. In J.P. Moatti, Y. Souteyrand, A. Prieur, T. Sandfort and P.
Aggleton (Eds) *AIDS in Europe: New Challenges for the Social Sciences*.
London: Routledge.

BROWN, M.P. (1997) *RePlacing Citizenship: AIDS Activism and Radical Democracy*. London: Guilford Press.

BURRINGTON, D. (1998) The public square and citizen queer: Toward a new
political geography. *Polity, 31*, 107–131.

CALLEN, M. (1983) *How to Have Sex in an Epidemic*. New York: News from the
Front Publications.

CARABINE, J. (1997) Heterosexuality and social policy. In D. Richardson (Ed.)
Theorising Heterosexuality: Telling it Straight. Buckingham: Open University
Press.

CARLAT, D.J., CARNARGO, C.A. Jr. and HERZOG, D.B. (1997) Eating disorders in males: A report on 135 patients. *American Journal of Psychiatry, 154*,
1127–1132.

CLARK, W. M. and SEROVICH J.M. (1997) Twenty years and still in the dark?
Content analysis of articles pertaining to gay, lesbian, and bisexual issues in
marriage and family therapy journals. *Journal of Marital and Family Therapy,
23*, 239–253.

COCHRAN, S.D. and MAYS, V.M. (1994) Depressive distress among homosexually active African American men and women. *American Journal of
Psychiatry, 151*, 524–529.

COHEN, M. and HUBERT, M. (1997) The place of time in understanding
sexual behaviour and designing HIV/AIDS prevention programs. In L. van
Campenhoudt, M. Cohen, G. Guizzardi and D. Hausser (Eds) *Sexual Interactions and HIV Risk: New Conceptual Persepectives in European Research*.
London: Taylor and Francis.

COYLE, A., MILTON, M. and ANNESLEY, P. (1999) The silencing of lesbian
and gay voices in psychotherapeutic texts and training. *Changes: An International Journal of Psychology and Psychotherapy, 17*, 132–143.

DEAN, M. (1999) *Governmentality: Power and Rule in Modern Society*. London:
Sage.

DEPARTMENT OF HEALTH (1999) *Saving Lives: Our Healthier Nation. Cm
4386*. London: HMSO.

DEVERELL, K. (1997) Professionalism and sexual identity in gay and bisexual
men's HIV prevention. In P. Aggleton, P. Davies and G. Hart (Eds) *AIDS:
Activism and Alliances*. London: Taylor and Francis.

DILLON, P., COPELAND, J. and PETERS, R. (1999) Exploring the relationship
between male homo/bisexuality, body image and steroid use. *Culture,
Health & Sexuality, 1*, 317–328.

DOUGLAS, N., WARWICK, I., KEMP, S. and WHITTY, G. (1997) *Playing It Safe:
Responses of Secondary School Teachers to Lesbian and Gay Pupils, Bullying, HIV
and AIDS Education and Section 28*. London: Terrence Higgins Trust.

DOYAL, L. and PENNELL, I. (1979) *The Political Economy of Health*. London:
Pluto Press.

FARIA, G. (1997) The challenge of health care social work with gay men and lesbians. *Social Work in Health Care, 25*, 65–72.

FOUCAULT, M. (1979) *The History of Sexuality, Volume 1: An Introduction.* London: Allen Lane.

FROCHLICH, K.L. and POTVIN, L. (1999) Health promotion through the lens of population health: Toward a salutogenic setting. *Critical Public Health, 9*, 211–222.

GARNETS, L., HANCOCK, K.A., COCHRAN, S.D., GOODCHILDS, J. and PEPLAU, L.A. (1991) Issues in psychotherapy with lesbians and gay men: A survey of psychologists. *American Psychologist, 46*, 964–972.

GOLDING, J. (1997) *Without Prejudice: MIND Lesbian, Gay and Bisexual Mental Health Awareness Research.* London: MIND Publications.

GREENE, B. (1994) Ethnic-minority lesbians and gay men: Mental health and treatment issues. *Journal of Consulting and Clinical Psychology, 62*, 243–251.

HARRISON, A.E. and SILENZIO, V.M.B. (1996) Comprehensive care of lesbian and gay patients and families. *Primary Care, 23*, 31–46.

HARRISON, S. (1998) The politics of evidence-based medicine in the United Kingdom. *Policy and Politics, 26*, 15–31.

HOYLE, E. and JOHN, P. (1995) *Professional Knowledge and Professional Practice.* London: Cassell.

KATZ, J. and PEBERDY, A. (Eds) (1992) *Promoting Health: Knowledge and Practice.* London: Macmillan.

KING, E. (1993) *Safety in Numbers.* London: Cassell.

KING, M. and BARTLETT, A. (1999) British psychiatry and homosexuality. *British Journal of Psychiatry, 175*, 106–113.

KITZINGER, C. (1997) Lesbian and gay psychology: A critical analysis. In D. Fox and I. Prilleltensky (Eds) *Critical Psychology: An Introduction.* London: Sage.

KUS, R.J. and LATCOVICH, M.A. (1995) Special interest groups in Alcoholics Anonymous: A focus on gay men's groups. In R.J. Kus (Ed.) *Addiction and Recovery in Gay and Lesbian Persons.* London: Harrington Press.

KUS, R.J. and SMITH, G.B. (1995) Referrals and resources for chemically dependent gay and lesbian clients In R.J. Kus (Ed.) *Addiction and Recovery in Gay and Lesbian Persons.* London: Harrington Press.

LUPTON, D. (1995) *The Imperative of Health: Public Health and the Regulated Body.* London: Sage.

McFARLANE, L. (1998) *Diagnosis: Homophobic. The Experiences of Lesbians, Gay Men and Bisexuals in Mental Health Services.* London: PACE.

MILTON, M. and COYLE, A. (1998) Psychotherapy with lesbian and gay clients. *The Psychologist, 11*, 73–76.

MOATTI, J.P., SOUTEYRAND, Y., PRIEUR, A., SANDFORT, T. and AGGLE- TON, P. (Eds) (2000) *AIDS in Europe: New Challenges for the Social Sciences.* London: Routledge.

MORGAN, K. S. and NERISON, R.M. (1993) Homosexuality and psychopoli- tics: An historical overview. *Psychotherapy, 30*, 133–140.

OPPENHEIMER, J. (1997) Movements, markets and the mainstream: Gay activism and assimilation in the age of AIDS. In J. Oppenheimer and H. Reckitt (Eds) *Acting on AIDS: Sex, Drugs and Politics.* London: Serpent's Tail.

PATTON, C. (1987) Resistance and the erotic: Reclaiming history, setting strat- egy as we face AIDS. *Radical America, 20*, 68–78.

PATTON, C. (1989) The AIDS industry: Construction of 'victims', 'volunteers', and 'experts'. In E. Carter and S. Watney (Eds) *Taking Liberties: AIDS and Cultural Politics*. London: Serpent's Tail.

PATTON, C. (1990) What science knows: Formations of AIDS knowledges. In P. Aggleton, P. Davies and G. Hart (Eds) *AIDS: Individual, Cultural and Policy Dimensions*. London: Falmer.

PERRY, T. and LUCAS, C.L. (1987) *The Lord is my Shepherd and He Knows I'm Gay*. Austin, TX: Liberty Press.

PETERSON, J.L. and CARBALLO-DIEGUEZ, A. (2000) HIV prevention among African-American and Latino men who have sex with men. In J.L. Peterson and R.J. DiClemente (Eds) *Handbook of HIV Prevention*. London: Kluwer Academic/Plenum.

PETERSON, J.L. and DiCLEMENTE, R.J. (Eds) (2000) *Handbook of HIV Prevention*. London: Kluwer Academic/Plenum.

PLUMMER, K. (1988) Organizing AIDS. In P. Aggleton and H. Homans (Eds) *Social Aspects of AIDS*. Lewes: Falmer Press.

PROCTOR, G. (1994) Lesbian clients' experience of clinical psychology: A listener's guide. *Changes: An International Journal of Psychology and Psychotherapy, 12*, 290–298.

ROBERTSON, A.E. (1998) The mental health experiences of gay men: A research study exploring gay men's health needs. *Journal of Psychiatric Mental Health Nursing, 5*, 33–40.

ROFES, E. (1998) *Dry Bones Breathe: Gay Men Creating Post-AIDS Identities and Cultures*. London: Harrington Press.

ROSE, N. (1999) *Governing the Soul: The Shaping of the Private Self*, 2nd ed. London: Free Association Books.

ROSS, M.W. and KELLY, J.A. (2000) Interventions to reduce HIV transmission in homosexual men. In J.L. Peterson and R.J. DiClemente (Eds) *Handbook of HIV Prevention*. London: Kluwer Academic/Plenum.

RYAN, B., CHERVIN, M. and MARSHALL-FOGIE, J. (2000) *Population Health and Gay Men's Health: A Discussion Paper*. Ottawa: Health Canada.

SANDERSON, T. (1986) *How To Be a Happy Homosexual: A Guide for Gay Men*. London: The Other Way Press.

SAPSFORD, R. (1998) Domains of analysis. In R. Sapsford, A. Still, D. Miell, R. Stevens and M. Wetherell (Eds) *Theory and Social Psychology*. London: Sage.

SCOTT, P. (1997) White noise: How gay men's activism gets written out of AIDS prevention. In J. Oppenheimer and H. Reckitt (Eds) *Acting on AIDS: Sex, Drugs and Politics*. London: Serpent's Tail.

SEABOLD, G. (1997) Surviving a partner's death deeply in the closet. In M. Shernoff (Ed.) *Gay Widowers: Life After the Death of a Partner*. London: Harrington Press.

SHERNOFF, M. (1997) Conclusion: Mental health considerations of gay widowers. In M. Shernoff (Ed.) *Gay Widowers: Life After the Death of a Partner*. London: Harrington Press.

SILVERSTEIN, C. and WHITE, E. (1977) *The Joy of Gay Sex: An Intimate Guide for Gay Men to the Pleasures of a Gay Lifestyle*. New York: Simon and Schuster.

STALL, R.D., PAUL, J.P., BARRETT, D.C., CROSBY, G.M. and BEIN, E. (1999) An outcome evaluation to measure changes in sexual risk-taking among gay men undergoing substance use disorder treatment. *Journal of Studies in Alcohol, 60*, 837–845.

STEVENS, P. (1992) Lesbian healthcare research: A review of the literature from 1970–1990. *Healthcare for Women International, 13*, 91–120.

UHRIG, L.J. (1986) *Sex Positive: A Gay Contribution to Sexual and Spiritual Union.* Boston, MA: Alyson Publications.

UNGVARSKI, P.J. and GROSSMAN, A.H. (1999) Health problems of gay and bisexual men. *Nursing Clinics of North America, 34*, 313–331.

VAN CAMPENHOUDT, L., COHEN, M., GUIZZARDI, G. and HAUSSER, D. (1997) *Sexual Interactions and HIV Risk: New Conceptual Perspectives in European Research.* London: Taylor and Francis.

WARWICK, I., OLIVER, C. and AGGLETON, P. (2000) Sexuality and mental health promotion: Lesbian and gay young people. In P. Aggleton, J. Hurry and I. Warwick (Eds) *Young People and Mental Health.* Chichester: John Wiley and Sons.

WARWICK, I., ORR, K. and WHITTY, G. (1995) *Local HIV Prevention Needs Assessments for Gay and Bisexual Men: A Review and Recommendations for Action.* London: Health Education Authority.

WATNEY, S. (1989) Taking liberties: An introduction. In E. Carter and S. Watney (Eds) *Taking Liberties: AIDS and Cultural Politics.* London: Serpent's Tail.

WATNEY, S. (1994) *Practices of Freedom.* London: Rivers Oram Press.

WEATHERBURN, P., DAVIES, P., HICKSON, F.C., HUNT, A.J., McMANUS, T.J. and COXON, A.P. (1993) No connection between alcohol use and unsafe sex among gay and bisexual men. *AIDS, 7*, 115–119.

WEEKS, J. (2000) *Making Sexual History.* Cambridge: Polity Press.

WILLIAMSON, I.R. (2000) Internalized homophobia and health issues affecting lesbians and gay men. *Health Education Research, 15*, 97–107.

WILTON, T. (2000) *Sexualities in Health and Social Care.* Buckingham: Open University Press.

WORLD HEALTH ORGANIZATION EUROPE (1998) *Health 21: An Introduction to The Health for All Policy Framework for the WHO European Region.* Copenhagen: World Health Organization Regional Office for Europe.

WORLD HEALTH ORGANIZATION, HEALTH and WELFARE CANADA and the CANADIAN PUBLIC HEALTH ASSOCIATION (1986) *Ottawa Charter for Health Promotion.* Geneva: World Health Organization.

WORLD HEALTH ORGANIZATION and MINISTRY of HEALTH, REPUBLIC of INDONESIA (1997) *The Jakarta Declaration on Leading Health Promotion into the 21ˢᵗ Century.* Geneva: World Health Organization.

WRIGHT, C. and COYLE, A. (1996) Experiences of AIDS-related bereavement among gay men: Implications for care. *Mortality, 1*, 267–282.

WRIGHT, M.T. (1998) Beyond risk factors: Trends in European safer sex research. *Psychology and Human Sexuality, 10(3/4)*, 7–18.

Chapter 9

Psychopathology and the Social and Historical Construction of Gay Male Identities

Gary Taylor

Men[1] who identify – or who are struggling to identify – as gay[2] appear to be more vulnerable to certain forms of psychological and emotional distress than men who identify as heterosexual. Much of this distress, no doubt, results from factors which have nothing to do with sexual identity and everything to do with being human. Indeed, an insistence upon consistently sexualizing the emotional difficulties of gay men would constitute naïve reductionism and would be potentially oppressive. While sexuality may be a constituent part of a person's identity – especially when that sexuality is constructed as being in some way 'different' – we are not simply the uncomplicated product of our sexualities. Nevertheless, this inequitable distribution of psychological distress suggests that certain processes are operating here. Indeed, based upon observations from my own practice as a clinical psychologist, it would seem that many gay men present with difficulties, dilemmas and conflicts that are intrinsically tied to their sexual identities. Sometimes these difficulties appear to be a direct response to negative societal representations of and behaviours towards homosexuality. Sometimes they appear to be the consequence of participation within a specific subculture and an adherence to its reified expectations, norms and values.

In this chapter, I will argue that both these 'aetiologies' are inextricably linked and, most crucially, are instrumental in the formation of 'problematized identities' likely to give rise to psychological and emotional distress. This chapter is concerned with the social and historical construction of gay male identities and communities and offers, in part, a theoretical deconstruction of the internalization of negative representations of 'gayness'. It sets out to explore the way in which psychological, emotional and behavioural difficulties experienced by some gay men might arise from the way in which their (sexual) identities have been discursively constructed through the introjection of culturally and sub-culturally dominant, historically precedented values and beliefs. I intend to consider the aetiology, reification, perpetuation and possible function of these discourses, locating them within their historical and cultural contexts and explore the ways in which they might impact upon the psychological well-being and behaviour of gay men. While my thesis will draw upon a wide-ranging literature – including psychological research – it constitutes, at least in part, a series of observations and hypotheses based largely upon my experience of working as a clinical psychologist with gay men and, indeed, upon my experiences as a gay man. It represents an alternative way of examining sexual identity to that offered by Laura A. Markowe in her consideration of the development of lesbian identity in Chapter 4 and also sets the scene for Chapters 10 and 11 which examine therapeutic practice with lesbian and gay clients.

Despite a growing appreciation of the way in which our selves and our emotions are socially constructed (Harre and Gillett, 1994; Lupton, 1998; Fee 1999), understandings of the way in which historically-grounded cultural representations impact upon identity formation and might instigate and shape the presentation of emotional distress are largely absent from traditional accounts within social, developmental and clinical psychology. From within 'community psychology', attempts have been made to understand psychopathology in relation to such factors as social exclusion and disempowerment (Rappaport, 1977; Brown and Harris, 1978; Joffee and Albee, 1981). Further to this, a number of feminist theorists have begun to locate women's psychological development and distress within social and historical processes of oppression (for example, Showalter, 1985, 1997; Ussher, 1991; Hepworth, 1999). However, the notion that any psychological understanding of an individual's development and disorder necessitates a critical appreciation of social and historical forces of categorization and regulation remains a radical one. Consequentially, psychology, as an applied science, has been criticized for being

> instrumental in maintaining the societal status quo by endorsing and reflecting dominant social values, disseminating those values in the persuasive form of so-called value free scientific statements and providing an asocial image of the individual as essentially independent from sociohistorical circumstances. (Prilleltensky, 1989, p. 800)

In this chapter I intend to try to address such criticism through an exploration of the way in which the identities and psychological difficulties of gay men are socially constructed, being the product of social and historical forces, grounded, at least in part, within oppressive and deeply-ingrained social and historical processes of categorization, regulation and exclusion. In so doing, I will also consider the way in which psychology, far from being an objective and dispassionate observer, actually performs an ideological role in actively constructing the phenomena under its gaze.

Constructing the male homosexual

The social constructionist paradigm assumes that in forming and making sense of our identities, we draw upon the cultural images, representations and discourses that are available to us (Berger and Luckmann, 1967; Burr, 1995; Gergen, 1999). As a 'narrative therapist', I am interested in the stories people tell about themselves and others, the meanings they ascribe and the beliefs they hold (White and Epston, 1990; McNamee and Gergen, 1992; McLeod, 1997; Parker, 1999; Payne 1999; Crossley, 2000). I am interested in knowing where their stories come from, why they have chosen one narrative over another, what functions any particular narrative might serve and what its implications might be. From such a perspective, it becomes purposeful, in working therapeutically with gay men, to try to disentangle some of the multiple discourses – past and present – that converge in the contemporary cultural construction of 'gay male identities'. It becomes necessary to try to deconstruct the meanings that are ascribed to homosexuality and understand their heritage in order to consider the impact that these meanings might have upon the thinking, feeling and behaviour of those men who draw upon them in constructing and making sense of their sexualities.

Although the emergence of 'the homosexual' as a person and as an identity is a relatively recent (albeit fiercely contested) phenomenon, the occurrence of sex between men has, almost certainly, existed for as long as human history. Since at least the medieval period, sex between men has been perceived negatively; indeed, social historians have documented the cruelty with which the church and state have attempted to repress homosexual behaviour (Greenberg, 1988; Davenport-Hines, 1990; Spencer, 1995). Between the fourteenth and mid-nineteenth centuries, hundreds of thousands of men were executed in Europe and the Americas for engaging in the act of sodomy. Indeed, the term 'faggot' – an expression still used in reference to gay men – is derived from the kindling used to burn sodomites. Sodomy was considered a particularly heinous crime, meriting – like treachery and witchcraft – a tortuous death by such means as burning, fatal castration or being slowly dismembered alive or eaten by dogs (Greenberg, 1988; Davenport-Hines, 1990). In the UK, the death penalty for sodomy was only repealed in 1861 and, although the last execution was in 1836, in 1846 more death sentences were pronounced for sodomy than for murder (Davenport-Hines, 1990).

This genocidal extermination was legitimized by the church through its positioning of sodomy as 'unspeakably sinful'. It was demonized and likened to a plague, a pestilent and treacherous vice capable of corrupting the innocent. Within the Judeo-Christian tradition, sodomy came to represent the threat of the outsider to the established order. In being linked to non-procreative sexuality and the anus, it and, by association, homosexuality, became a symbol of disorder, disintegration and death. Similar discourses were employed by the Nazis in their extermination of as many as 50 000 homosexual men in the twentieth century (Plant, 1986). Some 150 years after the last execution for sodomy in Britain, the same discourses were employed in the midst of an AIDS hysteria as justification for the beating, imprisonment and castration of gay men, as both a punishment and as a means of containing the epidemic (Altman, 1986; DHSS, 1987; Dupras *et al.*, 1989; Davenport-Hines 1990; Garfield, 1994). For analytic theorist Julia Kristeva (1965), this positioning of sodomy and homosexuality may be interpreted as the enactment of abhorrence at the anus, its 'misappropriation', its repellent excreta and their symbolization of death and decay. Whatever its social or intra-psychic origins, it is a discourse which, based upon my own clinical practice, still appears to reverberate around the identities and practices of gay men, particularly in the context of the AIDS pandemic (Taylor, 2000).

Despite, or perhaps because of, its harsh repression, the eighteenth century saw the gradual emergence within European cities of a network of 'amenities' catering to the needs of those with a penchant for sodomy. With the advent of specialist taverns or 'molly houses', there began to emerge a community of mainly effeminate and cross-dressing men who appear to have evolved an identity, as well as specific subcultural codes and practices, based upon their 'preferred sexual behaviours' (Trumbach, 1977; Bray, 1982; Spencer, 1995). That these 'communities' should embrace effeminacy and transgress conventional notions of gender is perhaps a further indication of the potential threat posed by homosexuality. The act of sodomy was regarded – much as homosexuality is today – not just as an affront against God but, perhaps more importantly, as constituting an attack upon masculinity, patriarchy and the institutions of marriage and the family. The act of being fucked is associated with being female. Within a society that is so staunchly patriarchal and misogynous, such sexual 'passivity' is therefore negatively valued in the extreme, being equated with subordination, subjugation and emasculation. This conflation of 'true masculinity' with exclusive heterosexuality implies that one cannot be a real man and get fucked, that the homosexual must therefore be less than a man, for, in becoming the sexual object, he becomes 'as if a woman' and is expected to behave accordingly. His passivity renders him grossly inferior and shamefully perverse. Again, we have here the homosexual as symbolic of the threat of the outsider to the established order, the threat of disorder and disintegration of conventional and clearly delineated and polarized gender roles. It is also, I believe, a discourse that negatively impacts upon the psychological well-being of gay men and would appear to continue to inform the social identities and behaviours of at least some.

For Foucault, the homosexual was brought into being towards the end of the nineteenth century, not through a gradual process of self-evolution but as a result of pseudo-medical taxonomy. Whereas the sodomite had been a temporary behavioural aberration, the homosexual was now a species, 'a personage, a past, a case history...a life form...with indiscreet anatomy and possibly a mysterious physiology' (Foucault, 1979, p. 43). This shift from verb to noun, the classification of persons rather than behaviours, further served the purpose of legitimization; for in establishing homosexuality as a stigmatized and transgressive identity rather than simply a perverse behavioural aberration, the boundaries between permissible and impermissible conduct were fortified and the possibility for transgression constrained (McIntosh, 1968; Weeks, 1990). Its 'essentialization' also meant that psychology and medicine were legitimized as the primary ideological apparatuses for its regulation and further construction. For Foucault, the homosexual was 'invented' in order to define, stigmatize and, ultimately, regulate 'otherness' with the purpose of defining and reifying procreative sexualities and reinforcing a sexual hegemony subservient to the requirements of capitalism. Since discourse had become the instrument by which dissent might be managed, so it was that a language was evolved for that which for so long had been unspeakable; and so it was that 'the (male) homosexual' was constructed. In this sense, 'the homosexual' is almost unique for few peoples have been brought into the world *in order* to be pilloried.

The notion that homosexual behaviour might be rooted in the constitution of the 'afflicted individual' has appeared and reappeared throughout history. However, it was only towards the end of the nineteenth century that homosexuality was truly conceived as a pathological identity located in the body rather than a transient vice located in the spirit (Greenberg, 1995). This essentialist medicalization of the homosexual was informed by pre-existing discourses locating sodomy as indicative of moral degeneracy. Medicine tended to regard the homosexual as sick, as physically and constitutionally degenerate. Influential physicians, such as Krafft-Ebing (1886/1965), considered the homosexual to have a constitutional weakness, for example, that he evidenced an inherited neurological malformation of the brain which meant that he experienced the sexual drives of a woman but had the anatomy of a man. This 'third sex theory' – also popular with nineteenth century sexologists and would-be social reformers such as Havelock Ellis (1897), Karl Ulrichs, Karoly Benkert and Magnus Hirschfeld (Greenberg, 1988) – once again relied upon the conflation of gender and sexual behaviour and the well-established assumption that truly to be a man, one must be heterosexual. Perhaps unsurprisingly, homosexuality was also thought to coincide with transsexualism, transvestism and effeminacy, as well as with other 'perversions', including excessive masturbation, sadism, masochism, paedophilia and bestiality and a vast array of 'unmanly characterological flaws', including vanity, egocentrism, immaturity, cowardice and dishonesty (Krafft-Ebing, 1886/1965).

Numerous early medical conceptualizations of homosexuality proposed that sexual pathology was the consequence of inter-generational somatic degeneracy resulting from poverty, alcoholism, in-breeding, poor sanitation and environmental squalor (Krafft-Ebing, 1877; Charcot and Magnan, 1882; Magnan 1885; Tarnowsky, 1886; Moreau, 1887; Moll, 1891; Fere, 1899; Forel, 1905). Other quasi-Darwinist theories (Kiernan, 1884; Lydston, 1889), fuelled by bourgeois unease and colonialist eugenicism, speculated that homosexuals were evolutionarily retarded, phylogenic throwbacks. Such discourses, in positioning the homosexual as belonging to the 'dangerous classes', reaffirmed his ostracism whilst legitimizing such treatments as eugenic castration, vasectomy and compulsory sterilization. The homosexual had become a degenerate and diseased 'species' requiring stringent preventative containment. Such ideas may appear antiquated but they continue to inform contemporary popular discussion, for example in relation to the management of the AIDS pandemic, Section 28 of the 1988 Local Government Act (forbidding the promotion of homosexuality by local authorities), age of consent legislation, lesbian and gay parenting (see Chapters 5 and 6) and debates concerning homosexuality and military service. Indeed, let us not forget that homosexuality was classified by the World Health Organization – the agency responsible for the global co-ordination of HIV prevention – within its classification of disorders, as if it were a disease akin to typhus or yellow fever, right up until the publication of its tenth volume in 1992 (World Health Organization, 1992). Furthermore, researchers (such as LeVay, 1991, 1994; Hamer *et al.*, 1993) continue to explore the genetic, chromosomal and physiological basis of homosexuality and thereby (unwittingly or otherwise) provide the basis for a contemporary eugenic debate.

In re-conceptualizing the homosexual as, most probably, developmentally stunted by the intra-familial environment, Freud advanced the notion that homosexuality might not be the consequence of inherited constitutional degeneracy. Freud (1905/1974) did not regard homosexuals as inherently sick; indeed, he believed that they could be content and well adjusted (Freud, 1935/1963). He refused to analyse patients *simply because* they were homosexual, opposed attempts to prevent homosexuals from training as analysts and spoke out against their prosecution (Lewes, 1995). Nevertheless, his theories did rely upon normative and pejorative notions of homosexuality as developmentally inferior; the homosexual was still 'psychologically degenerate'. Moreover, in emphasizing and centralizing the significance of his sexual choice in the construction of his identity, Freud located this inferiority at the very core of the homosexual's sense of self. Sex was incorporated into the very essence of the individual: it was not just his sexual preferences that were disordered; it was everything about him. 'Nothing that went into his total composition was unaffected by his sexuality. It was everywhere present in him' (Foucault, 1979, p. 43). The introduction of such a notion into a society that considered the homosexual to be an undesirable and pathological deviant could only intensify his social exclusion and vilification. Although some analytic theorists have written with sensitivity and insight on the subject (for example, Isay, 1989; Lewes, 1995), Freudian theory was to precipitate increasingly intolerant, pathologizing and damaging essentialist analytic accounts of homosexuality (see Chapter 10).

Most psychoanalytic theorists, since Freud, have tended to conceive of homosexuality as arising from the internalization, repression and transformation of death wishes and sadistic urges induced by a failure to resolve pre-Oedipal wishes and conflicts satisfactorily (Lewes, 1995). This, combined with his narcissistic self love, means that the homosexual, according to prominent, contemporary psychoanalyst Charles Socarides (1968), 'is filled with aggression, destruction and self deceit...[homosexuality] is a masquerade of life...[involving] only destruction, mutual deceit, exploitation of the partner and the self' (p. 67). 'Homosexuality', according to Socarides, 'is a dread dysfunction, malignant in character, which has risen to epidemic proportions' (cited in Young, 1995, p. 44). The degenerate homosexual – described here in terms more suited to a disease or plague – is seen as incapable of creativity or love, for he is seen to have chosen the anus over the vagina, defilement and decay over creativity and life. He is turned not towards life but towards death and destruction. Such discourses are again informed by powerful and primitive signification involving the association of homosexuality with the anus and, therefore, with degeneration, disorder and decay (Kristeva, 1965). Some analytic theorists have even substantiated such claims of conflation by recourse to the alleged repressed homosexuality of the Nazis (Lewes, 1995). One can only wonder at what impact such theorizing – in legitimizing dominant cultural discourses of the homosexual as pathologically villainous and self-destructive – has had upon generations of gay, bisexual and homosexual men who have sought the help of psychoanalysts.

Popular culture and the media (Sanderson, 1995) have, of course, also been instrumental in the dissemination and promotion of such discourses. For example, representations of the homosexual as self-destructive, murderous, immoral and tragically fated are rife within twentieth century television, film and literature. The homosexual has been mostly absent from popular culture but – until quite recently – when he is present, he is doomed. The stories are familiar: the effeminate and murderous villain, the pitifully tragic and lonely homosexual – both are deeply flawed and destined for a premature death. The homosexual can never be happy or well adjusted in these representations and he can never be allowed to grow old. The price for his misdemeanours, his unnatural yearnings, his sinful conduct must always be paid and, ideally, this price should be death, preferably at his own hand – a divine retribution. Russo (1987) has catalogued the cinema's murderous love affair with the homosexual with an exhaustive 'necrology' of bloody and premature deaths, including 13 suicides (by cutting, hanging, jumping, shooting and overdosing), 21 murders (by stabbing, shooting, bludgeoning, beating, drowning and cannibalism), one execution and a castration. A similar list could be compiled from classic and popular literary works including *The Picture of Dorian Gray* (Wilde, 1890/1991), *Death in Venice* (Mann, 1913/1954), *Billy Budd* (Melville, 1924/1972), *Giovanni's Room* (Baldwin, 1956/1963) and works by Genet, Purdy, Kirby and countless others. Consider Mann's novel, in which Aschenbach – a solitary, rather lonely and repressed middle-aged man – is captivated by the beauty of a young boy, Tadzio. A plague (cholera) is moving towards Venice but Aschenbach, gripped by his obsession with the youth and his unrequited passion, is unable to tear himself away from the city or his certain fate. Both Aschenbach and Tadzio are condemned to delirious, convulsive and tormented deaths. In fiction, the homosexual rarely grows old and, if he does, he is generally portrayed as pitifully sad and quite alone. Whatever the story, he must always in some sense be a victim of his sexuality.

Despite the expansive subjugation of discourse and the rise of 'talking therapies' in the management of dissent, the twentieth century also witnessed the evolution of increasingly barbaric and physically intrusive therapies for the regulation of homosexuality (Katz, 1976; Spencer, 1995; Young, 1995). In contrast to psychoanalysis, behaviourism conceives of homosexuality as no more than a set of behaviours. It takes the position that homosexuality is a learned response and that, through the manipulation of contingencies of reinforcement, it can be modified. The most commonly used method of 'treatment' has been aversion therapy, involving the paired association of homosexual stimuli or arousal with a negative reinforcement (Feldman and MacCulloch, 1965, 1971). This 'therapy', sometimes forcibly imposed, has included using electric shock, often to the genitals, to diminish the recipient's sexual response (Young, 1995). Other medical treatments have included the use of psychopharmacology, electro-convulsive therapy and electrical and surgical lobotomy (Greenberg, 1988; Young, 1995).

As the processes and apparatus of regulation have shifted from church, to judiciary, to medicine, so homosexuality has changed from sin, to crime, to sickness. Specific meanings and beliefs have waxed and waned whilst subtly interweaving discourses have jostled for position. Nevertheless, underlying psychological and cultural representations – as this brief review has tried to demonstrate – have remained constant and almost entirely negative. Yet these are among the discourses that must be embraced or actively opposed by gay men in the construction of their own identities. Towards the end of the twentieth century, with the advent of the gay liberation movement and queer politics, alternative and more affirmative discourses had begun to challenge negative and prejudicial representations of homosexuality (Weeks, 1990). Despite this, these negative representations have been of primary significance in the construction of the male homosexual and – reflecting upon my own clinical practice – appear to continue to inform the identities and practices of at least some gay men. Indeed, it is my contention that the development and dissemination of these discourses and their consequential positioning of homosexuality have been crucial in substantiating negative representations of homosexuality and undermining the psychological and physical well-being of those who identify as gay. Medically, religiously, legally and culturally-reified negative representations of homosexuality have had a toxically corrosive impact upon our psychological health. Negative ideas – such that homosexuals are sick, degenerate, immoral, deviant, potentially dangerous and so on – also appear to have been instrumental in driving many gay men towards self-damaging and abusive behaviours, thus confirming the prophetic myth that the homosexual is self-destructive and unavoidably doomed.

Psychopathology amongst gay men

Studies, mostly carried out during the 1960s and early 1970s, which aimed to evaluate the psychological health of gay and homosexual men, were, for the most part, unequivocal and crucial in undermining the notion that homosexuality itself constitutes a pathology (Gonsiorek, 1977; Savin-Williams, 1990). However, such a position, perhaps due in part to its subservience to an ideological agenda, necessitates a minimization of the incidence of psychological distress found among gay men. And yet, an increasing number of epidemiological studies testify to a greater incidence of psychological morbidity among (at least some) gay male populations when compared to heterosexuals. For example, rates of depression, suicide, self harm, substance misuse, homelessness and school non-attendance, misconduct and criminal behaviour have been reported as higher amongst adolescents who identify as gay or lesbian (Hetrick and Martin, 1987; Saewyc et al., 1998; Lock and Steiner, 1999; see also Chapter 2). In one study, undertaken by the US Department of Health and Human Services in 1989, gay and lesbian youths were found to be five times more likely to attempt suicide than their heterosexual peers (cited in Rivers, 1995). However, it would seem that it is not just adolescents that are at greater risk of suicide; in a study of men aged 18 to 27, gay men were found to be nearly 14 times more likely than heterosexual men to have made an attempt (Bagley and Tremblay, 1997). Other studies have found a significantly lower level of general psychological well-being (Coyle, 1993) and a significantly higher life-time prevalence of depression among gay men (Cochran and Mays, 2000) as well as increased rates of suicidal thinking and behaviour (Herrell *et al.*, 1999). The incidence of depression and suicidality among older gay men has yet to be thoroughly and satisfactorily investigated (especially in the UK, but see American writings by Berger, 1982; Lee, 1991; Reed, 1995; Ehrenberg, 1996; Jacobson and Grossman, 1996), so while what little research that has been conducted remains equivocal, it is plausible to assume that this group too might experience a disproportionate degree of psychological ill-health. Several studies have also found a significantly higher prevalence of alcohol and substance misuse and dependency among gay men in comparison to the general population (Fiefield *et al.*, 1977; Ziebold and Mongeon, 1982; Stall and Wiley, 1988; Cabaj, 1989; McKirnan and Peterson, 1989; Lewis and Ross, 1995). For example, in the study by Cabaj (1989), 30 per cent of gay men reported being drug dependent compared to about ten per cent of the 'heterosexual group'. Gay men also appear more likely to develop an eating disorder; for example, from a clinical sample of 135 men with an eating disorder, 42 per cent of those diagnosed with bulimia identified as gay or bisexual (Carlat *et al.*, 1997).

Most of these studies fail to explore the aetiology of their participants' psychological distress and behavioural difficulties adequately. However, it seems probable that a disproportionate part of their disturbance is the consequence of material processes of ostracism and victimization; for example, the result of actual or feared exclusion from family, work and social groups or the threat or occurrence of physical assault or emotional abuse. It also seems likely that such disturbance would follow from the adoption of negative cultural representations of homosexuality – representations with the capacity to undermine gay men's self worth and reliance and which – as I have noted – consistently position the gay man as sick, inferior, degenerate, contaminated, immoral, emasculated, dangerous and 'the other'. Some research supports a link between psychological health problems and negative and discriminatory experiences (Meyer, 1995; DiPlacido, 1998), the degree of perceived stigmatization (Ross, 1990) and the internalization of homophobic attitudes and beliefs (Meyer and Dean, 1998). A number of psychological clinicians have also commented on the probable influence of negative societal attitudes and behaviours towards homosexuality in the precipitation of psychological difficulties among gay men (Weinberg, 1972; Marmor, 1980; Malyon, 1982; Gonsiorek, 1988; Isay, 1989; McHenry and Johnson, 1993; Lewes, 1995; Davies and Neal, 1996). However, from an empirical perspective, any possible dynamic – including those factors which might serve to mitigate the impact of such stressors – appears inadequately investigated and poorly understood.

This negative, alienating and essentialist societal positioning of homosexuality has been crucial in precipitating the emergence of more positive, empowering and politicized discourses and the creation of affirmative (lesbian and) gay cultures and communities, most notably towards the end of the twentieth century (Katz, 1976; Weeks, 1990). However, based upon therapies with gay men and participant observation of these gay cultures and communities, one wonders at the extent to which they too might hold the capacity to undermine the psychological well-being of those who identify as gay. In the subsequent discussion, and given the paucity of research in this area, I wish to offer hypotheses concerning the extent to which some gay men's emotional and behavioural difficulties might be grounded within the very communities that also serve to empower and affirm their sexualities and identities.

The problematic nature of gay identities and cultures

Gay communities, cultures and lifestyles may be seen as evolving as a consequence of the essentialist construction of 'a homosexual identity' and in response to negative and oppressive behaviours and discourses embraced by the wider community. The emergence of modern gay cultures appears to have given rise to more positive and affirming collective gay identities whilst generating discourses that challenge those versions of 'being gay' promulgated by the wider society. Gay cultures have the capacity to provide a different, oppositional set of meanings from which gay men might construct and make sense of their sexualities and have been vital in offering a sense of inclusion within a society which is otherwise ostracizing (Katz, 1976; Weeks, 1990). However, in terms of identity development and psychological well-being, these emergent cultures appear problematic in a number of respects. As well as offering the potential for liberation and empowerment, the rigid cultural and physical identification and delineation of individuals according to sexual identity also has the capacity to alienate and to accentuate difference. Indeed, this has been the historical function of the ghetto in the containment and regulation of minority cultures since at least the sixteenth century (Davenport-Hines, 1990). These cultures possess the potential to reaffirm the ostracized status of the gay man and to consolidate his position as 'the other', as beyond mainstream society. They also contribute to the further polarization and solidification of sexualities and, despite their relative diversity, to the idea of not only a prescribed gay identity but also an entire 'gay lifestyle'. This, in conjunction with rampant commercialism, has resulted in a homosexual orientation becoming the basis for the construction of an entire identity (Bronski, 1998). This can leave many men feeling alienated, not only from mainstream culture but also from a highly prescriptive, narrowly defined gay culture which does not reflect their own values, beliefs or behaviours.

Another problematic area concerns the questionable extent to which contemporary gay cultures have evolved and disseminated representations of sexuality which are truly oppositional to those embraced by the wider community: it sometimes seems that they are little more than subtle re-enactments or re-interpretations of those discourses previously employed in the societal regulation and oppression of homosexualities. For example, effeminacy seems to have been an integral part of homosexual subcultures since their emergence in the eighteenth century (Bray, 1992; Spencer, 1995). While 'effeminacy' might be regarded as potentially dissident and as actually challenging more traditional patriarchal notions of gender, it would also appear to follow from, and reinforce, negative societal beliefs, as outlined previously, concerning homosexuality as an emasculation. And yet discourses around 'effeminacy' and 'camp' remain fundamental constituent parts of gay male culture, providing both explicit and covert representations which gay men are able to draw upon in the construction of their identities (Sontag, 1983; Medhurst, 1997). While this in itself may not be problematic, one might wonder at the degree to which such identities and behaviours are informed by more covert discourses involving the negative emasculation of homosexuality.

Another area of difficulty concerns the degree to which gay male cultures have internalized representations of the homosexual as tragic, hopeless and doomed (which were examined earlier in relation to popular culture). Indeed, the very birth of the modern gay movement seems to embody this paradox. Within gay 'mythology', gay liberation is said to have begun one night in June 1969 (although – as was noted in Chapter 1 – the gay liberation movement actually emerged much more slowly over a long period), when a group of gay men, lesbians, transvestites and transsexuals refused to tolerate further police victimization and rioted outside the Stonewall bar in New York (Katz, 1976). It was also, and not coincidentally, the day after the burial of Judy Garland following her fatal overdose. In considering some of the traditional icons of gay male culture – such as Marilyn Monroe, James Dean and Oscar Wilde – it would seem that certain pre-requisites are essential; ideally, any candidate should have lived a tragic and doomed existence characterized by an elusive search for happiness and to have, perhaps most importantly, in some way, sown the seeds of their own destruction. Garland, with her drug addictions and drinking, her string of failed and abusive affairs and lifetime of depression, was a prime candidate. No doubt there are many reasons why some gay men might have a certain affinity with such figures but it is my contention that our romanticism and veneration of tragedy, misery and self destruction is, at least in part, illustrative of our identification with and internalization of damaging cultural representations of homosexuality.

Further interconnected and key aspects of dominant contemporary gay cultures which have become pivotal, and possibly problematic, in the formation of many gay male identities concern the importance of desire and the eroticization of the young male body, the commodification of identity and the prioritization of pleasure, particularly sexual pleasure. Popular gay culture is extremely body conscious and is awash with sexualized imagery, eroticizing the young and muscular male form. Such imagery establishes an idealized and, for many, unobtainable aesthetic which can only serve to foster feelings of alienation and inadequacy. Some gay men appear to develop consequential beliefs that they must be in possession of the required body in order to participate in 'the gay lifestyle' and in order to feel desirable and to be desired. Although this area is under-researched, it seems probable that such beliefs would contribute to some gay men's difficulties with self-esteem and consequential problems with eating, obsessive weight-training and the use and abuse of anabolic steroids.

Gay culture appears unashamedly celebratory in its prioritization and pursuit of pleasure. Whilst there is much of value in the philosophy and practices of hedonism, one also needs to consider the mechanisms which support this contemporary construction of certain gay male identities as well as the possible consequences. Bronski (1998) is among those who have argued that since the homosexual is regarded as having no value in terms of the reproduction of labour, his societal worth is measurable only by his capacity to consume. The contemporary homosexual has therefore been aggressively constructed, marketed and exploited as a consumer-based identity – one in which the acquisition of consumer goods and the pursuit of pleasure are offered as compensation for social inequality and emotional deprivation. It is community through consumption, emancipation through accumulation, liberation through hedonism, whereby equality is naïvely equated with spending power, the pursuit of pleasure and sexual plurality (Woods, 1995; Simpson, 1996; Bronski, 1998). Foregoing any discussion of the long-term impact this positioning might have in terms of its depoliticization of gay culture, in the immediate term it would appear to contribute to a lifestyle and potentially an identity centred around bars and clubs, the consumption of alcohol and illicit drugs and the pursuit of sex. Research focusing on alcohol and drug consumption has generally found that while gay and heterosexual men consume comparable amounts as young adults, gay men continue to consume large amounts for longer (Stall and Wiley, 1988; McKirnan and Peterson, 1989). This is presumably a reflection of the central and extended significance of 'bar and dance cultures' in the lives of many gay men. However, such a lifestyle seems problematic in a number of respects, not least in terms of the perpetuation of alcohol and substance misuse problems but also in terms of the maturation of gay men.

Many gay men appear to struggle with growing older, not least because it necessitates leaving behind fundamental elements of an established identity and reassuringly familiar behaviours but also because it requires the evolution of a new lifestyle, but one which is not readily endorsed or even represented within mainstream gay cultures (Berger, 1982; Lee, 1991). The paucity of visible representations of older gay men living happy and rewarding lives means that many gay men, cocooned within their often exclusively young and hedonistic subcultures, immersed within a wider homophobic or, at best, heterosexist culture, are unable to accommodate the possibility of a life beyond the present. If one's lifestyle, relationships, identity, even one's sense of self-worth all centre around the values and practices of a subculture pre-occupied with sex, hedonism and the celebration of youth, old age can seem a frightening void; as Ratigan (1996) has commented, within gay male culture 'the older you are the less you exist' (p. 161). In a society dedicated to the family, the perpetuation of labour and the continuation of the species, gay men, despite our growing realization that we too can choose to be parents, may come to feel superfluous. Most cultures are familiar with images of a heterosexual old age, a time during which we can surround ourselves with dutiful children and adoring grandchildren. Some of us are also fortunate enough to experience our own parents or grandparents growing older, usually paired into opposite sex couples, illustrating for us, at least occasionally, the possibility of a happy heterosexual future. But there are few, if any, positive representations of happy, well adjusted elderly gay men. Due to the heterosexism of our society, the ageism of most gay cultures (Bennet and Thompson, 1991), our rejection of traditional notions of the family and our choice not to be, or prevention from being, parents, we are denied any positive, meaningfully applicable, culturally sanctioned representations with which to imagine and construct our futures. Instead we are offered representations of the homosexual as destined, like Tadzio and Aschenbach, for an early death or a sad and lonely old age.

The AIDSification of gay sexualities

Although gay men are increasingly exposed to and are generally able to seek out positive and empowering representations of gayness, we are, nevertheless, immersed within a culture and – as I have argued – within subcultures that perpetuate restrictive and ultimately damaging representations. This has become especially true with the advent of AIDS. The identities of gay men are (or at least are often seen as) inextricably tied to our sexual practices which, in turn, have become inextricably linked to HIV/AIDS and its connotations of malignancy, contamination and death. Any understanding of contemporary notions of gayness therefore necessitates an understanding of the way in which AIDS has been constructed and positioned within scientific and cultural discourse. The understanding of any disease necessitates an understanding of its metaphorical intricacies and ramifications (Sontag, 1989). This is especially true of AIDS because of the potency and widespread dissemination of its signification (Altman, 1986; Patton, 1986; Watney, 1987).

From the outset, AIDS was positioned as a gay disease (Altman, 1986; Garfield, 1994). Indeed, it was initially given the name GRID – Gay Related Immune Deficiency; there was reference to 'gay cancers' and 'gay viruses'; it was conceived as a gay health crisis, a 'gay plague'. Early aetiological theories linked the disease to the very essence of homosexuality. Scientists speculated that the immune systems of promiscuous homosexual men were being overloaded and poisoned by the ingestion of huge quantities of semen. Another hypothesis was that GRID was caused by some genetic or constitutional defect unique to homosexuals (Altman, 1986). Meanwhile, social and religious commentators, in drawing upon notions of sin and retribution, speculated upon more divine causalities (Davenport-Hines, 1990). This 'gayification' of the emerging epidemic relied upon and, in turn, reified powerful pre-existing discourses positioning homosexuals as sinful, inherently sick, degenerate, diseased and doomed. Such associations have been powerfully reinforced by popular media representations of the epidemic, most prominently, blatantly and enduringly in the mid 1980s (Watney, 1987; Sanderson, 1995).

The expression of sexuality is crucial to many gay men in the creation of identity. Indeed, for many gay men, personal liberation is measured quantitatively in terms of numbers of sexual partners, drawing upon early liberationist notions of sexual plurality as a rejection of the values of heterosexual and patriarchal monogamy (Altman, 1986). However, the rallying cry of 'so many men, so little time' was to take on rather less joyous connotations with the advent of AIDS. Then, perhaps for the first time since the introduction of antibiotics, sex took on a different, more sinister, set of meanings. Since the identification of HIV as the causative agent in AIDS, semen has become a cultural and personal signifier, not so much of passion, connectedness or love, but of deathly toxicity and poison – something to be avoided, spat out. We are denied some of the beauty and unspoilt pleasure of our bodies and our sexualities; instead the phallus becomes a 'vial of poison'; the anus, again, a grave; the condom, or its absence, a reminder of the deadly infectiousness of sex and our propensity to kill and be killed. Given that sex is so crucial to many gay men's sense of self, its metaphorical and literal contamination has had a powerful impact upon the way in which we conceive ourselves, our practices and our futures. It has also, no doubt, contributed to the psychological and sexual problems of many gay and homosexual men. Our identities as gay men have become subjectively and culturally inextricably linked to AIDS and to its connotations of death, sickness and disease, so much so that some gay men find it hard to imagine a future in which they might not become infected (Odets, 1995). Such fatalistic thinking and feelings of inevitability about contracting HIV, regardless of behaviour, rely at least in part upon an internalization of negative and 'AIDSified' representations of gayness.

Many gay men living through the epidemic seem to experience the internalized sense of a destiny that includes HIV/AIDS. Equally, and perhaps until only recently, many people with HIV held an internalized sense of an imminent and unavoidable death. The medical-cultural construction of AIDS as always fatal, together with its positioning of people with AIDS as passive victims, no doubt hastened the death of many gay men with HIV through the suppression of their hope, agency and immunological functioning. As Luc Montagnier, the head of the French laboratory that isolated HIV, has commented, 'Psychological factors are critical in supporting immune function...by telling someone they are condemned to die, your words alone will have condemned them' (cited in Young, 1995, p. 250). Our society's homophobia and its vilification and ostracizing of people with HIV also, no doubt, negatively impacts upon individuals' psychological health, worsening their prognoses and increasing rates of medical non-adherence, substance misuse, self-harm, neglect, suicide and, indirectly, frequencies of unprotected sex.

Perhaps it should not surprise us that women – since they are so often defined by their bodies – should use them to vent and display unhappiness and distress, such as through cutting and starvation (Ussher, 1991; Hepworth, 1999). Perhaps it should be equally unsurprising to us that some gay men – since we are defined by our sexual practices and are living in the midst of a sexually transmissible, potentially fatal epidemic – should use sex as the medium through which to act out our unhappiness and distress. Our cultures are crucial in determining the 'battlegrounds' upon which we engage with and communicate our own personal suffering. Constructions of gay sexualities in the context of AIDS are such that some gay men who are experiencing psychological and emotional distress may use sex as a form of deliberate self-harm, punishment or sabotage. As Walt Odets, a gay clinical psychologist working in San Francisco, has commented, 'AIDS is such an available and psychologically meaningful way for a gay man to not survive, it is surprising how difficult it has been for us to acknowledge that some men engage in unprotected sex for precisely that purpose' (1995, p. 206).

Conclusion

In this chapter I have sought to disentangle some of the discourses which appear to give rise to or maintain at least some of the psychological and behavioural difficulties experienced by gay men. I have put forward an argument that these difficulties can best be understood through a deconstruction of historically precedented material and discursive, cultural processes of categorization, regulation and exclusion. Psychologists and therapists are clearly limited in the degree to which they can effect change in the actual material processes that contribute to the psychological difficulties of their clients. However, through gaining a greater understanding and appreciation of the way in which internalized culturally and subculturally-inspired 'representations of gayness' might function in the precipitation and exacerbation of emotional and behavioural disturbance, psychological clinicians will be better able to identify and, where appropriate, challenge such narratives. For whilst it would be naïve to assume that emancipation and empowerment are all that are needed to cure people of their malaise and dissuade them from engaging in self-injurious behaviour, it is my contention that the dissemination and the collective and individual internalization of negative 'representations of gayness' continues to compromise the psychological and physical well-being of gay men.

Notes

1. Much of my subsequent theorizing could equally apply to lesbians and indeed to other marginalized groups (see Chapter 4 for a consideration of some of the identity dilemmas that lesbian women may face). However, since I position myself as a gay man and since much of my clinical practice has been with gay men, in this chapter I concern myself only with a discussion of the problematic construction of gay male identities.
2. In the context of this chapter, the term 'gay' is used in reference to a self-ascribed identity; 'homosexual' is generally used in a behavioural sense to refer to men who predominantly have sex with men.

References

ALTMAN, D. (1986) *AIDS and the New Puritanism*. London: Pluto Press.
BAGLEY, C. and TREMBLAY, P. (1997) Suicidal behaviors in homosexual and bisexual males. *Crisis, 18*, 24–34.
BALDWIN, J. (1956/1963) *Giovanni's Room*. London: Transworld.
BENNET, K.C. and THOMPSON, N.L. (1991) Accelerated ageing and male homosexuality. In J.A. Lee (Ed.) *Gay Midlife and Maturity*. New York: Harrington Park Press.
BERGER, P.L. and LUCKMANN, T. (1967) *The Social Construction of Reality: A Treatise in the Sociology of Knowledge*. New York: Penguin Press.

BERGER, R.M. (1982) *Gay and Grey: The Older Homosexual Man*. Urbana, IL: University of Illinois Press.

BRAY, A. (1982) *Homosexuality in Renaissance England*. London: Gay Men's Press.

BRONSKI, M. (1998) *The Pleasure Principle*. New York: St Martin's Press.

BROWN, G.W. and HARRIS, T.O. (1978) *The Social Origins of Depression*. London: Tavistock.

BURR, V. (1995) *An Introduction to Social Constructionism*. London: Routledge.

CABAJ, R.P. (1989) AIDS and chemical dependency: Special issues and treatment barriers for gay and bisexual men. *Journal of Psychoactive Drugs, 21*, 387–393.

CARLAT, D.J., CAMARGO, C.A. and HERZOG, D.B. (1997) Eating disorders in males: A report on 135 patients. *American Journal of Psychiatry, 154*, 1127–1132.

CHARCOT, J.M and MAGNAN, V. (1882) Inversion du sens genital. *Archives de Neurologie, 3*, 53–60.

COCHRAN, S.D. and MAYS, V.M. (2000) Lifetime prevalence of suicide symptoms and affective disorders among men reporting same-sex sexual partners: Results from the NHANES III. *American Journal of Public Health, 90*, 573–578.

COYLE, A. (1993) A study of psychological well-being among gay men using the GHQ-30. *British Journal of Clinical Psychology, 32*, 218–220.

CROSSLEY, M.L. (2000) *Introducing Narrative Psychology: Self, Trauma and the Construction of Meaning*. Buckingham: Open University Press.

DAVENPORT-HINES, R. (1990) *Sex, Death and Punishment*. London: Collins.

DAVIES, D. and NEAL, C. (Eds) (1996) *Pink Therapy: A Guide for Counsellors and Therapists Working with Lesbian, Gay and Bisexual Clients*. Buckingham: Open University Press.

DHSS (1987) *AIDS: Monitoring Responses to the Public Education Campaign February 1986–February 1987*. London: HMSO.

DiPLACIDO, J. (1998) Minority stress among lesbians, gay men, and bisexuals: A consequence of heterosexism, homophobia, and stigmatization. In G.M. Herek (Ed.) *Stigma and Sexual Orientation: Understanding Prejudice Against Lesbians, Gay Men, and Bisexuals*. Thousand Oaks, CA: Sage.

DUPRAS, A., LEVY, J., SAMSON, J.M. and TESSIER, D. (1989) Homophobia and attitudes about AIDS. *Psychological Reports, 64*, 236–238.

EHRENBERG, M. (1996) Aging and mental health: Issues in the gay and lesbian community. In C.J. Alexander (Ed.) *Gay and Lesbian Mental Health: A Sourcebook for Practitioners*. New York: Harrington Park Press.

ELLIS, H. (1897) *Sexual Inversion*. London: Wilson and Macmillan.

FEE, D. (1999) *Pathology and the Post-modern: Mental Illness as Discourse and Experience*. London: Sage.

FELDMAN, M.P. and MacCULLOCH, M.J. (1965) The application of anticipatory avoidance learning to the treatment of homosexuality: I, Theory, techniques and preliminary results. *Behavior Research and Therapy, 3*, 165–183.

FELDMAN, M.P. and MacCULLOCH, M.J. (1971) *Homosexual Behaviour: Therapy and Assessment*. New York: Pergamon Press.

FERE, C. (1899) *L' Instinct Sexuel: Evolution et Dissolution*. Paris: Felix Alcan.

FOREL, A.H. (1905) *Die Sexualle Frage: Ein Naturwissenschaftliche, Psychologische, Hygienische und Soziologische Studie fur Gebildete*. Munich: E. Reinhart.

FOUCAULT, M. (1979) *The History of Sexuality, Volume 1: An Introduction.* London: Allen Lane.

FREUD, S. (1905/1974) Three essays on the theory of sexuality. In A. Richards (Ed.) *On Sexuality*, Volume VII of the Pelican Freud Library. London: Penguin Books.

FREUD, S. (1935/1963) Letter to an American mother. In H.M. Ruitenteck (Ed.) *The Problem of Homosexuality in Modern Society.* New York: E.P. Dutton.

GARFIELD, S. (1994) *The End of Innocence: Britain in the Time of AIDS.* London: Faber and Faber.

GERGEN, K.J. (1999) *An Invitation to Social Construction.* London: Sage.

GONSIOREK, J.C. (1977) Psychological adjustment and homosexuality. *JSAS Catalogue of Selected Documents in Psychology, 50,* 217–225.

GONSIOREK, J.C. (1988) Mental health issues of gay and lesbian adolescents. *Journal of Adolescent Health Care, 9,* 114–127.

GREENBERG, D.F. (1988) *The Construction of Homosexuality.* Chicago, IL: Chicago Press.

HAMER, D.H., HU, S., MAGNUSON, V.L., HU, N. and PATTATUCCI, A.M.L. (1993) A linkage between DNA markers on the X chromosome and male sexual orientation. *Science, 261,* 321–327.

HARRE, R. and GILLETT, G. (1994) *The Discursive Mind.* London: Sage.

HEPWORTH, J. (1999) *The Social Construction of Anorexia Nervosa.* London: Sage.

HERRELL, R., GOLDBERG, J., TRUE, W.R., RAMAKRISHNAN, V., LYONS, M., EISEN, S. and TSUANG, M.T. (1999) Sexual orientation and suicidality: A co-twin control study in adult men. *Archives of General Psychiatry, 56,* 867–874.

HETRICK, E.S. and MARTIN, A.D. (1987) Developmental issues and their resolution for gay and lesbian adolescents. *Journal of Homosexuality, 14(1/2),* 25–43.

ISAY, R.A. (1989) *Being Homosexual: Gay Men and Their Development.* London: Penguin.

JACOBSON, S. and GROSSMAN, A.H. (1996) Older lesbians and gay men: Old myths, new images, and future directions. In R.C. Savin-Williams and K.M. Cohen (Eds) *The Lives of Lesbians, Gays, and Bisexuals: Children to Adults.* Fort Worth, TX: Harcourt Brace.

JOFFEE, J.M. and ALBEE, G.W. (1981) Powerlessness and psychopathology. In J.M. Joffee and G.W. Albee (Eds) *Prevention Through Political Action and Social Change: Primary Prevention of Psychopathology,* Volume 5. Hanover, NH: University Press of New England.

KATZ, J.N. (1976) *Gay American History.* New York: Thomas Y. Crowell.

KIERNAN, J.G. (1884) Insanity: Lecture xxvi: Perversion. *Detroit Lancet, 7,* 481–484.

KRAFFT-EBING, R. VON (1877) Uber gewisse anomalien des geschlechtstviebes. *Arciv fur Psychiatrie und Neurrenkrankheiten, 7,* 291–312.

KRAFFT-EBING, R. VON (1886/1965) *Psychopathia Sexualis: A Medico-Forensic Study.* New York: G.P. Putnam's & Sons.

KRISTEVA, J. (1965) *Powers of Horror: An Essay on Abjection.* New York: Columbia.

LEE, J.A. (Ed.) (1991) *Gay Midlife and Maturity.* New York: Harrington Park Press.

LEVAY, S. (1991) A difference in hypothalamic structure between heterosexual and homosexual men. *Science, 253,* 1034–1037.

LEVAY, S. (1994) *The Sexual Brain.* London: Bradford.

LEWES, K. (1995) *Psychoanalysis and Male Homosexuality.* London: Jason Aronson.

LEWIS, L.A and ROSS, M.W. (1995) *A Select Body: The Gay Dance Party Subculture and the HIV Pandemic.* London: Cassell.

LOCK, J. and STEINER, H. (1999) Gay, lesbian and bisexual youth risks for emotional, physical and social problems: Results of a community based survey. *Journal of the American Academy of Child and Adolescent Psychiatry, 38,* 297–304.

LUPTON, D. (1998) *The Emotional Self: A Sociocultural Exploration.* London: Sage.

LYDSTON, G.F. (1889) Sexual perversion, satyriasis and nymphomania. *Medical and Surgical Reporter, 61,* 281–285.

MAGNAN, V. (1885) *Recherches sur les Centres Nerveux.* Paris: Masson.

MALYON, A.K. (1982) Psychotherapeutic implications of internalized homophobia in gay men. In J. Gonsiorek (Ed.) *Homosexuality and Psychotherapy: A Practitioner's Handbook of Affirmative Models.* New York: Haworth Press.

MANN, T. (1913/1954) *Death in Venice and Seven Other Stories.* New York: Vintage.

McHENRY, S. and JOHNSON, J. (1993) Homophobia in the therapist and gay or lesbian client: Conscious and unconscious collusions in self hate. *Psychotherapy, 30,* 141–151.

McINTOSH, M. (1968) The homosexual role. *Social Problems, 16,* 182–192.

McKIRNAN, D.J. and PETERSON, P.L. (1989) Alcohol and drug use among homosexual men and women: Epidemiology and population characteristics. *Addictive Behaviours, 14,* 545–553.

McLEOD, J. (1997) *Narrative and Psychotherapy.* London: Sage.

McNAMEE, S. and GERGEN, K.J. (Eds) (1992) *Therapy as Social Construction.* London: Sage.

MEDHURST, A. (1997) Camp. In A. Medhurst and S.R. Munt (Eds) *Lesbian and Gay Studies: A Critical Introduction.* London: Cassell.

MELVILLE, H. (1924/1972) *Billy Budd.* New York: Pocket Books.

MEYER, I.H. (1995) Minority stress and mental health in gay men. *Journal of Health and Social Behaviour, 36,* 38–56.

MEYER, I.H. and DEAN, L. (1998) Internalized homophobia, intimacy and sexual behavior among gay and bisexual men. In G.M. Herek (Ed.) *Stigma and Sexual Orientation: Understanding Prejudice Against Lesbians, Gay Men, and Bisexuals.* Thousand Oaks, CA: Sage.

MOLL, A. (1891) *Die Kontrare Sex Uaelempfindung.* Berlin: Fischer.

MOREAU, P. (1887) *Des Aberations du Sens Genetique.* Paris: Asselin.

ODETS, W. (1995) *In the Shadow of the Epidemic: Being HIV Negative in the Age of AIDS.* London: Cassell.

PARKER, I. (Ed.) (1999) *Deconstructing Psychotherapy.* London: Sage.

PATTON, C. (1986) *Sex and Germs: The Politics of AIDS.* Boston, MA: South End Press.

PAYNE, E. (1999) *Narrative Therapy: An Introduction for Counsellors.* London: Sage.

PLANT, R. (1986) *The Pink Triangle: The Nazi War Against Homosexuals.* New York: Henry and Holt.

PRILLELTENSKY, I. (1989) Psychology and the status quo. *American Psychologist, 44,* 795–802.

RAPPAPORT, J. (1977) *Community Psychology: Values, Research and Action.* New York: Holt, Rinehart and Winston.

RATIGAN, B. (1996) Working with older gay men. In D. Davies and C. Neal (Eds) *Pink Therapy: A Guide for Counsellors and Therapists Working with Lesbian, Gay and Bisexual Clients.* Buckingham: Open University Press.

REED, J.D. (1995) Development in late life: Older lesbian and gay lives. In A.R. D'Augelli and C.J. Patterson (Eds) *Lesbian, Gay, and Bisexual Identities Over the Lifespan: Psychological Perspectives*. New York: Oxford University Press.

RIVERS, I. (1995) Mental health issues among lesbians and gay men bullied in school. *Health and Social Care in the Community, 3*, 380–383.

RUSSO, V. (1987) *The Celluloid Closet: Homosexuality in the Movies*. New York: Harper and Row.

SAEWYC, E.M., BEARINGER, L.H., HEINZ, P.A., BLUM, R.W. and RESNICK, M.D. (1998) Gender differences in health and risk behaviours among bisexual and homosexual adolescents. *Journal of Adolescent Health, 23*, 181–188.

SANDERSON, T. (1995) *Mediawatch*. London: Cassell.

SAVIN-WILLIAMS, R.C. (1990) *Gay and Lesbian Youth: Expressions of Identity*. New York: Hemisphere.

SHOWALTER, E. (1985) *The Female Malady: Women, Madness and English Culture 1830–1980*. London: Virago.

SHOWALTER, E. (1997) *Hystories, Hysterical Epidemics and Modern Culture*. London: Picador.

SIMPSON, M. (Ed.) (1996) *Anti-Gay*. London: Freedom Editions.

SOCARIDES, C. (1968) *The Overt Homosexual*. New York: Jason Aronson.

SONTAG, S. (1983) *A Susan Sontag Reader*. London: Penguin.

SONTAG, S. (1989) *AIDS and its Metaphors*. London: Penguin.

SPENCER, C. (1995) *Homosexuality: A History*. London: Fourth Estate.

STALL, R. and WILEY, J. (1988) A comparison of alcohol and drug use patterns of homosexual and heterosexual men. *Drug and Alcohol Dependence, 22*, 63–73.

TARNOWSKY, B. (1886) *Die Krankhaften Erscheinungen des Geschlectsinnes: Eine Forensich-Psychiatrische Studien*. Berlin: Hirschwald.

TAYLOR, G.W. (2000) Deathmaking and gay sexualities in the age of AIDS. *Changes: An International Journal of Psychology and Psychotherapy, 18*, 49–61.

TRUMBACH, R. (1977) London sodomites; Homosexual behaviour and western culture in the eighteenth century. *Journal of Social History, 11*, 1–33.

USSHER, J.M. (1991) *Women's Madness: Misogyny or Mental Illness*. Hemel Hempstead: Harvester Wheatsheaf.

WATNEY, S. (1987) *Policing Desire: Pornography, AIDS and the Media*. London: Comedia.

WEEKS, J (1990) *Coming Out: Homosexual Politics in Britain from the Nineteenth Century to the Present*. London: Quartet Books.

WEINBERG, G. (1972) *Society and the Healthy Homosexual*. New York: St Martin's Press.

WHITE, M. and EPSTON, D. (1990) *Narrative Means to Therapeutic Ends*. New York: W.W. Norton.

WILDE, O. (1890/1991) *The Picture of Dorian Gray*. London: Penguin.

WOODS, C. (1995) *State of a Queer Nation: A Critique of Gay and Lesbian Politics in 1990s Britain*. London: Cassell.

WORLD HEALTH ORGANIZATION (1992) *The ICD 10 – Classification of Mental and Behavioural Disorders*. Geneva: World Health Organization.

YOUNG, I. (1995) *The Stonewall Experiment: A Gay Psychohistory*. London: Cassell.

ZIEBOLD, T.O. and MONGEON, J.E. (1982) *Gay and Sober: Directions for Counselling and Therapy*. New York: Harrington Park Press.

Chapter 10

Lesbian and Gay Affirmative Psychotherapy: Defining the Domain

Martin Milton, Adrian Coyle and Charles Legg

When the American Psychiatric Association decided in 1973 to remove homosexuality as an official diagnostic category from its *Diagnostic and Statistical Manual of Mental Disorders*, this represented a formal recognition of a changing social outlook on homosexuality and prepared the way for further changes in the mental health field. One such change is the development of 'lesbian and gay affirmative psychotherapy' (but see Gonsiorek's, 1996, consideration of its earlier theoretical roots) – hereafter referred to as 'affirmative therapy'. This development can be seen as a response to the problematic way in which psychotherapeutic work with lesbian and gay clients has historically been discussed in the psychotherapeutic literature (Milton and Coyle, 1999) and the negative therapeutic experiences consistently encountered by lesbians and gay men (Garnets *et al.*, 1991; Proctor, 1994; Golding, 1997; Annesley and Coyle, 1998; McFarlane, 1998; Milton and Coyle, 1998a). An affirmative approach to therapeutic practice developed slowly at first but there now exists a sizeable literature on this topic (see Milton and Coyle, 1998b, for a resource list). Despite this, there remains a lack of consensus concerning what constitutes lesbian and gay affirmative perspectives and practices within therapy. Some have conceptualized affirmative therapy as a distinct way of working with particular stances that must be taken; for example, raising experiences of oppression to consciousness and undoing conditioning associated with negative stereotypes of lesbians and gay men (Clark, 1987). Others have conceptualized affirmative practice as a non-discriminatory, contextually aware attitude when working with lesbian and gay clients that can be incorporated into mainstream psychotherapeutic theories and practices (Malyon, 1982; Davies and Neal, 1996, 2000; Ellis, 1997; Shelley, 1998). The challenge presented by both these viewpoints is to 'update' established therapeutic models or to develop new theories and practices that attend to the diversity of experience represented by lesbian and gay sexualities (Malley and Tasker, 1999).

Literature on affirmative therapy: common characteristics

In more specific terms, the literature on affirmative therapy presents a number of qualities that are said to characterize affirmative approaches. One quality that is regarded as central – and sometimes so fundamental that it is not explicitly stated – is the therapist's ability to view lesbian and gay sexualities as being as normal, natural and healthy as any other sexual orientation (Isay, 1989; Hitchings, 1994, 1997; Young, 1995; Davies, 1996; Haldeman, 2000; Morrow, 2000). Another quality commonly ascribed to affirmative therapists is that they should be of the opinion that sexuality *per se* is not the cause of the psychological difficulties presented by lesbian and gay clients (Kingdon, 1979; Malyon, 1982; Garnets *et al.*, 1991; Milton and Coyle, 1998a; Haslam, 2000). However, it is deemed acceptable to believe that negative social evaluations of and responses to lesbian and gay sexualities may cause or exacerbate clients' distress. Hence, a contextual focus is thought to be important as it assists therapists in assessing whether problems are primarily related to personal dynamics or to anti-lesbian and gay prejudice (Gonsiorek, 1985; Falco, 1991; Young, 1995; Dworkin, 2000). This differentiation is held to be significant for clinical formulation, treatment planning and the selection of a therapeutic focus (Tasker and McCann, 1999).

The affirmative therapist's ability to empathize with the experience of their lesbian and gay clients is said to be important in increasing the therapist's understanding of their clients (Stein, 1988; Moon, 1994; Davies, 2000). Therefore it is suggested that the therapist should be knowledgeable about lesbian and gay sexualities (McWhirter and Mattison, 1985; Rochlin, 1985; Cabaj, 1988; Buhrke, 1989; Isay, 1989; Murphy, 1991; Ratigan, 1995; Liddle, 1996; Browning *et al.*, 1997; Shannon and Woods, 1997; Milton and Coyle, 1998a; Gray, 2000) and particularly about the stresses associated with being lesbian or gay in discriminatory contexts (Malyon, 1982; Falco, 1991; Greene, 1994; Hancock, 1995; Young, 1995; McCarn and Fessinger, 1996; Annesley and Coyle, 1998; Davies, 2000; Hancock, 2000; Izzard, 2000). Matching therapists and clients on the basis of their sexual identity – and also in terms of gender – is often discussed as one specific way of facilitating therapists' understanding of the experiences of the client, particularly of experiences that highlight the differences between lesbian/gay and heterosexual lives (Riddle and Sang, 1978; Gartrell, 1984; Moon, 1994; Leitman, 1995; Liddle, 1996; Annesley and Coyle, 1998). However, the potential disadvantages of such matching have also been recognized (Hitchings, 1994), including the possibility that a commonality of sexual identity between therapist and client may be overridden by other important differences – for example, in gender, culture and ethnicity – and so may not be as therapeutically useful as might first appear (Brauner, 2000; Morrow, 2000). A final common theme in the literature concerns the need for the therapist to be open about and comfortable with their own sexual identity in order to avoid personal issues related to sexual identity becoming entangled with their clients' issues (McWhirter and Mattison, 1985; Falco, 1991; Garnets *et al.*, 1991; Hayes and Gelso, 1993; Hitchings, 1994; Brown, 1996; Liddle, 1996; Davies, 2000; Dworkin, 2000; Izzard, 2000; Perlman, 2000).

Exploring the domain empirically

Although these commonalities can be discerned in the literature on affirmative therapy, questions remain concerning the definitions and meanings accorded to affirmative practice by practitioners who believe themselves to be working affirmatively and clients who believe themselves to have experienced affirmative practice. While one would expect some correspondence between the views of practitioners and clients and the literature on affirmative therapy, there may also be differences. These might arise partly from the gap that routinely exists between theory and practice and partly from the fact that lesbian and gay affirmative therapy remains a 'work in progress' and so challenges that have been encountered and developments that have been devised by practitioners and clients may not yet have filtered into the professional literature. In an attempt to explore empirically what is meant by lesbian and gay affirmative therapy, we interviewed 14 therapists who described themselves as practising in an affirmative way and 18 clients who had received affirmative therapy. To be eligible for the study, 'clients' had to self-identify as lesbian or gay and had to have experienced psychotherapy for at least three months with an appropriately qualified therapist. During this experience the clients needed to have felt that matters related to their sexuality had been attended to in a sensitive and productive manner. 'Therapist' participants needed to have been accredited by at least one professional accrediting body (for example, the British Association for Counselling, the British Psychological Society's Divisions of Clinical or Counselling Psychology or the United Kingdom Council for Psychotherapy) and be working from a position that they felt was lesbian and gay affirmative.

The sample included male (N=14) and female (N=4) clients, heterosexual female therapists (N=3), lesbian therapists (N=2) and gay male therapists (N=9); no heterosexual male therapists responded to invitations to participate. In terms of ethnicity, all but one of the participants identified as 'white'; the only non-white participant (a client) defined himself as Indian. The mean age of the therapists was 43 years (range 28–64; standard deviation 11.9) and of the clients, 37 years (range 24–58; standard deviation 8.6). The majority of participants had been educated to postgraduate level (13 therapists – 92.9 per cent; 9 clients – 50 per cent). The mean length of time since the therapists had achieved accreditation was 3.1 years (range 0.5–8; standard deviation 2.1). As shown in Table 10.1, the range of theoretical approaches used/experienced was diverse. Note that the orientation categories in Table 10.1 are those reported by participants and are not mutually exclusive; also several participants reported experiences with more than one model. Clients reported entering therapy to address a range of problems, including addiction, anxiety, depression, bereavement, 'coming out' and sexuality-related issues and family and relationship problems.

Table 10.1: Theoretical orientations of therapist participants and theoretical orientations experienced by client participants.

Theoretical Orientation	Therapist Participants	Client Participants
Cognitive-Behavioural	1 (2.2%)	3 (6.5%)
Existential-Phenomenological	1 (2.2%)	2 (4.4%)
Gestalt	1 (2.2%)	2 (2.2%)
Humanistic	3 (6.6%)	10 (21.8%)
Integrative	7 (15.2%)	1 (2.2%)
Jungian	0	1 (2.2%)
Neuro-Linguistic Programming	1 (2.2%)	0
Psychoanalytic	2 (4.4%)	4 (8.7%)
Psychosynthesis	1 (2.2%)	2 (4.4%)
Systemic	2 (4.4%)	0
Transactional Analysis	0	1 (2.2%)
Don't Know	0	1 (2.2%)

Most participants were interviewed in their places of work or in their homes. The interview schedule for therapists included questions about their training, ideas about what constitutes affirmative practice, what leads them to see their current practice as affirmative, the benefits and limitations of working in this way and the role of their theoretical orientation in helping or hindering affirmative practice. The interview schedule for clients explored their ideas about what constitutes affirmative practice and focused on questions about their experiences of affirmative and non-affirmative therapy, including the factors that drew them to therapy, whether and how their sexuality was raised and the perceived usefulness of their affirmative therapy. Interviews were audiotaped and the tapes were transcribed verbatim. Data were analysed using grounded theory techniques with the aim of producing a coherent account that was attentive to the connections between different aspects of the data set (Glaser and Strauss, 1967; Pidgeon, 1996; Pidgeon and Henwood, 1996).

In the rest of this chapter, a selective overview of the analysis is presented in order to provide a sense of what were identified as key issues in lesbian and gay affirmative psychotherapy. In the quotations that are cited, empty square brackets indicate where material has been omitted and three dots indicate a short pause; material that has been added for clarification appears within square brackets; words in upper case lettering convey emphasis. Pseudonyms are used to indicate the sources of the quotations and participants are identified either as 'a client' or 'a therapist' (where this is not immediately apparent from the context).

Contextual factors

Contextual factors were said to be crucially important for lesbian and gay affirmative psychotherapy, which mirrors a theme in some therapeutic literature (Cohn, 1989; Safran, 1990a, 1990b; Samuels, 1993; Stolorow *et al.*, 1994; Morrow, 2000). These factors can be located within the therapeutic setting, the therapeutic encounter and the wider sociopolitical domain and they shape the possibility of the therapy being lesbian and gay affirmative. Participants discussed a range of contextual factors. Here we will focus on the practices and policies of the setting in which therapy takes place and the gender and sexual identity of the therapists (and clients).

The setting
The physical setting in which therapy takes place and the practices associated with the organization that provides the therapy often have an impact on clients' initial experiences of therapy. Some participants felt that therapy settings can sometimes encourage an open expression of sexuality-related issues. For example, Zoe (a client) noted how a student counselling service had managed this by including sexuality issues on the therapy centre's intake form as 'something you could tick. [It] was quite nice and easy to do it that way'. Other participants

noted that the setting could limit the degree to which practitioners might work in a lesbian and gay affirmative manner by censuring an acceptance and open discussion of lesbian and gay experience. Reflecting on his experience of practice with an adolescent male, Ross (a therapist) commented 'I would have been heavily censured by the organization I was working in [if I had discussed gay sexuality] because [ ] I would have been seen as encouraging his homosexuality, which would not have been acceptable within that organization'.

Gender

For some, the gender of the therapist was thought to be an important consideration in affirmative therapy. However, some other participants viewed it as irrelevant. Where gender was experienced as important, it was felt to be crucial to the manner in which a therapist is chosen and was said to influence the issues that can be worked on. Male and female therapists were represented as bringing different gender-based qualities to the therapeutic encounter, often mirroring the stereotypical ways in which men and women tend to be viewed in everyday life. Male therapists were also seen as better able to withstand some of the material that the client might bring. For example, Grant (a client) said 'I felt I could perhaps talk a bit more openly with a man, and uh, talk about my homosexuality more to a man than I could to [a woman]'. By contrast, female therapists were sometimes seen in terms of stereotypically 'feminine' qualities such as being nurturant. For example, Sam (a client) felt that, in choosing a female therapist, he had 'wanted some sort of mothering in a way, some supporting' and reckoned that the reported absence of sexual tension in his relationship with his female therapist had facilitated this.

Sexual identities and matching

Various views were expressed by participants on the question of whether lesbian and gay affirmative therapists need to be lesbian or gay themselves, i.e., whether therapists and clients need to be matched in terms of sexual identity. Some participants (both therapists and clients) argued that it is not necessary for a therapist to be lesbian or gay in order to provide affirmative therapy. Indeed, some participants suggested that particular benefits might accrue from working with a heterosexual affirmative therapist who can to some extent represent the heterosexual world within the therapeutic context. As Adam (a client) put it, 'to have a straight person who is on my side – it could actually help with my relationship with the world out there'.

A few participants expressed the view that lesbian and gay affirmative therapy can only be provided by lesbian and gay therapists because of the difficulties faced by heterosexuals in understanding and empathizing with lesbian and gay experiences. This was acknowledged to be a controversial view and one therapist felt that he had 'set the cat among the pigeons' (Brad) by having voiced it in the past. However, other participants did attend to the therapeutic benefits that might be available from having a lesbian or gay therapist working with a lesbian or gay client. For example, affirmative therapists who are themselves lesbian or gay and who are 'out' within the therapeutic context were seen as potentially embodying a challenge to pathologizing stereotypes and providing hope that negative views of lesbian and gay sexuality can be overcome. As Maggie (a lesbian therapist) put it, 'As a therapist you are in a powerful position and you can be a lesbian, which is a not good thing [in the eyes of society and perhaps in the eyes of the client too] – [ ] possibly [by being an "out" lesbian therapist] there's a way to make it a [ ] slightly gooder thing'. The fact that the therapist is lesbian or gay was also seen as providing them with an authority within affirmative therapy that may not be available to the heterosexual therapist.

Another viewpoint on this issue was that, although there are challenges involved, heterosexual therapists may be able to provide lesbian and gay affirmative therapy. As Maggie (a therapist) put it, 'It's possible but I think it's hard'. This view was accompanied by a discussion of particular issues that heterosexual therapists would need to explore before being able to provide this sort of therapy. For example, Alec (a client) felt it was important that 'the therapist has spent some time exploring their sexuality and [is] non-judgemental and accepting – then they should be OK whether they are gay or straight'. Liam (a therapist) applied this need for self-reflection and self-exploration to heterosexual *and* lesbian and gay therapists, saying that, in order to practise affirmatively, 'any therapist will need to have explored their own sexuality – probably important for any gay therapist to have explored their heterosexuality and probably for any heterosexual therapist to have found at least a small part of themselves that might loosely be described as gay'.

Disclosure of sexual identity

In common with other therapist participants, Ben (a therapist) discussed the importance of knowing about a client's sexual identity early in therapy so that this information would be available to the therapeutic process: 'Almost all the time I would know the sexual orientation...I always thought that was an important part'. Some clients spoke of having appreciated this and disclosed their sexuality at an early stage: Ewan (a client) said he 'raised it in one of the initial sessions' and Greg (a client) said he raised it 'right from the very beginning. The very first time I ever saw him, I said I needed to talk about it'.

Participants also recognized that disclosure can feel risky to both clients and therapists. Sam (a client) said 'It is risky to tell anybody in a way, [ ] risky for me to look at it', as disclosure has various implications for both self and other – something that has been well charted in the literature on 'coming out' (for example, Cass, 1979; Coleman, 1982; Weinberg, 1983; Lewis, 1984; Minton and McDonald, 1984; Harry, 1993; see also Chapter 4). Some of the participants felt that it should be left to clients to raise the issue of their sexuality. Tony (a therapist) said 'I think it is up to the client to raise [their sexuality] and they always do. [ ] I have no special pre-arranged way of dealing with [it]'. However, others felt that at times it might be important for therapists to search actively for information about a client's sexual identity. Several therapists commented on this and provided examples of how they might do this. Ross said that when working with adolescents, he 'would never ask [ ] if they had a boyfriend or girlfriend because it just rules out other possibilities. [I would ask] do they have a partner or do they have someone special they are seeing at the minute? I put it in a gender-neutral way'. Likewise, Liam described asking a client: 'So tell me [ ] – when you go to the gym, do you notice that you find some of the people – the men or the women – interesting and sexually attractive?'. Both Ross and Liam felt that these approaches allowed space for a variety of possible sexual identities to be discussed. Not to seek information about the client's sexual identity was seen by some as a form of not attending to lesbian and gay sexualities and colluding with what they saw as the routine silencing of lesbian and gay sexualities in therapeutic contexts.

Participants argued that general self-disclosure by therapists might be particularly useful when working with lesbian and gay clients as it is a way of potentially diminishing the power differential between therapist and client. Thus Jennifer (a therapist) said: 'I might be a little bit more self-disclosing because a gay client might need to know where I am coming from. [ ] Often they have an expectation of people being prejudiced and they might ask about that. I suppose in order to lessen the power between us I would be a bit more self-disclosing'. Self-disclosure was thus represented as one way that a client can experience the therapist as being safe to engage with. On the same theme, Jennifer related an example of how she used self-disclosure to help build a therapeutic relationship when working with a lesbian client: 'One gay client I disclosed being Jewish to – turned out that she was Jewish and that was a link between us but that wasn't really to do with her being gay. [ ] [It was more to do with] an understanding of what it is like to be slightly outside the mainstream'.

On the issue of the therapist disclosing their sexual identity to their clients, only one therapist expressed the view that the role of the therapist is to 'make it explicit that [ ] their sexuality – like everything else – is [ ] on the table for discussion' (Anna). Other therapists did not offer general recommendations about always or never disclosing; instead they stressed the importance of being willing to consider disclosure. Contraindications were mentioned as occasionally there are times when it may not be useful for the therapist to self-disclose; this was considered in relation to the needs of the client. Liam gave an example of how he might decide that it is not therapeutic or important to disclose his sexual identity: with 'clients who are very ambivalent about they may be gay, they may not be gay and [where] they are doing some kind of struggle and they don't know about me for the moment, [ ] unless they ask I will leave that'.

Sexual feelings

Several client participants suggested that, while clients desire to know about their therapists and while this is likely to play a role in establishing effective therapeutic relationships, this desire might include sexual interest in the therapist. Such interest was not seen as dependent on the sexual identity of the therapist; Adam recounted that this had been an aspect of his therapy with a heterosexual woman. As he put it, 'The groin stuff came with it. [ ] I did also feel very sexually attracted towards her but it was much more...it wasn't just like "Phwoah, I fancy you" – it was "WOOOMPH – good grief"'.

While these feelings were seen as a potentially important facilitating aspect of therapy, the accounts provided by the participants also acknowledged that sexual feelings, or even the potential thereof, can create anxiety in and be a hindrance to therapy. Ewan (a client) described how he had decided against seeing a gay male therapist: 'Obviously he was the same gender as me and the same sexual orientation and it would almost be...as if it would be too near the knuckle'. Participants also noted that sexual feelings are not always directly experienced between therapist and client but are discussed more generally. Patrick (a client) described how, in order to 'normalize' his (Patrick's) passionate sexual activity, his therapist had talked about 'having sex with his wife all weekend when they first met [ ] and it was a bit of an unthreatening fantasy because if he had told me that he was gay himself and spent the entire weekend shagging his boyfriend [ ] when he first met him, that might have been a bit too – that might have freaked me out a bit'.

Knowledge of lesbian and gay experiences

Participants considered differences between lesbian/gay and heterosexual experiences and suggested that different issues and therapeutic processes may exist for people of different sexual identities. Natalie (a therapist) attempted to outline some of these differences. She identified 'different expectations in a relationship, different role models and things people aspire to [ ] perhaps different norms – [ ] the meaning it [the person's sexual identity] has in that person's social circle and the meaning it might have to their commitment to the relationship'. Participants felt that affirmative therapists should be highly knowledgeable about these and other issues, including lesbian and gay sexual behaviour, lesbian and gay relationships (and the variety of potential relationship structures) and the experience of negotiating a marginalized sexual identity, including 'internalized homophobia'. On the topic of lesbian and gay relationships, Adam (a client) said 'I am not sure that the world is quite the same for a gay couple as it is for a straight couple...polygamy in straight relationships may be more problematic than in gay relationships'. Ewan (a client) felt it was particularly important that the therapist have 'a good understanding of problems that could face lesbians and gay men' as he thought this would assist the therapist in recognizing the impact of sexuality on the experiences available to the client. Participants believed it was important for the therapist's knowledge to be grounded in experience of some kind rather than being gained through intellectual/academic methods alone. Adam (a client) felt that his therapist had been able to convey experiential understanding because she 'had a brother who was gay and maybe...that by a process of osmosis she kind of [knew]'.

Some participants reported negative experiences arising from their therapists' lack of knowledge of lesbian and gay contexts. The most common of these related to therapists seeing 'open' relationships (i.e., relationships that were not sexually exclusive) as problematic and an inevitable source of conflict. Adam (a client) said that he had 'an open relationship and I think I got a vibe that her [the therapist's] feeling was that our relationship was insubstantial, that it was weak, that it needed to be propped up by affairs outside of the relationship [ ] I had the feeling it had something to do with a...heterosexual's eye view of what an ideal relationship should be'.

Linking to the question of matching, participants suggested that lesbian and gay therapists have more 'accurate' awareness of their lesbian and gay clients' experiences than heterosexual therapists. However, Ross (a therapist) noted that a shared sexuality does not guarantee a similarity of experience and does not automatically confer a shared understanding. He said 'I have had clients say that "You must know what I'm talking about here" and I have [ ] said "I kinda know what you're talking about from my own experience but I'm not sure it's exactly the same and I guess some of the questions that I am wondering about in relation to what you're raising are something about the difference between your experience and my experience"'.

Safety

Participants linked the conveying of an appropriate understanding of lesbian and gay experiences by therapists to the creation of a sense of safety for clients. When considering therapist self-disclosure, we noted that this too may be a means of creating a safe therapeutic context. Client participants also connected a sense of safety with a non-judge-mental stance and with therapists attending to the experiences of constructing and maintaining lesbian or gay identity. As Greg (a client) put it, 'I wanted to talk about what it was like to be gay. I wanted it to be safe about being gay, to express it'. The topic of 'coming out' is part of the content of many therapeutic encounters with lesbians and gay men. For many client participants, therapy was one of the first places where they had voiced the possibility of a lesbian or gay identity. Grant said that in therapy 'I admitted for the very first time to any strangers my sexual orientation...I must say it was very positive'.

Linking once again to the question of matching, participants noted that clients (and others) may assume that therapy with a heterosexual therapist will be unsafe. Jennifer (a therapist) noted that 'the fact of being straight can set up barriers, whatever my attitude. I may have areas that I am not aware of even though I might try'. These concerns were also voiced by client participants. For example, Mark (a client) said 'I didn't believe that a straight person would be able to under-stand my experience of my sexuality and accept it and really understand what is happening for me'. Tania (a client) felt that 'some heterosexual people [therapists] [ ] would make judgements'. Similar-ly, Kyle (a client) suggested that 'if [the therapist] was straight, I'd be assuming that he was automatically against me'. It is important not to suggest that views such as these are purely an aspect of the client's anxiety or projection. Reflecting on their experiences, participants were clear that many heterosexual people do struggle to understand lesbian and gay sexualities and experiences. Oliver (a client) remembered how two previous therapists 'clearly did not understand and it was as though I had to explain everything and check out "Do you know what I mean?"'. A result of such an experience can be that the client pathol-ogizes himself or herself: as Oliver put it, the client may be left wondering 'Are my problems so bad that my counsellor can't under-stand? – I must really be screwed up'.

Professional literature and training

The scientific and professional literature on therapy is something 'external' to therapeutic relationships that is influential in developing practitioners and was seen as having an impact on the degree to which they are able to be lesbian and gay affirmative. Participants noted that this is due to the influence of the literature on training, supervision and theories of practice. Many participants suggested that training was generally lacking in relation to its coverage of working with lesbian and gay clients and therefore it was difficult to talk openly about sex-uality-related issues in training (see also Coyle *et al.*, 1999). Participants ssed the view that the professional therapeutic literature is characterized either by an absence of or limited and stagnant views of lesbian and gay experience and development and of therapeutic practice with lesbian and gay clients. For example, referring to one particular body of literature, Hannah (a therapist) said 'I don't find that counselling provides much diversity in the knowledge that's presented about lesbian and gay theory...I find it quite boring actually. I find it quite tedious [ ] saying the same thing over and over again'. Whereas Hannah felt that the literature in this particular domain was of limited use, she believed that lesbian and gay affirmative practice could be strengthened by attention to the sociological literature, as it 'provides me with a useful resource of information [ ] It's like suddenly going from black and white to colour'.

Jack (a therapist) also reflected on how little lesbian and gay issues had been addressed in his clinical psychology training. He remarked that the total coverage of lesbian and gay issues occurred 'in part of the two or three days on HIV [where] there is [ ] an hour's lecture on homosexuality'. This example highlights the medicalized context within which participants said lesbian and gay sexuality was sometimes presented.

Theoretical models of therapy

Participants viewed theoretical models of therapy as being of great importance although they also saw the 'models' question as a complex issue. Brad (a therapist) felt that lesbian and gay affirmative therapists are 'open to questioning the theory. They aren't dogmatic and highly opinionated [ ] It is an open-minded examining of theory'. There was also support for the importance of moving from a stance of 'theory as truth' to theory as 'frameworks and that's really it...[ ] They are quite useful in that respect but to read into them a way of working as being the only way of working is quite dangerous really' (Hannah, a therapist). Participants suggested that one way of being circumspect about notions of 'truth' was to have an awareness of a range of theoretical models rather than being limited to one – 'something about [being] aware of other models of working and constantly building on that', as Ross (a therapist) put it.

Clients and therapists spoke of a number of specific psychotherapeutic theories and considered their potential for shaping lesbian and gay affirmative practice (see Davies and Neal, 2000, for a systematic consideration of this from the perspective of therapists reflecting on their own theoretical approaches; see also Fassinger, 2000). Not surprisingly, therapists often focused on the positive aspects of their own theoretical orientation and stressed its affirmative potential. However, some therapists were also able to point to possible limitations in their approach's affirmative potential and some discussed the possible benefits of approaches other than their own.

Reflecting on his own experiences in therapy, Oliver (a client) felt that 'humanistic and transactional analysis-influenced therapists have seemed to be more affirmative'. Liam (an integrative and humanistic therapist) suggested that humanistic models might be able to achieve this as they 'don't hold an illness/sickness view of homosexuality'. The particular qualities and principles of the orientation were thought to assist in challenging such a view. Humanistic therapy was said to have 'a very strong anti-discrimination value embedded in its core philosophy. [ ] It's absolutely crystal clear and so there's a real commitment there' (Anna, an integrative therapist). Jack (a cognitive-behavioural therapist) agreed with this view when he said 'Rogerian, humanist, existential lend itself very much to a gay affirmative stance...ideas of kind of fulfilling your human potential...being a whole person and getting back to active listening...a fertile ground for gay affirmative practice'. Gestalt therapy was viewed as respectful of lesbian and gay sexuality as it was said to allow flexibility and to recognize the value of difference. Mark (a client) suggested that 'Gestalt is very positive to people who are different. [ ] [It] would respect people who are in minorities and who view things differently'. On being asked to describe how a therapeutic model might assist the therapist's attempts to be lesbian and gay affirmative, Brad (an integrative/existential-phenomenological therapist) referred to phenomenological psychotherapy. He believed that 'the whole idea of phenomenology and dialogic relationship is very useful. That the purpose of the therapist is to enter into the phenomenological world of the client [ ] to understand the client – that in itself is extremely curative'.

Several therapist participants considered the stance that cognitive-behavioural therapy takes towards lesbian and gay sexuality in relation to its potential to be lesbian and gay affirmative. It was generally seen as non-pathologizing but, more specifically, Jack (a cognitive-behavioural therapist) felt that 'it assists because it has a pretty much a value neutral, pragmatic rather than a dogmatic stance...and because it doesn't have much to say about early developmental processes'. Participants felt that systemic therapy was useful because of the attention that it pays to the relationship between the contexts of the client, the family and the therapist. Maggie (a systemic therapist) expressed the view that 'a systemic orientation is [ ] very useful in assuming that the circumstances of your external world and the circumstances of your internal world are not in fact separate, discrete entities...that they [ ] inevitably [ ] affect each other and are affected by each other' (for more on this approach, see Chapter 11).

Participants expressed concern about the manner in which psychoanalytic theory was seen to pathologize or ignore lesbian and gay sexuality (see Chapter 9 for a brief discussion of this). However, Mark (a client) acknowledged the diversity of outlooks represented by the umbrella term 'psychoanalytic theory' and chose to problematize one particular version of it, saying that 'traditional psychoanalytic theory is very homophobic and anti-gay and people coming from that traditional theoretical training are going to be harder to work with if not impossible'. Jon (a psychoanalytic therapist) stated that his 'first [thrice weekly] training analysis had to be abandoned after 18 months. It became apparent that the therapist wasn't going to "pass" a trainee who was a practising gay man. Only a "cure" to heterosexuality would have passed me' (see Phillips *et al.*, 2001, for comments from psychoanalytic practitioners on lesbian and gay sexualities which exemplify this pathologizing outlook). Regardless of the degree to which any model is or can be lesbian and gay affirmative, there was also a recognition of a relationship between the practitioner's values and therapeutic skills and the affirmative potential of the therapy.

Therapist flexibility

We have noted above that some participants advocated a flexible, non-dogmatic, questioning stance towards theoretical models of therapy within affirmative practice. Participants also pointed out that flexibility is required because affirmative therapists need to assist clients with a wide range of difficulties and not just issues that are clearly related to sexual identity. As a group, client participants spoke of having sought therapy in response to diverse difficulties. For example, Ulli said he had experienced 'chronic anxiety, recurring depression, panic feelings and social phobia, alcohol abuse and sex addiction'. Such diverse presentations require lesbian and gay affirmative therapists – like most other therapists – to be able to identify and conceptualize a wide range of clinical difficulties. To do this, it was believed that therapists would need to adopt a flexible stance to the client's presenting problems and to therapeutic theory. The participants stressed that this stance would be characterized by its non-pathologizing manner and by its refusal to view sexuality as the necessary cause of the presenting problems. Providing an example of this, Kyle (a client) said of his therapist 'She'll actually say...whatever but it won't be related to my sexuality – it'll be related to other things...other relationships that may have happened in my past'. Linking back to the need for therapists to be knowledgeable about lesbian and gay experiences, it was felt that, in order to develop a comprehensive analysis of clients' difficulties, therapists require 'a good understanding of problems that could face lesbians and gay men [whether they be] because of...family, religious beliefs...different cultural attitudes to homosexuality [or the] problems that people can have at work [ ] because of homophobia' (Ewan, a client). Such flexibility and non-dogmatism in the conceptualization of presenting problems was seen as important because of its perceived potential in facilitating a collaborative working alliance and an increased ability to be empathic.

Outcomes

Some participants suggested that what constitutes positive outcomes in affirmative therapy would be similar to what constitutes positive outcomes in any therapy. However, others identified two particular goals that they felt were important in affirmative therapy, i.e., the development of more positive views of lesbian and gay sexuality and improved relationships with self and others.

Being able to challenge clients appropriately was seen as a significant part of the process of helping clients to develop more positive views of lesbian and gay sexuality. Challenging was primarily seen as an active stance in which the meanings associated with the client's narrative are questioned. Related to the creation of new meaning were the participants' views that therapists can model different ways of being for clients. As Tom (a therapist) put it, 'The most important thing I can do is to model something positive about being gay – that it is possible to be a gay man or a lesbian and be healthy and well and reasonably stable and secure'. However, the concept of modelling was also questioned: Maggie (a therapist) disagreed with the concept entirely, saying 'I find the whole idea of role modelling completely dodgy. I think if you used your therapist as a role model you'd be dead in the water'.

Participants contended that strategies such as challenging and modelling can open up a consideration of the diversity of experience encompassed by the terms 'lesbian' and 'gay man'. This was said to facilitate the building of client confidence in developing and/or facing a sense of their own uniqueness. Participants' reflections on therapeutic practice suggested that it may be that these actions invite the client to reconsider their stereotypes and assumptions about the nature of their own and other lesbian and gay identities, permitting the identification of new possibilities. Challenging and questioning were not confined to *clients'* views, however. Some participants also pointed to the need for therapists to challenge and question their own views and involve themselves in 'scrutinizing one's belief systems and prejudices' (Ross, a therapist), allowing therapists 'to be as conscious as possible of the risks of stereotyping, prejudice and trying to deal with our own tendency to be prejudiced' (Anna, a therapist).

The second major outcome that participants felt was particularly pertinent to affirmative therapy was the development of a capacity for good relationships with oneself and with others – both 'others' in clients' intimate worlds and more general 'others'. Connected with this, it was seen as important that therapeutic meetings should be experienced as a personal (rather than technical) encounter for both participants. It was believed that when therapy allows the client to consider and experience diverse relationships with the therapist, the client may gain insight and skill in developing new ways of relating. Jack (a therapist) extended this to include the potential for clients to build better relationships with other lesbians and gay men whom they will meet in the future; he said that he hoped his clients would develop 'a greater acceptance of other gay men or lesbian women...more of a kind of awareness of diversity rather than using the stereotyped images'.

Participants also felt that if a client develops a relationship as a lesbian or gay man with the therapist and encounters acceptance, respect and affirmation, this increases the likelihood of the client being able to accept, respect and affirm himself/herself. Jack (a therapist) said that he hoped his clients would experience 'greater self acceptance – a...freeing up of shame or distress around sexual identity'. For Oliver (a client), the attainment of self-acceptance had been a prime reason for seeking therapy; he explained that he had done so in the hope that he would be able 'to feel a greater sense of ease with myself'.

Promoting and developing affirmative therapy

The implications of some of the key findings will now be considered but, first, it is necessary to reflect upon the status of these findings. Qualitative research tends to aim for a diversity of participants rather than representative samples, with the intention of exploring the research phenomenon from multiple perspectives. This study achieved diversity on some important dimensions, including the theoretical orientation of the therapists. However, the numbers of female therapists and clients were small relative to the numbers of male therapists and clients; no heterosexual male therapists were recruited at all; and all but one of the participants were white. While it would be possible to suggest reasons for the lack of response from male heterosexual therapists and from therapists and clients from minority ethnic communities, this would be mere speculation. If more time had been available, we would have adopted a theoretical sampling strategy – which involves seeking out different perspectives on the research topic to elaborate and enrich an emergent theoretical account (Glaser and Strauss, 1967) – and would have actively sought to recruit heterosexual male therapists and more non-white and female participants. It is worth noting, however, that the heterosexual male perspective is not entirely absent from the study as some client participants provided accounts of experiences with heterosexual male therapists. Qualitative research on any topic tends to proceed by constructing an increasingly comprehensive picture of the research topic through a series of small-scale, complementary studies, with each extending the insights gained from previous work. We therefore hope that other researchers will extend the analytic account that we have offered by focusing on the views and experiences of those whose voices are missing from or minimally represented in our study.

Despite these limitations, various tentative conclusions concerning the nature of lesbian and gay affirmative therapy can be drawn from the study's findings. Perhaps the most important conclusion is that, on the basis of these participants' views, lesbian and gay affirmative therapy cannot be considered a therapeutic approach analogous to psychodynamic, person-centred or cognitive behavioural approaches, for example, which are grounded in elaborated theories of human development, well-being and distress. Instead, participants' accounts indicate that lesbian and gay affirmative therapy is grounded in certain concepts, skills and qualities of being (many of which characterize good practice with any client group), underpinned by a belief in the acceptability of lesbian and gay sexualities and a thorough understanding of the nature, dynamics and challenges of these sexualities. It might therefore be justifiably defined as a therapeutic 'stance' rather than a theoretically-driven therapeutic approach. Although – as noted earlier – this conceptualization has already featured in the literature on lesbian and gay affirmative therapy, this study has succeeded in grounding it in and elaborating it through accounts of (experiences of) therapeutic practice. This conclusion about the nature of affirmative therapy may, of course, need to be revised or amended in the light of future research which adds new perspectives to the analytic account offered here.

The extent to which (and ease with which) this affirmative stance can be incorporated within different schools of therapeutic theory and practice will vary according to the core assumptions of these schools, with some requiring more significant amendment than others in order to accommodate an affirmative stance. This is a potentially problematic issue because the greater the change that is required, the greater the likelihood of it being resisted, not only because of anti-lesbian and gay prejudice but also because fundamental change may be seen as eroding the very basis of a particular therapeutic tradition. This has been witnessed in attempts to reformulate psychodynamic theories in the light of feminist theory, which has led to debates about whether the end products can still be considered psychodynamic (Schoenewolf, 1997). In addition, queries have been raised about whether these attempts can really be said to have addressed the problems that led psychodynamic approaches to be seen as colluding with and reinforcing women's subjugation (Hollway, 1989; Frosh, 1994). Similarly, it is easy to imagine a situation where disagreement would arise over whether a particular theoretical approach has changed too much or too little in an attempt to be lesbian and gay affirmative. If affirmative practice is considered to be worth striving for within any particular theoretical tradition, change may be unavoidable and such change needs to start with a critical analysis of what may be core assumptions of that tradition. The lessons learned from the development of feminist therapeutic practice may prove valuable in directing, negotiating and advancing this process of change (Dutton-Douglas and Walker, 1988; Brown, 1994; Enns, 1997; Seu and Heenan, 1998). The reflections of therapeutic practitioners on their theoretical approaches in this study and, more especially, the critical reflections on a range of theoretical approaches and the consequent recommendations for affirmative practice in such literature as Davies and Neal (2000) and Fassinger (2000) indicate that this process is already well under way. It is not enough for therapists to separate practice from theory, i.e., to practise in a non-pathologizing way with lesbian and gay clients without challenging pathologizing theory within which their practice may be located – a pattern apparent among some psychoanalytic practitioners in a study by Phillips *et al.* (2001). This achieves little in terms of effecting institutional change.

The promotion of lesbian and gay affirmative therapeutic practice is dependent upon the provision of lesbian and gay affirmative therapeutic training. Therapist participants in the present study highlighted deficiencies in the coverage accorded to working with lesbian and gay clients in their training. As all therapeutic practitioners may potentially encounter lesbian and gay clients, staff on basic and post-qualification therapeutic training courses need to consider how they can ensure they foster competence in lesbian and gay affirmative practice among trainees (see Phillips, 2000, for recommendations concerning training). This will require staff to develop and refine their own competence in this domain and become skilled in disseminating it to trainees. It will also involve creating adequate space within curricula to address issues relevant to lesbian and gay functioning and well-being, such as those outlined by participants in this study when discussing the knowledge of lesbian and gay experiences that affirmative therapists require (for example, knowledge of lesbian and gay sexual behaviour, lesbian and gay relationships and the experience of negotiating a marginalized sexual identity). In addition, it has been suggested that training courses should provide arenas where trainees can explore their own sexualities and sexual prejudices (Izzard, 2000), thereby fostering the critical self-reflection that some participants felt was required in order for therapists to practise affirmatively.

One feature that is notable by its absence from the data set reported in this chapter is any real critique of the concept of affirmative therapy. As affirmative therapy becomes increasingly established, critical analysis becomes not only inevitable but also necessary for its continued development. Some analyses have already raised important questions about an affirmative stance. For example, du Plock (1997) has claimed that affirmative therapy carries with it a set of assumptions about and views of lesbian and gay sexualities which may overwrite the subjectivities of clients in a prescriptive way, giving the power of definition to the therapist; he has taken issue with the idea that therapy (and particularly his own existential-phenomenological approach) should be 'affirming' anything. It has also been claimed that affirmative therapy in the USA has become caught up in identity politics, retreating into an intellectual ghetto divorced from the psychological mainstream (Gonsiorek, 2000). The challenges presented by such analyses should be seen as potentially 'nourishing' for affirmative practice and need to be engaged with seriously if affirmative approaches are to mature and increase in sophistication.

However, the need to engage with informed critical analyses of affirmative therapy should not be used as an excuse for doing nothing to address the negative therapeutic experiences that have been consistently reported by lesbians and gay men in the research literature. If serious and concerted attempts are made in therapeutic training to promote the knowledge and develop (at least some of) the outlooks and qualities identified in this study (and elsewhere) as characterizing an affirmative approach, the likelihood of lesbians and gay men routinely encountering sensitive, informed, non-pathologizing, validating and life-enhancing therapeutic services would be greatly increased. In the light of trauma that has been inflicted upon lesbians and gay men by so-called 'therapeutic' and other 'mental health' services in the past (see Chapters 8 and 9), surely this is a situation that is worth striving for as a matter of urgency.

References

ANNESLEY, P. and COYLE, A. (1998) Dykes and psychs: Lesbian women's experiences of clinical psychology services. *Changes: An International Journal of Psychology and Psychotherapy, 16*, 247–258.

BRAUNER, R. (2000) Embracing difference: Addressing race, culture and sexuality. In C. Neal and D. Davies (Eds) *Issues in Therapy with Lesbian, Gay, Bisexual and Transgender Clients*. Buckingham: Open University Press.

BROWN, L. (1994) *Subversive Dialogues: Theory in Feminist Therapy*. New York: Basic Books.

BROWN, L. (1996) Ethical concerns with sexual minority patients. In R. Cabaj and T. Stein (Eds) *Textbook of Homosexuality and Mental Health*. Washington, DC: American Psychiatric Press.

BROWNING, C., REYNOLDS, A.L. and DWORKIN, S.H. (1997) Affirmative psychotherapy for lesbian women. In D.R. Atkinson and G. Hackett (Eds) *Counseling Diverse Populations*, 2nd ed. Boston, MA: McGraw Hill.

BUHRKE, R. (1989) Training issues for counseling psychologists in working with lesbian women and gay men. *Counseling Psychologist, 19*, 216–234.

CABAJ, R. (1988) Homosexuality and neurosis: Considerations for psychotherapy. *Journal of Homosexuality, 15(1–2)*, 13–23.

CASS, V.C. (1979) Homosexual identity formation: A theoretical model. *Journal of Homosexuality, 4(3)*, 219–235.

CLARK, D. (1987) *The New Loving Someone Gay*. Berkeley, CA: Celestial Arts.

COHN, H. (1997) The place of the actual in psychotherapy. *Free Associations, 18*, 49–61.

COLEMAN, E. (1982) Developmental stages of the coming-out process. In W. Paul, J.D. Weinrich, J.C. Gonsiorek and M.E. Hotvedt (Eds) *Homosexuality: Social, Psychological, and Biological Issues*. Beverly Hills, CA: Sage.

COYLE, A., MILTON, M. and ANNESLEY, P. (1999) The silencing of lesbian and gay voices in psychotherapeutic texts and training. *Changes: An International Journal of Psychology and Psychotherapy, 17*, 132–143.

DAVIES, D. (1996) Towards a model of gay affirmative therapy. In D. Davies and C. Neal (Eds) *Pink Therapy: A Guide for Counsellors and Therapists Working with Lesbian, Gay and Bisexual Clients*. Buckingham: Open University Press.

DAVIES, D. (2000) Person-centred therapy. In D. Davies and C. Neal (Eds) *Therapeutic Perspectives on Working with Lesbian, Gay and Bisexual Clients*. Buckingham: Open University Press.

DAVIES, D. and NEAL, C. (Eds) (1996) *Pink Therapy: A Guide for Counsellors and Therapists Working with Lesbian, Gay and Bisexual Clients*. Buckingham: Open University Press.

DAVIES, D. and NEAL, C. (Eds) (2000) *Therapeutic Perspectives on Working with Lesbian, Gay and Bisexual Clients*. Buckingham: Open University Press.

du PLOCK, S. (1997) Sexual misconceptions: A critique of gay affirmative therapy and some thoughts on an existential-phenomenological theory of sexual orientation. *Journal of the Society for Existential Analysis, 8(2)*, 56–71.

DUTTON-DOUGLAS, M.A. and WALKER, L.E.A. (Eds) (1988) *Feminist Psychotherapies: Integration of Therapeutic and Feminist Systems*. Norwood, NJ: Ablex.

DWORKIN, S.H. (2000) Individual therapy with lesbian, gay, and bisexual clients. In R.M. Perez, K.A. DeBord and K.J. Bieschke (Eds) *Handbook of Counseling and Psychotherapy with Lesbian, Gay, and Bisexual Clients*. Washington DC: American Psychological Association.

ELLIS, M.L. (1997) Who speaks? Who listens? Different voices and different sexualities. *British Journal of Psychotherapy, 13*, 369–383.

ENNS, C.Z. (1997) *Feminist Theories and Feminist Psychotherapies: Origins, Themes, and Variations*. New York: Harrington Park Press/Haworth Press.

FALCO, K.L. (1991) *Psychotherapy with Lesbian Clients: Theory into Practice*. New York: Brunner/Mazel.

FASSINGER, R.E. (2000) Applying counseling theories to lesbian, gay, and bisexual clients: Pitfalls and possibilities. In R.M. Perez, K.A. DeBord and K.J. Bieschke (Eds) *Handbook of Counseling and Psychotherapy with Lesbian, Gay, and Bisexual Clients*. Washington DC: American Psychological Association.

FROSH, S. (1994) *Sexual Difference: Masculinity and Psychoanalysis*. London: Routledge.

GARNETS, L., HANCOCK, K.A., COCHRAN, S.D., GOODCHILDS, J. and PEPLAU, L.A. (1991) Issues in psychotherapy with lesbians and gay men: A survey of psychologists. *American Psychologist, 46*, 964–972.

GARTRELL, N. (1984) Combating homophobia in the psychotherapy of lesbians. *Women & Therapy, 3*, 13–29.

GLASER, B.G. and STRAUSS, A.L. (1967) *The Discovery of Grounded Theory: Strategies for Qualitative Research*. Chicago, IL: Aldine.

GOLDING, J. (1997) *Without Prejudice: MIND Lesbian, Gay and Bisexual Mental Health Awareness Research*. London: MIND Publications.

GONSIOREK, J.C. (Ed.) (1985) *A Guide to Psychotherapy with Gay and Lesbian Clients*. New York: Harrington Park Press.

GONSIOREK, J.C. (1996) Mental health and sexual orientation. In R.C. Savin-Williams and K.M. Cohen (Eds) *The Lives of Lesbians, Gays, and Bisexuals: Children to Adults*. Fort Worth, TX: Harcourt Brace.

GONSIOREK, J. (2000) Foreword. In D. Davies and C. Neal (Eds) *Therapeutic Perspectives on Working with Lesbian, Gay and Bisexual Clients*. Buckingham: Open University Press.

GRAY, J. (2000) Cognitive-behavioural therapy. In D. Davies and C. Neal (Eds) *Therapeutic Perspectives on Working with Lesbian, Gay and Bisexual Clients*. Buckingham: Open University Press.

GREENE, B. (1994) Lesbian and gay sexual orientations: Implications for clinical training, practice, and research. In B. Greene and G.M. Herek (Eds) *Lesbian and Gay Psychology: Theory, Research, and Clinical Applications*. Thousand Oaks, CA: Sage.

HALDEMAN, D.C. (2000) Therapeutic responses to sexual orientation: Psychology's evolution. In B. Greene and G.L. Croom (Eds) *Education, Research, and Practice in Lesbian, Gay, Bisexual, and Transgendered Psychology: A Resource Manual*. Thousand Oaks, CA: Sage.

HANCOCK, K.A. (1995) Psychotherapy with lesbians and gay men. In A.R. D'Augelli and C.J. Patterson (Eds) *Lesbian, Gay, and Bisexual Identities Over the Lifespan: Psychological Perspectives*. New York: Oxford University Press.

HANCOCK, K.A. (2000) Lesbian, gay, and bisexual lives: Basic issues in psychotherapy training and practice. In B. Greene and G.L. Croom (Eds) *Education, Research, and Practice in Lesbian, Gay, Bisexual, and Transgendered Psychology: A Resource Manual*. Thousand Oaks, CA: Sage.

HARRY, J. (1993) Being out: A general model. *Journal of Homosexuality, 26(1)*, 25–39.

HASLAM, D. (2000) Analytical psychology. In D. Davies and C. Neal (Eds) *Therapeutic Perspectives on Working with Lesbian, Gay and Bisexual Clients*. Buckingham: Open University Press.

HAYES, J.A. and GELSO, C.J. (1993) Male counselors' discomfort with gay and HIV infected clients. *Journal of Counseling Psychology, 40*, 86–93.

HITCHINGS, P. (1994) Psychotherapy and sexual orientation. In P. Clarkson and M. Pokorny (Eds) *The Handbook of Psychotherapy*. London: Routledge.

HITCHINGS, P. (1997) Counselling and sexual orientation. In S. Palmer and G. McMahon (Eds) *Handbook of Counselling*. London: Routledge.

HOLLWAY, W. (1989) *Subjectivity and Method in Psychology: Gender, Meaning and Science*. London: Sage.

ISAY, R.A. (1989) *Being Homosexual: Gay Men and their Development*. London: Penguin.

IZZARD, S. (2000) Psychoanalytic psychotherapy. In D. Davies and C. Neal (Eds) *Therapeutic Perspectives on Working with Lesbian, Gay and Bisexual Clients*. Buckingham: Open University Press.

KINGDON, M.A. (1979) Lesbians. *Counseling Psychologist, 8*, 44–45.

LEWIS, L.A. (1984) The coming-out process for lesbians: Integrating a stable identity. *Social Work, Sept-Oct*, 464–469.

LIDDLE, B. (1996) Therapist sexual orientation, gender and counseling practices as they relate to ratings of helpfulness by gay and lesbian clients. *Journal of Counseling Psychology, 43*, 394–401.

MALLEY, M. and TASKER, F. (1999) Lesbians, gay men and family therapy: A contradiction in terms? *Journal of Family Therapy, 21*, 3–29.

MALYON, A.K. (1982) Psychotherapeutic implications of internalized homophobia in gay men. In J. Gonsiorek (Ed.) *Homosexuality and Psychotherapy: A Practitioner's Handbook of Affirmative Models*. New York: Haworth Press.

McCARN, S.R. and FASSINGER, R.E. (1996) Revisioning sexual minority identity formation: A new model of lesbian identity and its implications for counseling and research. *Counseling Psychologist, 24*, 508–534.

McFARLANE, L. (1998) *Diagnosis: Homophobic. The Experiences of Lesbians, Gay Men and Bisexuals in Mental Health Services.* London: PACE.

McWHIRTER, D. and MATTISON, A. (1985) Psychotherapy for gay male couples. In J.C. Gonsiorek (Ed.) *A Guide to Psychotherapy with Gay and Lesbian Clients.* New York: Harrington Park Press.

MILTON, M. and COYLE, A. (1998a) Psychotherapy with lesbian and gay clients. *The Psychologist, 11*, 73–76.

MILTON, M. and COYLE, A. (1998b) Reference library on counselling psychology: Lesbian and gay affirmative therapy. *Counselling Psychology Review, 13(4)*, 36–40.

MILTON, M. and COYLE, A. (1999) Lesbian and gay affirmative psychotherapy: Issues in theory and practice. *Sexual and Marital Therapy, 14*, 43–59.

MINTON, H.L. and McDONALD, G.J. (1984) Homosexual identity formation as a developmental process. *Journal of Homosexuality, 9(2–3)*, 91–104.

MOON, L. (1994) Counselling with lesbians and gay men. *Changes: An International Journal of Psychology and Psychotherapy, 12*, 277–283.

MORROW, S.L. (2000) First do no harm: Therapist issues in psychotherapy with lesbian, gay, and bisexual clients. In R.M. Perez, K.A. DeBord and K.J. Bieschke (Eds) *Handbook of Counseling and Psychotherapy with Lesbian, Gay, and Bisexual Clients.* Washington DC: American Psychological Association.

MURPHY, B.C. (1991) Educating mental health professionals about gay and lesbian issues. *Journal of Homosexuality, 22(3–4)*, 229–246.

PERLMAN, G. (2000) Transactional analysis. In D. Davies and C. Neal (Eds) *Therapeutic Perspectives on Working with Lesbian, Gay and Bisexual Clients.* Buckingham: Open University Press.

PHILLIPS, J.C. (2000) Training issues and considerations. In R.M. Perez, K.A. DeBord and K.J. Bieschke (Eds) *Handbook of Counseling and Psychotherapy with Lesbian, Gay, and Bisexual Clients.* Washington DC: American Psychological Association.

PHILLIPS, P., BARTLETT, A. and KING, M. (2001) Psychotherapists' approaches to gay and lesbian patients/clients: A qualitative study. *British Journal of Medical Psychology, 74*, 73–84.

PIDGEON, N.F. (1996) Grounded theory: Theoretical background. In J.T.E. Richardson (Ed.) *Handbook of Qualitative Research Methods for Psychology and the Social Sciences.* Leicester: BPS Books.

PIDGEON, N.F. and HENWOOD, K.L. (1996) Grounded theory: Practical implementation. In J.T.E. Richardson (Ed.) *Handbook of Qualitative Research Methods for Psychology and the Social Sciences.* Leicester: BPS Books.

PROCTOR, G. (1994) Lesbian clients' experience of clinical psychology: A listener's guide. *Changes: An International Journal of Psychology and Psychotherapy, 12*, 290–298.

RATIGAN, B. (1995) Inner world, outer world: Exploring the tensions of race, sexual orientation and class and the internal world. *Psychodynamic Counselling, 1*, 173–186.

RIDDLE, D.I. and SANG, B. (1978) Psychotherapy with lesbians. *Journal of Social Issues, 34*, 84–100.

ROCHLIN, M. (1985) Sexual orientation of the therapist and therapeutic effectiveness with gay clients. In J.C. Gonsiorek (Ed.) *A Guide to Psychotherapy with Gay and Lesbian Clients*. New York: Harrington Park Press.

SAFRAN, J.D. (1990a) Towards a refinement of cognitive therapy in light of interpersonal theory: I. Theory. *Clinical Psychology Review, 10*, 87–105.

SAFRAN, J.D. (1990b) Towards a refinement of cognitive therapy in light of interpersonal theory: II. Practice. *Clinical Psychology Review, 10*, 107–121.

SAMUELS, A. (1993) *The Political Psyche*. London: Routledge.

SCHOENEWOLF, G. (1997) Towards a viable theory of female development. *Changes: An International Journal of Psychology and Psychotherapy, 15*, 1–12.

SEU, I.B. and HEENAN, M.C. (Eds) (1998) *Feminism & Psychotherapy: Reflections on Contemporary Theories and Practices*. London: Sage.

SHANNON, J.W. and WOODS, W.J. (1997) Affirmative psychotherapy for gay men. In D.R. Atkinson and G. Hackett (Eds) *Counseling Diverse Populations*, 2nd ed. Boston, MA: McGraw Hill.

SHELLEY, C. (Ed.) (1998) *Contemporary Perspectives on Psychotherapy and Homosexualities*. London: Free Association Books.

STEIN, T. (1988) Theoretical considerations in psychotherapy with gay men and lesbians. *Journal of Homosexuality, 15(1–2)*, 75–95.

STOLOROW, R., ATWOOD, G. and BRANDCHAFT, B. (Eds) (1994) *The Intersubjective Perspective*. Northvale, NJ: Jason Aronson.

TASKER, F. and McCANN, D. (1999) Affirming patterns of adolescent sexual identity: The challenge. *Journal of Family Therapy, 21*, 30–54.

WEINBERG, T.S. (1983) *Gay Men, Gay Selves: The Social Construction of Homosexual Identities*. New York: Irvington.

YOUNG, V. (1995) *The Equality Complex – Lesbians in Therapy: A Guide to Anti-Oppressive Practice*. London: Cassell.

Chapter 11

Family Therapy with Lesbian and Gay Clients

Maeve Malley and Damian McCann

This chapter examines the relationships of lesbians and gay men within the context of families and family therapy. Although attention is focused on the intimate relationships of lesbians and gay men within a variety of contexts, i.e., family of origin, couple relationships and 'family of choice', these are examined against a larger framework for thinking and practice. Following the empirical consideration of the characteristics of lesbian and gay affirmative therapy offered in Chapter 10, the extent to which family and systemic therapy, as a body of thinking and a treatment modality, is both relevant and responsive to the needs of lesbians and gay men will be assessed.

The family in the context of society

It is generally recognized that the family, as a system, exerts a powerful organizing influence on the development and well-being of its members. It is precisely because of this that the family has been the subject of much government interference and legislation, intended to reinforce dominant ideologies and values. As Shelley (1998) states 'the deeper moral, political and stereotypic views on homosexuality that the wider population adheres to are overwhelmingly posited against same-sex practice' (p. 1). The family, therefore, can be viewed as a 'sitting duck', vulnerable to the powerful discourses within society which espouse a heterosexist ideology, while at the same time being a reinforcer of these beliefs and practices. It is in this most basic sense that the family is a conduit between the public and private domains. According to Goldenberg and Goldenberg (1996), the family is a 'cybernetically rule-governed system', the interactions of whose members typically follow organized established patterns based upon the family structure: 'These patterns enable each person to learn what is permitted or expected of him or her as well as others in family transactions' (p. 44). In other words, these patterns form the basis of the family's tradition and its relationship with the outside world.

Furthermore, given the social stigma associated with homosexual lifestyles, it is hardly surprising that lesbians and gay men continue to struggle for real acceptance within the family and the wider community (Strommer, 1990). For many, the solution has been to develop alternative 'families of choice' (Weston, 1991; Weeks *et al.*, 1996) and to rely more heavily on supports within the multi-generational lesbian and gay communities (Slater and Mencher, 1991). However, as Johnson and Colucci (1999) note:

> even though the construct of 'family' is being applied more often to lesbian and gay life, dominant opinion maintains that their structures are idiosyncratic and strikingly different from those of heterosexual family life. (p. 346)

At the same time, a willingness is needed to challenge attempts by the moral majority to invalidate new and exciting trajectories that may bear fruit for future generations of lesbians and gay men in the context of their relationships with others.

The family in the context of therapy

Given the inherent tensions and dilemmas for lesbians and gay men within the context of family relationships, as the internal dynamics of the family vie with larger socio-political agendas, it is not surprising that some lesbians and gay men turn to therapy for help. However, the extent to which therapeutic services are equipped to meet the needs of lesbians, gay men and their families remains open to debate, especially since a number of recent studies cast doubt on the ability of a range of mental health services to work therapeutically with this particular client group (see Garnets *et al.*, 1991; Proctor, 1994; Golding, 1997; Annesley and Coyle, 1998; McFarlane, 1998; Milton and Coyle, 1998). It is against this backdrop that the relevance and usefulness of a family and systemic approach will be assessed, particularly since, like many other therapeutic approaches, family therapy has been slow to address the specific needs of lesbians and gay men both in theory and in practice. Nevertheless, as a therapeutic modality, family therapy has the potential to offer a less reductive, pathologizing and linear response to problems of living. In addition, recent developments in family and systemic practice – particularly the shift towards greater transparency and collaboration in the therapeutic endeavour – offer at least the potential for a more respectful therapeutic space in which lesbians and gay men can think and work.

More than simply another treatment method, family therapy represents a 'whole new way of conceptualising human problems, of understanding behaviour, the development of symptoms, and their resolution' (Sluzki, 1978, p. 366). In contrast to individual or intrapsychic-based models, family therapy is essentially concerned with the relationships between people as a basis for understanding and explaining human suffering. It encompasses a philosophy of how to observe and frame relational events and, in addition, provides a method of description that explicitly makes connections between people and their wider social context (Gorell Barnes, 1998). Therefore, even when working with an individual, a family therapist will be interested in and concerned with understanding that individual in the context of other significant relational systems. A central and organizing belief held by family therapists is that the therapeutic endeavour is a mutual search for shared meaning through social conversational processes in which the therapist is also part of the system. According to Goldenberg and Goldenberg (1996), 'Instead of providing answers to the family's problems, the therapist and family members together search for meaning and in the process "re-author" lives and relationships' (p. 14).

The shift away from a belief in an objective reality where therapy, as an activity, is about finding a single explanation or truth, towards a more reflective stance in which the endeavour is invested with a search for shared meaning, locates family therapy within a social constructionist framework. Social constructionism insists that we take a critical stance towards our taken-for-granted ways of understanding the world (Burr, 1995). This perspective is also concerned with the ways in which people interact in the course of their everyday lives, since it is through these shared processes that versions of knowledge are constructed. In addition, it is generally recognized that these negotiated understandings take a variety of forms, reinforcing not one, but many constructions of the world.

A brief case example will highlight these ideas in action. Let us assume that a family, consisting of two parents and a daughter, present for therapy in the context of a struggle relating to an acceptance of the daughter's lesbianism. In such a situation, the therapist, together with members of the family, will attempt to explore the beliefs underlying the struggle as a basis for moving the system towards greater acceptance. The therapist would not be interested in trying to understand or provide explanations for the daughter's lesbianism unless, of course, this were relevant or appropriate. For example, if the 'block' in the system concerned a belief that the daughter's lesbianism was caused by the father's absence from home during her childhood, then the therapist might invoke other knowledge bases supporting a multi-causal approach as a basis for challenging unhelpful assumptions. At the same time, the therapist would also attempt to work with the level of internalized homophobia and heterosexism within the system as a means of challenging the negative views held by the family in relation to lesbianism. In that sense, the family's own private struggle would be placed in the context of a larger conversation that is taking place within society.

Family and systemic practitioners, therefore, see the issue of power as central to any exploration of meaning and are also curious about the ways in which this plays itself out in the therapeutic domain. Unable to rely on neat, functional explanations in which everyone within the system shares equal power and therefore equal responsibility in regard to the emergence and resolution of problems within systems, family therapists have had to 'rethread the needle'. This, of course, has particular relevance to the subject in hand since it is precisely the failure of many therapists, past and present, to attend properly to context – both their own and that of lesbian and gay clients – that has led to practice which is at best described as inadequate and at worst homophobic and potentially abusive.

However, the increased visibility of lesbian and gay clients within the therapeutic domain, together with pressure from family and systemic therapists themselves, has to some extent forced training institutions and practitioners to think beyond comfortable and familiar heterosexist constructions of family life and relationships, thereby promoting a more lesbian and gay affirmative therapeutic stance. Although it is beyond the scope of this chapter to provide a more comprehensive explanation of the theory and practice of family therapy, it is useful to remind ourselves of the potential benefits of adopting a systemic approach to therapeutic work with lesbians and gay men:

- A systemic approach challenges a rigid and positivistic view of people and problems and suggests a propositional 'as if' view where the emphasis is on understanding the context (circumstances and relationships) where the problem occurs (Dallos and Draper, 2000).
- The search for shared meaning through dialogue also frees practitioners from the pressure of having to get things right, although this may, at times, be in conflict with the more potentially prescriptive forms of 'lesbian and gay affirmative' therapy.
- The recognition that the therapist is indeed part of the system brings with it a more self-reflective stance which, in theory at least, offers the potential for greater accountability. In other words, the therapist's curiosity about the client's thinking and behaviour cuts both ways.
- The willingness of systemic therapists to grapple with the thorny issues of power and difference, both within theory and practice, gives lesbians, gay men and their families a more empowered setting in which to explore issues relevant to them and their lives.

Further illustrations of the ways in which family therapists are facing up to the challenge of working with lesbians and gay men will be considered later in the chapter. However, this brief account should assist the reader in better understanding the application of the theory of family therapy in practice (for a more detailed description of family and systemic practice, see Goldenberg and Goldenberg, 1986; Jones, 1993; Gorell Barnes, 1998; Dallos and Draper, 2000).

Family therapists in the context of therapy

Over the past twenty years, there has been has been an increasing recognition that the therapeutic setting is not a 'neutral' or 'objective' one and an acknowledgement that counselling, psychology, psychiatry and psychotherapy theory and training often incorporate negative or 'homophobic' attitudes (Clark 1987; Iasenza, 1989; Shelley, 1998). Psychotherapy generally is not a neutral activity; it holds power at its centre and – like it or not – is pervaded by beliefs presented as 'fact' or 'truth' (Davison, 1991). These beliefs necessarily tend towards those of the prevailing social orthodoxy, which still emphasize both heterosexist and homophobic dogma (Siegel and Walker, 1996). Those professionals to whom lesbians and gay men may turn for assistance will, in all probability, be representative of the wider society in their attitudes (Annesley and Coyle, 1995). Not surprisingly, family therapists may also exhibit a tendency to reflect the prevailing belief structures and those of their family and their peer group (Ryder, 1985). It is worth noting that familial attitudes towards lesbians and gay men tend to reflect both the views of the wider societal context and the particular religious, political, ethnic, cultural and class perspectives of the family as well as transmitted intergenerational family beliefs (Greene, 1994). As Fine and Turner (1991) note, therapists have been 'slow to take an analytical position about how the politics from their own clinical work is influenced by dominant beliefs from their own cultural system' (p. 319).

Peer attitudes, in the case of family therapists, are also liable to be affected by the prevailing attitudes debated within the professional body to which they belong, modified by any training they have done and the contexts in which they have worked since they finished their initial professional training. It has also been hypothesized that some professional 'helping' backgrounds will be less challenging than others to heterosexist and homophobic attitudes and belief structures; whether this is because of the type of candidates attracted to professions characterized by more 'traditional' attitudes or because of the homogenizing effect of the belief structures present within these professions is unclear (Malley, 1996). Most family therapists fall into the wider group of 'health care professionals' – social workers, nurses, doctors, psychiatrists, psychologists, psychotherapists – and it is realistic to assume that they will share some characteristics and attitudes of these professional groups. Studies have sampled the attitudes towards homosexuality of several relevant professional groups and have concluded that homophobic attitudes still tend to be present amongst health professionals (see Malley and Tasker, 1999, for an overview of this research).

Many commentators have noted the psychoanalytic roots of family therapy (Hoffman, 1981; Barker, 1992) and some psychoanalytic ideas have been seen as particularly pathologizing of lesbian and gay identities (Bieber *et al.*, 1962; Socarides, 1978; Silverstein, 1991; Nicolosi, 1993). Certainly, a failure to be unequivocal in the condemnation of discrimination against lesbians and gay men as training candidates (and training analysts) has bedevilled psychoanalytic training organizations in both the UK and the USA (O'Connor and Ryan, 1993; Ellis, 1994; Orbach, 1995; Mendoza, 1997) but it is equally important to note that there are psychoanalytically-trained psychotherapists who have written about working with lesbians and gay men in a non-pathologizing way (for example, Cornett and Hudson, 1985; Lewes, 1988; Isay, 1989; O'Connor and Ryan, 1993; Ratigan, 1998). Without labouring the point, it seems unsafe simply to assume that homophobic or heterosexist attitudes in this whole area are becoming less prevalent, since several studies indicate that, post AIDS, attitudes may, in fact, have become more negative than they were previously (Schwanberg, 1990).

Less pathologizing attitudes may range from a well-intentioned liberalism – which has its own limitations – to a simple lack of awareness of the special 'cultural context' (Crawford, 1988) of many lesbians and gay men. Such a lack of awareness specifically within the field of family therapy may be evidenced by the fact that a search of family therapy publications for papers on sexuality will not yield a particularly rich harvest. Clark and Serovich's (1997) content analysis of articles published in 17 journals in the marriage and family therapy area between 1975 and 1995 revealed that only 77 out of more than 13 000 articles focused on lesbian, gay and/or bisexual issues or used sexual orientation as a variable. There are, however, some notable exceptions (Krestan and Bepko, 1980; Collins and Zimmerman, 1983; Shernoff, 1984; Crawford, 1988; Dahlheimer and Feigal, 1991; Markowitz, 1991; Ussher, 1991; Hewson, 1993; Stacy, 1993; Green and Bobele, 1994; Hardman, 1995; Green *et al.*, 1996; Long, 1996). Green and Bobele's (1994) paper discusses the 'silence in the field' (of family therapy) regarding sexuality in general, in contrast to the (valid) emphasis given, within systemic theory, to gender and ethnicity as centrally defining of experience in life and in therapy. This may be because of the less 'visible' nature of sexuality as a variable or because of still-prevailing negative judgements directed at lesbians and gay men (Clark and Serovich, 1997).

Although liberal humanism has been influential in opposing the pathologization of sexual minorities because 'everyone has equal human rights', it has been widely confused with the notion that lesbians, bisexuals and gay men are 'just the same as everyone else' (Kitzinger, 1987). While those subscribing to these views are likely to hold neutral or even positive attitudes towards lesbians and gay men, the danger of this lack of differentiation is that heterosexual-based patterns (such as family life cycle patterns) will be imposed upon lesbian and gay relationships. Consequently, different ways of relating within same-gender relationships are at best ignored and at worst discriminated against (Kitzinger and Coyle, 1995; Hardman, 1997; see also Chapter 10).

There is also an increasing awareness that our therapeutic assumptions are often based around the norms of the 'dominant' culture. Therefore, we may need to adapt our theory and our practice when we work with clients who are not White, male and heterosexual. A lack of consideration of sexuality as a crucially defining element of experience may go hand-in-hand with an assumption that systemic theory and models of practice, framed for and with the heterosexual population, are automatically and instantly applicable to the lesbian and gay population. In the therapeutic context, the liberal humanistic view has contributed to the idea that family life cycle models of normative family functioning can be generally applied, with little modification, to family therapy with lesbians and gay men and their families. Also, it has led to expectations that no special knowledge of lesbian or gay sexualities is needed and that therapeutic techniques and interventions for working with heterosexual clients can simply be translated for working with lesbians and gay men (Brown, 1996). These views have only recently begun to be challenged within family therapy (Siegel and Walker, 1996).

Lesbians and gay men in the context of the family

Incorporating both families of origin and families of choice, lesbians and gay men are well positioned to experience the joys and trepidations that all other human beings encounter within these most influential domains. However, the hostility and lack of acceptance from the dominant heterosexual social context add an additional layer of complexity that, in itself, may account for the decision of some lesbians and gay men to approach therapists for help and assistance. Developmental issues pertaining to lesbians and gay men in the context of their families and their relationships with others will now be considered. Three areas of family life will be highlighted and frameworks for practice will be offered.

i) Disclosure issues

Unlike gender, race and other obvious physical characteristics which give fundamental information about an individual's status within society, sexual orientation remains hidden. This, together with the fact that heterosexuality is usually assumed unless otherwise stated, creates the phenomenon know as 'coming out' (see Chapter 4). Initially this involves the individual coming to terms with her or his sexual orien-

tation. This is usually followed at some stage by the individual disclosing to family or friends that she or he is lesbian or gay. A number
of models describing how lesbians and gay men come out have been
formulated (Ponse, 1978; Cass, 1979; Troiden, 1979; Woodman and
Lenna, 1980; Coleman, 1982; Sophie, 1982; Lewis, 1984; Roth, 1985;
Golden, 1987; Hanley-Hackenbruck, 1989; Martin, 1991; Hollander and
Haber, 1992; Neisen, 1993; Scrivner and Eldridge, 1995; Morales, 1996;
Tepper, 1996). However, as Cain (1991) points out, many lesbians and
gay men are neither entirely 'out' nor entirely 'not out' but engage in a
complex process of 'information management' regarding their sexuality. This can be affected – as can the coming out process generally – by
a number of variables, such as gender, race, location, social values and
attitudes and individual factors (De Monteflores and Schultz, 1978;
Hanley-Hackenbruck, 1989; Newman and Muzzonigro, 1993; Greene,
1994; Morales, 1996). Tasker and McCann (1999) note that:

> coming out to others will be a long-term process of informing others
> about a lesbian, bisexual or gay sexual identity, and not allowing various
> presumptions of heterosexuality to jeopardize self esteem. (p. 37)

For some, the task may feel unmanageable and many may fear rejection or indeed guilt, believing that a parent will blame him or herself
for their daughter's or son's homosexuality. This point is further
underlined by Cramer and Roach (1988) who draw attention to the fact
that coming out to parents is one of the most difficult tasks the lesbian
or gay person faces in the identity formation process; other accounts
show that the situation is equally problematic when coming out to
friends. Reinforcing this point, Weston (1991) makes a crucial observation when she says:

> claiming a gay identity in the presence of parents or siblings frequently
> involved an anxiety-filled struggle to bring speech about sexual identity
> (if not sex) into the cultural domain of the 'family'. (p. 43)

This issue is complicated by the fact that cultural stereotypes represent
lesbian and especially gay sexualities as being primarily concerned
with sexual acts whereas heterosexuality is seen in terms of families
and relationships. To some extent, this may account for one possible
parental response to the news that a son or daughter is lesbian or gay,
i.e., a parent's obsessive anxiety about a son (or – less likely – a daughter) contracting HIV and developing AIDS. It may also be a factor in
the resurgence of anxiety when a son or daughter, who previously
experienced acceptance within the family in being out but un-part-
nered, upsets the fragile balance by actually forming a new gay or
lesbian relationship.

Apart from the fact that 'coming out' is not a single event and has to
be negotiated and renegotiated, it is also worth noting that there will

be great variations in the timing of lesbians and gay men disclosing their sexual orientation within the family. For some, the actual disclosure will take place in adolescence, while for others it may not take place until much later in life. In addition, there may be a graduated disclosure, with siblings often being told first, followed by mothers and then fathers. The extent to which parents and siblings feel able to accept and endorse a daughter's or son's lesbian or gay identity will depend to a large extent on the quality of the relationship prior to disclosure, as well as the level of openness and acceptance generally within the family in regard to diversity. Where love and acceptance are valued over social conformity, then the capacity of the family to work towards acceptance will be increased.

Although the anxiety associated with coming out – particularly to parents – is near universal (Strommen, 1989), it is suggested that lesbians and gay men who are able to come out to members of their family of origin will have higher self-esteem than those who feel they cannot (Savin-Williams, 1989). Research also indicates that self-esteem is higher in those lesbians and gay men who are able to be out in what they feel to be the important contexts of their lives (Cass, 1979; Coleman, 1982; Savin-Williams, 1989; Neisen, 1993; Browning *et al.*, 1997; Shannon and Woods, 1997) since this may permit a felt connection and involvement with lesbian and gay communities which has also been identified as a protective factor for the psychological well-being of lesbians and gay men (Kurdek and Schmitt, 1987; Hayes *et al.*, 1992; Greene, 1994; DiPlacido, 1998).

A clinical example may illustrate some of the complexities inherent in the whole issue of visibility, invisibility and coming out:

Clare (aged 52) and Siobhan (aged 38) have been in a relationship for almost two years. They have had a 'long-distance' relationship for most of this time as they lived 200 miles apart, until Clare moved very recently to a house very close to Siobhan's. They had met while Clare was teaching at a summer school, which Siobhan attended. Neither has previously had a lesbian relationship; both were formerly married and have four children between them. Clare's sons are 31 and 28 and her daughter is 25; Siobhan has one daughter of 13. Clare was divorced 15 years ago; her ex-husband has very little contact with her but the children visit him relatively frequently (he lives abroad) and Siobhan's husband was killed in an industrial accident five years ago. She maintains close contact with her husband's family, who live in Ireland.

The issues that have brought the couple into therapy are manifold but all relate to issues of visibility and the sanctions, difficulties and consequences – both positive and negative – therein.

Clare feels that she has had to make many of the compromises in the relationship, as it is she who has moved house and changed jobs to be closer to her lover. Siobhan was unwilling to move cities as this would have involved uprooting her daughter and changing schools at what she felt to be a crucial stage in her daughter's adolescence. It is for this reason also – the desire not to cause 'upset' – that she is unwilling to tell her daughter about the relationship. Indeed, the only person she has told about the relationship is her older sister, who was 'neutral' in her response but advised Siobhan to tell no one else in the family.

Clare feels that she cannot be 'out' at work until she has established herself in her new post and she has no lesbian or gay friends living nearby. Her daughter is aware of her relationship, as is her younger son, but neither have told their partners or children. Siobhan feels that Clare has 'less to lose' by making the relationship known more generally and feels that Clare is pushing for them to live together in the near future. She feels that her daughter could be ostracized at school if the relationship were apparent, aside from the degree of rejection that she would anticipate from the extended family network, including her husband's family, whom she fears might apply for custody of the child and would certainly cut all contact. Clare feels that Siobhan is 'over-reacting' and is actually much less committed to the relationship than she (Clare) is; Clare feels also that Siobhan dictates the terms of the relationship but that Siobhan feels very rejected if Clare makes plans to go and visit friends or family, which takes her away from Siobhan.

The fact of Clare and Siobhan's gender means that this relationship starts from a point of invisibility, in that a societal myopia renders (sexual) relationships between women less visible than in any other pairing. Societal views may also see them as particularly deviant when the women involved are mothers and carers (both women have elderly parents as well as children). Women will often feel less powerful in their places of work, will tend to be less economically self-sufficient and will have greater difficulty in being assertive about their social, sexual and emotional needs, particularly if these seem to conflict with those of another. In a context where a couple is cut off from the support of a lesbian or gay community, issues of isolation can be particularly acute. When a couple may be at different life cycle stages and may have a different perspective on the value or necessity of 'outness' in different contexts, a sense of alienation may pervade the relationship. Issues of internalized homophobia, defining self in terms of the needs of others and of not having 'models' of how it is possible to be a 'good enough' parent, child, sibling or colleague, while simultaneously being visible as a lesbian or as part of a lesbian couple or family, need to be acknowledged and disentangled. We will return to the specific issues of family and parenting at a later stage.

In the scenario above, we have assumed that Clare and Siobhan were able to present as a couple to therapy but this will often not be the case. The extent to which family therapists as a professional group facilitate and work with disclosure issues in the context of therapy is unknown. However, anecdotal evidence gleaned from family therapists in a variety of settings would suggest that they are either unaware of the fact that they are working with lesbians and gay men or they simply do not know how to ask. At the very least, this would suggest a degree of discomfort or over-sensitivity that will be unhelpful to lesbians and gay men within the context of therapy. Furthermore, stereotypes that may still hold currency amongst family therapists – of lesbians and gay men as isolated, lonely and self-hating individuals (Long, 1996), particularly as they grow older – may deter family therapists from asking, for fear that they will be entering unfamiliar and frightening territory. Family therapists may be helped in knowing that the construction of 'families of choice', that can provide a consistent and enduring source of support and connection, is a particularly creative and often constructive response to the losses that can accrue as a consequence of being 'out' in an inhospitable context (Weston, 1991; Weeks *et al.*, 1996). Some studies of ageing indicate that the protective effect of such an acquired, chosen 'family' may in fact be greater than that associated with a connection to biological or nuclear heterosexual families (Berger, 1982; Quam and Whitford, 1992; Berger and Kelly, 1996). These families of choice may include lovers, ex-lovers, ex-lovers' lovers, biological family, the biological family of friends, lovers or ex-lovers, children related by blood, children not related by blood, ex-heterosexual partners, friends and others.

Given the broad tapestry on which lesbians and gay men weave relationships with family and friends, family therapists reliant on narrow definitions of affiliation may unwittingly be communicating important information to lesbian and gay clients that actually encourages non-disclosure. Inevitably, this raises issues about the authenticity of the therapeutic encounter in which the therapist and client are engaged. Of particular importance, however, is the central question of whether family therapists in the first instance feel able to affirm a lesbian or gay lifestyle, since this will be essential to developing a meaningful and effective working relationship with family members who are lesbian or gay or, for that matter, members of the lesbian and gay community itself. At the same time, the greater visibility of lesbian and gay clients within the context of therapy places greater demands on therapists as a whole, that they at least reflect critically upon aspects of their practice that may be unhelpful or harmful (as well as identifying aspects that may be beneficial) to this particular client group.

ii) Couple relationships

Like heterosexual couples, lesbians and gay men also fall in and out of love. However, the relationships of lesbians and gay men are generally conducted against a backdrop of uncertainty within the various contexts in which the relationship functions. Johnson and Colucci (1999) suggest that:

Lesbians and gays are more typically painted as eternally single adults cruising from one failed relationship to another or as underground couples coming into the light only in the 'gay ghettos'. (p. 346)

Therapists faced with lesbian and gay couples requesting help with their relationships will need to separate myth from reality. They will also need to draw on specific models of couple-relating if the therapy is to have coherence and direction. We need to recognize that some of our core therapeutic models may be essentially 'heterosexist' or irrelevant to a lesbian or gay male population – templates for heterosexual relationships that have limited value or that do not easily fit lesbian or gay relationships. Until recently, the most influential family life cycle model offered to family therapists was that developed by Carter and McGoldrick (1980, 1989). However, this was essentially a template based on heterosexual couple and family formation and parenting. Family and systemic therapists have tended to rely heavily on a family life cycle model since this provides a developmental overview, which has been helpful in organizing the therapist's thinking. While models of relationship may be equally useful in working with lesbians and gay men, it is important that these should be appropriate and that therapists should have the ability to acknowledge the limitations of most models. As Slater says (1995), as a cautionary preface to her own lesbian life cycle model:

> The very act of generalising about lesbians' lives excludes some women from the discussion, creating new (albeit wider) parameters of 'normal' versus 'abnormal' ways of being. The last thing lesbian families need is yet another source – this time perhaps from within their own community – telling them that their lives are atypical or off-course. (p. 11)

She suggests, however, a model of the lesbian couple and family over time and identifies some of the issues that each stage may bring. The model moves from the issues involved in the formation of the couple (with a clear presumption of sexual monogamy) through on-going couplehood, the middle years, generativity and issues for older lesbians. A similar model has been suggested for gay men, with slightly different stages – blending, nesting, maintaining, collaborating, trusting, and re-partnering. While the value of these models may be that they can provide some kind of relationship 'template' for lesbians, gay men and their therapists, this is also their disadvantage. While it is clearly an advantage to derive these models from lesbian and gay relationships as they exist, rather than deriving these models from heterosexual templates and applying them to lesbian and gay relationships, it may also ignore the wider variation of relationships available to lesbians and gay men, since the creation of models may demand simplification and the homogenization of difference. These models also tend to be derived from the experiences of White, middle-class lesbians and gay men, as these are often the most visible and researched populations (Greene, 1998), which may further exclude already excluded and 'invisibilized' groups of lesbians and gay men. While it would be counter-productive to ignore models that have been derived from lesbian and gay populations, it is important to realize that they may be partial and reductionist and that they may simply give a snapshot of what one part of a visible population may be doing at a certain point in time, rather than indicating some determined truth about lesbians, gay men and their relationships. One small example will highlight the issues involved:

> David (aged 33) and Michael (aged 29) are struggling in their relationship, for which they seek therapy. They have, as a couple, been together for just over a year. David is a confident and experienced gay man who has little involvement with his family of origin. Michael, on the other hand, is very involved with his parents and sister and it is only in the past two years that Michael has actually 'come out' and begun to frequent gay venues. The relationship between David and Michael is marked by a high level of conflict and Michael fears that David is seeing other men.

Given such a presentation, in what ways is the family life cycle helpful? Although Carter and McGoldrick's (1999) expanded family life cycle text includes a chapter on lesbians, gay men and their families (Johnson and Colucci, 1999) which deconstructs the original model and is helpful in addressing a range of contemporary issues affecting lesbians and gay men, many family therapists will undoubtedly struggle to understand and make sense of the above presentation within these terms. Without some consideration of the individual developmental model and the way in which this connects to the couple's developmental framework, the therapist working with David and Michael may be in danger of being drawn into the content rather than the context of the arguments. Furthermore, the therapist must also be aware of current debates relating to the sexual practices of gay men if she or he is to connect with the issues involved in David and Michael's situation. Indeed, gay male relationships receive little attention in Carter and McGoldrick's (1989) family life cycle model, but are specifically mentioned in the context of a discussion of the impact of HIV/AIDS on the family. HIV and AIDS undeniably have serious implications for individuals and families, both in terms of the stigma attached to the condition and coping with illness within the family; nevertheless, HIV and AIDS are not the defining feature of gay relationships. While therapists will need to increase their knowledge and awareness of the problems arising from sero-positive status, it does a disservice to lesbian, gay male and heterosexual couples, families and individuals to assume that these problems will apply only to gay men and that these are the only problems for gay men. For a fuller description of life cycle models specific to lesbians and gay men and the ways in which these intersect with other important systems, see McWhirter and Mattison (1984, 1988), Slater and Mencher (1991) and Slater (1995).

Johnson and Colucci (1999) do flag up some more generally applicable issues, particularly the debate concerning fusion and distance in lesbian and gay male relationships and the whole question of closeness and distance in regard to family of origin. As with many other issues in lesbian and gay relationships, clinical judgements on 'closeness' were derived from the patterns of heterosexual relationships, on the assumption that these are automatically transferable to lesbian or gay male relationships (Burstow, 1992; Walker and Goldner, 1995). Consequently, lesbian relationships have often been characterized within systemic therapy as 'over-close' or 'fused' whereas gay male relationships are judged to be 'distant' or 'detached' (Krestan and Bepko, 1980; Goodrich *et al.*, 1988; Klinger, 1996). The actual experience of 'distance' or 'closeness' within lesbian and gay relationships seems to allow for a greater degree of flexibility and is a source of satisfaction in the relationship (Green *et al.*,1996; Hill, 1999). Furthermore, it is also important for therapists to recognize that role flexibility and equality within relationships are qualities that are particularly valued among lesbians and gay men (Blumstein and Schwartz, 1983; Peplau, 1991).

iii) Families of lesbians and gay men

With the increase in lesbians and gay men parenting children within the context of families (see Chapters 5 and 6), it is hardly surprising that family and systemic therapists are beginning to see some of these families in their consulting rooms. Although the issues raised in the families of lesbians and gay men may be similar to those encountered in heterosexual families, therapists must broaden their perspective to ensure that they have the necessary understanding and skills to work with complex co-parenting arrangements, for example, where a heterosexual birth father is objecting to his daughter aged ten being exposed to her mother's lesbian lover, who is about to give birth to a child conceived by donor insemination where the gay father will have an active role in the parenting of the child.

Given the ignorance about lesbian and gay parenting, it may be helpful to consider possible routes to parenthood (see Chapter 5 for a more detailed consideration). Firstly, lesbians and gay men may bear children in the context of a heterosexual relationship or marriage. Secondly, lesbian women may give birth to a child following sexual intercourse with a man or by means of donor insemination. Thirdly, gay men may enlist the help of a surrogate mother. Fourthly, lesbians and gay men, using any of the above means, may together decide on a co-parenting arrangement. Fifthly, lesbians and gay men may – formally or informally – foster or adopt through the usual legal channels. Family and systemic therapists must therefore consider the implications of these lesbian and gay parenting scenarios within their clinical practice. A case example will be used to draw out some of the issues involved and provide some 'food for thought':

Jill and Donna are longstanding partners and for the past year have been considering parenthood. Donna (aged 39) is very keen to have a baby and Jill (aged 49), although somewhat reluctant, can see that mother-hood is important for Donna and agrees to Donna placing an advert for a gay male couple interested in a co-parenting arrangement. Jim (aged 28) and Alan (aged 40) respond to the advert and a series of meetings ensue, as they together begin to work through the issues involved. For instance, although it is agreed that Jim will be the donor father, Alan will also have an active role in parenting the child. Consideration has also been given to the legal arrangements and the level of contact both men will have with the baby. However, with the arrangements in place, Alan decides that he cannot go through with it. He feels that he has been placed under pressure by Jim, who at one stage threatened to leave their four year relationship if Alan did not agree to him parenting a child.

Donna and Jill are feeling desperate about this turn-of-events and are now getting into difficulties within their own relationship. For this reason, Donna makes enquiries about therapists in her area. A friend rec-ommends a family and systemic therapist who has had some experience of working with lesbian couples. The therapist has an initial meeting with Donna and Jill together. Working from a position of 'curiosity', she discovers a pattern of conflict between the partners whenever they are faced with difficulties. There is also the pressure from Donna's 'biologi-cal clock', which seems to intensify her rage with Alan. At the same time, the therapist is aware that Donna and Jill have the necessary skills to negotiate their way out of 'tight spots', since they succeeded in reaching an agreement over Donna having a child. The therapist also wonders whether Donna and Jill's struggle might be helpful to them in under-standing something of Jim and Alan's difficulties and whether there might be a way of helping all four of them reach closure or make use of an opportunity to rethink.

In suggesting a joint meeting with Donna, Jill, Jim and Alan, the ther-apist is very interested in exploring the beliefs about parenting held by all four parties concerned. The therapist is already hypothesizing that part of the difficulty for Alan is that he may be worried that he will be pushed into the background as Jim joins with Donna and Jill around the planned birth and care of the new-born. She also wonders whether Alan has had a real opportunity to put his case in a way that allows him to feel that he has a voice and that he can make a decision for himself. Could Alan be saying something important for the whole system? Donna speaks to the two men about attending therapy and they agree to go along for one meeting. During that meeting, Jim is very critical of Alan's reluctance to go ahead with the arrangement. With the pressure off, Donna and Jill help Alan to put some of his fears into words and together they begin to think about these.

It is clear to Alan that Donna and Jill are committed to him and Jim being involved and that their advert wasn't a ruse to have the baby and run. Alan had not before this point been able to put his fears into words because Jim would immediately feel that Alan was trying to prevent him moving forward in his life. In other words, from Jim's point of view, Alan was being too conventional and too conservative and Jim's heightened sense of awareness over this issue prevented him from seeing that Alan might have genuine concerns for both of them. The therapist offered to continue working with them around the question of a baby but she also suggested seeing them separately if there were specific issues for the men or the women that would not be appropriate to work on as a group.

Conclusion

This chapter has highlighted a range of issues which family and systemic therapists need to be aware of if they are to provide ethically-based practice that is responsive to the needs of lesbians, gay men and their families. Research is currently being conducted into the training and practice of family and systemic therapists in regard to therapy offered to lesbians and gay men. It is no longer acceptable to assume that therapists are, by virtue of their core training, equipped to work with this client group or that even co-constructed conversations operate in a neutral or non-political context. Therapists are being challenged to think beyond the constraints of dominant heterosexist thinking and it has been the aim of this chapter to expand the thinking and practice base of family and systemic therapists. We will leave the reader to decide how successful we have been in achieving our aim.

References

ANDERSON, S.C. and ANDERSON, D.C. (1988) Working with lesbian alcoholics. *Social Work, 30*, 518–525.

ANNESLEY, P. and COYLE, A. (1995) Clinical psychologists' attitudes to lesbians. *Journal of Community & Applied Social Psychology, 5*, 327–331.

ANNESLEY, P. and COYLE, A. (1998) Dykes and psychs: Lesbian women's experiences of clinical psychology services. *Changes: An International Journal of Psychology and Psychotherapy, 16*, 247–258.

BARKER, P. (1992) *Basic Family Therapy*. Oxford: Blackwell.

BERGER, R.M. (1982) The unseen minority: Older gays and lesbians. *Social Work, 27*, 236–242.

BERGER, R.M. (1983) What is a homosexual? *Social Work, 28*, 132–135.

BERGER, R.M. and KELLY, J.J. (1996) Gay men and lesbians grown older. In R.P. Cabaj and T.S. Stein (Eds) *Textbook of Homosexuality and Mental Health*. Washington DC: American Psychiatric Press.

BIEBER, I., DAIN, H.J., DINCE, P.R., DRELLICH, M.G., GRAND, H.G.,

GUNDLACH, R.H., KREMER, M.W., RIFKIN, A.H., WILBUR, C.B. and BIEBER, T.B. (1962) *Homosexuality: A Psychoanalytic Study.* New York: Basic Books.

BLUMSTEIN, P. and SCHWARTZ, P. (1983) *American Couples: Money, Work, Sex.* New York: William Morrow.

BROWN, L.S. (1996) Preventing heterosexism and bias in psychotherapy and counseling. In E.D. Rothblum and L.A. Bond (Eds) *Preventing Heterosexism and Homophobia.* London: Sage.

BROWNING, C., REYNOLDS, A.L. and DWORKIN, S.H. (1997) Affirmative psychotherapy for lesbian women. In D.R. Atkinson and G. Hackett (Eds) *Counseling Diverse Populations*, 2nd ed. Boston, MA: McGraw Hill.

BURR, V. (1995) *An Introduction to Social Constructionism.* London: Routledge.

BURSTOW, B. (1992) *Radical Feminist Therapy.* London: Sage.

CAIN, R. (1991) Stigma management and gay identity development. *Social Work, 36,* 67–73.

CARTER, B. and McGOLDRICK, M. (1980) *The Family Life Cycle: A Framework for Family Therapy.* New York: Gardner Press.

CARTER, B. and McGOLDRICK, M. (1989) *The Changing Family Life Cycle: A Framework for Family Therapy.* London: Allyn & Bacon.

CASS, V.C. (1979) Homosexual identity formation: A theoretical model. *Journal of Homosexuality, 4(3),* 219–235.

CLARK, D. (1987) *The New Loving Someone Gay.* Berkeley, CA: Celestial Arts.

CLARK, W.M. and SEROVICH, J.M. (1997) Twenty years and still in the dark? Content analysis of articles pertaining to gay, lesbian and bisexual issues in marriage and family therapy journals. *Journal of Marital and Family Therapy, 23,* 239–253.

COLEMAN. E. (1982) Developmental stages of the coming-out process. In W. Paul, J.C. Gonsiorek and M.E. Hotvedt (Eds) *Homosexuality: Social, Psychological, and Biological Issues.* Beverly Hills, CA: Sage.

COLEMAN, E. (1990) The married lesbian. In F.W. Bozett and M.B. Sussman (Eds) *Homosexuality and Family Relations.* New York: Harrington Park Press.

COLLINS, L.E. and ZIMMERMAN, N. (1983) Homosexual and bisexual issues. *Family Therapy Collections, 5,* 82–100.

CORNETT, C.W. and HUDSON, R.A. (1985) Psychoanalytic theory and affirmation of the gay lifestyle. *Journal of Homosexuality, 12(1),* 97–108.

CRAMER, D.W. and ROACH, A.J. (1988) Coming out to mom and dad: A study of gay males and their relationships with parents. *Journal of Homosexuality, 15(3–4),* 79–91.

CRAWFORD, S. (1988) Cultural context as a factor in the expansion of therapeutic conversation with lesbian families. *Journal of Strategic and Systemic Therapies, 7(3),* 2–11.

DAHLHEIMER, D. and FEIGAL, J.D. (1991) Bridging the gap. *Networker, Jan/Feb,* 44–53.

DALLOS, R. and DRAPER, R. (2000) *An Introduction to Family Therapy: Systemic Theory and Practice.* Buckingham: Open University Press.

DAVISON, G.C. (1991) Constructionism and morality in therapy for homosexuality. In J.C. Gonsiorek and J.D. Weinrich (Eds) *Homosexuality: Research Implications for Public Policy.* Newbury Park, CA: Sage.

DeMONTEFLORES, C. and SCHULTZ, S. (1978). Coming out: Similarities and differences for lesbians and gay men. *Journal of Social Issues, 34,* 59–72.

DiPLACIDO, J. (1998) Minority stress among lesbians, gay men, and bisexuals:

A consequence of heterosexism, homophobia, and stigmatization. In G.M. Herek (Ed.) *Stigma and Sexual Orientation: Understanding Prejudice Against Lesbians, Gay Men, and Bisexuals.* Thousand Oaks, CA: Sage.

ELLIS, M.L. (1994) *Lesbians, Gay Men and Psychoanalytic Training.* London: Free Association Books.

FINE, M. and TURNER, J. (1991) Tyranny and freedom: Looking at ideas in the practice of family therapy. *Family Process, 30,* 307–320.

GARNETS, L., HANCOCK, K.A., COCHRAN, S.D., GOODCHILDS, J. and PEPLAU, L.A. (1991) Issues in psychotherapy with lesbians and gay men: A survey of psychologists. *American Psychologist, 46,* 964–972.

GOLDEN, C. (1987) Diversity and variability in women's sexual identities. In Boston Lesbian Psychologies Collective (Ed.) *Lesbian Psychologies.* Urbana, IL: University of Illinois Press.

GOLDENBERG, I. and GOLDENBERG, H. (1996) *Family Therapy: An Overview.* Pacific Grove, CA: Brooks/Cole.

GOLDING, J. (1997) *Without Prejudice: MIND Lesbian, Gay and Bisexual Mental Health Awareness Research.* London: MIND Publications.

GOLDNER, V. (1985) Feminism and family therapy. *Family Process, 24,* 31–47.

GOODRICH, T.J., RAMPAGE, C., ELLMAN, B. and HALSTEAD, K. (1988) *Feminist Family Therapy.* New York: W.W. Norton.

GORELL BARNES, G. (1998) *Family Therapy in Changing Times.* Basingstoke: Macmillan.

GREEN, R.J., BETTINGER, M. and ZACKS, E. (1996) Are lesbian couples fused and gay male couples disengaged? Questioning gender straight jackets. In J. Laird and R.J. Green (Eds) *Lesbians and Gays in Couples and Families: A Handbook for Therapists.* San Francisco, CA: Jossey-Bass.

GREEN, S.K. and BOBELE, M. (1994) Family therapists' response to AIDS: An examination of attitudes, knowledge and contact. *Journal of Marital and Family Therapy, 20,* 349–367.

GREENE, B. (1994) Ethnic-minority lesbians and gay men: Mental health and treatment issues. *Journal of Consulting and Clinical Psychology, 62,* 243–251.

GREENE, B. (1998) Family, ethnic identity, and sexual orientation: African-American lesbians and gay men. In C.J. Patterson and A.R. D'Augelli (Eds) *Lesbian, Gay, and Bisexual Identities in Families: Psychological Perspectives.* New York: Oxford University Press.

HAMMERSMITH, S.K. and WEINBERG, M.S. (1973) Homosexual identity: Commitment, adjustment, and significant others. *Sociometry, 36,* 56–79.

HANLEY-HACKENBRUCK, P. (1989) Psychotherapy and the 'coming out' process. *Journal of Gay & Lesbian Psychotherapy, 1,* 21–39.

HARDMAN, K. (1995) Family therapy with lesbian client systems. *Context, 23,* 22–23.

HARDMAN, K.L.J. (1997) Social workers' attitudes to lesbian clients. *British Journal of Social Work, 27,* 545–563.

HAYES, R.B., TURNER, H. and COATES, T.J. (1992) Social support, AIDS related symptoms, and depression among gay men. *Journal of Consulting and Clinical Psychology, 60,* 463–469.

HEWSON, D. (1993) Heterosexual dominance in the world of therapy? *Dulwich Centre Newsletter, 2,* 14–20.

HILL, C.A. (1999) Fusion and conflict in lesbian relationships? *Feminism & Psychology, 9,* 179–185.

HOFFMAN, L. (1981) *Foundations of Family Therapy.* New York: Basic Books.

HOLLANDER, J. and HABER, L. (1992) Ecological transition: Using Bronfenbrenner's model to study sexual identity change. *Health Care for Women International*, *13*, 121–129.

IASENZA, S. (1989) Some challenges of integrating sexual orientations into counselor training and research. *Journal of Counseling and Development*, *68*, 73–76.

ISAY, R.A. (1991) The homosexual analyst: Clinical considerations. *The Psychoanalytic Study of the Child*, *46*, 199–216.

JOHNSON, T.W. and COLUCCI, P. (1999) Lesbians, gay men, and the family life cycle. In B. Carter and M. McGoldrick (Eds) *The Expanded Family Life Cycle: Individual, Family, and Social Perspectives*. Needham Heights, MA: Allyn & Bacon.

JONES, E. (1993) *Family Systems Therapy: Developments in Milan-Systemic Therapies*. Chichester: John Wiley.

KITZINGER, C. (1987) *The Social Construction of Lesbianism*. London: Sage.

KITZINGER, C. and COYLE, A. (1995) Lesbian and gay couples: Speaking of difference. *The Psychologist*, *8*, 64–69.

KLINGER, R.L. (1996) Lesbian couples. In R.P. Cabaj and T.S. Stein (Eds) *Textbook of Homosexuality and Mental Health*. Washington DC: American Psychiatric Press.

KRESTAN, J. and BEPKO, C.S. (1980) The problem of fusion in the lesbian relationship. *Family Process*, *19*, 277–289.

KURDEK, L. and SCHMITT, J.P. (1987) Perceived emotional support from family and friends for members of homosexual, married and cohabiting couples. *Journal of Homosexuality*, *14(3–4)*, 57–68.

LAIRD, J. (1996) Invisible ties: Lesbians and their families of origin. In J. Laird and R.J. Green (Eds) *Lesbians and Gays in Couples and Families: A Handbook for Therapists*. San Francisco, CA: Jossey-Bass.

LEWES, K. (1988) *Psychoanalysis and Male Homosexuality*. London: Jason Aronson.

LEWIS, L.A. (1984). The coming-out process for lesbians: Integrating a stable identity. *Social Work*, *29*, 464–469.

LONG, J.K. (1996) Working with lesbians, gays, and bisexuals: Addressing heterosexism in supervision. *Family Process*, *35*, 377–388.

MALLEY, M. (1996) *Lesbians, Gay Men and Family Therapy: A Contradiction in Terms?* Unpublished MSc thesis, Institute of Family Therapy/Birkbeck College, University of London.

MALLEY, M. and TASKER, F. (1999) Lesbians, gay men and family therapy: A contradiction in terms? *Journal of Family Therapy*, *21*, 3–29.

MARKOWITZ, L.M. (1991) Homosexuality: Are we still in the dark? *Networker*, *Jan/Feb*, 27–35.

MARTIN, H.P. (1991) The coming-out process for homosexuals. *Hospital and Community Psychiatry*, *42*, 158–162.

McFARLANE, L. (1998) *Diagnosis: Homophobic. The Experiences of Lesbians, Gay Men and Bisexuals in Mental Health Services*. London: PACE.

McWHIRTER, D.P. and MATTISON, A.M. (1984) *The Male Couple: How Relationships Develop*. Englewood Cliffs, NJ: Prentice-Hall.

McWHIRTER, D.P. and MATTISON, A.M. (1988) Psychotherapy for gay male couples. In J.P. De Cecco (Ed.) *Gay Relationships*. New York: Harrington Park Press.

MENDOZA, S. (1997) Genitality and genital homosexuality: Criteria of selection of homosexual candidates. *British Journal of Psychotherapy, 13*, 384–394.

MILTON, M. and COYLE, A. (1998) Psychotherapy with lesbian and gay clients. *The Psychologist, 11*, 73–76.

MORALES, E. (1996) Gender roles among Latino gay and bisexual men: Implications for family and couple relationships. In J. Laird and R.J. Green (Eds) *Lesbians and Gays in Couples and Families: A Handbook for Therapists*. San Francisco, CA: Jossey-Bass.

NEISEN, J.H. (1993) Healing from cultural victimization: Recovery from shame due to heterosexism. *Journal of Gay & Lesbian Psychotherapy, 2*, 49–63.

NEWMAN, B.S. and MUZZONIGRO, P.G. (1993) The effects of traditional family values on the coming out process of gay male adolescents. *Adolescence, 28*, 213–226.

NICOLOSI, J. (1993) *Healing Homosexuality: Case Stories of Reparative Therapy*. London: Jason Aronson.

O'CONNOR, N. and RYAN, J. (1993) *Wild Desires and Mistaken Identities: Lesbianism and Psychoanalysis*. London: Virago.

ORBACH S. (1995) Beware the prejudiced analyst. *The Guardian Weekend, April 29th*, 8.

PEPLAU, L.A. (1991) Lesbian and gay relationships. In J.C. Gonsiorek and J.D. Weinrich (Eds) *Homosexuality: Research Implications for Public Policy*. Newbury Park, CA: Sage.

PONSE, B. (1978) *Identities in the Lesbian World*. Westport, CT: Greenwood.

POTTER, S.J. and DARTY, T.E. (1981) Social work and the invisible minority. *Social Work, 26*, 187–192.

PROCTOR G. (1994) Lesbian clients' experience of clinical psychology: A listener's guide. *Changes: An International Journal of Psychology and Psychotherapy, 12*, 290–298.

QUAM, J.K. and WHITFORD, G.S. (1992) Adaptation and age-related expectations of older gay and lesbian adults. *The Gerontologist, 32*, 367–374.

RATIGAN, B. (1998) Gay men and psychoanalysis: Queer bedfellows? In C. Shelley (Ed.) *Contemporary Perspectives on Psychotherapy and Homosexualities*. London: Free Association Books.

ROTH, S. (1985) Psychotherapy with lesbian couples. *Journal of Marital and Family Therapy, 11*, 273–286.

RYDER, R.G. (1985) Professionals' values in family assessment. *Counseling and Values, 30*, 24–34.

SAVIN-WILLIAMS, R.C. (1989) Coming out to parents and self-esteem among gay and lesbian youths. *Journal of Homosexuality, 18(1–2)*, 1–35.

SCHWANBERG, S.L. (1990) Attitudes towards homosexuality in American health care literature 1983–87. *Journal of Homosexuality, 19(3)*, 117–136.

SCRIVNER, R. and ELDRIDGE, N.S. (1995) Lesbian and gay family psychology. In R.H. Mikesell, D.D. Lusterman and S.H. McDaniel (Eds) *Integrating Family Therapy: Handbook of Family Psychology & Systems Therapy*. Washington DC: American Psychological Society.

SHANNON, J.W. and WOODS, W.J. (1997) Affirmative psychotherapy for gay men. In D.R. Atkinson and G. Hackett (Eds) *Counseling Diverse Populations*, 2nd ed. Boston, MA: McGraw Hill.

SHELLEY, C. (1998). Introduction. In C. Shelley (Ed.) *Contemporary Perspectives on Psychotherapy and Homosexualities*. London: Free Association Books.

SHERNOFF, M. (1984) Family therapy for lesbian and gay clients. *Social Work, 29*, 393–396.

SIEGEL, S. and WALKER, G. (1996) Conversations between a gay therapist and a straight therapist. In J. Laird and R.J. Green (Eds) *Lesbians and Gays in Couples and Families: A Handbook for Therapists*. San Francisco, CA: Jossey-Bass.

SILVERSTEIN, C. (1991) Psychological and medical treatments of homosexuality. In J.C. Gonsiorek and J.D. Weinrich (Eds) *Homosexuality: Research Implications for Public Policy*. Newbury Park, CA: Sage.

SLATER, S. (1995) *The Lesbian Family Life Cycle*. London: Free Press.

SLATER, S. and MENCHER, J. (1991) The lesbian family life cycle: A contextual approach. *American Journal of Orthopsychiatry, 61*, 372–383.

SLUZKI, C.E. (1978) Marital therapy from a systems perspective. In T.J. Paolino and B.S. McGrady (Eds) *Marriage & Marital Therapy: Psychoanalytic, Behavioural, & Systems Theory Perspectives*. New York: Brunner/Mazell.

SOCARIDES, C.W. (1978) *Homosexuality*. New York: Jason Aronson.

SOPHIE, J. (1982) Counseling lesbians. *The Personal Guidance Journal, Feb*, 341–345.

STACY, K. (1993) Exploring stories of lesbian experience in therapy. *Dulwich Centre Newsletter, 2*, 2–13.

STROMMEN, E.F. (1989) 'You're a what?': Family member reactions to the disclosure of homosexuality. In F.W. Bozett (Ed.) *Homosexuality and the Family*. New York: Harrington Park Press.

STROMMEN, E.F. (1990) Hidden branches and growing pains: Homosexuality and the family tree. In F.W. Bozett and M.B. Sussman (Eds) *Homosexuality and Family Relations*. New York: Harrington Park Press.

TASKER, F. and McCANN, D. (1999) Affirming patterns of adolescent sexual identity: The challenge. *Journal of Family Therapy, 21*, 30–54.

TAYLOR, I. and ROBERTSON, A. (1994) A sensitive question. *Nursing Times, 90(51)*, 31–32.

TEPPER, K. (1996) The 'coming-out' process as differentiation: A Bowenian perspective for the gay or lesbian client. *Progress: Family Systems Research and Therapy, 5*, 73–82.

TROIDEN, R.R. (1979). Becoming homosexual: A model of gay identity acquisition. *Psychiatry, 42*, 362–373.

USSHER, J. (1991) Family and couples therapy with gay and lesbian clients: Acknowledging the forgotten minority. *Journal of Family Therapy, 13*, 131–148.

WALKER, G. and GOLDNER, V. (1995) The wounded prince and the women who love him. In C. Burck and B. Speed (Eds) *Gender, Power and Relationships*. London: Routledge.

WEEKS, J., DONOVAN, C. and HEAPHY, B. (1996) *Families of Choice: Patterns of Non-Heterosexual Relationships: A Literature Review* [Social Science Research Papers 2]. London: South Bank University.

WESTON, K. (1991) *Families We Choose: Lesbians, Gays, Kinship*. New York: Columbia University Press.

WISNIEWSKI, J.J. and TOOMEY, B.G. (1987) Are social workers homophobic? *Social Work, 32*, 454–455.

WOODMAN, N.J. and LENNA, H.R. (1980) *Counseling with Gay Men and Women: A Guide for Facilitating Positive Life-Styles*. San Francisco, CA: Jossey-Bass.

Chapter 12

'I've Always Tolerated It But...': Heterosexual Masculinity and the Discursive Reproduction of Homophobia

Brendan Gough

The focus of this chapter is mainly on the negative perceptions and actions marshalled by heterosexual men against homosexual men (for discussion on discourse, prejudice and lesbian women, see Kitzinger, 1987). The term 'homophobia' has been used by various researchers to describe prejudiced ideals and practices deployed with reference to lesbians and gay men (for example, Weinberg, 1972; MacDonald, 1976; Friend, 1992). It refers to a fear of homosexuality in others (and probably oneself) and frequently implies verbal and physical aggression towards individuals (self-)identified as lesbian or gay (see Pharr, 1988; but also see Kitzinger and Perkins, 1993, for a critical discussion of homophobia). Male homophobia in relation to gay men is perhaps most evident in situations (at school, work, in the pub, doing sport, etc.) where heterosexual men are together in groups. In these contexts, there seems to be a huge investment in asserting heterosexual and masculine credentials, a project bolstered by 'humorously' locating 'weakness' in other men (see Epstein, 1997). First hand accounts from gay men depicting a range of victimizing experiences attest to the painful consequences of homophobia whilst sets of statistics on 'gay-bashing' and related crimes point to its prevalence (see Love, 1998).

In addition, there is much evidence of prejudice and discrimination against gay communities inflicted by men and male-dominated institutions such as the law, medicine, the military and religious groups (see Herek, 1989, 1998; Blumenfeld, 1992). However, this is by no means a purely contemporary phenomenon. Several writers have traced the socio-historical origins of homophobia to the explicit legal and scientific-medical criminalization and pathologization of homosexual activities in the late nineteenth century (Weeks, 1989; Lofstrom, 1997. This form of institutional homophobia was reflected in the 'scientific' view of homosexuality as a form of mental illness requiring such 'cures' as aversion therapy shock treatments. Despite the declassification of homosexuality as a mental illness and the growing visibility and confidence of gay communities since the 1970s, widespread public acceptance has proved elusive; indeed, homophobia has burgeoned over the past twenty years (Segal, 1990).

Clearly, prejudice against gay men (and lesbian women) constitutes a serious social problem which requires attention from 'critical' psychology researchers interested in raising awareness and creating the conditions for social change. My own research on men, masculinity and discourse has been influenced by feminist and critical social psychologies (Parker, 1992; Wilkinson and Kitzinger, 1995; Wilkinson, 1996) which emphasize the social construction of gender and sexuality and favour discourse analysis as a way of interrogating prevailing social norms. These positions are discussed below when I introduce my work on homophobia. Firstly, however, I will attempt to contextualize this work by highlighting recent significant cultural events and contemporary research on heterosexual men and homophobia.

Homophobia in contemporary society

The increasing visibility of lesbian and gay culture evident in recent times has been accompanied by a powerful homophobic backlash, illustrated by the concerted efforts of dominant groups and institutions towards the recriminalization of same-sex sexual behaviour. In the UK in 1988, legislation was passed by the then Conservative government – Section 28 of the Local Government Act – which aimed to outlaw the 'promotion' of homosexuality in schools, whilst in the USA, Republican politicians and various moral-religious groups have pursued a conservative agenda in advocating anti-lesbian and anti-gay policies. For example, with regard to changes in USA government legislation concerning lesbians and gays in the military, Adam (1994) has noted implicit irrational constructions of lesbians and gay men as threats to discipline and cohesion, in spite of simultaneous commendation for services to the state; the same constructions were evident in parallel debates in the UK.

The emergence of the AIDS epidemic in the 1980s seemed to have provided an opportunity to reinforce a conservative homophobic agenda as gay men became scapegoated as diseased and sinful, reaping just desserts for their 'immoral promiscuity'. The campaign to reinstate 'family values' in the wake of 1970s liberalism which politicians in the UK and the USA had been promoting thus gathered renewed impetus as public uncertainty and panic were exploited (see Smart, 1992). Even when it was acknowledged that heterosexual people could be affected, such victims were largely portrayed as innocent (as opposed to more culpable homosexuals – see Weeks, 1989). It has also been claimed that national governments have failed to open up discussion and raise awareness about sex and sexuality, preferring to frame public information literature on HIV/AIDS in terms of sex-death connections or phallocentric heterosexual norms (see Holland *et al.*, 1991; McFadden, 1995).

Various surveys now attest to the prevalence of homophobia, especially among heterosexual men. A common finding, for example, is that heterosexual men score more highly than women on measures of homophobia (for example, the 'Index of Homophobia') towards gay men (see Kite, 1984; Kite and Whitley, 1998). In addition, correlations have been produced between homophobia and various measures of traditionally 'masculine' dis/inclinations, such as lack of self-disclosure, touching and intimacy in general (see Monroe *et al.*, 1997). However, implicit in such questionnaire studies is the notion that prejudiced 'attitudes' are located within particular individuals, a problematic focus from a discourse analytic perspective (which I adopt) which highlights the ways in which social and cultural ideals are taken up and reworked by individuals and groups (see Parker, 1989, 1992).

However, there has been research investigating homophobia as a social phenomenon, with evidence suggesting widespread prejudice amongst groups of mainly young, working-class, heterosexual men located at various institutional sites. For example, research on male bonding activities in sporting contexts has noted patterns of sexist, racist and homophobic discourse (for example, Fine, 1987; Lyman, 1987). Research with adolescent males in a work context also points to frequent instances of homophobia which maintain hierarchies between different groupings (see Haywood and Mac an Ghaill, 1997). Most work in this area has concentrated on educational arenas as sites where homophobia is marshalled to differentiate between groups of males and to consolidate forms of heterosexual masculinities. It is in this context that many writers have emphasized the connection between homophobia and misogyny:

> to call a boy a 'poof' is derogatory but this term, in denoting lack of guts, suggests femininity – weakness, softness and inferiority. (Lees, 1987, p. 180)

The use of insults like 'poof' and 'nancy boy' by males has been documented in both primary (for example, Epstein, 1997) and secondary school (for example, Mac an Ghaill, 1994) contexts through ethnographic observation of male interactions and recording the stories of 'victims' of such abuse. Consider the comments of Miles, a secondary school pupil who did not inhabit a traditionally masculine position within his school:

> It's a sort of stigma, ain't it? A quiet person in a class would be called 'gay' or summat. I was for a time 'cos I was fairly quiet in the classroom and for a while everyone was callin' me gay...I think my grades have

suffered because of disruptive members of the class. (From Kehily and Nayak, 1997, p. 83)

Clearly, talk and 'humour' based on homophobia and directed at 'other' males is used by boys and men to define and regulate what Carrigan *et al.* (1985) term 'hegemonic masculinities' – with painful consequences for non-macho or 'sissy' men (see Hunter, 1992, for an interesting piece on prejudice against 'feminine' heterosexual men). 'Hegemonic masculinities' refer to currently dominant forms of masculinity which derive from and serve to reinforce divisions between men and between men and women to the benefit of privileged groups, usually white, heterosexual, middle-class males and to the detriment of 'legitimate' others, such as women and gay men (see Connell, 1995; Gough, 1998). Heterosexuality is one readily available 'hegemonic' institution/discourse within which many heterosexual males in the 1990s deploy negative portrayals of male homosexuality as a means of (self-)policing their masculinities. However, little research has examined homophobia among older, middle-class men who might display greater investment in presenting themselves as liberal or 'politically correct' – for example, in a university context. Questions arise here concerning whether and how homosexuality in general and gay men in particular can be subjected to abuse and ridicule where institutional and cultural norms exist promoting tolerance and equal rights (see Billig, 1988; Gill, 1993). For example, in an article based on research with male university students, I noted that sexism and anti-feminism were sometimes couched within a repertoire of tolerance (as in 'Feminism is fine but...') (Gough, 1998). The sample analysis which follows therefore highlights patterns of homophobic discourse within a contemporary university setting and discusses their importance for constructing heterosexual masculinities.

The study

Data collection

Three group discussions were conducted with men, each lasting approximately one and a half hours. The participants were all second year university Psychology students aged between 20 and 50 and mostly from the Yorkshire and Humberside region of the north of England. In terms of occupational background, whether of self or parents, the participants could be described as working class, with links to the mining and steel industries common. Of course, the notion of class – like masculinity – is fragmented and it is not clear (nor was it pursued here) whether the students would define themselves as middle class in relation to university or working class in relation to family background. Again, although not explicitly reported, it was quite obvious that the participants located themselves as heterosexual.

Apart from the concern to explore talk in an all-male context, group discussions were selected instead of the more standard individual interviews in order to explore how a range of ideas around gender and sexuality were negotiated between men. The use of this focus group format highlights the impact of social interaction on the navigation of culturally available ideas as participants strive to make sense of particular phenomena (see Carey, 1995; Millward, 2000). This is important as the oppression of lesbian and gay people often follows from the reproduction of such socially shared understandings, as in the discursive collusion in which boys frequently indulge to position other boys as weak and effeminate (for example, Fine, 1987).

The students were enlisted informally when I made a general request for volunteers following a teaching session I had delivered. I simply announced that I wanted to carry out some discussions with men about masculinity in the 1990s. Fortunately the response was enthusiastic and I proceeded to organize the recording sessions. All three discussions were subsequently conducted in a room at the university and recorded with permission on a standard tape recorder with microphone attachment and then transcribed. Discussion one involved five participants (including myself), discussion two had three participants and discussion three involved four people.

In the interests of 'naturalistic' conversation, little emphasis was placed on structuring the talk. However, as there were certain areas I wanted to explore with the groups, I prepared an interview schedule which covered the following topics: social background, identity, university life, feminism, relationships with wo/men, equality, sexuality and aspirations for the future. As it transpired, the discussions did proceed quite fluently with minimal need to refer to my schedule.

Discourse analysis

In examining the qualitative data, I used a combination of constructionist grounded theory and discourse analysis. In the past, these two approaches have been seen as incompatible but it is becoming more acceptable to combine the two in productive ways (see Henwood, 1993; Lugton, 1997; Willott and Griffin, 1997). The transcripts were initially 'read' using the method of grounded theory whereby each segment of text is categorized in detail (Glaser and Strauss, 1967; Pidgeon, 1996; Pidgeon and Henwood, 1996). In this way several themes which are grounded in the talk of the participants are 'identified', combined and contrasted. When this is done, the analyst brings to bear their personal experience and theoretical position upon the material, although in practice it is difficult to avoid doing this from the outset; indeed, such ideas may be recorded on 'memo' cards during the process. This link between theory and data is emphasized by Pidgeon (1996) who highlights the researcher's role in constructing the themes, a move which can facilitate links with discourse analysis, an explicitly constructionist approach.

Having produced a set of themes, the next step moves into a form of 'discourse analysis' (Burman and Parker, 1993) whereby each theme is considered in turn and examined in terms of the different ways in which it is talked about. Recurrent patterns of discourse – which Potter and Wetherell (1987) term 'interpretative repertoires' – are then identified. Within feminist and critical social psychologies, there are different approaches to the analysis of texts and there is some variation in terminology. For example, the term 'discourse' is preferred to 'interpretative repertoire' by Parker (1992) and Billig *et al.* (1988) use the term 'ideological dilemma' to emphasize the co-existence of and conflict between two or more culturally valued ideas around a given object. Distinctions notwithstanding, all approaches tend to converge on exploring and expressing the multiple and often contradictory accounts from which people draw in their talk as well as connecting these to (the reproduction of) ideological practices (see, for example, Coyle, 2000, for an overview and Parker, 1992, for an extended discussion of the debates around modes of discourse analysis). Thus, the analysis which follows attempts to identify multiple and conflicting accounting strategies used by the male interviewees in talking about homosexuality and related issues. Specifically, given the extent to which the texts invoked interpretative repertoires used to bolster inequality and uphold heterosexist practices, the focus is on this ideological dimension to the talk.

My interest in interrogating discourse which could be seen to bolster inequality and uphold heterosexist practices ties in with my identification as a critical social psychologist. The analysis which follows must also be regarded in the light of other positions which I inhabit, i.e., white, male and heterosexual – positions shared with the research participants. Whilst such commonalities can facilitate comfortable and smooth interactions, other differences between myself and the participants (for example, differences in roles as tutor-student and researcher-participant) and between the students themselves (in terms of age, marital status, etc.) can militate against consensus and collusion. The analysis then should be read with these issues in mind, issues which are reflexively discussed in the final section.

In the quotations that are presented in the analysis, dots within square brackets ([.]) indicate a pause, with the number of dots providing a rough guide to the duration of the pause; text within square brackets is either clarificatory information or – where it was difficult to discern what was said with certainty – probable content; and where text is underlined, this indicates where the speaker spoke with emphasis. All speakers are identified by pseudonyms in the quotations and I (as the interviewer) am identified as 'Bren'.

Homophobic talk

A general perusal of the transcripts would suggest that, although the participants were inclined to present homosexuality as something alien and/or problematic, great efforts were often made to soften such claims lest accusations of prejudice be forthcoming. The following list documents the most common ways of speaking about homosexuality:

- *'tolerance'*: the speaker professes a liberal attitude to homosexuality while also producing statements that could be regarded as homophobic (as in 'I've always tolerated it but...').
- *'privacy'*: the speaker expresses disapproval of public displays of (homo)sexuality.
- *'difference'*: the speaker draws clear distinctions (between lesbian and gay persons and sexual acts, gay men and lesbian women, homosociality and homosexuality).
- *'individualism'*: the speaker construes sexuality as personal choice (unconnected to ideology and power relations).

This is not to suggest that more blatantly anti-lesbian and anti-gay remarks were not made – consider the following comments:

Bren	[..] what are your thoughts on homosexuality?
Eric	Petrified of it
Bren	Petrified of it?
Eric	I hate it. I am totally homophobic – take them out and shoot them all
	(extract 1, discussion 1)

Joe	Does it [homosexuality] disgust you?
Trev	Yeah, big time. I don't give a toss as long as I don't see it [..] I don't care if they do it behind bars [laughs] – Freudian slip, behind closed doors [..]
	(extract 2, discussion 3)

Unambiguous homophobic declarations are made in both cases which variously profess fear, hostility (in the first instance), repulsion and the importance of keeping homosexuality at a distance (in the second case). The emphasis on invisibility and privacy around (homo)sexual practice in the second extract is quite dominant across the three discussions, a theme to which we will return later. On the other hand, it would be an oversight to imply that gay-friendly sentiments were not expressed, as the following examples make clear:

Will   I think they're very brave, especially when they're comin' out of the closet [..] because we have a society that's not specifically run for homosexuality in itself and gay people, they're gonna be labelled and stereotyped [..] so they're very brave to do what they do.

(extract 3, discussion 2)

Glen   and if you've never slept with another man then how can you know for sure that you're not? And that you're just doin' what you've been socialized to do because it was the only option open to you?

(extract 4, discussion 1)

Both extracts make use of a socialization account of sexuality to highlight dominant norms and restrictions relating to homosexual practice. This engenders some admiration and sympathy for gay 'people' on the part of the first speaker whilst the second emphasizes the cultural barriers which police sexual expression and identity. Of course, this socialization repertoire would have been very much available to the participants in their social science context at college. Yet, it is fair to report that most talk around homosexuality favoured pejorative terminology framed by 'rational' argument(s). For example, the following brief extract makes use of a number of the repertoires outlined above:

Martin   If it's, if it's treated like conventional heterosexuality, you've got your partner and you keep it to yourself and it's not flaunted, I've always tolerated it but what annoys me is when you see these gay marches, they're all dressed up in these perverted leathers, whatever it is, bondage gear – if they wanna do that in their own home then that's alright, but I think they're gettin' themselves a bad name when they all turn up dressed as transvestites and they've got the tights on like 'Rocky Horror Picture Show' and they're walkin' down street; you just look at 'em and you think 'What are they?' and they look like monsters, if they were just dressed fairly conventionally, just say 'Look, I'm homosexual, accept me' I'd have no problem whatsoever – you're not tryin' to rape me, you're not tryin' to force it on me, I accept it, but it's that perversion that they seem to put over, not all of 'em, I mean it's a public minority, but it's that that I don't accept. If it was a heterosexual march and everybody was, like, in bondage gear and handcuffs, it's not on this [..] you can't have this walkin' down the street. It goes off, you know it happens, you accept that [...] but for them to force that on people, now whether they're dressin' to that extent to make a point, this is what you gotta accept.

(extract 5, discussion 1)

Martin's contribution here comes soon after the topic of homosexuality has been raised and contains several statements which could easily be read as prejudiced, such as comparing gay marchers to monsters or constructing gay men as potential rapists. However, these themes of abnormality and danger are embedded in and enabled by reference to certain heterosexual ideals. Firstly, 'normal' (hetero)sexuality is equated with privacy ('you keep it to yourself') and restraint ('it's not flaunted'). The implication – soon to be made explicit – is that 'deviant' homosexuality is bound up with unacceptable public displays and, as such, should be controlled. What is interesting here is that the overt attack on gay marchers is prefaced with the speaker positioning himself as liberal ('I've always tolerated it but...') – there is a concern not to be perceived as homophobic. There would be no need for such disclaimers if the context permitted openly prejudiced expression; perhaps Martin is being careful in constructing his arguments because of the prevailing middle class university context augmented by the presence of a course tutor. So, the upshot of the first few lines is that homosexuality is fine if it conforms to – is policed by – heterosexual conventions.

In projecting the gay other(s), this participant makes particular reference to disapproved dress ('perverted leathers...bondage gear...dressed as transvestites') – as if to suggest that deviance is self-evidently written on the body; after all, no 'normal' person would resort to such style. However, such practices are again deemed acceptable in the context of the unseen domestic space ('if they wanna do that in their own home then that's alright'). The main issue then centres around privacy; it is not outlandish fashion *per se* which offends most, although this aspect does seem difficult to stomach (as in the 'monsters' reference and the subsequent claim that 'conventional' dress would attract more support); rather, the major crime lies in the public 'flaunting' of such images ('walkin' down the street' blatantly).

Another dimension to Martin's perceptions of gay men is then presented – the threat of rape ('you're not trying to force it on me...'). The gay other is imbued with potential power and strength, a common enough depiction in heterosexual folklore – consider, for example, heterosexual fear and nervous joking provoked by a jail sentence, joining the navy, attending public school, etc. – and one which conflicts, ironically, with equally popular images of gay men as effeminate and weak. Perhaps sensing that his talk could be understood as prejudiced, Martin moves to minimize the potential for such accusations towards the end of his speaking turn. Firstly, he proceeds to confine his attribution of perversion to a 'public minority'; next, he acknowledges and makes to accept such 'perversion' as fact; and finally he concedes that public 'perversion' may well be geared towards highlighting important political realities. In the midst of these pronouncements, however, it could be argued that homophobic talk is reinforced. A hypothetical 'heterosexual march' is imagined to suggest the absurdity of the sort of gay parades/charades which Martin speaks of and to underline the notion of the ordinary heterosexual 'bloke' rationally choosing to avoid such displays. The implicit theme here of sexuality as individual expression and responsibility is developed more explicitly in other extracts.

Most themes present-ed in Martin's talk are reproduced in other texts. The next extract, taken from discussion 3, follows a debate between two participants where one of them is openly challenged by the other to defend ostensibly homophobic comments:

Joe	and I know, like, a few gay lads that work at the club and when they see me they come up to me and give me a kiss on the cheek
Trev	Oh no! Uhhh, I just couldn't, it's just not..
Joe	I call you 'love' and 'flower' but you don't get offended do you?
Trev	Yeah, I mean
Joe	But what if I turned round and said I was gay? Would you instantly dislike me because of it?
Trev	No, I mean I've got, I have one gay friend and [I wasn't chuffed about it] I'm not bothered – as long as they don't come on to me.
Joe	So what makes you think that any homosexual's gonna come on to you?
Trev	Well, I'm not bothered if they come on to me [..] as long as they don't! [laughter] No [..]
Joe	Is it just that it would repulse you to give a guy a kiss?
Trev	Oh yeah, big time, yeah
Joe	But why?
Trev	It's just disgustin', I just can't stand it [..] I just don't think it's right
Joe	What about a couple of girls snoggin'?
Trev	No, it's not [..]
Joe	If they were attractive?
Trev	If they were attractive, if they were attractive it [laughter] No, it has its sexual tone yeah, but
Joe	What about if it was two attractive blokes?
Trev	There's no such thing, is there?
Joe	Two of the guys from Levi ads with six pack and, all

	muscly and that
Trev	I just don't [understand it] I don't know, I can't help it, not that I'm that [bothered] anyway, I just can't stand it, it's just not [on] [..] bit close to the mark.

(extract 6, discussion 3)

Initially, Trev openly expresses disbelief and horror around being kissed (on the cheek) by gay friends, thereby aligning himself with a tightly male heterosexual/homophobic identity, in contrast to Joe's self-positioning as gay-friendly. The availability of these two identities here cautions against simplistic portrayals of university or middle-class contexts as either liberal or conservative – the current historical context (the group discussions took place in 1996) seems to offer both possibilities for presenting sexuality. However, as the focus of the chapter is on patterns of homophobic discourse, we will attend more closely to Trev's talk around homosexuality.

When challenged by Joe, Trev attempts to protest liberal credentials, to establish that he is relaxed about homosexuality – the now familiar appeal to egalitarian values. However, these claims warrant further statements which can be regarded as prejudiced – in this case a projection of gay men as predators interested in corrupting (decent) heterosexuals. In responding to his friend's polite interrogations and the dilemmas posed, Trev attempts to position himself simultaneously as traditionally masculine and progressively tolerant. Humour is used as a device which enables the taboo (homophobic) statements to be articulated but read as innocuous, thereby helping to protect the speaker from accusations of prejudice.

The denigrated gay other is again furnished with disturbing power, perhaps deriving from socially mediated fears and fantasies. When this myth of the gay threat and the rejection of men kissing are then questioned by Joe, Trev falls back on expressions of disgust before couching his defence in moralistic terms. It is interesting that portrayals of homosexuality as morally suspect still exert fascination for some men. A popular distinction is then drawn between all-male and all-female sex, with the latter, predictably, rendered much more acceptable and enjoyable. As for the all-male variety, Trev goes so far as to deny the possibility that two heterosexual men could find each other attractive. A line is thus drawn around heterosexuality which disallows even the slightest hint of homoeroticism and which marks off homosexuality as a separate, dysfunctional alterior zone.

In his final utterance, Trev professes perplexity on the subject of male-on-male attraction; it is something which he dismisses and which, allegedly, causes little concern. Yet, he immediately contradicts this disaffected stance by delivering a passionate rebuttal. There is a sense of disgust reported that seems to go beyond cool rationality and which evokes psychoanalytic discourse around unconscious anxieties and desires ('a bit close to the mark'). So, with this extract we encounter a range of strategies which discursively project gay men as deficient and damaging and which seek to erect defences and boundaries to distinguish between acceptable and unacceptable sexualities.

This attempt to distance oneself from the ravages of homosexuality is more explicit in the next extract, where a concerted effort is made to define homosociality as nonsexual. When presented with the idea of bisexuality being universal, there is some cautious agreement initially ('to some extent') before it is contested with a humorous reference to repression (by Will) and then constructed as only one misguided view from a range of more plausible alternatives (by Mike). The homoerotic dimension associated with bisexuality is, of course, where the 'problem' lies, to which the subsequent attempts to warrant all-male relationships as devoid of sexual desire attest. Mike proceeds to provide his preferred interpretation of behaviour – 'male bonding' – which could be (in his view, mistakenly) construed in sexual terms.

Bren	What about Freud's idea that everyone is bisexual?
Tony	To a certain extent
Will	It must be really repressed in me B, I'm sorry [laughter]
Mike	I'd see that as an interpretation because, like, people say 'Aye, you're drunk with each other and it's all male bonding together' and people put that down as camaraderie if you like, but it's just guys bein' guys, but it's [..]
Tony	Just an aspect of guys bein' together, it's <u>degrees</u> isn't it?
Mike	'Cos people, it's not like you're attracted, I would say there's guys that I would respect, guys, like brothers and stuff, but definitely not sexual feeling [later]
Will	I'm not <u>aware</u> of having sort of gay feelings, I'm just not aware of it, I mean I'm a happily married man with a family and that's [..] I can't say, I mean I was married before and I didn't have any different thoughts then, so I just can't comprehend it, I mean what [..] I'm not aware of it
Tony	I suppose you can actually say that some men are quite attractive, to actually look at [..] but as far as taking it any further than that, I mean not sexually attractive, I don't think
Bren	So there's a distinction there then
Tony	Mmm, yeah

(extract 7, discussion 2)

In a very short time several ideas are proposed which seem designed to deflect explanations based on the erotic. Firstly, alcohol is immediately cited as a factor, as if to say that displays of affection between men do not (and should not?) take place under 'normal' sober circumstances; male-to-male emotional expressions are therefore viewed as fleeting aberrations connected to a loss of reason under the influence of alcohol. Interestingly, when male-to-male sexual activity has in fact occurred, research suggests that alcohol (ab)use may be cited to deflect potential ascriptions of gay sexual identities (Hencken, 1984). However, the normality of such behaviour (in the context of alcohol?) is then underlined by virtue of the notion of 'male bonding', as if it is self-evidently understood that 'just guys bein' guys' is plainly natural and social. This vague appeal to norms around masculinity is echoed and developed slightly by Tony who emphasizes the concept of 'degrees' to distinguish between acceptable and deviant (i.e., homoerotic) displays. Ironically, the notion of 'degrees' implies a continuum, i.e., a lack of qualitative difference between homosocial and homosexual activities.

Mike then elaborates the distinction thesis on more explicit lines by eschewing the idea of finding men attractive. His earlier notion of 'camaraderie' is extended by a lexicon of homosociality where terms like 'respect' and 'brotherly' are invoked to describe male relationships. In so doing, distance is placed between self and other men and between men generally; a taboo is reinforced around sexual desire for other men, underlined by the 'brother' reference, which could be used in the sense of family or in terms of Black youth subculture (in both cases, the desire to sleep with your 'brother' is deemed strictly out of bounds). The account culminates in an overt denial of any sexual dimension to relations between men. Mike's high level involvement with a university sports team could be significant here in his greater effort to construct male activities and togetherness as homosocial; implications of homosexuality, if accepted, would possibly present more threats – hence his defensiveness.

A little later in the proceedings, the others conspire in the process of maintaining distinctions between the homosocial and the homoerotic. Will reiterates his claim of having no conscious 'gay feelings' which is then warranted by highlighting his heterosexual credentials (married with family) – as if it is obvious that conforming to heterosexual norms precludes homosexual desire. Again a clear boundary is erected and the possibility of bisexuality dismissed. Tony then appears to make a concession by admitting in theory that attraction between men is conceivable but moves to qualify this by restricting attraction to a form of dispassionate visual appreciation (echoes of 'respect' again). This point is further underlined by remarks which foreclose possibilities inherent in male-to-male attraction of homoerotic desire and activity. So, this last extract then suggests a monumental project of denying desire between heterosexual men and projecting this onto the gay male other(s) where it is safely contained. Various distinctions are made which drive this point home.

In the final extract, some of the earlier themes are repeated but some new variations are also presented. For example, there is a claim that lesbians and gay men are prejudiced and a suggestion that heterosexual people need to be protected from public displays of homosexuality. Trev makes to ridicule Joe's gay-friendly rhetoric by asserting that this perspective should not be claimed by heterosexuals: tolerance and support for lesbians and gay men ought to be exclusively located in the 'poof' world. This remark is framed as humour, signalled by the knowing deployment of a standard term of abuse ('poof') – a term known to be offensive and used to transgress politically correct boundaries and hence provoke mirth – but his subsequent talk dispenses with such attempts at diversion as he switches to serious mode. In this vein, Trev issues an attack on lesbian and gay identity and visibility by means of the claim that any prejudice lies with lesbians and gay men rather than the heterosexual majority ('they're not pro-straight'). This sentiment is prefaced and softened (or perhaps enabled) by an expression of tolerance regarding 'different' categories of sexuality and a denial of extremism on the part of gays ('they're not anti-straight').

Joe	I think I used to be homophobic, definitely, I think that's [i.e., tolerance] the way forward.
Trev	[laughs] Yeah, if you're a poof [laughter] No, a lot of it does piss me off, like all this gay pride and shit, I mean you can call people straight, bi and what-have-you, I know they're not anti-straight but at the same time they're not pro-straight either.
Joe	No, but if like, men and women can walk down the street and hold hands and kiss then why can't they do it? I mean it's only because we're socialized to say it's wrong, so if we change to say that it's right to snog whoever you want and it's up to you, there'd be no problem.
Trev	Yeah, but you have to think about other people, it would repulse a lot of people.
Joe	Yeah, but what I'm sayin' is it only repulses them because we're taught it's wrong.
Trev	Yeah, it is, it is.
Joe	If, if you were taught to eat your own faeces was right and you [..] that might be a good psychology experiment
Trev	Yeah
Joe	Gave them praise for doin' it, then outsiders would think it's just, disgustin' but they, you know, that's fine, see what I mean?

Trev   I know what you mean, but that's, I mean, I just don't
            see it as right
Joe   Do you not want to change, do you not want to see
            that it's [..] 'cos you can, people can change.
Trev   Yeah, in a way I can understand it, but in another way
            it's just like there's em, yeah, as long as it just doesn't
            get in my face I'm not bothered really, if I don't see it,
            it would <u>seem</u> OK, but it's just not. I, I don't disagree
            with it, like, fundamentally – well, I suppose actually
            I do, yeah [laughter] but I don't disagree in a way that
            I can't understand it because I don't think they should
            do it but at the same time I know certain people can't
            help it so I can understand it, but I still don't think
            they should do it [..] but I can't stand all those
            'wannabe queers', people like that, it's like
Joe   Who want to be camp cos it's cool
Trev   Yeah

                                                    (extract 8, discussion 3)

So, the gay male other, who under contemporary cultural norms
around political correctness etc. is widely regarded as an oppressed
victim, is here positioned in the role of oppressor and, by implication,
it is heterosexuals who are the real victims. This strategy of rebutting
accusations of prejudice by projecting it on to the targets of subjection
has been documented with respect to men's talk about ethnic groups
(for example, Billig, 1988) and women (for example, Gill, 1993; Gough,
1998).

   Joe then challenges Trev's apparent lack of tolerance of homosexuality by invoking a repertoire of (hetero)sexuality as socialization,
thereby asserting an arbitrary and restrictive fashioning of sexual practices and identities. This discourse is widely used across texts and is
not rejected by Trev but he quickly moves to present another defence –
a repertoire promoting sensitivity to the offended feelings of 'ordinary'
(heterosexual) people. The theme of the heterosexual as victim of
abnormal gay displays is thus continued, with the advantage that the
speaker has positioned himself as considerate about heterosexual
others but not, of course, about the other other (gay men). Obviously,
this presentation of self as other-oriented renders it difficult to make
charges of homophobia stick.

   When Joe counters with a renewed emphasis on the socialization
repertoire to account for heterosexual disgust at gay visibility, Trev
rejects this explanation by speaking from a discourse of asocial reality
– homosexuality is asserted to be simply, universally, immoral. That
homosexuality is wrong constitutes an incontrovertible fact tied to the
nature of things rather than social convention. When further challenged, Trev tones down his argument by professing insight into Joe's

point of view and locating the immorality discourse within his own perceptions (rather than 'nature' or 'reality') – 'I just don't see it as right'. He then goes on to make a crucial distinction between intellectual and emotional acceptance of homosexuality which allows him to retain potentially homophobic remarks whilst professing 'understanding'. Familiar appeals to invisibility and privacy in the realm of (homo)sexual matters are repeated to give the impression of qualified tolerance ('as long as it doesn't get in my face').

A curious additional repertoire is suggested – homosexuality as beyond 'their' control – as if to paint lesbians and gay men as immature deviants deserving of sympathy and correction who are unskilled in the self-discipline required of and attained by ordinary decent heterosexual people. Before and after this remark, professed understanding is emphasized; the speaker clearly does not wish to be viewed as homophobic whilst knowingly presenting ideas which could be heard as such. Finally, another construction of the gay other is forwarded – homosexuality as self-conscious strategic presentation in the interests of acceptance within fashionable circles. This repertoire is reproduced in all three discussions and may well be a currently popular perception of the gay other by heterosexual men, with the attendant negative implications of shallowness and simulation. On this point, agreement is secured with Joe and the conversation moves on with less debate. So, with this extract, we encounter some recurring themes and additional repertoires deployed in the service of projecting the gay other as disturbed and dangerous.

Conclusion

As the preceding analysis suggests, some heterosexual (white, middle-class) men in the UK continue to fear and devalue homosexuality. In this way, the presentation of a heterosexual, 'masculine' self is implicitly attained (normal, rational, disciplined, etc.), once again highlighting the dependence of hegemonic forms of masculinity on the derogated other for self-definition (see Connell, 1995; Coyle and Morgan-Sykes, 1998; Gough, 1998).

The perceived threat from gay men could be connected to some heterosexual male perceptions of contemporary culture as 'emasculating' in the wake of feminism and gay politics (for example, Bly, 1991; Farrell, 1994). Indeed, elsewhere in the texts, there was a common perception of the university environment as 'pro-women' (see Gough, 2001). If this is the case, then all-male gatherings such as this research context (but more typically in the pub or club) could be regarded as 'safe' places where men revert to traditional gender displays felt to be frowned on by wider society. Of course, it is difficult and perhaps frustrating that the talk of such a small sample cannot be generalized to larger groups of men, although similar themes have been encountered with other samples of male university students (for example, see Gough and Edwards, 1998). Clearly, more research is required which explores constructions of the 'gay other' among groups such as Black and Asian men, working class men, professional men, etc. In order to challenge the maintenance and promotion of homophobic ideals in mundane talk, it becomes important to identify, contextualize and problematize the range of discursive strategies deployed. In addition, it would be interesting to investigate how heterosexual men were viewed from gay male perspectives.

The men's talk here is interesting in that much of it betrays an effort simultaneously to obscure and articulate statements easily viewed as prejudiced; there is a concern to deflect accusations of homophobia in a cultural climate often perceived as pro-equality and anti-discrimination (see Billig, 1988). Perhaps this portrait of prevailing norms is exacerbated within a higher educational context and, specifically, in a social science setting, where notions of ideology, power, inequalities, etc. would be familiar (the participants had all taken sociology and social psychology modules). It can also be argued that the attempt to avoid overt expressions of prejudice would be facilitated by a relatively advanced repertoire of arguments and concepts gleaned from the university domain, a point which challenges liberal notions of the educational process as an inherently enlightening experience.

The present analysis both highlights the utility of discourse analysis in interrogating ideological talk around homosexuality as well as the need to examine further the nature and range of repertoires used to protect and promote heterosexuality at the expense of homosexuality. Yet, certain issues tend to arise from such work which are difficult to resolve. For example, it could be argued that the present study has 'given voice' to a group of homophobic men and, as such, has contributed to, rather than challenged, ideals commonly regarded as politically dubious. Further, there is the degree to which the researcher (in this case myself) has colluded in the texts which have been (co)produced and which could promote discrimination. Certainly, during the course of the group discussions, I found myself guiltily giggling at some of the remarks presented whilst at other times remaining silent and experiencing feelings of tension in the face of the prevailing talk.

Yet, it would seem impossible to extricate oneself completely from cultural resources which circulate and are drawn upon to make sense of complex phenomena such as sexuality. In other words, explanations of homophobia should not revolve around deficient personalities as much as dominant ideals which exert power and fascination over (in this instance) a group of men positioned as white and heterosexual (the researcher included). Of course, the weight which is ascribed to society and individuals in accounting for prejudice is very much a matter for debate. Despite these and other concerns (for example, differences and tensions between researcher and researched, etc. – see Wilkinson and

Kitzinger, 1996) however, discourse analytic studies such as this provide useful, critical insights into the quotidian reproduction of ideology and inequalities around homosexuality in this particular case and around gender and sexuality more generally. Such analyses could usefully feed into initiatives to combat homophobia and other forms of prejudice with men and boys in a variety of settings (see Salisbury and Jackson, 1996).

References

BILLIG, M. (1988) The notion of prejudice: Some rhetorical and ideological aspects. *Text, 8*, 91–110.

BILLIG, M., CONDOR, S., EDWARDS, D., GAME, M., MIDDLETON, D.J. and RADLEY, A.R. (1988) *Ideological Dilemmas: A Social Psychology of Everyday Thinking*. London: Sage.

BLUMENFELD, W.J. (1992) *Homophobia: How We All Pay the Price*. Boston, MA: Beacon Press.

BLY, R. (1991) *Iron John: A Book About Men*. New York: Addison-Wesley.

BURMAN, E. and PARKER, I. (Eds) (1993) *Discourse Analytic Research: Repertoires and Readings of Texts in Action*. London: Routledge.

CAREY, M.A. (Ed.) (1995) Issues and applications of focus groups [special issue]. *Qualitative Health Research, 5*, 413–530.

CARRIGAN, T., CONNELL, R.W. and LEE, J. (1985) Towards a new sociology of masculinity. *Theory & Society, 14*, 551–604.

CONNELL, R.W. (1995) *Masculinities*. Cambridge: Polity Press.

COYLE, A. (2000) Discourse analysis. In G.M. Breakwell, S. Hammond and C. Fife-Schaw (Eds) *Research Methods in Psychology*, 2nd ed. London: Sage.

COYLE, A. and MORGAN-SYKES, C. (1998) Troubled men and threatening women: The construction of 'crisis' in male mental health. *Feminism & Psychology, 8*, 263–284.

EHRENREICH, B. (1983) *The Hearts of Men: American Dreams and the Flight from Commitment*. London: Pluto Press.

EPSTEIN, D. (1997) Boyz' own stories: Masculinities and sexualities in schools [1]. *Gender and Education, 9(1)*, 105–115.

FALUDI, S. (1992) *Backlash: The Undeclared War Against Women*. London: Chatto and Windus.

FARRELL, W. (1994) *The Myth of Male Power*. New York: Fourth Estate.

FINE, G. (1987) *With the Boys: Little League Baseball and Preadolescent Culture*. Chicago, IL: University of Chicago Press.

FRIEND, R.A. (1992) Choices, not closets: Heterosexism and homophobia in schools. In L. Weis and M. Fine (Eds) *Silenced Voices: Issues of Gender, Class and Race in Today's Schools*. Albany, NY: State University of New York Press.

GILL, R. (1993) Justifying injustice: Broadcasters' accounts of inequality. In E. Burman and I. Parker (Eds) *Discourse Analytic Research: Repertoires and Readings of Texts in Action*. London: Routledge.

GLASER, B.G. and STRAUSS, A.L. (1967) *The Discovery of Grounded Theory: Strategies for Qualitative Research*. Chicago, IL: Aldine.

GOUGH, B. (1998) Men and the discursive reproduction of sexism: Repertoires of difference and equality. *Feminism and Psychology, 8*, 25–49.

GOUGH, B. (2001) 'Biting your tongue': Negotiating masculinities in contemporary Britain. *Journal of Gender Studies, 10,* 169–185.

GOUGH, B. and EDWARDS, G. (1998) The beer talking: Four lads, a carry out and the reproduction of masculinities. *Sociological Review, 46,* 409–435.

HAYWOOD, C. and MAC AN GHAILL, M. (1997) A man in the making: Sexual masculinities within changing training cultures. *Sociological Review, 45,* 576–591.

HENCKEN, J.D. (1984) Conceptualizations of homosexual behavior which preclude homosexual self-labeling. *Journal of Homosexuality, 9(4),* 53–63.

HENWOOD, K. (1993) Women and later life: The discursive construction of identities within family relationships. *Journal of Aging Studies, 7,* 303–385.

HEREK, G.M. (1989) Hate crimes against lesbians and gay men. *American Psychologist, 44,* 948–955.

HEREK, G.M. (Ed.) (1998) *Stigma and Sexual Orientation: Understanding Prejudice Against Lesbians, Gay Men, and Bisexuals.* Thousand Oaks, CA: Sage.

HOLLAND, J., RAMAZANOGLU, C., SCOTT, S., SHARPE, S. and THOMSON, R. (1991) *Pressure, Resistance, Empowerment: Young Women and the Negotiation of Safer Sex.* London: Tufnell Press.

HUNTER, A. (1992) Same door, different closet: A heterosexual sissy's coming-out party. *Feminism and Psychology, 2,* 367–385.

KEHILY, M.J. and NAYAK, A. (1997) Lads and laughter: Humour and the production of heterosexual hierarchies. *Gender and Education, 9(1),* 69–87.

KINSMAN, G. (1987) *The Regulation of Desire: Sexuality in Canada.* Montreal: Black Rose Books.

KITE, M.E. (1984) Sex differences in attitudes towards homosexuals: A meta-analytic review. *Journal of Homosexuality, 10(1/2),* 69–81.

KITE, M.E. and WHITLEY, B.E. (1998) Do heterosexual women and men differ in their attitudes toward homosexuality? A conceptual and methodological analysis. In G.M. Herek (Ed.) *Stigma and Sexual Orientation: Understanding Prejudice Against Lesbians, Gay Men, and Bisexuals.* Thousand Oaks, CA: Sage.

KITZINGER, C. (1987) *The Social Construction of Lesbianism.* London: Sage.

KITZINGER, C. and PERKINS, R. (1993) *Changing Our Minds: Lesbian Feminism and Psychology.* London: Onlywomen Press.

LEES, S. (1987) The structure of sexual relations in school. In M. Arnot and G. Weiner (Eds) *Gender and the Politics of Schooling.* London: Hutchinson.

LEES, S. (1993) *Sugar and Spice: Sexuality and Adolescent Girls.* London: Penguin.

LOFSTROM, J. (1997) The birth of the queen/the modern homosexual: Historical explanations revisited. *Sociological Review, 45,* 24–42.

LOVE, P.G. (1998) Cultural barriers facing lesbian, gay and bisexual students at a Catholic college. *Journal of Higher Education, 69,* 298–324.

LUGTON, J. (1997) The nature of social support as experienced by women treated for breast cancer. *Journal of Advanced Nursing, 25,* 1184–1191.

LYMAN, P. (1987) The fraternal bond as joking relationship: A case study of the role of sexist jokes in male group bonding. In M.S. Kimmel (Ed.) *Changing Men: New Directions in Research on Men and Masculinity.* Newbury Park, CA: Sage.

MAC AN GHAILL, M. (1994) *The Making of Men: Masculinities, Sexualities and Schooling.* Buckingham: Open University Press.

MACDONALD, A.P. (1976) Homophobia: Its roots and meanings. *Homosexual Counseling Journal, 3,* 23–33.

McFADDEN, M. (1995) *Female Sexuality in the Second Decade of AIDS*. Unpublished PhD thesis, Queen's University, Belfast.

MILLWARD, L.J. (2000) Focus groups. In G.M. Breakwell, S. Hammond and C. Fife-Schaw (Eds) *Research Methods in Psychology*, 2nd ed. London: Sage.

MONROE, M., BAKER, R. and ROLL, S. (1997) The relationship of homophobia to intimacy in heterosexual men. *Journal of Homosexuality, 33(2)*, 23–36.

PARKER, I. (1989) *The Crisis in Modern Social Psychology and How To End It*. London: Routledge.

PARKER, I. (1992) *Discourse Dynamics: Critical Analysis for Social and Individual Psychology*. London: Routledge.

PHARR, S. (1988) *Homophobia: A Weapon of Sexism*. Little Rock, AR: Chardon Press.

PIDGEON, N. (1996) Grounded theory: Theoretical background. In J.T.E. Richardson (Ed.) *Handbook of Qualitative Research Methods for Psychology and the Social Sciences*. Leicester: BPS Books.

PIDGEON, N. and HENWOOD, K. (1996) Grounded theory: Practical implementation. In J.T.E. Richardson (Ed.) *Handbook of Qualitative Research Methods for Psychology and the Social Sciences*. Leicester: BPS Books.

POTTER, J. and WETHERELL, M. (1987) *Discourse and Social Psychology: Beyond Attitudes and Behaviour*. London: Sage.

SALISBURY, J. and JACKSON, D. (1996) *Challenging Macho Values: Practical Ways of Working with Adolescent Boys*. London: Falmer.

SEGAL, L. (1990) *Slow Motion: Changing Masculinities, Changing Men*. London: Virago.

SEIDLER, V.J. (1989) *Rediscovering Masculinity: Reason, Language and Sexuality*. London: Routledge.

SMART, C. (1992) *Historical Essays on Marriage, Motherhood and Sexuality*. London: Routledge.

WEEKS, J. (1985) *Sexuality and its Discontents*. London: Routledge.

WEEKS, J. (1989) *Sex, Politics and Society: The Regulation of Sexuality Since 1800*. London: Longman.

WEINBERG, G. (1972) *Society and the Healthy Homosexual*. New York: St Martin's Press.

WILKINSON, S. (Ed.) (1996) *Feminist Social Psychologies: International Perspectives*. Buckingham: Open University Press.

WILKINSON, S. and KITZINGER, C. (Eds) (1995) *Feminism and Discourse: Psychological Perspectives*. London: Sage.

WILKINSON, S. and KITZINGER, C. (Eds) (1996) *Representing the Other: A 'Feminism & Psychology' Reader*. London: Sage.

WILLOTT, S. and GRIFFIN, C. (1997) 'Wham, bam, am I a man?': Unemployed men talk about masculinities. *Feminism & Psychology, 7*, 107–128.

Chapter 13

Student Support for Lesbian and Gay Human Rights: Findings from a Large-scale Questionnaire Study

Sonja J. Ellis

Human rights are 'the rights of all people at all times and in all situations' (Cranston, 1962, p. 49). Human rights include first and foremost 'the right to life' and second, any rights which maintain the existence and quality of that life, for all people, independent of individual differences such as class, race, sex, sexual orientation, religion and (dis)ability. Consequently, human rights are generally considered universal and egalitarian (i.e., they apply to all people equally), indivisible (they cannot be separated from one another) and inalienable (they cannot be taken away or foregone) (for example, see Donnelly, 1993; Jones, 1994). International documents, such as the Universal Declaration of Human Rights (UDHR) (United Nations, 1948) and the European Convention for the Protection of Human Rights and Fundamental Freedoms (Council of Europe, 1950), have been instituted as guidelines for governmental policy and practice with the aim of ensuring that the human rights of all people are respected.

The socio-political climate for lesbians and gay men

In no country of the world – not even in the UK – are lesbians and gay men legally afforded the full range of human rights that heterosexual persons are. At the time of writing, consensual sexual acts between two women or two men are illegal in 41 countries; sex between men is illegal in a further 40 countries (see Amnesty International, 1997; International Lesbian and Gay Association [ILGA], 1999); and in only a handful of countries (for example, South Africa, Ecuador and Fiji) does the national constitution explicitly offer protection from discrimination on the basis of sexual orientation (see ILGA, 1999). In some countries, homosexual acts are punishable by physical beatings or even the death penalty (Wilets, 1994; Amnesty International, 1997).

Regardless of the official legal status of homosexual acts, lesbians and gay men in many countries are the target of state-sanctioned violence or social and ethnic cleansing (Khush, 1993; ILGA, 1998; OrdoÒez and Elliott, 1998) and many more become the victims of hate-motivated crimes (for example, see Federal Bureau of Investigation [FBI], 1995), or domestic violence (for example, see Rosenbloom, 1996; Thadani, 1996). The supposedly inalienable right to life, liberty and security of person is threatened or taken away from lesbians and gay men simply because of who they/we are and who they/we love and because they/we express that love in public, violate gender norms, disclose their/our identities and/or fight for lesbian and gay rights (see International Gay and Lesbian Human Rights Commission [IGLHRC], 1995; Rosenbloom, 1996; Amnesty International, 1997).

However, human rights violations against lesbians and gay men are not restricted to physical violence. Across the globe, lesbians and gay men are frequently denied human rights to privacy, dignity and respect (see IGLHRC, 1995; Rosenbloom, 1996; Amnesty International, 1997); equal access to employment and favourable work conditions (for example, see Kitzinger, 1991; Hayfield, 1995; Lesbian and Gay Employment Rights, 1998; Stonewall, 1998); the right to freedom of expression and assembly (for example, see Khush, 1993; Dunton and Palmberg, 1996; Amnesty International, 1997); and are invariably denied access to and discriminated against in relation to reproductive technologies, adoption services and custody of their/our own or their/our partners' children (see Hayfield, 1995; 'Key dates in lesbian...', 1997): for a detailed summary of all these issues and more, see Rosenbloom (1996), Amnesty International (1997) and Ellis (1999).

Psychology and lesbian and gay human rights

Although a human rights framework has predominantly been employed in work from a political-legal perspective, it has also been of interest to psychologists. A number of psychologists have discussed human rights in relation to psychological practice (for example, Rosenzweig, 1988; Burden, 1993; Olkin, 1997), psycholegal studies (for example, Melton, 1989, 1992), trauma following human rights violations (Becker, 1995; Silove, 1999) and children's rights (for example, Drexel, 1994; Penn and Coverdale, 1996; Wessells, 1997). More commonly, though, mainstream psychologists have tended to explore attitudes towards and/or social understandings of human rights. Some have investigated understandings of human rights among specific populations, such as children (for example, Wade, 1994; Ruck *et al.*, 1998), or in cross-national contexts (for example, Clémence *et al.*, 1995; Doise *et al.*, 1999) or non-western cultures (for example, Atolagbe and Otubanjo, 1984; Macek *et al.*, 1997). Others have explored people's constructions of human rights (for example, Diaz-Veizades *et al.*, 1995; Stainton Rogers and Kitzinger, 1995) and whether situational and ideological contexts make a difference to people's attitudes (Moghaddam and Vuksanovic, 1990). Some studies (for example, Doise *et al.*, 1994; Macek *et al.*, 1997) have also undertaken a cursory exploration of responsibility for enforcing human rights, finding that a large proportion of respondents view the enforcement of human rights as a governmental rather than a personal responsibility.

Conversely, studies of moral reasoning have predominantly focused on people's attitudes about specific rights issues, such as euthanasia (for example, Lee *et al.*, 1996) or the death penalty (for example, Ellsworth and Gross, 1994) and people's political attitudes towards particular groups of people, such as feminists (for example, Sotelo, 1997). However, among mainstream work on rights and moral reasoning, there appears to be an absence of work on people's understandings of and support for lesbian and gay (human) rights.

Within lesbian and gay psychology, the study of attitudes towards lesbians and gay men is also well-established. Many studies have investigated and documented the attitudes towards lesbians and gay men of particular groups of individuals, such as psychologists and mental health professionals (for example, Annesley and Coyle, 1995), social workers (for example, Wisniewski and Toomey, 1987; Berkman and Zinberg, 1997), medical trainees and professionals (for example, Douglas *et al.*, 1985; Klamen *et al.*, 1999), students (for example, Matchinsky and Iverson, 1996; Donnelly *et al.*, 1997; Proulx, 1997; Schellenberg *et al.*, 1999) and resident assistants (D'Augelli, 1989). Analyses of differences in attitudes among members of sub-groups have tended to indicate that males (for example, D'Augelli, 1989; Chng and Moore, 1991; Seltzer, 1992; Donnelly *et al.*, 1997; Klamen *et al.*, 1999; Schellenberg *et al.*, 1999), those with religious affiliations (for example, Seltzer, 1992; Berkman and Zinberg, 1997; see also Herek, 1994; Eliason, 1995) and those who have few lesbian or gay acquaintances (for example, Klamen *et al.*, 1999) are significantly more likely to hold negative attitudes towards lesbians and gay men. Studies have also suggested that attitudes towards gay men are significantly more negative than attitudes towards lesbians (for example, see Berkman and Zinberg, 1997; Schellenberg *et al.*, 1999).

By comparison, only a few studies (for example, D'Augelli, 1989; Pratto *et al.*, 1994; Eliason, 1996; Malaney *et al.*, 1997) have explored levels of support for lesbian and gay rights issues, usually as part of a larger study of social attitudes or as a study of the social climate for lesbians and gay men within a particular environment. The findings of these studies indicate variable levels of support for the different rights of lesbians and gay men. For example, in one study (Malaney *et al.*, 1997), the majority of students surveyed agreed that lesbians and gay men should be allowed to teach in schools, marry and have their relationships legally recognized, but were less inclined to support the rights of lesbians and gay men to serve in the military or to adopt children. Similarly, in another study (Eliason, 1996) up to 26 per cent of university staff surveyed indicated that they did not support the right of lesbians and gay men to teach children and only 53 per cent said they would endorse the extension of health care benefits to same sex partners.

However, these studies have tended to focus on only a small range of issues – such as parenting, serving in the armed forces and employment issues – and have not explored people's views in relation to (human) rights issues such as the right to life, the right to asylum and the right to freedom of expression and access to information. It would appear then that, to date, no study has comprehensively explored support for human rights as they apply to lesbians and gay men. Despite the frequently-cited limitations of psychological research routinely employing students, a student sample was specifically targeted for the study reported in this chapter in order to allow for comparison with other studies employing student samples and because – as Brendan Gough notes in Chapter 12 – students are typically routinely exposed to liberal perspectives within a university setting and would therefore be expected to express more liberal attitudes towards lesbian and gay issues than might be expected of their non-student counterparts.

Results will be presented from a large-scale questionnaire study exploring support for lesbian and gay human rights among university students. In this chapter, 'support' will be explored by considering (i) levels of endorsement of lesbian and gay human rights issues and (ii) individuals' sense of personal responsibility for creating positive social change for lesbians and gay men. The former analysis will draw on quantitative research data and the latter on qualitative responses.

Method

A convenience sample of 627 students from 14 universities across England, Scotland and Northern Ireland completed the questionnaire for this study. As would be expected from a sample of predominantly psychology and social science students, the majority of participants were young (78 per cent were under 25), white (87 per cent), heterosexual (90 per cent), female (83 per cent) undergraduate (97 per cent) students.

A composite questionnaire constructed for a larger study looking at support for and reasoning about lesbian and gay human rights issues was employed in this study (and is available from the author[1]) (Ellis, 2001). The questionnaire in its entirety comprised three sections: (i) attitudes towards lesbian and gay issues, (ii) position in relation to lesbian and gay rights and (iii) moral dilemmas pertaining to lesbian and gay issues. Data from the first two sections are discussed here.

Section one comprised 35 items constituting two separate (five-point) Likert-type scales: the Support for Lesbian and Gay Human Rights scale (SLGHR) (developed by the author, Celia Kitzinger and Sue Wilkinson) and the Attitudes Towards Lesbians and Gay Men Scale – Short Form (ATLG-S) (see Herek, 1994).The SLGHR scale was developed from surveys and interview schedules used in previous studies on lesbian and gay issues (for example, Maney and Cain, 1997), human rights issues (for example, Diaz-Veizades *et al.*, 1995; Doise *et al.*, 1999) and moral issues (for example, Ellsworth and Gross, 1994; Kahn, 1997). Items were composed in order directly to reflect the content of each article of the UDHR which could apply to lesbians and gay men (*qua* lesbians and gay men).

Section two explored participants' sense of personal responsibility for creating positive social change for lesbians and gay men. It comprised two related but differently focused questions : (i) 'If lesbians and gay men are unjustly treated in our society, do you feel it is your personal responsibility to help create positive changes?' (adapted from McClosky and Brill, 1983) and (ii) 'Would you be willing to join with others to help create social change for lesbians and gay men?'. These were designed to obtain an indication of respondents' reported willingness to act in relation to lesbian and gay human rights. Respondents were also asked to respond to these questions on a five-point scale from 'most definitely' through to 'definitely not' for the former and 'extremely willing' to 'extremely unwilling' for the latter and to explain their answers in the spaces provided.

Support and perceived responsibility for lesbian and gay human rights: empirical findings

To explore the extent to which respondents indicated support for lesbian and gay rights, analyses of three aspects of the questionnaire are outlined. First, the relationship between attitudes towards lesbians and gay men (as measured by the ATLG-S) and support for lesbian and gay human rights (measured by the SLGHR scale) was examined by correlation. Second, responses to individual items of the SLGHR scale were analysed in terms of levels of endorsement of lesbian and gay human rights issues. Finally, the qualitative data on respondents' positions in relation to lesbian and gay rights were analysed to explore their sense of responsibility for ensuring that lesbian and gay human rights are respected.

Attitudes towards lesbians and gay men and support for lesbian and gay human rights

In this study, a Cronbach reliability analysis revealed a high level of internal reliability for the ATLG-S ($\alpha = 0.93$), comparable to that reported in previous studies which have employed the scale (for example, Campbell *et al.*, 1997; see also Herek, 1994). The SLGHR scale also showed an exceptionally high level of internal reliability for this sample ($\alpha = 0.94$).

A highly statistically significant relationship was found between attitudes towards lesbians and gay men and support for lesbian and gay human rights ($r = 0.86$, $N = 585$, $p < 0.001$). Thus, the more negative a participant's attitude towards lesbians and gay men, the less likely he/she was to indicate support for lesbian and gay human rights.

Endorsement of lesbian and gay human rights issues

A descriptive analysis of responses showed that 96 per cent of respondents were willing to endorse the statement 'a person's sexual orientation should not block that person's access to basic rights and freedoms' and support was very high for basic personal freedoms. A large majority of respondents agreed or strongly agreed that 'lesbians and gay men should not be fined or arrested for engaging in consenting sexual acts of whatever nature in the privacy of their own homes' (89.4 per cent) and that 'no one in any country of the world should be arrested, detained, or exiled simply for being lesbian or gay' (94.4 per cent). A large majority *dis*agreed that 'a country should have the right to impose the death penalty on lesbians and gay men if that is consistent with that culture's values and beliefs' (89.8 per cent).

However, levels of endorsement for political rights were inconsistent and ranged from around 90 per cent agreeing or strongly agreeing that 'a man's homosexuality or a woman's lesbianism should not be raised as an issue in a court of law, unless the case under consideration directly relates to homosexual acts', whilst fewer than two thirds agreed or strongly agreed that 'lesbians and gay men should be granted asylum in another country when homosexuality is persecuted in their own'. This is despite the fact that the UDHR states that 'the right to seek and to enjoy in other countries asylum from persecution' (article 14) is a basic human right and that Amnesty International recognises lesbians and gay men as prisoners of conscience (see Amnesty International UK, 1999).

Although employment rights of lesbians and gay men were generally well supported, support for lesbians' and gay men's right to serve their country in the armed forces was somewhat lower than for other items, with almost one in ten (8.8 per cent) agreeing or strongly agreeing that 'it is not appropriate for lesbians and gay men to serve in the armed forces'.

Support for social rights was moderately high but with some lack of support for freedom of expression. A quarter of participants (24.9 per cent) failed to support lesbians' and gay men's right to 'flaunt their sexuality in public at marches and demonstrations' and a substantial minority (14.4 per cent) agreed or strongly agreed that 'lesbians and gay men should only be allowed to express their views as long as they don't offend or upset the majority'. Although 79.1 per cent agreed or strongly agreed that 'it should be acceptable for lesbian and gay male couples openly to express their affection for their partners in public without fear of harassment or violence', this leaves one in five of this young student sample not supporting this right. In fact, 8.6 per cent disagreed or strongly disagreed that lesbians and gay men should have this right.

Freedom of expression and access to information within educational settings attracted variable support: 83.1 per cent of respondents agreed or strongly agreed that 'children should be taught respect for the rights of lesbians and gay men', yet fewer than 55 per cent of respondents agreed or strongly agreed that 'books promoting lesbianism and gay male homosexuality as a positive lifestyle should be freely available in school libraries' and that 'university modules...should explicitly include lesbian and gay male perspectives'. Nearly a quarter of respondents (24.0 per cent) agreed or strongly agreed that 'society has a right to prevent lesbians and gay men who want to speak in schools from actively promoting homosexuality as equivalent to heterosexuality' and fewer than half disagreed or strongly disagreed with this.

Levels of support for the right to marry and found a family (article 16 of the UDHR) were relatively low. For example, 14.4 per cent of respondents disagreed or strongly disagreed that 'lesbian and gay couples should be legally permitted to marry' and nearly a quarter (22.5 per cent) disagreed or strongly disagreed that 'lesbian and gay couples should have all the same parenting rights as heterosexuals'. On this latter item, fewer than half agreed or strongly agreed with it; hence, support for lesbian and gay parenting rights was found to be limited.

Although a majority of respondents endorsed most statements on the SLGHR scale, support was much stronger for global human rights than it was for specific applications of those rights in particular situations.

Responsibility for lesbian and gay human rights

Support for lesbian and gay rights was also explored in terms of the extent to which respondents believed that it was their personal responsibility to create positive social change for lesbians and gay men. Of the

521 written responses to the question 'If lesbians and gay men are unjustly treated in our society, do you feel it is your personal responsibility to help create positive changes?', 42 per cent[2] expressed the view that lesbian and gay issues were *not* their personal responsibility. Most invoked disinterest by way of explanation: 'it does not concern me'; 'I'm not directly involved'; 'it does not affect me'; 'it is not my problem'; 'it's not really my business'; 'I see the lesbian and gay issue as irrelevant to my life'; 'don't want the hassle'; 'I don't feel strongly about this issue'; 'I don't care'. Responsibility for improving human rights was attributed to lesbians and gay men: 'they should take responsibility themselves'; 'it is their place to fight for it'; 'it's their responsibility, not mine'; 'I feel it is up to the gay community to create positive changes'.

Other respondents expressed a sense of powerlessness about their own ability to effect social change. This included responses such as 'I don't think I have the ideas or will to actively promote homosexuality'; 'I do not think I would be able to do anything'; 'I do not have the power to make a change'; 'I don't think my personal view would have a huge effect'; 'I would not know how to create useful positive changes'.

Finally, moral prohibition characterized many responses which disavowed responsibility. Responses reflecting this theme focused on notions of lesbianism and gay male homosexuality as perverse, sinful, unnatural and a matter of choice. For example, 'I don't think homosexuality is right, as I see it as a choice'; 'I can't condone homosexuality'; 'it is a sin – it is not natural'; 'I think such sexual behaviour is a perversion and should not be encouraged'; 'homosexuality of any kind is a serious wrong deviation from what should be'.

However, responses from 53 per cent of respondents indicated that they *did* feel some sense of personal responsibility for helping to create positive social change for lesbians and gay men. The majority of respondents saw their sense of personal responsibility as related to individual (rather than political) action: 'I try not to discriminate myself'; 'by not condemning them myself or isolating them'; 'by not personally saying anything harmful'; and by adopting 'a positive attitude towards them in social circumstances'. Others justified their sense of responsibility in terms of liberal acceptance or tolerance of lesbians and gay men. For example, 'it is the responsibility of everyone to accept gays and lesbians for who they are and what they are'; 'it is a "live and let live" opinion that other people would benefit in sharing'; 'the sexuality of people should just be accepted. It should not need promoting'. Conversely, some viewed their personal responsibility as including the education of others, especially children; for example, 'it's my personal responsibility to ensure that my children have a positive attitude'; 'I feel it is my personal responsibility to pass my views on to my children'; and responsibility for 'educating people in their perception of others' sexual orientation'.

Personal responsibility was often conditional. For example, 'if I heard people talking negatively about lesbians or gay men I would speak out, but I would not go around preaching lesbian and gay rights'; 'I believe that been [sic] lesbian or gay is a human right and as long as they do not influence with their behaviour'; 'I would advocate that people have a right to choose their sexual orientations as long as they don't force others to convert'. Similarly, respondents who suggested that they would actively challenge prejudice typically confined their responsibility to challenging only blatant discrimination: for example, 'I feel you must say something to someone in a situation where they are openly discriminating against lesbian/gay people in an offensive way'; 'I have a duty as a fellow human to defend [sic] outright discrimination'.

Relatively few respondents saw their personal responsibility in explicitly political terms. However, respondents taking a political approach framed their personal responsibility for lesbian and gay rights in terms of a social (or collective) responsibility for social change. For example, 'I think homophobia is equally as unacceptable as racism or any other form of prejudice. It is everyone's responsibility to promote human rights in all circumstances'; 'in our society we value equality and freedom from discrimination so it is everyone's responsibility to help create positive changes'; 'I believe it is the responsibility of all of us [ ] to make a united effort to abolish unfair and unjust treatment within our societies'.

A few respondents gave responses which indicated the interconnectedness of lesbian and gay human rights with the rights of all people as human beings. For example 'since I'm not gay, it doesn't affect me personally, but giving all people equal rights benefits society, it benefits everyone indirectly'; 'if gays and lesbians are disadvantaged and treated unfairly it ultimately effects [sic] society as a whole'; 'any restrictions on the freedom of lesbians and gay men is a restriction of the life-style choice of all'. As one respondent put it:

> As a member of an ethnic minority I understand that it can be disempowering to have someone else fighting your battles, nonetheless under certain circumstances it would be damaging to my own sense of sense [sic] if I were to witness discrimination etc and not act.

In summary, just over half of respondents viewed themselves as personally responsible for creating positive social change for lesbians and gay men but only a few gave responses which indicated an active commitment to supporting lesbian and gay rights.

Students' views of lesbian and gay human rights: reflections and recommendations

The purpose of this study was to explore support for lesbian and gay human rights through an examination of students' endorsement of lesbian and gay human rights issues and their sense of personal responsibility for ensuring positive social change for lesbians and gay men. Although few previous studies have comprehensively investigated lesbian and gay rights issues, the findings from this study were comparable to those of other studies in some respects. For example, questions relating to parenting issues and marriage yielded similar levels of endorsement as in some studies (for example, Malaney *et al.*, 1997) but received lower levels of endorsement than in other studies (for example, Annesley and Coyle, 1995). However, compared to other studies, respondents in this study showed greater support for issues such as the extension of spousal benefits to lesbian and gay couples (for example, see Eliason, 1996) and allowing lesbians and gay men to serve in the military (Malaney *et al.*, 1997). Although these differences are likely to be attributable to cultural differences (Malaney *et al.*'s and Eliason's studies were undertaken in the United States), in light of the sociopolitical climate for lesbians and gay men in the UK, it is unlikely that support for lesbian and gay rights is as strong as is suggested by a cursory reading of the data (Diaz-Veizades *et al.*, 1995).

Although most items on the SLGHR scale received majority endorsement, a comparison of individual human rights issues showed a lack of consistency in levels of support, even for items pertaining to the same or similar human rights. Whilst basic personal freedoms and employment rights received high levels of endorsement, support for social and (certain) political rights was somewhat lower. For example, despite almost unanimous agreement with the statement 'a person's sexual orientation should not block that person's access to basic rights and freedoms', fewer than two thirds of respondents were willing to endorse lesbians' and gay men's rights to asylum and marriage and the provision of books which positively portray lesbians and gay men in school libraries; fewer than half of respondents were willing to have lesbian and gay perspectives represented in school classrooms and university courses and to extend full parenting rights to lesbians and gay men. This would also seem to indicate that respondents were willing to endorse global liberal principles of non-discrimination but were less willing to endorse specific lesbian and gay human rights issues. This suggests an impoverished understanding of human rights principles and how they translate into practical applications.

It is interesting to note that a number of the least well supported issues are those which relate closely to key debates which have proved contentious in UK politics (for example, lesbian and gay parenting, same-sex marriage, the age of consent and the provision of affirmative education about lesbian and gay sexualities in schools). The pattern of responses also seems to suggest that people view lesbian and gay human rights as encompassing basic personal freedoms but not necessarily social and political rights, indicating that respondents do not conceptualize lesbian and gay human rights as a universal and indivisible package. However, what we cannot tell from these data is whether this conceptualization is specific to lesbian and gay rights or whether it applies equally to human rights issues generally.

It is also noteworthy that issues not receiving a high level of endorsement were not so much opposed but rather respondents were unwilling to indicate a committed response one way or the other, evident in the inflated endorsement of 'unsure/neutral' responses. Theory around racism (for example, see McConahay *et al.*, 1981; Schuman *et al.*, 1985) and sexism (for example, see Campbell *et al.*, 1997; Masser and Abrams, 1999) suggests that the current cultural climate makes it unlikely that respondents (especially university-educated individuals) will openly espouse prejudicial attitudes.

Regarding respondents' willingness to act in relation to lesbian and gay human rights, the sense of disinterest or powerlessness expressed in many of these responses can be related to the findings of Doise *et al.* (1994) and Macek *et al.* (1997), whose respondents were also reluctant to view the enforcement of human rights as their responsibility, seeing it instead as a governmental concern. However, the findings here do not conclusively indicate whether this is particular to lesbian and gay issues or to creating positive social change for any group (for example, women or ethnic minorities) – something which could usefully be explored in future research.

Overall, the findings of this study seem to indicate an affirmation of egalitarianism as a socially desirable value but a lack of commitment to it when it clashes with one's ideological beliefs (see Schuman *et al.*, 1985) or when given the opportunity for praxis. The lack of support for lesbian and gay human rights is worrying in that if lesbian and gay rights are not supported in principle, they are unlikely to be supported in practice. Our attention might therefore turn to how we can educate students in relation to lesbian and gay issues as human rights issues and indeed in relation to human rights in general.

Not surprisingly, the present study found that a positive attitude towards lesbians and gay men was strongly related to greater support for lesbian and gay human rights. It would seem then that it would be advantageous to work towards developing positive attitudes towards lesbians and gay men. This could be achieved by more frequently making lesbian and gay issues an integral part of the social science curriculum, through exposure to lesbian and gay perspectives in the classroom (for example, see Buhrke, 1989; Wells, 1989; Chng and Moore, 1991), by inviting lesbian and gay speakers (for example, see Geasler *et al.*, 1995; Long, 1996; Berkman and Zinberg, 1997) and through provision of lesbian and gay resources (for example, see Schreier, 1995; Long, 1996; Milton and Coyle, 1998).

However, the findings of this study also point to the need for education in human rights. Human rights education includes an understanding of what human rights are, how they are implemented and, above all, individual responsibility for upholding and defending them. Numerous resources and syllabi for human rights education are freely available at the Human Rights Education Associates website (http://www.hrea.org/). Guides to human rights activism (for example, Long, 2001) – including those specific to lesbian and gay human rights (for example, Amnesty International UK, 1999) – are also a good place from which to begin education focused on action.

Lesbian and gay issues are increasingly appearing on the international human rights agenda and recent policy changes (for example, the legalisation of same-sex marriages in the Netherlands; the equalising of the age of consent for gay men and heterosexuals in the UK) have been won on grounds of human rights. In this current sociopolitical climate, then, it is important for students to be educated both in lesbian and gay awareness as well as in human rights. To do so would go a considerable way to encouraging political action and facilitating positive social change for lesbians and gay men.

Notes

1. The author can be contacted at <S.J.Ellis@shu.ac.uk>
2. In this section, percentages do not add up to 100 as five per cent of responses were unclear.

Acknowledgements

Thanks are owed to Sue Wilkinson and Celia Kitzinger for their supervision of the PhD research from which material in this chapter is drawn. The financial assistance of the Loughborough University Faculty of Social Sciences and Humanities and the UK Committee of Vice-Chancellors and Principals (CVCP) Overseas Research Student Grant CRB/97026001 is gratefully acknowledged.

References

AMNESTY INTERNATIONAL (1997) *Breaking the Silence: Human Rights Violations Based on Sexual Orientation*. London: Amnesty International.
AMNESTY INTERNATIONAL UK (1999) *'The Louder We Will Sing': Campaigning for Lesbian and Gay Human Rights*. London: Amnesty International.
ANNESLEY, P. and COYLE, A. (1995) Clinical psychologists' attitudes to lesbians. *Journal of Community & Applied Social Psychology*, 5, 327–331.
ATOLAGBE, E.O. and OTUBANJO, F. (1984) Attitudes of Nigerian college students towards fundamental human rights. *Social Behavior and Personality*, 12, 91–96.
BECKER, D. (1995) The deficiency of the concept of posttraumatic stress when

dealing with victims of human rights violations. In R.J. Kleber, C.R. Figley and B.P.R. Gelsons (Eds) *Beyond Trauma: Cultural and Social Dynamics*. New York: Plenum.

BERKMAN, C.S. and ZINBERG, G. (1997) Homophobia and heterosexism in social workers. *Social Work, 42*, 319–332.

BUHRKE, R.A. (1989) Incorporating lesbian and gay issues into counselor training: A resource guide. *Journal of Counseling and Development, 68*, 77–80.

BURDEN, R. (1993) Taking a human rights perspective: Some basic implications for the practising school psychologist. *School Psychology International, 14*, 195–198.

CAMPBELL, B., SCHELLENBERG, E.G. and SENN, C.Y. (1997) Evaluating measures of contemporary sexism. *Psychology of Women Quarterly, 21*, 89–102.

CHNG, C.L. and MOORE, A. (1991) Can attitudes of college students towards AIDS and homosexuality be changed in six weeks? The effects of a gay panel. *Health Values, 15(2)*, 41–49.

CLÉMENCE, A., DOISE, W., DE ROSA, A.S. and GONZALEZ, L. (1995) La représentation sociale des droits de l'homme: Une recherche internationale sur l'étendue et les limites de l'universalité. *Journal International de Psychologie, 30*, 181–212.

COUNCIL OF EUROPE (1950) *Convention for Protection of Human Rights and Fundamental Freedoms* [document]. Retrieved July 28th 1998 from the world wide web: http://www.coe.fr/eng/legaltxt/5e.htm

CRANSTON, M. (1962) *Human Rights Today*. London: Ampersand.

D'AUGELLI, A.R. (1989) Homophobia in a university community: Views of prospective resident assistants. *Journal of College Student Development, 30*, 547–552.

DIAZ-VEIZADES, J., WIDAMAN, K.F., LITTLE, T.D. and GIBBS, K.W. (1995) The measurement and structure of human rights attitudes. *The Journal of Social Psychology, 135*, 313–328.

DOISE, W., SPINI, D. and CLÉMENCE, A. (1999) Human rights studied as social representations in a cross-national context. *European Journal of Social Psychology, 29*, 1–29.

DOISE, W., SPINI, D., JESUINO, J.C., NG, S.-H. and EMLER, N. (1994) Values and perceived conflicts in the social representation of human rights: Feasibility of a cross-national study. *Swiss Journal of Psychology, 53*, 240–251.

DONNELLY, J. (1993) *International Human Rights*. Boulder, CO: Westview.

DONNELLY, J., DONNELLY, M., KITTELSON, M.J., FOGARTY, K.J., PROCACCINO, A.T. and DUNCAN, D.F. (1997) An exploration of attitudes on sexuality at a northeastern urban university. *Psychological Reports, 81*, 677–678.

DOUGLAS, C.J., KALMAN, C.M. and KALMAN, T.P. (1985) Homophobia among physicians and nurses: An empirical study. *Hospital and Community Psychiatry, 36*, 1309–1311.

DREXEL, J. (1994) Human rights of street children in Brazil. *Educational and Child Psychology, 11(4)*, 31–34.

DUNTON, C. and PALMBERG, M. (1996) *Human Rights and Homosexuality in Southern Africa*, 2nd ed. Uppsala, Sweden: Nordiska.

ELIASON, M.J. (1995) Attitudes about lesbians and gay men: A review and implications for social service training. *Journal of Gay and Lesbian Social Services, 2*, 73–90.

ELIASON, M.J. (1996) A survey of the campus climate for lesbian, gay, and bisexual university members. *Journal of Psychology and Human Sexuality, 8(4)*, 39–58.

ELLIS, S.J. (1999) Lesbian and gay issues are human rights issues: The need for a human rights approach to lesbian and gay psychology. *BPS Lesbian & Gay Psychology Section Newsletter, issue 3*, 9–14.

ELLIS, S.J. (2001) *Denying Equality: People's Understanding of and Reasoning about Human Rights in Relation to Lesbian and Gay Issues.* Unpublished PhD thesis, Loughborough University.

ELLSWORTH, P.C. and GROSS, S.R. (1994) Hardening of the attitudes: Americans' views on the death penalty. *Journal of Social Issues, 50(2)*, 19–52.

FEDERAL BUREAU OF INVESTIGATION (1995) *Hate Crimes Statistics* [document]. Washington, DC: Federal Bureau of Investigation. Retrieved July 25th 1999 from the world wide web: http://www.fbi.gov

GEASLER, M.J., CROTEAU, J.M., HEINEMAN, C.J. and EDLUND, C.J. (1995) A qualitative study of students' expression of change after attending panel presentations by lesbian, gay, and bisexual speakers. *Journal of College Student Development, 36*, 483–492.

HAYFIELD, A. (1995) Several faces of discrimination. In V. Mason-John (Ed.) *Talking Black: Lesbians of African and Asian Descent Speak Out.* London: Cassell.

HEREK, G.M. (1994) Assessing heterosexuals' attitudes toward lesbians and gay men: A review of empirical research with the ATLG scale. In B. Greene and G.M. Herek (Eds) *Lesbian and Gay Psychology: Theory, Research, and Clinical Applications.* Thousand Oaks, CA: Sage.

INTERNATIONAL GAY AND LESBIAN HUMAN RIGHTS COMMISSION (1995) *The International Tribunal on Human Rights Violations Against Sexual Minorities.* San Francisco, CA: International Gay and Lesbian Human Rights Commission.

INTERNATIONAL LESBIAN AND GAY ASSOCIATION (1998) *ILGA: International News* [documents]. Brussels: International Lesbian and Gay Association. Retrieved August 26th 1998 from the world wide web: http://www.ILGA.org/information/

INTERNATIONAL LESBIAN AND GAY ASSOCIATION (1999) *World Legal Survey* [document]. Brussels: International Lesbian and Gay Association. Retrieved May 1999 from the world wide web: http://www.ilga.org/Information/Legal_survey/ilga_world-legal-surveyper cent20introduction.htm

JONES, P. (1994) *Rights.* London: Macmillan.

KAHN, P. (1997) Children's moral and ecological reasoning about the Prince William Sound oil spill. *Developmental Psychology, 33*, 1091–1096.

KEY DATES IN LESBIAN SHARON BOTTOMS' FOUR-YEAR CUSTODY AND VISITATION BATTLE (1997, 8 May) [newspaper excerpt]. *The Journal.* Retrieved August 27th 1998 from the world wide web: http://www.jrnl.com/news/97/May/jrn20080597.html

KHUSH (1993) Fighting back: An interview with Pratibha Parmar. In R. Ratti (Ed.) *A Lotus of Another Color: An Unfolding of the South Asian Gay and Lesbian Experience.* Boston, MA: Alyson.

KITZINGER, C. (1991) Lesbians and gay men in the workplace: Psychosocial issues. In M.J. Davidson and J. Earnshaw (Eds) *Vulnerable Workers: Psychosocial and Legal Issues.* London: John Wiley.

KLAMEN, D.L., GROSSMAN, L.S. and KOPACZ, D.R. (1999) Medical student homophobia. *Journal of Homosexuality, 37(1)*, 53–63.

LESBIAN AND GAY EMPLOYMENT RIGHTS (1998) *Annual Report 1997–98*. London: Lesbian and Gay Employment Rights.

LEE, Y.-T., KLEINBACH, R., HU, P.C., PENG, Z.-Z. and CHEN, X.-Y. (1996) Cross-cultural research on euthanasia and abortion. *Journal of Social Issues, 52*, 131–148.

LONG, J.K. (1996) Working with lesbians, gays, and bisexuals: Addressing heterosexism in supervision. *Family Process, 35*, 377–388.

LONG, S. (2001) *Making the Mountain Move: An Activist's Guide to How International Human Rights Mechanisms Can Work for You* [document]. San Francisco, CA: International Gay and Lesbian Human Rights Commission. Retrieved January 26th 2001 from the world wide web: http://www.iglhrc.org/news/factsheets/unguide.html

MACEK, P., OSECKA, L. and KOSTRON, L. (1997) Social representations of human rights among Czech university students. *Journal of Community & Applied Social Psychology, 7*, 65–76.

MALANEY, G.D., WILLIAMS, E.A. and GELLER, W.W. (1997) Assessing campus climate for gays, lesbians, and bisexuals at two institutions. *Journal of College Student Development, 38*, 365–375.

MANEY, D.W. and CAIN, R.E. (1997) Preservice elementary teachers' attitudes toward gay and lesbian parenting. *Journal of School Health, 67*, 236–241.

MASSER, B. and ABRAMS, D. (1999) Contemporary sexism: The relationships among hostility, benevolence, and neosexism. *Psychology of Women Quarterly, 23*, 503–517.

MATCHINSKY, D.J. and IVERSON, T.G. (1996) Homophobia in heterosexual female undergraduates. *Journal of Homosexuality, 31(4)*, 123–128.

McCLOSKY, H. and BRILL, A. (1983) *Dimensions of Tolerance: What Americans Believe about Civil Liberties*. New York: Russell Sage Foundation.

McCONAHAY, J.B., HARDEE, B.B. and BATTS, V. (1981) Has racism declined in America? It depends on who is asking and what is asked. *Journal of Conflict Resolution, 25*, 563–579.

MELTON, G.B. (1989) Public policy and private prejudice: Psychology and law on gay rights. *American Psychologist, 44*, 933–940.

MELTON, G.B. (1992) The law is a good thing (Psychology is, too): Human rights and psychological jurisprudence. *Law and Human Behavior, 16*, 381–398.

MILTON, M. and COYLE, A. (1998) Psychotherapy with lesbian and gay clients. *The Psychologist, 11*, 73–76.

MOGHADDAM, F.M. and VUKSANOVIC, V. (1990) Attitudes and behavior toward human rights across different contexts: The role of right-wing authoritarianism, political ideology, and religiosity. *International Journal of Psychology, 25*, 455–474.

OLKIN, R. (1997) The human rights of children with disabilities. *Women and Therapy, 20(2)*, 29–42.

ORDOÒEZ, J.P. and ELLIOTT, R. (1998) 'Cleaning up the Streets': Human Rights Violations in Colombia and Honduras [article]. Belgium: International Lesbian and Gay Association. Retrieved August 26th 1998 from the world wide web: http://www.ILGA.org/Information/cleaning_up_ the_streets_.htm

PENN, M.L. and COVERDALE, C. (1996) Transracial adoption: A human rights perspective. *Journal of Black Psychology, 22*, 240–245.

PRATTO, F., SIDANIUS, J., STALLWORTH, L.M. and MALLE, B.F. (1994) Social dominance orientation: A personality variable predicting social and political attitudes. *Journal of Personality and Social Psychology, 67*, 741–763.

PROULX, R. (1997) Homophobia in northeastern Brazilian university students. *Journal of Homosexuality, 34(1)*, 47–56.

ROSENBLOOM, R. (Ed.) (1996) *Unspoken Rules: Sexual Orientation and Women's Human Rights*. London: Cassell.

ROSENZWEIG, M.R. (1988) Psychology and United Nations human rights efforts. *American Psychologist, 43*, 79–86.

RUCK, M.D., KEATING, D.P., ABRAMOVITCH, R. and KOEGL, C.J. (1998) Adolescents' and children's knowledge about rights: Some evidence for how young people view rights in their own lives. *Journal of Adolescence, 21*, 275–289.

SCHELLENBERG, E.G., HIRT, J. and SEARS, A. (1999) Attitudes towards homosexuals among students at a Canadian university. *Sex Roles, 40*, 139–152.

SCHREIER, B.A. (1995) Moving beyond tolerance: A new paradigm for programming about homophobia/biphobia and heterosexism. *Journal of College Student Development, 36*, 19–26.

SCHUMAN, H., STEEH, C. and BOBO, L. (1985) *Racial Attitudes in America: Trends and Interpretations*. Cambridge, MA: Harvard University Press.

SELTZER, R. (1992) The social location of those holding anti-homosexual attitudes. *Sex Roles, 26*, 391–398.

SILOVE, D. (1999) The psychosocial effects of torture, mass human rights violations, and refugee trauma: Toward an integrated conceptual framework. *Journal of Nervous and Mental Disease, 187*, 200–207.

SOTELO, M.J. (1997) Political tolerance among adolescents towards feminists. *Feminism & Psychology, 7*, 517–528.

STAINTON ROGERS, R. and KITZINGER, C. (1995) A decalogue of human rights: What happens when you let the people speak. *Social Science Information, 34*, 87–106.

STONEWALL (1998) *Stonewall Factsheet: Discrimination at Work*. London: Stonewall.

THADANI, G. (1996) *Sakhiyani: Lesbian Desire in Ancient and Modern India*. London: Cassell.

UNITED NATIONS (1948) *The Universal Declaration of Human Rights* [document]. Geneva: United Nations. Retrieved July 24th 1998 from the world wide web: http://www.un.org/Overview/rights.html

WADE, R.C. (1994) Conceptual change in elementary social studies: A case study of fourth graders' understanding of human rights. *Theory and Research in Social Education, 23*, 74–95.

WELLS, J.W. (1989) Teaching about gay and lesbian sexual and affectional orientation using explicit films to reduce homophobia. *Journal of Humanistic Education and Development, 28*, 18–34.

WESSELLS, M.G. (1997) Armed conflict and children's rights. *American Psychologist, 52*, 1385–1386.

WILETS, J.D. (1994) International human rights law and sexual orientation. *Hastings International and Comparative Law Review, 18*, 1–120.

WISNIEWSKI, J.J. and TOOMEY, B.G. (1987) Are social workers homophobic? *Social Work, 32*, 454–455.

Chapter 14

Lesbian and Gay Awareness Training: Challenging Homophobia, Liberalism and Managing Stereotypes

Elizabeth Peel

Lesbian and gay awareness training emerges out of a long tradition within lesbian and gay activism and is rooted in the idea that negative attitudes and behaviours towards lesbians and gay men can be challenged and changed through education. The notion is that, via exposure to lesbians and gay men and to the realities of lesbian and gay lives, people's prejudices and fears can be overcome. This chapter has two purposes: first, I chart the historical development of lesbian and gay awareness education and training within and beyond psychology and second, after highlighting existing caveats in the literature, I explore some of the crucial themes for those lesbians and gay men involved in conducting lesbian and gay awareness training. Using extracts from interviews with trainers, the focus is on the dilemmas they face and how some of their key concerns – including homophobia, liberalism and stereotypes – relate to the representation of training presented in lesbian and gay psychology and the literature on attitude change. Note that, due to limitations of space, some contested concepts – such as 'homophobia' – will be employed without examining and responding to the critiques which they have attracted (see Kitzinger and Perkins, 1993, for a critical consideration of 'homophobia').

Attempts to educate people about lesbian and gay experience in order to change negative attitudes and behaviours (and hence improve lesbian and gay lives) can be traced back at least to the late 1800s and the pioneering work of the sexologist Havelock Ellis (see Chapter 1). His 'scientific' work (notably the volumes entitled *Studies in the Psychology of Sex*) and his involvement with pro-'lesbian and gay' organizations aimed to promote tolerant attitudes towards homosexuals (Weeks, 2000). Later, in 1928, Radclyffe Hall's novel, *The Well of Loneliness*, and the attendant media furore brought homosexual issues to public attention and intensified the plea for tolerance. So too did the educational work of the Mattachine Society (which – together with the lesbian group, the Daughters of Bilitis – began in the 1950s) which lobbied for equal rights and aimed to promote the 'respectable' face of homosexuality. The society, for example, advised its members to dress 'appropriately': 'men should don white shirts, suits and ties and women should appear in skirts and dresses' (Jivani, 1997, p. 161).

A groundswell of radical change occurred in the late 1960s with the growth of the lesbian and gay liberation movement (whose philosophy was embodied by organizations such as the National Gay and Lesbian Task Force), whose goals were political as well as educational (Blumenfeld and Raymond, 1993). Gay Liberation Front Women (1977) emphasized their dedication to 'changing attitudes, institutions, and laws that oppress lesbians, using all or any methods from reform to revolution' (p. 202). The radical rhetoric of the 1970s (informed by feminist activism) provided a more confrontational and challenging alternative to previous assimilationist strategies, captured in Shelley's (1977) words: 'Look out, straights. Here comes the Gay Liberation Front, springing up like warts all over the bland face of Amerika' (p. 31). The place of training and education in lesbian and gay activism parallels the approach adopted by the lesbian and gay lobbying group, Stonewall, in Britain (for more information, see www.stonewall.org.uk), which works within the existing political system in order to change it. At the other end of the spectrum, the British queer rights direct activism group, Outrage, attempts to disrupt the existing social system through being 'unapologetic and provocative' (see www.outrage.org.uk), holding 'kiss-ins' and demonstrations. Awareness training embodies the former approach; it is at the more 'palatable', mild end of the continuum of lesbian and gay strategies for social change – 'the time-honored, nonviolent means of social change, the alternative to revolution' (Gilligan, 1993, p. 162).

Education about lesbian and gay issues was also encouraged within psychology after the establishment of 'affirmative' lesbian and gay psychology in the early 1970s. Ever since the germinal stages of the development of the American Psychological Association's Division 44 (the US equivalent of the British Psychological Society's Lesbian and Gay Psychology Section), an educative role for the organization was emphasized (Morin and Rothblum, 1991). In confronting institutionalized heterosexism, it has been recommended that education should occur at all levels of research and practice; therapists particularly should be exposed 'to alternative thinking (i.e. lesbian and gay issues)' (Sang, 1989, p. 95). Research which explores heterosexuals' attitudes towards lesbians and gay men has been described as a clear example of research which is 'on the offense' regarding lesbian and gay human rights (Morin, 1977 p. 635). Much that has been published in the field explicitly aims to enlighten the reader. For instance, Savin-Williams and Cohen (1996) state that they wish to 'promote an increased awareness and understanding' (p. v) about lesbians and gay men. However, the majority of discussion around the need for education and training on sexuality occurs either within educational (for example, D'Augelli, 1992; Epstein, 1994; Epstein and Johnson, 1998) or professional contexts (for example, in psychiatry – Townsend *et al.*, 1995; in nursing – Irwin, 1992, Gray *et al.*, 1996; and in teaching – Casper *et al.*, 1996, Bohan, 1997). The professions which have given slightly more space to the discussion of sexuality training are social work (for example, Gochros, 1984; Van Soest, 1996; Burgess *et al.*, 1997 – but see below) and counselling and psychotherapeutic psychology (for example, Graham *et al.*, 1984; Buhrke, 1989; Buhrke and Douce, 1991; Mobley, 1998; Milton and Coyle, 1999 – but see Coyle *et al.*, 1999).

Education may be an efficacious method of social change – and indeed has been postulated as a method of prejudice reduction in the field of racial equality (for example, Weiner and Wright, 1973; Bethlehem, 1985) – but unfortunately lesbian and gay issues tend to be marginalized or completely ignored in discussion of equality issues (Hill, 1995). Teaching about lesbian and gay issues has garnered much less institutional support than training addressing other equal opportunities issues, a situation not aided by a lack of legislative backing and the assumption that 'sexuality has no legitimate place at work' (Martin and Collinson, 1999, p. 295). The invisibility of sexuality is also part of the problem: as Hill (1995) remarks, 'unlike other prejudices, heterocentric assumptions are so beguiling they go undetected by even the most equity-sensitive individuals' (p. 146). Multicultural and anti-racist education is much better integrated into schools and workplace training (Figueroa, 1991), as is training on sexism and disablism. It has been noted that a career within disability equality training is possible (Campbell and Oliver, 1996) – a situation unlikely in sexuality education. Legally in the UK, workplaces are obliged to provided equal opportunities training covering only race, gender and disability. The quantity of discussion of lesbian and gay issues appears relatively small in generic sexuality or equal opportunities courses, often being only accorded one lecture, if given any coverage at all (Townsend *et al.*, 1995).

The establishment of pro-lesbian and gay education is problematic. For example, Munt (1996), after establishing her course entitled 'lesbian literature', was advised by her establishment either to 'advertise the course pseudonymously, or not run it at all' (p. 235). Professional training does not appear to be more advanced or explicit. Within social work training in anti-discriminatory practice, for instance, there is a tendency to overlook lesbian and gay issues. Conversely, it has been suggested that any lesbian and gay awareness training should contain a discussion of gender roles and sexism (for example, Simoni, 1996). Integrating a number of equal opportunities issues in training is currently in vogue within 'helping' professions but lesbian and gay issues are disadvantaged. After examining 128 British social work reports, Trotter and Gilchrist (1996), for instance, remarked that anti-discriminatory practice courses get 'fudged' and 'anti-heterosexist and non-homophobic practice is generally not made explicit' (p. 75).

The detailed analysis of the content of discussions about lesbian and gay issues in these various educational contexts could provide a means to understand the construction of pro- and anti-gay arguments. However, any discussion of the specific nature and content of training is (generally) limited to training manuals (for example, Stewart, 1999). Therefore, exploring trainers' reflections on the process of lesbian and gay awareness training is essential to begin to ascertain how training works and what aspects of it are problematic for trainers themselves (as lesbians or gay men and as educators), for participants and ultimately for social change. Before exploring the key themes and dilemmas for lesbian and gay awareness trainers (surrounding homophobia, liberalism and stereotypes) in my research data, the content of training and educational strategies will be described and critiqued. I draw first on the literature in the area and later – after introducing the trainers and their motivations for conducting training – I outline the lesbian and gay awareness trainers' own discussions of training design.

What constitutes lesbian and gay awareness training?

The lesbian and gay psychological literature is relatively silent about the construction, design and process of lesbian and gay awareness training (Van de Ven, 1995). However, a number of components are thought to be desirable within training, including the identification of lesbian and gay stereotypes, the replacement of stereotypes with 'positive' or factual information, experiential work, encouraging empathy, recognizing heterosexual privilege and adopting practical strategies for challenging heterosexism.

The theoretical underpinnings of much lesbian and gay psychological discussion of attitude change come from conventional social psychological theory (for instance, Herek, 1984), which is germane to understanding lesbian and gay awareness training, given that social communication has been viewed as '*the* determinant of attitude change' (Jaspars, 1978, p. 278, emphasis in original). Much attitude change research is premised on Festinger's (1957) cognitive dissonance theory which assumes that attitudes should be congruent with each other and that unbalanced or conflictual attitudes will result in change. One key information-processing model of change focuses on the source and nature of a particular message and the characteristics of the receiver of the message (Hovland *et al.*, 1949; Eagly and Chaiken, 1993; Haynes, 1993). This has generated empirical research demonstrating the efficacy of an expert speaker (Jaspars, 1978) and the importance of a message giver being perceived as credible and trustworthy by the receiver (Hovland *et al.*, 1953). Furthermore, the process of persuasion has been said to involve a central and peripheral route: the central route to persuasion involves the audience cognitively attending to and concentrating on a message, while the peripheral route relies on extraneous factors for acceptance of a message, such as non-verbal cues or the attractiveness of the message giver (Petty and Cacioppo, 1986). Contact is often cited as an essential method for reducing prejudice, premised on the notion that prejudiced attitudes are grounded in misinformation and rooted within the individual. In this case, positive instances of contact between groups (in contexts where the groups have equal status, joint goals and fairly intimate contact) can work to reduce negative attitudes (for example, Bethlehem, 1985). As we will see later, these theories of attitude change are echoed in lay theories of change implicit in trainers' own accounts of the issues involved in training.

Method

The data to be reported in this chapter were collected over an eleven-month period (from November 1998 to October 1999) and consist of 15 individual interviews with trainers – ten with gay men and five with lesbians. Interviews lasted for an hour on average, resulting in 350 pages of transcript. All of the interviewees were white and aged 30–55 years and all but one were able-bodied. They had a wide range of experience of conducting lesbian and gay awareness training (ranging from 1 to 20 years) and the groups they trained included social/youth workers, probation officers, nurses, police staff, academics, students, council workers, trade union staff, housing workers, teachers, psychologists and psychotherapists. Interviewees often commented that the interview was the first time they had discussed their training or reflected on their practice, other than with close friends or colleagues who acted as co-trainers.

The interview data were tape recorded and transcribed orthographically. In analysing the data, the transcripts were read and re-read to identify prevalent themes. This thematic analysis is based (in part) on Potter and Wetherell's (1987) approach to discourse analysis and the resultant analytic themes closely resemble what they call 'interpretative repertoires'. Repeated readings of the transcripts revealed three key themes: challenging homophobia, liberalism and managing stereotypes. These particular themes were drawn from the data as talk about these issues was pervasive and also they were seen as problematic or presenting dilemmas for the trainers. Before exploring these themes in some detail, general training issues, motivations for conducting training and training content are discussed. Throughout the presentation of the analysis, the names of the participants have been replaced by pseudonyms. Empty square brackets reveal where material has been omitted from quotations; material within square brackets has been added for purposes of clarification.

Motivation(s) for conducting awareness training

Awareness training's ultimate project is to challenge normative understandings of sexuality, to make the unspeakable not only speakable but also accountable and to 'try to weave in [to training] some sort of practical steps people can take, so it just doesn't seem this kind of airy fairy notion of [ ] "be nice to puffs"' (Ron). All of the trainers had personal (as well as professional) motivations for conducting training, for example, a need to be heard or the desire to redress the power imbalance between sexualities. Ben described facilitating training as a 'little revenge thing', which he attributed to the fact that 'people attempted to impose heterosexuality upon me. I was, I felt invisible [ ] and so it's about a redress of that. It's about saying "Well alright, now it's time to shut up and listen"'.

Other interviewees saw training as a providing a space for group members to reflect on their heterosexist beliefs – described by Anthony as being 'misunderstood and maligned and judged'. Enabling participants 'to think through this and [ ] to be able to try and make better sense of gay people's experiences' (Anthony) was seen as important. Katie began training because she wanted 'people to think' and the perceived slow progress of societal change provided her with continuing motivation. She suggested that if society changed and lesbianism was as accepted as heterosexuality, 'I would think, "Right, pack up your textbook and go home, girl". But I don't see much evidence that it has'.

For Emily, training is essential for 'equality and equity for everybody', whilst Simon saw it as 'the final frontier in terms of providing training to professionals'. Ron aimed to ensure that lesbians and gay men 'get a quality service, the same as everybody else', whilst Dee saw awareness training as a pragmatic way to change the world: 'to remind people in any situation they're not powerless [ ] Letting people see there's layers of oppression and we have an ability to make sure the issues are on the agenda'. Lou saw herself as involved in training because 'it's going to have a knock-on effect'. She felt 'people are going to go back in their lives and say something next time they hear something [anti-lesbian or gay]'. We can see here, in trainers' explanations for conducting training, lay conceptions relating to the problematic link between attitude and behaviour that has been noted in social psychological theory (for example, Ajzen and Fisbein, 1980). An emphasis on making group members 'think' (Katie), which can be conceived as the attitudinal component, was closely tied to a concern for 'practical steps' (Ron), i.e., a behavioural change, which might empower individuals to challenge homophobia and result in a 'quality service' for lesbian and gay clients.

We can see here trainers' belief that, once pervasive heterosexism is better understood, the door is opened for challenge. However, Anthony was also concerned about the low appeal of awareness training: 'Most people don't want to know. [ ] I'm concerned that therapists don't want to know. If they're working with queer clients they really need to know more about that cultural group'. Despite this, Anthony was committed (along with the other trainers) to try to increase training 'in the workplace. [ ] We need to repeal Section 28 [of the 1988 Local Government Act which forbids the promotion of homosexuality as a 'pretended family relationship' by any local authority] so that we can be doing it in schools', whilst being aware of the need to ensure wider conditions for social change, such as 'getting an equal age of consent [for gay men] and [ ] some basic human rights legislation' (see Chapter 13 on this issue).

Training design and content

Trainers described using a relatively homogeneous set of exercises and group work formats within training. A key aspect was seen as giving 'people thought-provoking exercises, sometimes role plays and sometimes experiences' (Katie). A questionnaire/guided visualization entitled 'Do you need treatment?' (which inverts questions typically asked of lesbians/gay men, such as 'What caused your homosexuality?', which becomes 'What caused your heterosexuality?'), language exercises, stereotypes exercises and various quizzes and questionnaires and knowledge-providing tasks were commonly mentioned. Interviewees addressed many aspects of training content raised in the literature. Identification of stereotypes was often discussed: Daniel reported using a 'How to spot a homo' quiz, whilst Ron described using a stereotypes exercise as a method to challenge (usually negative) stereotypical views held by group participants:

> Get the group to draw a typical lesbian or a typical gay man. [ ] You get very clichéd images. You get women in dungarees with shaved hair and tattoos and looking butch. And you get either very camp, effete, fairy gay men or clones in shirts with moustaches, and [ ] then you kind of make people think a bit – 'These are the ideas I have of lesbians and gay men but how do I get those ideas?'.

Language exercises were also used to acknowledge stereotypical and derogatory terms for lesbians/gay men. These typically involved asking the group to list all the terms, words, names, etc. they had heard under the headings 'lesbians', 'gay men' and 'bisexuals' (and some-times 'heterosexuals'). The length and content of the lists were compared and used as a basis for discussion. Challenging overt con-demnation by contextualizing 'facts' about lesbian and gay oppression was also commonly reported. For example, Daniel described how he deals with religious homophobia:

> The Bible's thrown at you [ ] – homosexuality is a sin that cries out to heaven [ ] So another thing is 'Which of these are classed as a sin in Leviti-cus [a book in the Bible]? – a) eating pork b) eating shrimps c) wearing clothes made from more than one material and d) a man having long hair. Pick the one that's a sin in Leviticus'. Well the only one that isn't is (d) but (d) is a sin in Deuteronomy [another book of the Bible].

Encouraging participants to reflect on their own homophobia formed part of trainers' attempts to challenge heterosexual privilege. Katie rec-ommended drawing a 'life graph', which encouraged participants to understand what societal messages they received about sexuality. Dee used a 'life stories' exercise where participants talked about their lives without mentioning key elements (such as partner and social life) 'to clearly demonstrate how [lesbian and gay] people's lives are restrict-ed'. Lou used guided visualization to encourage heterosexual participants to reflect on their privilege: 'you are heterosexual but you're in the minority; the world is a lesbian and gay world. [ ] You paint the picture of what we face at the moment'. Exercises aimed at increasing group members' ability to empathize with lesbians and gay men and enhance their awareness of discrimination were juxtaposed with exercises designed to challenge their homophobia. For instance, Anthony reported asking participants to write a 'coming out' letter in order to have them 'imagine some of the sorts of experiences that go into [ ] leading a life that nobody else really knew about and then trying to tell someone about it'. Anthony also described giving group members 'homowork' to increase their empathy for lesbian and gay experience: he suggested 'they read *Gay Times* in public or go and buy it in the shop and see how they feel. [ ] And if they don't feel like doing it, why is that? What does that say for them about that, their own inter-nalized fear and homophobia?'.

Additionally, trainers spoke of using tasks that addressed societal inequality, for instance, the 'Smartie game'. Here participants adopt a role (for example, a disabled gay man) and gain Smarties (sweets/candy) if they can easily perform various social activities in that role (such as getting married) 'and of course, the white, heterosex-ual, middle class male has got a whole lot of Smarties and the black lesbian's got none' (Daniel). Although experiential tasks were supple-mented with factual information, trainers also talked about practical applications of training and addressed 'very specific action planning where people are committed to going away and looking at issues' (Dee). The trainers' discussion of the process and content of their training provides a context for the key themes that were identified as pervasive in the interviews. We will start by considering the theme of 'homophobia'.

Homophobia: 'lager louts' and religiosity

Explicit homophobia was not often encountered by trainers because they suspected that people with strongly heterosexist views ('really offensive people' – Katie) absented themselves from lesbian and gay awareness training sessions. As Katie said, 'There are always people who have gone to the dentist – that's a nice safe excuse, isn't it? You know, "Sorry I've got a dental appointment"'. Nonetheless, several trainers had experienced situations in which overtly anti-lesbian and anti-gay sentiments were expressed. Anthony described one instance:

> There were two scally lads – this is in Liverpool – there were two scally lads who just kept feeding off each other in terms of their homophobia and their lager loutish attitudes and they were expressing some really offensive attitudes – that 'gay people should be shot' and 'gay people clearly spread AIDS' [ ] and all the negative stereotypes that sort of you'd expect of the worst kind of straight lager lout-type footie fan.

In addition religious arguments were frequently cited as providing the vehicle for heterosexism, which trainers found 'really really difficult' to challenge because such anti-lesbian and anti-gay arguments (such as 'homosexuality is a sin') are not made in relation to 'disability awareness, race or gender awareness in the same way' (Emily). Their lay theories regarding the problematic nature of strongly-held religious views intuitively fit with attitude change research that suggests that changing a more extreme attitude is more difficult than changing a neutral one (Jaspars, 1978). Ben commented on the hypocrisy concealed in homophobia rooted in religious faith:

> Christians we've had on the courses have always said 'I would never be prejudiced against someone and I'd never [ ] queer bash somebody [ ] or think that someone should lose their job or anything like that but I think it's an immoral sin' and [ ] God is going to cast us all into a pit of eternal flame.

On the other hand, there was some respect for 'honesty' and participants who were willing to express overtly heterosexist beliefs and follow the injunction to 'be homophobic [ ] Let's just be honest about it and let's just understand it' (Ben). Several trainers talked about the value of having anti-lesbian and anti-gay views voiced in training sessions: 'I always feel it's positive to hear it because I think [ ] if you do have a bigot saying stuff, they're probably voicing it for a number of other people who are too quiet, too nervous, too liberal whatever, to be saying it' (Anthony). Similarly, Ron thought that having homophobic views expressed would 'spice it up' because if participants are being 'nicey nicey, "Oh yes [ ] we all think the same way and we all agree", it doesn't give you a lot to work on really'. The value that trainers accorded to homophobic views being expressed in training relates to the cognitively-based attitude literature, in which homophobia is seen as being a relatively stable and fixed belief, rooted within the individual, which can therefore be 'brought out' in training (see Billig, 1987).

The trainers' talk addressing individualized (infrequently expressed) homophobia also has resonance with the common-sense and psychotherapeutic ideas that 'working through' and talking about deep-seated or troubling issues is an essential aid to resolving them (Epstein and Steinberg, 1998). It can be seen from the trainers' discussion of homophobia within training that, by attributing the problem to specific (and 'extreme') individuals and seeing homophobic ideas as useful for the training process, they are able to reframe the problem of homophobia in an educationally useful light. The trainers emphasized, when dealing with homophobic views, the necessity to 'build bridges' (Anthony) and stressed the similarity of lesbians and gay men to other marginalized groups. For example, when trying to undermine religious-based homophobia coupled with a black cultural identity, Anthony reported using the argument '"You have [a] cultural history that's really rich and it's been really persecuted and we have one too and let me tell you about some of the examples of how our cultural history has been eradicated or changed or challenged or persecuted"'. However, whilst not wishing to undermine the significance of overtly homophobic views in lesbian and gay awareness training, trainers saw liberal attitudes as a more widespread, insidious and problematic challenge to effective training.

Liberalism: minimizing the importance of sexuality

Although it may appear to be a positive stance, liberalism can be deployed as a method of social control (Kitzinger, 1989). Lesbian feminists, such as Kathie Sarachild (1974), have suggested that liberal views enable individuals 'to sit on the fence, avoid taking sides, to denounce polarization, confrontation and the use of force. It is the perfect tool for the oppressor's use' (cited in Kramarae and Treichler, 1992, p. 231). The trainers pointed to two 'types' of liberalism, i.e., the common-sense notion of liberalism as a broadminded non-prejudicial perspective and a more negative view of liberal ideology as a way of masking prejudice. Trainers viewed liberal, open-minded attitudes as a desired result of training but also as a hindrance because participants in training were said to espouse liberalism to 'demonstrate [ ] that they don't have a problem' (Ben). All the trainers were wary of this; as Simon said, 'If everyone's too right on, I just think "mmm"'.

The trainers gave many examples of liberal sentiments that were expressed by heterosexual group members, such as: 'I treat everyone the same' (Katie); 'Everything's okay because there's more people on TV [ ] everything's hunky-dory' (Simon); 'We've got characters in East Enders and things [and] we're a lot more laid back that I don't think this is an issue any more' (Dee); 'Some of my best friends are gay' (Saul); 'There's not a homophobic bone in my body' (Ben); and 'I don't go round shouting that I'm heterosexual' (Katie). It has been noted within lesbian and gay psychology that ignoring differences between sexualities and assuming an equivalent status of heterosexuality and homosexuality deny the significance of sexual identity for many lesbians and gay men (Messing *et al.*, 1984). Daniel expressed the opinion that this tendency arises because it is 'less easy for educated people to voice prejudices about lesbians and gays publicly any more. They may still have them but they're subsumed as it were', which results in 'cultural amnesia', in that attitudes towards distinctive lesbian and gay cultures are hidden by liberal rhetoric (see also Chapter 12).

Trainers described the constant verbalizing of liberal views as 'a load of crap and really dangerous' (Lou), which 'makes me very frustrated' (Dee); Saul said 'I want to smack people when they say that [express views characterized by liberalism]'. Liberalism was often seen by trainers as a mask or smokescreen – 'liberal defenses' (Andy) – to hide underlying heterosexism. Trainers suggested reasons why participants 'keep this mantra going of, you know, I'm a nice liberal' (Ben). Saul, for instance, speculated about why group members try to make sexuality a 'non-issue':

> What they're actually saying is 'I don't feel comfortable with this' but they aren't brave enough to actually say 'I need to learn'. What they're actually doing is really colluding with the heterosexist hegemony that's been around you know forever. [ ] Sorry, phooey, it is not a non-issue – it is a major issue for a lot of people. [ ] They've [participants] got a very surface understanding of what's going on and it's usually about providing an excuse so they can disengage so they don't have to deal with it.

Ben also said 'they're really trying to close it [discussion] down' and Katie suggested that liberalism occurs 'because they're struggling – not because they're clever'. Displays of liberalism were said to be used to avoid addressing the issues. Katie described a situation where a female trainee was 'getting off on being a gay man's friend rather than doing any work, so if he'd said "The world is made of green cheese" or something, she'd have said "Oh yes and it's really gay green cheese"'. For

Daniel, 'It's like the people who say, "Oh I don't see people as black so that isn't an issue for me". When people say that, I'm immediately suspicious and think "Yes it is, and you've got a big problem here"'. Lou saw liberalism as 'really dangerous' and so she aimed to challenge the 'sameness argument' – 'challenge this whole fuckwittery about "I treat everybody the same"'. Trainers reported undermining liberalism by emphasizing the unique and different qualities of lesbian and gay identities and by 'throwing in some statistics about homophobic attacks' (Simon). Overall, trainers wanted trainees to 'go away [ ] thinking there is an issue here [ ] It's not good enough to treat lesbians and gay men as the same as everyone else and assume that heterosexist model' (Emma).

Liberalism in training is problematic for trainers not only for the reasons outlined above but also because if participants genuinely do not hold prejudicial views of lesbians and gay men, then training is redundant, as are trainers. Conventional social psychological work on attitudes and prejudice (with regard to race) has found that people perceive their own attitudes to be less prejudicial and more enlightened than what they perceive to be the norm (for example, Banton, 1959). This could explain the prevalence of liberal ideology that the trainers report being voiced by participants but it suggests (as the trainers themselves do) that individuals' 'real' attitudes are more prejudiced than they are prepared to admit. Both the trainers and the psychological literature point to the likelihood of liberalism being a 'defense' to mask underlying heterosexism. Of course, this could be read as a rhetorical move on the part of the trainers to ensure an enduring need for lesbian and gay awareness training/trainers. However, if we accept that 'the ideology of heterosexual superiority infests itself in all levels of communicative practice [and] the resistance to opening up these spaces is enormous' (Nakayama, 1998, p. 117 and p. 119), then liberalism and making lesbian and gay sexualities a 'non-issue' can be viewed as a subtle manifestation of heterosexism in lesbian and gay awareness training.

Managing stereotypes: ambassadors, models and walking visual aids

Traditional social psychologists have frequently assumed that prejudicial and bigoted thinking is characterized by the deployment of stereotypes (see Billig, 1995); this notion was foregrounded in trainers' discussions of stereotypes. Trainers were very aware of being an 'ambassador' (Katie), 'model' (Anthony) or a 'walking visual aid' (Lou) in the training context and all had given serious consideration to the extent to which they could (or wanted to) represent to trainees 'the acceptable face of homosexuality' (Ron). Although it has been acknowledged that 'the instructor might need to take the lead in dispelling myths or stereotypes' (Newman, 1989, p. 207), how trainers managed the issue of stereotypes and represented themselves as members of the group they were discussing was a pertinent issue.

Both trainers and the literature link discussion of stereotypes with the 'contact hypothesis' – prevalent in standard social psychological work on discrimination and prejudice – because training was seen as bringing 'people into contact with gay sensibility, gay politics, gay issues' (Ben). As was noted earlier, the 'contact hypothesis' suggests that under certain conditions, contact between members of a majority and minority social group can reduce the bias of the in-group (i.e., heterosexuals) towards the out-group (i.e., lesbians and/or gay men). It has been suggested (when designing contact studies) that lesbians and gay men should 'create a target out-group member who is the optimal blend of typicality and likableness' (Simon, 1998, p. 75). There are, however, inherent dangers with this approach, as there is a 'tendency for the programmer [trainer] to become personally identified with the topic' (Schreier, 1995, p. 25) or, as Ron described it, 'the trap that you can fall into is that people see you as kind of representative'. Simon highlighted the dilemma of disliking being seen only as a gay man, while being aware of the benefits of group members having contact with him: 'I hate this, but it's actually true for someone who has never spent seven and a half hours with a gay man, for example – just to have that experience can be life-changing'.

More broadly, trainers felt that 'gay people are more visible now than they were' and, as a result, 'it's rare to find somebody in a group now who has never had any contact with gay people' (Anthony), whether that contact is personal or via the media. D'Augelli (1992) suggests education should assume the 'exceptionality' of lesbians and gay men. He writes: 'the pedagogical goal is to describe the many variations of exceptional development among lesbians and gay men, instead of subtly devaluing these *differences* as disabilities' (p. 217, emphasis added). Thus trainers' embodiment of lesbian or gay stereotypes was seen as potentially accentuating the differences between lesbians or gay men and heterosexuals but this was offset by stressing similarity and commonality (in appearance and ideology) with heterosexuals as well. In other words, trainers managed stereotypes and issues surrounding their own appearance by drawing on arguments about both difference from and similarity to heterosexuals (although an over-reliance on the latter argument carries the risk of slipping into a liberal denial of difference). For instance, Ben said he communicates to trainees a similarity argument that 'lesbians and gay men aren't beamed down from planet homosexual. We come from the same backgrounds; we come from the same ideological positions [as heterosexuals]'. Other trainers felt they minimized the difference between lesbians or gay men and heterosexuals and thus undermined stereotypes by appearing 'ordinary' and fostering the view that 'he's just an ordinary guy who does all the things everybody else does', unlike 'Quentin Crisp or Julian Clary'. Daniel said he 'always' facilitates training in his 'school teacher outfit [ ] to show that really I'm just ever so boring and ordinary'. Others found presenting an image of lesbians and gay men as 'normal' and similar to heterosexuals to be problematic; Ron said he found it 'really awful'. He continued:

> I feel like one of these people from [ ] the Mattachine Society in America in the 50s or 60s. But they were very much like 'We must dress conservatively and behave demurely and you know sort of like show that we're just normal people and that we're nice and we're not sort of child abusers and we can just live quiet little lives and not disturb anyone'.

Conversely, others said they consciously did not alter their appearance for the training context: for example, Ben said 'I just dress scruffily because I always dress scruffily'. Saul described the need to 'present me' as important because 'part of the control issue around heterosexism is we're told that we can hide. I could choose to grow my hair longer and shave my goatee off [ ] [but] if I'm dishonest, then they've won'. However, regardless of the nature of the image trainers discussed presenting, they also oriented to the effect of stereotypes. For instance, Emma said she looked 'dykey' and thought 'I'm really obvious now – I wonder what difference that'll make?'. The pressure to conform to or challenge stereotypes was ultimately a dilemma for the trainers, whether they represented them visually and refuted them verbally or vice versa. In training, Ron 'found' himself 'wearing a checked shirt and jeans and [ ] the people in the group actually drew me [ ] I'm sat there going "No no, that's an awful stereotype" and I'm sat there being it'. Lou, again, saw the contradiction: 'What I want to do is blow some of the stereotypes and I do have a small giggle at myself because I probably [represent quite a lot of them]. I have short hair, I wear trousers, I'm in a man's jacket, I'm wearing a waistcoat, I have sensible shoes [laughs]'.

It can be seen, therefore, that trainers report adopting different strategies to manage the dilemma of conforming to or distancing themselves from prevalent stereotypes of lesbians and gay men. Social psychological and lay theory converge again here, as implicit in their discussion of stereotypes is an emphasis on the peripheral route to attitude change, which relies on appearance and other extraneous factors (as was noted earlier). Whereas problems associated with strongly defended homophobic views and liberal arguments may present difficulties for trainers operating on the central route towards attitude change, the extent to which trainers are perceived as representative of lesbians and gay men – and, by extension, 'expert', credible or likeable – will impact on the peripheral route to change in participants' attitudes (see Haynes, 1993; Aronson *et al.*, 1999).

Thus the issues of homophobia, liberalism and stereotypes were presented as dilemmatic for trainers; they saw the issues as both positive and negative in training. Homophobia was constructed as potentially useful when it is expressed in a training context because it highlights that prejudice exists and it 'spices it up a bit', whilst being difficult to challenge in some respects. Liberalism was viewed as a positive outcome of training, yet was perceived as a difficulty because it masks heterosexism and ignores the unique qualities of lesbian or gay sexuality. Similarly, stereotypes were seen as positive when they can be deployed by the trainers to educational effect but purely stereotypical thinking in group members was seen as negative and as glossing over the individuality of lesbians and gay men. Additionally, trainers drew on (primarily) an individualized notion of prejudice, which parallels attitude change research. In essence, then, the approach to heterosexism reduction explored here is constructed through dilemmatic accounts of homophobia, liberalism and stereotypes, which hinge on an individualistic conception of prejudice against lesbians and gay men.

From research to practice: some reflections on lesbian and gay awareness training

Education is, of course, one strategy amongst many that can be used to advance the status of lesbians and gay men in society. One criticism levelled at training, usually from group participants but also from trainers, is that it entails 'preaching to the converted' – discussing lesbian and gay issues with already enlightened, liberal individuals working in 'helping' professions. Some studies have found an increase in homophobia as a result of education (for example, Sedahley and Ziemba, 1984) or no significant change in attitudes. However, a number of other evaluations report positive change as a result of education (Anderson, 1982; Cerny and Polyson, 1984, cited in Wells, 1991; Stevenson, 1988; Newman, 1989; Rudolph, 1989; D'Augelli, 1992).

Despite this, training is essential; challenging manifestations of subtle heterosexism (such as 'displays' of liberalism) are as important and difficult as eliminating more overt signs of homophobia. The consensus is that, although specific training programmes have had mixed results, education about lesbian and gay issues is valuable. For instance, in a Brazilian context, one primary school teacher said: 'Some of my students say that homosexuals should have their throats slit – and that is why I teach. I believe that education is the way to change the world' (Proulx, 1997, p. 55). Currently, however, the importance of and need for education is stressed but there is a paucity of information on how this should be developed and achieved. Often research suggests that training is an important strategy to reduce homophobia and heterosexism, and prejudice needs to be overcome (for example, Smith, 1993; Eliason, 1995, 1996). However, an explication of how this is to be achieved is largely absent. The exploration of training offered here goes a little way towards rectifying this.

The themes prevalent in trainers' talk point to some ways of improving the efficacy of training. Drawing on attitude change research which suggests that the cognitive aspects of attitudes will be changed through cognitive arguments and similarly that emotion-based components of attitudes will be altered through affective messages (Aronson *et al.*, 1999), the reported synthesis of using 'facts' and personal anecdotes in training may be useful in effecting change. If, as trainers suggest, liberal views are prevalent within the training context, then creating counter-arguments within a liberal ideological framework may be most effective in challenging heterosexist views couched within this framework (Jaspars, 1978). However, this means that attempts to formulate radical arguments are further marginalized in lesbian and gay awareness training, which may have negative polit-ical consequences (see Leidholt and Raymond, 1990). The themes addressed here are infused with individualized notions of attitude and heterosexism, within a context imbued with liberal ideology, yet within these constraints trainers appear to be carving out some space for change.

By arguing for the difference of lesbians and gay men from hetero-sexuals in certain contexts (for example, when challenging liberal arguments) and yet emphasizing the similarity of all sexualities in response to other arguments (for example, religion-based homopho-bia), trainers may be working directly with beliefs, using the central route to attitude change (Petty and Cacioppo, 1986), which arguably increases the likelihood of a sustained reduction in heterosexist atti-tudes (Haynes, 1993). Therefore (thinking optimistically) arguments located within the framework of normative heterosexuality might work to undermine heterosexist beliefs by indirectly questioning the 'homophobic', 'liberal' or 'stereotyped' view.

Acknowledgements

I am grateful to the trainers I interviewed for this research, whose insights and expertise have been very valuable. I would also like to thank Celia Kitzinger for supervising the PhD research on which I have drawn in this chapter and Celia Kitzinger, Adrian Coyle and Victoria Clarke for their constructive comments on an earlier draft of the chap-ter. My family and Michelle Rundle also deserve mention for their support. This research was supported by ESRC grant number R00429834612.

References

AJZEN, I. and FISHBEIN, M. (1980) *Understanding Attitudes and Predicting Social Behavior*. Englewood Cliffs, NJ: Prentice-Hall.

ANDERSON, C.L. (1982) The effect of a workshop on attitudes of female nursing students toward male homosexuality. *Journal of Homosexuality, 7(1)*, 57–69.

ARONSON, E., WILSON, T. and AKERT, R. (1999) *Social Psychology*. New York: Longman.

BANTON, M. (1959) *White and Coloured*. London: Cape.

BETHLEHEM, D. (1985) *A Social Psychology of Prejudice*. London: Croom Helm.

BILLIG, M. (1987) *Arguing and Thinking: A Rhetorical Approach to Social Psychology*. Cambridge: Cambridge University Press.

BILLIG, M. (1995) *Banal Nationalism*. London: Sage.

BLUMENFELD, W.J. and RAYMOND, D. (1993) *Looking at Gay and Lesbian Life*. Boston, MA: Beacon Press.

BOHAN, J. (1997) Teaching on the edge: The psychology of sexual orientation. *Teaching of Psychology, 24*, 27–32.

BUHRKE, R.A. (1989) Incorporating lesbian and gay issues into counselor training: A resource guide. *Journal of Counseling & Development, 68*, 77–80.

BUHRKE, R.A. and DOUCE, L.A. (1991) Training issues for counseling psychologists in working with lesbian women and gay men. *Counseling Psychologist, 19*, 216–234.

BURGESS, R., HEALEY, J., HOLMAN, J., HYDE, P., McBRIDE, S., MILBURN, H., MILLICAN, K., NNAJI, J., PREST, P., SPENCE, J., STAINSBY, P., TROTTER, J. and TURNER, K. (1997) Guilty by association: Challenging assumptions and exploring values around lesbian and gay issues on a diploma in social work course. *Social Work Education, 16*, 97–108.

CAMPBELL, J. and OLIVER, M. (1996) *Disability Politics: Understanding Our Past, Changing Our Future*. London: Routledge.

CASPER, V., CUFFARO, H., SCHULTZ, S., SILIN, J. and WICKENS, E. (1996) Towards a most thorough understanding of the world: Sexual orientation and early childhood education. *Harvard Educational Review, 66*, 271–293.

COYLE, A., MILTON, M. and ANNESLEY, P. (1999) The silencing of lesbian and gay voices in psychotherapeutic texts and training. *Changes: An International Journal of Psychology and Psychotherapy, 17*, 132–143.

D'AUGELLI, A.R. (1992) Teaching lesbian/gay development: From oppression to exceptionality. *Journal of Homosexuality, 22(3–4)*, 213–227.

EAGLY, A.H. and CHAIKEN, S. (1993). *The Psychology of Attitudes*. Fort Worth, TX: Harcourt Brace.

ELIASON, M. (1995) Attitudes about lesbians and gay men: A review and implications for social service training. *Journal of Gay & Lesbian Social Services, 2(2)*, 73–90.

ELIASON, M. (1996) A survey of the campus climate for lesbian, gay, and bisexual university members. *Journal of Psychology and Human Sexuality, 8(4)*, 39–58.

EPSTEIN, D. (Ed.) (1994) *Challenging Lesbian and Gay Inequalities in Education*. Buckingham: Open University Press.

EPSTEIN, D. and JOHNSON, R. (1998) *Schooling Sexualities*. Buckingham: Open University Press.

EPSTEIN, D. and STEINBERG, D.L. (1998) American dreamin': Discoursing liberally on *The Oprah Winfrey Show*. *Women's Studies International Forum*, 21(1), 77–94.

FESTINGER, L. (1957) *A Theory of Cognitive Dissonance*. New York: Harper and Row.

FIGUEROA, P. (1991) *Education and the Social Construction of 'Race'*. London: Routledge.

GAY LIBERATION FRONT WOMEN (1977) Lesbians and the ultimate liberation of women. In K. Jay and A. Young (Eds) *Out of the Closets: Voices of Gay Liberation*. New York: First Jove/HBJ.

GILLIGAN, C. (1993) Joining the resistance: Psychology, politics, girls, and women. In L. Weis and M. Fine (Eds) *Beyond Silenced Voices: Class, Race, and Gender in United States Schools*. Albany, NY: State University of New York Press.

GOCHROS, H. (1984) Teaching social workers to meet the needs of the homosexually orientated. In R. Schoenberg and R. Goldberg (Eds) *Homosexuality and Social Work*. New York: Haworth Press.

GRAHAM, D., RAWLINGS, E., HALPERN, H. and HERMES, J. (1984) Therapists' needs for training in counseling lesbians and gay men. *Professional Psychology: Research and Practice*, 15, 482–496.

GRAY, D., KRAMER, M., MINICK, P., McGEHEE, L., THOMAS, D. and GREINER, D. (1996) Heterosexism in nursing education. *Journal of Nursing Education*, 35, 204–210.

HALL, R. (1928/1982) *The Well of Loneliness*. London: Virago.

HAYNES, N. (1993) *Principles of Social Psychology*. Hove: Lawrence Erlbaum.

HEREK, G.M. (1984) Beyond 'homophobia': A social psychological perspective on attitudes toward lesbians and gay men. *Journal of Homosexuality*, 10(1–2), 1–21.

HILL, R. (1995) Gay discourse in adult education: A critical view. *Adult Education Quarterly*, 45, 142–158.

HOVLAND, C., JANIS, I. and KELLEY, H.H. (1953) *Communication and Persuasion*. New Haven, CT: Yale University Press.

HOVLAND, C., LUMSDAINE, A.A. and SHEFFIELD, F.D. (1949) *Experiments on Mass Communication: Studies in Social Psychology in World War II*, vol. III. Princeton, NJ: Princeton University Press.

IRWIN, R. (1992) Critical re-evaluation can overcome discrimination: Providing equal standards of care for homosexual patients. *Professional Nurse*, April, 435–438.

JASPARS, J. (1978) Determinants of attitudes and attitude change. In H. Tajfel and C. Fraser (Eds) *Introducing Social Psychology: An Analysis of Individual Reaction and Response*. London: Penguin

JIVANI, A. (1997) *It's Not Unusual: A History of Lesbian and Gay Britain in the Twentieth Century*. London: Michael O'Mara Books.

KITZINGER, C. (1989) The regulation of lesbian identities: Liberal humanism as an ideology of social control. In J. Shotter and K.J. Gergen (Eds) *Texts of Identity*. London: Sage.

KITZINGER, C. and PERKINS, R. (1993) *Changing Our Minds: Lesbian Feminism and Psychology*. London: Onlywomen Press.

KRAMARAE, C. and TREICHLER, P. (Eds) (1992) *Amazons, Bluestockings and Crones: A Feminist Dictionary*. London: Pandora Press.

LEIDHOLT, D. and RAYMOND, J. (1990) (Eds) *The Sexual Liberals and the Attack on Feminism.* New York: Pergamon.

MARTIN, P. and COLLINSON, D. (1999) Gender and sexuality in organizations. In M. Feree, J. Lorber and B. Hess (Eds) *Revisioning Gender.* Thousand Oaks, CA: Sage.

MESSING, A., SCHOENBERG, R. and STEPHENS, R. (1984) Confronting homophobia in health care settings: Guidelines for social work practice. In R. Schoenberg and R. Goldberg (Eds) *Homosexuality and Social Work.* New York: Haworth Press.

MILTON, M. and COYLE, A. (1999) Lesbian and gay affirmative psychotherapy: Issues in theory and practice. *Sexual and Marital Therapy, 14*, 43–59.

MOBLEY, M. (1998) Lesbian, gay, and bisexual issues in counseling psychology training: Acceptance in the millennium? *Counseling Psychologist, 26*, 786–796.

MORIN, S. (1977) Heterosexual bias in psychological research on lesbianism and male homosexuality. *American Psychologist, 32*, 629–637.

MORIN, S. and ROTHBLUM, E. (1991) Removing the stigma: Fifteen years of progress. *American Psychologist, 46*, 947–949.

MUNT, S. (1996) Beyond backlash: Lesbian studies in the United Kingdom. In B. Zimmerman and T. McNaron (Eds) *The New Lesbian Studies: Into the 21st Century.* New York: The Feminist Press.

NAKAYAMA, T. (1998) Communicating heterosexism. In M. Hetcht (Ed.) *Communicating Prejudice.* Thousand Oaks, CA: Sage.

NEWMAN, B. (1989) Including curriculum content on lesbian and gay issues. *Journal of Social Work Education, 3*, 202–211.

PETTY, R. and CACIOPPO, J.T. (1986) *Communication and Persuasion: Central and Peripheral Routes to Attitude Change.* New York: Springer-Verlag.

POTTER, J. and WETHERELL, M. (1987) *Discourse and Social Psychology: Beyond Attitudes and Behaviour.* London: Sage.

PROULX, R. (1997) Homophobia in northeastern Brazilian university students. *Journal of Homosexuality, 34(1)*, 47–56.

RUDOLPH, J. (1989) Effects of a workshop on mental health practitioners' attitudes toward homosexuality and counseling effectiveness. *Journal of Counseling & Development, 68*, 81–85.

SANG, B. (1989) New directions in lesbian research, theory, and education. *Journal of Counseling & Development, 68*, 92–96.

SAVIN-WILLIAMS, R.C. and COHEN, K.M. (Eds) (1996) *The Lives of Lesbians, Gays, and Bisexuals: Children to Adults.* Fort Worth, TX: Harcourt Brace.

SCHREIER, B. (1995) Moving beyond tolerance: A new paradigm for programming about homophobia/biphobia and heterosexism. *Journal of College Student Development, 36*, 19–26.

SERDAHELY, W. and ZIEMBA, G. (1984) Changing homophobic attitudes through college sexuality education. *Journal of Homosexuality, 10(1–2)*, 109–116.

SHELLEY, M. (1977) Gay is good. In K. Jay and A. Young (Eds) *Out of the Closets: Voices of Gay Liberation.* New York: First Jove/HBJ.

SIMON, A. (1998) The relationship between stereotypes of and attitudes towards lesbians and gays. In G.M. Herek (Ed.) *Stigma and Sexual Orientation: Understanding Prejudice Against Lesbians, Gay Men, and Bisexuals.* Thousand Oaks, CA: Sage.

SMITH, G.B. (1993) Homophobia and attitudes toward gay men and lesbians by psychiatric nurses. *Archives of Psychiatric Nursing, 7*, 377–384.

STEVENSON, M. (1988) Promoting tolerance for homosexuality: An evaluation of intervention strategies. *Journal of Sex Research, 25,* 500–511.

STEWART, C. (1999) *Sexually Stigmatized Communities: Reducing Heterosexism and Homophobia – An Awareness Training Manual.* Thousand Oaks, CA: Sage.

TOWNSEND, M., WALLICK, M. and CAMBRE, K. (1995) Gay and lesbian issues in U.S. psychiatry training as reported by residency training directors. *Academic Psychiatry, 19,* 213–218.

TROTTER, J. and GILCHRIST, J. (1996) Assessing DipSW students: Anti-discriminatory practice in relation to lesbian and gay issues. *Social Work Education, 15,* 75–82.

VAN DE VEN, P. (1995) A comparison of two teaching modules for reducing homophobia in young offenders. *Journal of Applied Social Psychology, 25,* 632–649.

VAN SOEST, D. (1996) The influence of competing ideologies about homosexuality on nondiscrimination policy: Implications for social work education. *Journal of Social Work Education, 32,* 53–63.

WEEKS, J. (2000) *Making Sexual History.* Cambridge: Polity Press.

WEINER, M.J. and WRIGHT, F.E. (1973) Effects of undergoing arbitrary discrimination upon subsequent attitudes toward a minority group. *Journal of Applied Social Psychology, 3,* 94–102.

WELLS, J. (1991) What makes a difference? Various teaching strategies to reduce homophobia in university students. *Annals of Sex Research, 4,* 229–238.

Index

05219165